Theorizing Black Theatre

Theorizing Black Theatre

Art Versus Protest in Critical Writings, 1898–1965

HENRY D. MILLER
Foreword by JAMES V. HATCH

McFarland & Company, Inc., Publishers
Jefferson, North Carolina, and London

LIBRARY OF CONGRESS CATALOGUING-IN-PUBLICATION DATA

Miller, Henry (Henry D.)
　　Theorizing black theatre : art versus protest in critical writings, 1898–1965 / Henry D. Miller ; foreword by James V. Hatch.
　　　　p.　　cm.
　　Includes bibliographical references and index.

　　ISBN 978-0-7864-5937-7
　　softcover : 50# alkaline paper ∞

　　1. American drama — African American authors — History and criticism.　2. American drama — 20th century — History and criticism.　3. African American theater — United States — History — 20th century.　4. African Americans — Intellectual life — 20th century.　5. African Americans in literature.　6. Racism in literature.　7. Civil rights in literature.　8. Politics in literature.　I. Title.
　　PS338.N4M45　2011
　　812'.509896073 — dc22　　　　　　　　　　2010041612

British Library cataloguing data are available

© 2011 Henry D. Miller. All rights reserved

No part of this book may be reproduced or transmitted in any form or by any means, electronic or mechanical, including photocopying or recording, or by any information storage and retrieval system, without permission in writing from the publisher.

On the cover: A scene from the 1936 film adaptation of Marc Connelly's Pulitzer Prize–winning play *The Green Pastures* (Warner Bros./Photofest)

Manufactured in the United States of America

McFarland & Company, Inc., Publishers
　Box 611, Jefferson, North Carolina 28640
　　www.mcfarlandpub.com

To the memory of my parents:
Hortense E. Miller (1921–2000) and
Henry J. Miller (1921–1975)

And the late professor emeritus Charles Gattnig
of the City College, City University of New York

* * *

Also to the African American theatre people who have,
sometimes unknowingly, personally taught me a
great deal about the main crafts of the theatre —
acting, playwriting, and directing:

Marilyn Tsouristakis, Claire Leyba, Philip Hayes Dean,
Roger Furman, Maxwell Glanville, Stanley Greene, Ted Butler,
Ed Ellison, Ossie Davis, Simon Bly, James Baldwin,
Leecinth Hunkins, Louise Mike, Rose Philip,
Dr. Barbara Holmes, Esther Rolle, Alice Childress,
Lofton Mitchell, Oscar Brown, Jr., Frances Foster,
Earl Hyman, Marjorie Eliot, Arthur French, Jr.,
William Jay Marshall, Frank Robinson Adu, and
Arthur Woodley.

Table of Contents

Acknowledgments — viii
Foreword by James V. Hatch — 1
Preface — 3
Introduction — 7

I — The Dawn of Black Dramatic Theory and the Art or Propaganda Debate Goes Public, 1898–1916 — 21

II — "The New Negro" and the High Harlem Renaissance: Core of 20th Century Black Dramatic Theory, 1917–1929 — 51

III — Black Theory in the Great Depression and Beyond, 1930–1949, Part I — 86

IV — Black Theory in the Great Depression and Beyond, 1930–1949, Part II — 117

V — Civil Rights vs. Integration and the Persistence of Art-Theatre Drama, 1950–1959 — 140

VI — The Rise of Black Arts Theory and the Persistence of Art-Theatre Drama, 1960–1965 — 179

VII — Back to the Future: Conclusion — 217

Chapter Notes — 235
Bibliography — 253
Index — 267

Acknowledgments

This book would not have been possible without the guidance and encouragement of James V. Hatch, professor emeritus of the Graduate School and University Center of the City University of New York. In my greatest hours of doubt, Professor Hatch insisted that my voice was needed in the continuing discourse on African American drama and theatre.

The tireless and cheerful assistance of Sharon M. Howard, a senior librarian at the Schomburg Center for Research in Black Culture in New York, and Leida I. Torres and Joellen P. Elbashir, both of the Moreland-Spingarn Research Center at Howard University in Washington, D.C., is deeply appreciated. Also, special thanks go to William Branch for leading me to the illuminating 1959 conference of Negro writers in which he was a participant.

Finally, the proofreading and handwriting deciphering ability of my wife, Stephanie Miller, a retired New York City public school principal, has gone a long way in the effort to make this book a readable tool for those who have an interest in American theatre.

Foreword by James V. Hatch

In the Introduction to this book, Henry Miller states his mission clearly: "This book attempts to offer a more comprehensive view of twentieth-century black dramatic theory than now exists." The key phrase here is "a more comprehensive ... twentieth-century black dramatic theory."

More than two thousand years ago Aristotle set down the principles and purposes of Greek drama. Over the centuries as new dramatic forms evolved, other philosophers, dramaturges, directors, and sundry academics redefined the "rules" as to what made a "good" play. These male critics and scholars, whether European or American, reflected the tastes of their class: kings, court dramatists, literary academics; even in America, the university professors, newspaper critics and Broadway producers, few of whom were African American, placed the taste of Europe in the mouths of white audiences until the early twentieth century. Suddenly there was an explosion of African American "folk plays," many written by black women high school teachers. Clearly these new playwrights did not adhere to European taste or formula. Indeed, in many of their plays, the protagonists were women! Some writers staged the struggle of slaves, share croppers, or the working class, all from their own families' experiences.

In the 1920s two black scholars took notice. W.E.B. Du Bois and Alain Locke, both graduates of European universities, soon agreed to disagree. W.E.B. Du Bois, founder and editor of *Crisis Magazine,* called upon playwrights to teach, to prepare black audiences for the racial and political struggles that lay ahead. Alain Locke, a classics professor at Howard University, objected. Theatre should not be a pulpit for preaching politics, but rather an art to woo its audiences into appreciating the beauty of its African roots. Locke won disciples—Eulalie Spence, and the poet Jean Toomer. Du Bois, too, won adherents—Willis Richardson and Georgia Douglas Johnson. The debate goes on today.

Professor Miller brings valuable insights and fresh ideas to black dramaturgy. First, because he himself was raised by a working class family in the

South Bronx, he understands the black struggles against racism, a familiar factor in all the black arts. Second, because as a very young man he enrolled himself in Harlem's community theatres as an actor, a director, and playwright, he understands black theatre and its audiences. Third, Miller earned his Ph.D. in theatre history at the City University of New York. From these studies, he discovered that most books on the history of dramatic theory discuss only produced plays. While this selection serves mainstream drama, a number of worthy black plays were never produced; he has included some of the neglected dramas in order that the reader may discover them too.

African American dramaturgy now, at last, has its own black mentor who has fulfilled his promise to give us a "more comprehensive view of twentieth-century black dramatic theory."

James V. Hatch is professor emeritus of theatre at the Graduate School and University Center of the City University of New York. He is the author of several books on African American theatre, and has received numerous awards, including two Obie awards for contributions to Off Broadway theatre.

Preface

From the "git-go," using one of the terms of the black vernacular into which I was born, I had to be encouraged to write this book, or rather to write the doctoral dissertation from which it comes. From my years of advanced study of the entire theatre, it seemed to me that in my area of specialization, African American theatre (the love of my life since I was fourteen), the voices from inside of traditional black American life were overwhelmingly dominated by voices from outside of it. And those dominant voices, it seemed to me, even in much of the work written by black scholars and thinkers, spoke more about a kind of protest writing that ended up being a response to the objects of protest (the white mainstream majority) than about a black definition of the nature and purpose of dramatic art. Over my years of study, more than one notable and respected college professor had informed me that African American drama is overwhelmingly about the historical protestations of American blacks to gain political and social equality. For a number of the scholars in the field, black American drama is fundamentally a matter of protest and not primarily a matter of art. And this point of view was supported by a considerable body of African American protest dramas.

Yet, as kids on the streets of the then notoriously underprivileged South Bronx, in stark contradiction to the protest dictum, my wife and I became involved in the theatre as a major point of early adolescent interest, not to get white folks straight about all they had done to us, but simply because the theatre art form fascinated us. Of course, the notion of art as a reasonable, even rewarding pursuit had been lodged in our pre-adolescent brains by two working-class fathers who painted not only their South Bronx apartments but also still lifes, modernist abstracts, and modernist portraiture; in my wife's case, this pursuit of art was done when her father wasn't waiting tables at a New York City millionaire's club and, in my case, when my father wasn't working on the railroad or as a merchant seaman.

Later, along with Glynn Turman, the original little boy "Travis" in *A*

Raisin in the Sun, Ben Vereen, and a number of notable African American theatre artists, my wife graduated from New York City's High School of Performing Arts. After college, she elected to take her training in the theatre arts to the field of education — her first love — and into inner-city schools in the South Bronx and Harlem where children like ourselves, then as now, are so much in need of a decent education. However, I also had an elocutionist uncle, Walter Sherman Fluellen, one of my mother's three brothers, who also dabbled in the graphic arts and wrote dramatic poetry, that is, when he wasn't employed as a glorified stock clerk at a New York company appropriately called Empire Shield. My uncle performed his poetry in a number of black churches, pretty much laying folks in the aisles. And it was no accident that my uncle's middle name was in honor of the Civil War Union general who burned down Atlanta, Georgia, which rather tellingly happened to be the home of my mother's family before arriving in — or should I say escaping to — New York. At any rate, it was my uncle's writing and performances that gave me the childhood realization that the theatre arts, come hell or high water, was something that one day simply had to be the profession to which I would devote my life. Yet, my uncle, with the middle name that lets you know what my mother's family thought of "good ole Georgia," wrote and performed very little of what could be called protest poetry. Similarly, my father, almost consumed with an appreciation of modern jazz, abstracted on his canvases that world of black music when he wasn't painting still lifes of flowers and fruit to improve his management of colors and textures in oil. For the most part, the black family artwork, along with my father's devotion to African American Jazz, that first made me think seriously about the theatre arts as a life's pursuit was composed of the black "Inner-Life" concerns, which, as we shall see in this book, were first identified by W.E.B. Du Bois, then championed almost until his death by Alain Leroy Locke: religious and philosophical issues, questions of individual morality, family relationships, the celebration of life (in the form of a new grandson in my father-in-law's painting of my son), and black American music.

By the time I began my formal advanced theatre studies, I had been a leading actor in the New Heritage Repertory Theatre, one of Harlem's major Black Arts, Civil Rights companies; I had directed over thirty Off Off Broadway and Regional Theatre stage productions in New York City and Atlanta; founded theatre companies in the South Bronx and Harlem; made an internationally exhibited half-hour film; graduated from film school; taught college-level play and screen writing in professional, non-academic workshops; and written a couple of award-winning one-act African American dramas. Through all of this, my early family introduction to art had been with me, informing and shaping the many thousands of aesthetic choices I had to make over the years.

So, as indicated above, it seemed to me that in the arena of advanced theatre studies in which I was trying to "do my thing," especially as relates to the nature of African American drama, the traditional black family voices that had inspired and guided me, initially delivering me to the theatre arts, were all but mute. For much of my time in theatre doctoral studies, and most especially when I had to write the document on which this book is based, I felt like a guest at the wrong tea party. Thus, this book comes to you largely due to the persuasive powers of Professor Emeritus James V. Hatch, co-author with the late Errol Hill of the 2003 award-winning *A History of African American Theatre*, and one of the leading scholars of black American theatre of our time. Professor Hatch — whose voice you will hear repeatedly throughout this book — convinced me that my Harlem/South Bronx–inspired voice was necessary to a much needed expansion of a continuing and critical discourse on African American theatre and drama.

So, the tension between art and protest that first dawned on me while sitting in my father's tiny music room in our South Bronx apartment, enraptured by the sounds of Charlie Parker visually counterpointed by my father's wall-painting of Lester Young, is probably what this book is really about. It is a tension that has deeply informed my life as a theatre artist and a lifelong student of the theatre, and that has dominated twentieth-century African American drama. In keeping with my training as a dramatist, using Stanislavski's imagery, I have tried to make this art or protest issue the "through-line," the connective tissue of every aspect of this book. I have also tried to write a book devoid of the typical politically correct evaluations of the "usual suspects," a book not simply for black students of the black theatre but for all students of American drama and all those toiling in the wonder of the broader field of American Cultural Studies. Perhaps now, at the beginning of a new century in which the United States is sure to become a truly multicultural nation, and as an African American occupies the Oval Office, this is a book whose time has come. Let the reader be the judge.

Introduction

Post-Slavery Classicism, 1865–1900

An introduction to the prevailing ideas about drama in progressive nineteenth-century Negro America is necessary to any meaningful discussion of twentieth-century African American dramatic theory. Nineteenth-century notions of the nature and proper uses of black drama in Negro America were, in the main, the product of the educational backgrounds of a group of thinkers and practitioners who laid the early foundations of twentieth-century Black dramatic theory.

In "Theatre in Historically Black Colleges: A Survey of 100 Years," James V. Hatch writes that "with the ink of capitulation hardly dry at Appomatox, the Protestants' American Missionary Association flew into the conquered South and built a series of denominational schools" for the new Freedmen. To introduce their future teachers and ministers to the rhetorical beauties of what was then called "the art of declamation," the Missionary schools required the study of Shakespeare, the Bible, the Greeks, and the usual Roman orators. Thus, in Negro America following the Civil War, a kind of Post-Slavery American Classicism (and Romanticism) became central to the education of what William Easton, in the preface to his play *Dessalines*, later called a "new emancipation literati."[1] The Missionary schools, or schools very much like them, educated the members of the new emancipation literati who were to have the greatest influence on early twentieth-century African American dramatic theory: W.E.B. Du Bois (1868–1963), Alain Locke (1885–1954), Montgomery Gregory (1887–1971), Will Marion Cook (1869–1944), Robert A. Cole (1868–1911), James Weldon Johnson (1871–1938), and Archibald Grimké (1849–1930). Du Bois had gone to Fisk, a Missionary school; Johnson graduated from two of the Association's schools: Florida's Stanton School and Atlanta University. Cole is reported to have attended Atlanta University, and Cook graduated from Oberlin College. Du Bois, Locke, Gregory, and Grimké were also Harvard graduates.

The educational career of the biologist Ernest Just (1883–1941), founder of Howard University's Howard Players (1909) is, perhaps, one of the better illustrations of Post-Slavery Classicism. Just attended the denominational school Kimball Union Academy in New Hampshire (1899). At Kimball, he pursued a classical course of study in preparation for a career as a scholar of Greek antiquity. Unlike the other Protestant schools, Kimball, early on, saw the importance of theatre as an educational tool, and there Just performed in the school's production of Goldsmith's eighteenth-century comedy *She Stoops to Conquer*. Just continued his classical studies until, in his third semester at Dartmouth (1904), he changed his major course of study to the Sciences.[2]

The Post-Slavery Classicism of the schools that Just, Du Bois, Johnson, and the others attended was a peculiarly American synthesis of Classical and Romantic ideas. In the 1893 preface to his play *Dessalines*, Easton exemplified this American mixture of the Classical and the Romantic, setting forth a combination of a Horatian and a neoclassical Aristotelian view of the cathartic purpose of drama and revealing the value he accorded Shakespeare's drama — which formed much of the inspirational foundation of early German Romanticism: "In ancient Rome, the drama was made the reformer of private vices and public morals.... The stage in those days, as it is today, was a mirror for despots to view their own iniquity." Humorously, Easton continues: "Othello, once the pride of the ambitious colored histrionic, has sadly metamorphosed his once singularly dark complexion and now holds the boards, the victim of a very mild sunburn." The Romantic American classicism of Shakespeare had taken hold in large segments of progressive Negro America long before the onset of the Civil War. We have as evidence of this phenomenon the work of the African American Shakespearean actor James Hewlett at the all-black African Grove Theatre in New York City in the 1820s, and the subsequent career of Ira Aldridge, an early member of the African Grove and a Shakespearean actor who achieved international notice by the 1850s.[3] However, as Hatch has indicated, it was the North's victory over the South that institutionalized in southern Negro America the "classicism" which, for the most part, had been characteristic of the education of a relatively small, northern Negro elite.

W.E.B. Du Bois, in his "Prelude" to *Star of Ethiopia* (1913), used what many Americans of his generation would have termed, but for the race of his dramatic figures, the "classical" imagery and tone of the Royal Entries and Pageants of late Medieval and early Renaissance Europe: "The lights of the Court of Freedom blaze. A trumpet blast is heard and four heralds, black and of gigantic stature, appear with silver trumpets and standing at the four corners of the temple of beauty...." In the Romantic tradition of Keats, Du Bois privileged the element of "beauty" in art, or rather, as shall be seen later, the elements of "Truth and Beauty" in art.

The nineteenth-century reverberations of the Post-Slavery Classicism of the missionary schools and their non-denominational counterparts continued well into the twentieth century. On 20 April 1915, in the pages of the *New York Age*, James Weldon Johnson extolled the virtues of Shakespeare's words using as his examples passages from *Macbeth*, *Romeo and Juliet* and *Henry V*. During the Harlem Renaissance, Alain Locke, in "The Drama of Negro Life," (1926) appears to be calling for Negro plays which would be, in some sense, modeled after classical drama: Here Locke writes that there are circumstances in Negro life analogous to many issues taken up in classical tragedy.[4] In this same essay, Locke reveals a telling sliver of his Aristotelian training in his criticism of Willis Richardson's play *The Chip Woman's Fortune* (1923). Locke writes that the play needed "more ... *pity and terror*." Twelve years later, during the Great Depression, the poet-dramatist Owen Dodson seemed to follow Locke's earlier suggestion in his *Divine Comedy* (1938), a drama replete with the classical techniques of allegory, verse, and adaptations of the Greek chorus. In this work, classically based aesthetic strategies were used in an attempt to lift the Depression inspired troubles of ordinary Negroes to the Aristotelian cathartic heights of the pity and terror with which Locke was concerned.

Dodson's case is perhaps special in that it provides a clear insight to the flow of elements of Post-Slavery Classicism from the nineteenth to the twentieth century. In *Sorrow Is the Only Faithful One: The Life of Owen Dodson*,[5] James Hatch writes that Dodson was the son of parents born five years after the end of the Civil War, and that his parents, Nathaniel and Sarah, provided for Dodson and his siblings a Brooklyn, New York home in which a "Baptist devotion to the Bible embodied a reverence for literacy." Dodson's mother had been a Virginia schoolteacher; his father had graduated from Virginia's Wayland Seminary, which "rigorously imposed upon its Negroes ... oratory, Bible study ... ethics, as well as Latin, [and] Greek." Wayland, as might be expected, was "subsidized by northern missionaries." Dodson's parents were full-fledged members of Easton's "new Emancipation literati." The aesthetic values of those Literati had been, so to speak, imbibed by Dodson with his mother's milk.

As a graduate of Yale Drama School (1938), a stage director, and a professor of drama at Howard University for twenty-five years, Dodson's life and work influenced the work of major African American theatre thinkers and practitioners of the forties, fifties, and sixties. Hatch reports that Langston Hughes, James Baldwin, Frank Silvera, Ted Shine, Gordon Heath, and Richard Wesley (member of the New Lafayette Players, ca. 1969) are but a few of the black theatre people with whom Dodson shared his vast knowledge of the traditional theatre. Dodson's 1968 essay "Playwrights in Dark Glasses" uses, among others, Shakespeare and Aristophanes as models for African American drama and advances the classically based aesthetics of "universality," and "inevitability" as necessary elements of important African American drama.[6]

The Missionary and other non-denominational schools with classically oriented curricula helped to create the Post-Slavery Classicism of which Dodson and others were direct descendants. When evaluating the progress of African American dramatic theory, it is wise to remember that much of what contemporary scholarship considers the "classical" elements of "universality," "inevitability," and "humanism" occurred on the African continent in the world's oldest extant drama, ancient Egypt's *Abydos Passion Play* (1868 B.C.), more than a millennium before these "classical" elements dominated fifth and sixth century Greek drama.[7] Further, from John Mbiti's *African Religions and Philosophies*, it can be seen, too, that the so-called classical elements of "universality" and "humanized" gods hold sway in virtually all of the rest of traditional Africa as well. All of this means that Post-Slavery Classicism was not wholly a matter of newly freed slaves assimilating the imposed classical, "Eurocentric" dogma of their white Protestant teachers. The Freedmen, still, at least in part, a culturally African people, undoubtedly experienced a general, if unspecified, affinity with the philosophical assumptions of "humanism," and "universality" underlying their classical training. Similarly, in our own time, we must consider, too, that August Wilson's seemingly Aristotelian inspired remarks that "the common values of American theatre that we share [mainstream and black drama] are plot ... dialogue ... characterization ... design"[8] may not be merely the result of Wilson's assimilation of the principles of the European "well-made play." Rather, this remark may well be, from a traditional African American vantage point, a contemporary result of fundamental African philosophical assumptions about the humanist and universal nature of the cosmos and therefore about the nature of dramatic art.

At the end of the nineteenth century and the beginning of the twentieth, Booker T. Washington was "the one recognized spokesman of his ten million fellows," writes W.E.B. Du Bois, "and one of the most notable figures in a nation of seventy millions."[9] By the turn of the century, it was Washington's self-help "programme of industrial education" and "conciliation of the South" that dominated progressive Negro thought. Washington had an avid interest in theatrical movie making, perhaps because the mastery of early film's technology required something akin to the industrial training he advocated. Washington's death in 1915 may have changed the course of African American film history.[10] He died just before his personal secretary, Emmett Scott, signed an agreement with the Advance Motion Picture Company of Chicago to have

Washington's Tuskegee Institute and National Negro Business League co-produce a cinematic answer to D.W. Griffith's *Birth of a Nation*. Without Washington's leadership, Scott eventually lost control of the project.

Washington's "self-help" message did find its way into one early black drama, Joseph S. Cotter, Sr.'s *Caleb the Degenerate* (1901).[11] But the Post-Slavery Classicism that had led a growing number of Negro intellectuals to see drama as a necessary avenue of Negro expression had, apparently, held little interest for Washington. The effects of Post-Slavery Classicism did not take hold in Negro intellectual life until after Washington's death and its seeds did not fully flower until the period known as the Harlem Renaissance (c. 1919–1929).

Model Studies

There is an almost alarming paucity of books relating to Black dramatic theory in the broad field of American theatre studies. The model studies for this book are Samuel A. Hay's *African American Theatre: An Historical and Critical Analysis* (1994), and Marvin Carlson's *Theories of the Theatre: A Historical and Critical Survey, from the Greeks to the Present* (1993).

In terms of methodology, this book is heavily indebted to Carlson's historical and critical survey of existing theories of the theatre, and the resulting discourse between theorists and theatre thinkers. Hay, perhaps for the first time in a scholarly book, takes up the art or propaganda debate first formulated in Alain Locke's article, "Art or Propaganda?" published in the periodical *Harlem* in 1928. And, in taking up this art or propaganda battle and identifying its primary combatants, W.E.B. Du Bois and Alain Locke, Hay's work offers a broad, if limited, view of twentieth-century black dramatic theory. A third of Hay's work here is devoted to non-theoretical issues, such as, theatre "development," "governance," and a proposed "national endowment of African American Theatre." Excluding these non-theoretical concerns, this book attempts to offer a more comprehensive view of twentieth-century black dramatic theory than now exists.

Who's In and Who's Out

In keeping with the discourse between theorists found in Carlson's *Theories of the Theatre*, for most of the periods of African American theatre covered in this book there are but two pertinent historical figures who can reasonably be described as theorists: the seminal sociologist W.E.B. Du Bois and, like

Aristotle, the philosopher Alain Leroy Locke. Yet, neither Locke, Du Bois, nor any other historical figure in African American arts and letters until Amiri Baraka (LeRoi Jones) in the 1960s would have described themselves as theatre theorists. Nevertheless, the historical record shows that Du Bois and Locke each had a pervasive and singular influence on Negro arts at a time when formative and enduring questions about those arts, including the drama, were first being posed. In addition to participating in the Negro theatre arts since 1913 and almost single-handedly invoking the arts and letters credo of the early Harlem Renaissance, Du Bois was also editor of the *Crisis Magazine*, the NAACP organ that was, from its founding in 1909 to the 1930s, the most widely read publication in Negro America. Thus, Du Bois' views on politics and the arts were widely absorbed by a mostly grateful national Negro public. Similarly, it is seldom remembered that in addition to Alain Locke's efforts to encourage the establishment of a Negro Art-Theatre from about 1916 almost until his death in 1954, he was the first African American Rhodes Scholar — a status he held for some forty years — and this fact alone gave him a formidable influence over the thinking of the Negro intelligentsia of his day. Du Bois and Locke, were, in fact, the chief combatants in the art or propaganda debate that dominated African American drama for most of the twentieth century. Therefore, for the purposes of this book, they are here treated as the primary theorists of twentieth-century black dramatic theory.

Also of paramount importance are the plays treated in this book; the overwhelming majority of them are produced works. In my experience as a practitioner in African American theatre arts beginning in the 1960s and my researches as a theatre scholar, it is almost a rule of thumb that produced dramas, as compared to unproduced ones, have an overwhelming influence on the development of dramatic theory. None of the closet dramas written in the Civil Rights period of the late 1950s and the 1960s affected the way we think about the nature of African American drama as did Lorraine Hansberry's *A Raisin in the Sun* (1958) or Charles Gordone's Pulitzer prize–winning *No Place to Be Somebody* (1969). Indeed, historically, Seneca's most notable closet tragedies have inspired a relatively tiny discourse on the development of dramatic theory as compared to Shakespeare's plays, which form the foundation of the entire field of Romantic dramatic theory. For these reasons and the obvious fact that not every play written by an African American author in the first 65 years of the twentieth century can be reasonably covered in one book, with a few exceptions, what is dealt with here are produced dramatic works, generally the greatest indicators of the art or propaganda debate that dominated twentieth-century black dramatic theory.

Two notable exceptions to this rule are the short plays by an often unsung playwright of the early twentieth century, Mary Burrill (1884–1946). Burrill's *They That Sit in Darkness* (1919) was written at a time when it was against the law to distribute birth control information to American women, and it is, perhaps, the first American play — and definitely the first extant African American drama — to take up this, then as now, controversial subject. Burrill's *Aftermath* (1919) seriously foreshadows the militant activist drama of the Black Arts movement of the 1960s when her central character, a black soldier returning home from World War I, leaves his home, gun in hand, to avenge the lynching of his father while he was busy fighting for freedom abroad. Although there appears to be no extant production record of these works, I have included treatments of them in this book as evidence of the diversity and militancy of early African American protest drama.

Finally, on this issue of what's in and what's out of this book, the omission here of one of the pre-eminent African American essayists and novelists, Zora Neale Hurston (1891–1960), needs some explanation. In fact, Hurston's mostly unproduced ten writings for the stage in the Library of Congress suggest a crying need for a new title about her work: *The Closet Dramas of Zora Neale Hurston*. Of her known produced plays, *Mule Bone* and *Sermon in the Valley* (repeatedly produced at Cleveland's Karamu House and its Charles Gilpin Players in the 1930s), *Mule Bone* was controversially co-authored with Langston Hughes, and I have been unable to unearth an extant play script or review of *Sermon in the Valley*.[12]

Perhaps more importantly, the *Mule Bone* controversy between Hurston and Hughes proved to be more than a battle over copyright ownership and Hurston's alleged plagiarism of Hughes' work. It was, perhaps, the first sign of Hurston's growing estrangement from the leadership of the already waning Harlem Renaissance with its cadre of theatre producers and book publishers — only Alain Locke took her side in the controversy. The *Mule Bone* controversy was also the beginning of the obscurity from which she would be posthumously retrieved by Alice Walker in 1973. Tragically, in the field of black drama, her influence over the progress of black dramatic theory in the periods covered in this book was, at best, minimal, especially when compared to black women dramatists of produced plays like Angelina Grimké (1880–1958) in the early twentieth century, or Eulalie Spence (1894–1981) of the Harlem Renaissance, and, of course, Alice Childress (1916–1994) and Lorraine Hansberry (1930–1965) in the 1950s. Given the 1970s revival of Hurston's literary achievements and the Broadway production of *Mule Bone* in 1991, a critical examination of her work in the theatre may prove to have had a far greater influence on African American drama of the '70s and beyond than it ever had on the historical periods treated here.

Needs

Perhaps no event in contemporary theatre history better demonstrates the need for a critical historical analysis of twentieth-century African American drama than the August Wilson–Robert Brustein encounter in New York in January of 1997. That rather theatrical Town Hall debate was the culmination of a cultural and theoretical battle that had been carried on for more than six months in, among other places, the pages of *American Theatre* and *The New Republic*.[13] Wilson, "America's most celebrated black playwright," and Brustein, perhaps "America's most contentious critic," represented, respectively, what appears to be the natural opposition between a call for the development of a "unique and specific black dramatic art" and "the continued evolution of so-called universal values" in the American theatre.[14] These broad oppositions were, perhaps for theatrical effect, admittedly overstated. Wilson later said that the essence of his side of the argument "comes down to just how we [African Americans] are going to participate in the American theatre." He added that "if we had 9 or 10 theatres instead of one, our contribution would be larger.... Blacks do not have a history of going to the theatre and you need to develop that audience." Brustein, too, apparently in a less combative mood, agreed with Wilson that foundations aiming to expand African American presence in the American theatre should give money earmarked for that purpose to black theater organizations rather than targeting it to mainstream venues, "like the Arena Stage and the Hartford Stage Company."

But this debate, however overstated, does dramatically call into question the very nature of the culturally inspired theoretical assumptions that lie just beneath the surface of African-American drama. If, as Brustein would have it, black drama and theatre should be absorbed into the great American mainstream, it would seem a worthwhile idea to know, in fact, just what it is that mainstream would be absorbing. Conversely, if black American theatre is to pursue a course of development beyond the mainstream — that is, in African American controlled theatre institutions, as Wilson suggests — then here, too, an examination of the history of black dramatic theory would seem to be an essential tool to those plotting such a course. In fact, such an investigation would undoubtedly shed a defining light on which road, Wilson's or Brustein's, is likely to prove to be the road best traveled.

Here, in the quest for that "road best traveled," it will be seen that for the first sixty-five years of the twentieth century black dramatic theory has been dominated by a great debate which defined black drama as art on the one hand and as propaganda on the other. The art or propaganda question has, of course, been an enduring feature of general dramatic theory in both the nineteenth and twentieth centuries. But, in an African American history replete with overt and covert struggles for social and political equality, the art or propaganda debate, arguably, reached a magnitude and importance found in no other area of twentieth-century dramatic theory. In this context, a brief look at some of the assumptions of two influential African American contributors to that great debate will provide an introduction to the central issues with which this book is concerned.

In 1903, while Brander Matthews (1852–1929), a white college professor, was positing an unbreakable bond between performance and the written drama or the text, W.E.B. Du Bois was pondering the implications of what he termed Negro "double consciousness."[15] Matthews was named by Columbia in 1899 as the first professor of dramatic literature in an English speaking university, and Du Bois, by 1920, would become black America's most influential thinker and spokesman on African American life. His "double consciousness" question, the inner opposition of being both an American and a "Negro," posited a kind of cultural duality with which every black American had to contend. In 1903, Du Bois' issue of "double consciousness" seemed beyond Matthews' assumptions about the nature of drama, wholly in the realms of sociology and psychology. But "double consciousness" would, nevertheless, deeply inform the progress of twentieth-century black dramatic theory.

In "Sweet Meat from LeRoi [Jones]: The Dramatic World of Amiri Baraka," Sandra L. Richards writes that "like Genet in *The Blacks* [and Brecht in most of his more noted work], Jones seems to suggest that art is often an artificial construct designed to distract its recipients from the chaotic whirl of life outside the creative realm."[16] If she is right — there is, as will be seen later, much in Baraka's theory and practice that substantiates this contention — Richards' comments, more than sixty years after Du Bois articulated his notion of "double consciousness," capture in the man once considered black America's most militant and influential literary and theatre theorist a form of Du Bois' double consciousness.

In the "Negro" or, in Du Bois' terms, the Negro or African half of the African American, there is a fundamental contradiction with the modernist notion that "art is a construct devised to distract its recipients from" anything in the real world. For the "Negro" and his ancestors, that is, without their Euro-American cultural accoutrements, it is a matter of ancient habit that art is used to both define and transcend the ultimate vagaries of the real world to a set of almost cosmic, universal human values in which one finds joy in sorrow, humor in misfortune, and solace and even rejuvenation in death. All of this can, of course, be traced to the varying religious beliefs supporting most of traditional West African (and Asian) cosmological design. And, a deeper investigation than I am able to make here of the black American musical art forms, "Blues" and "Jazz," would substantiate for all but the most intransigent that these persistent aesthetic imperatives were not erased by the experience of slavery. In "Africanisms in African-American Music," Portia K. Maultsby's comprehensive treatment of her subject opens a broad window on the extensive scholarship which supports the argument for African American retention of some of the more enduring aesthetic elements of African cosmological design — especially when Maultsby's findings are coupled with Margaret Creel's "Gullah Attitudes toward Life and Death," Robert Hall's "African Religious Retentions in Florida," and George Brandon's "Sacrificial Practices in Santeria, an African-Cuban Religion in the United States."[17]

Again, comparing the purely African or Negro view of art to the modernist view with which Richards has identified Baraka, the separation between the real and the non-real worlds is, on the whole, a far more penetrable barrier in traditional Africa and African America than it ever was in modernist Europe.[18] In the African system of beliefs retained in traditional black America, art is not so much an "artifice" as it is a discourse with existential cosmic forces, a conversation, if you will, between humankind and the gods (the same might be said for traditional art in Asia). Rather obvious evidence of this fact can be found in the largely African and Native American inspired "magical realism" in the award-winning literature of both Toni Morrison and Gabriel Garcia Marquez, or in one less than casual observation of a traditional African American New Orleans funeral.[19] Thus, Richards' finding suggests that Baraka's thought defines black dramatic art in essentially Euro-American modernist theoretical terms, while much older and relevant African and African American assumptions about art are apparently ignored; this is a vivid demonstration of what Du Bois meant by "double consciousness." After almost three hundred years, Du Bois knew that the Negro in America was not simply a Negro. He or she had become an American, too. Thus, the cultural constructs of Europe and America hold sway in the African American consciousness alongside what Du Bois called "Negro-ness."

The first African American drama published in the United States, William Wells Brown's (1814–1884), *The Escape: Or Leap to Freedom* (1858),[20] found no joy in the sorrow of slavery and little humor in the misfortune of those who suffered it. *The Escape* was not an attempt at transcendence to the cosmic values presiding over real-world contradictions in traditional African belief systems. Rather, it depicted the overwhelmingly real-world social and political issue of slavery. Aesthetically, *The Escape* has much in common with the nineteenth-century Euro-American melodrama that Brown, an actual escaped slave, had obviously used as his model. Du Bois himself came to see much of mainstream regular drama as a propaganda tool used skillfully by those who meant to deny the Negro full citizenship. But he did not see regular drama as a kind of opiate of the masses, as did a number of the modernists. A child of mid–nineteenth century romanticism, Du Bois probably would have found unworthy the aesthetic strategies devised to counteract the alleged "opiate effect," such as distancing the audience, calling attention to the theatrical apparatus, and almost violently "breaking the fourth wall," etc.

Just as the hope of helping to abolish slavery pushed William Wells Brown to write a play, the deteriorating status of Negro life in late nineteenth and early twentieth-century America shaped Du Bois' approach to dramatic theory. In his *Black Theatre USA*, James Hatch makes the point that the deterioration of Negro life that Du Bois faced at the turn of the century had begun with the actual end of Reconstruction in 1879. "The withdrawal of Federal Troops from the South allowed the reinstitution of slavery conditions," and this began the South-to-North Negro migration which reached its height during and just after World War I. In the United States, circumstances had, of necessity, placed Du Bois ahead of many of our contemporary theatre artists in using drama to call attention to real-world social and political issues.

It should be remembered here, too, that there was much in Du Bois' career in theatre and drama (and in Baraka's, too) that gives the lie to the "great divide" between mainstream and black dramatic theory which provided so much theatricality to the Wilson-Brustein debate. David Levering Lewis writes that Joel Elias Spingarn (1875–1939), the World War I Chairman of the NAACP, an American German Jew, "was probably the only white man Du Bois regarded as a true friend," and that, along with James Weldon Johnson, Spingarn was "one of the few people occasionally able to influence" Du Bois. More importantly for the considerations here, Spingarn was also, Lewis writes, "an inspired teacher of literature at Columbia [University in New York], renowned for his lectures on 'The New Criticism.'"[21] Marvin Carlson writes that in 1910 Spingarn called for

> a rejection of all the traditional rules, concepts of genre, moral judgments of art, history of themes — indeed of historical concerns of any kind — and for a criticism that recognizes every work as a fresh attempt at expression, an individual creation "governed by its own laws."

As for Matthews' "unbreakable bond" of performance and the text, Spingarn was the American disciple of Benedetto Croce (1866–1952), and Croce considered performance one of the drama's "externals" and that "the effect of certain plays could be attained simply by reading them." Spingarn supported Croce's view, considering performance as merely a part of "theatre conditions," which, along with "theatre audiences, have no more relation to drama as an art than a history of publishing has to poetry."[22]

How much of his position Spingarn passed along to Du Bois is likely something we shall never know — Du Bois' actual writings on dramatic theory are almost painfully lean. But Spingarn's rejection of all "traditional rules" and determination to see "every work as a fresh attempt at expression" did provide an intellectual rationale for Du Bois which freed his theory of all traditional theoretical considerations. A Harvard scholar and steeped in academic traditions, Du Bois was likely in need of such an intellectual foundation for what he needed Negro drama to become, which was, of course, an effective implement in the Negro's struggle for full citizenship. However, the tortuous connecting currents of American dramatic theory are brought into even clearer focus by the realization that, in a theoretical sense, Croce's and Spingarn's position was, in fact, a closely related forerunner of a well-known "Black Arts" militant position or assumption of the 1960s. This assumption found all-white (in Spingarn's words) "traditional rules, concepts of genre, moral judgments of art, history of themes" inapplicable to the drama or the lives of black people. Thus, using a line of reasoning not too distant from Croce's and Spingarn's, Larry Neal would derive as a "motive" for "Black Arts" drama ("the Black thing") the "destruction of the white thing."[23]

In Brown's Protest nineteenth-century melodrama and in the politically motivated and modernist aesthetics of Du Bois, Baraka, and Neal, Euro-American theoretical assumptions about the nature of drama were, in many ways, the coin of the aesthetic realm. In the often Kafka-esque, "double consciousness" world of post-slavery racism, reworkings of these Euro-American theoretical assumptions were used — as in the Spingarn-Neal positions — to delineate, even foster, a so-called Black militant dramatic art which also situated itself in opposition to the entire Euro-American cultural project. And this, of course, is a stunning manifestation of "double consciousness" on its deepest theoretical and psychological level, the very issue that W.E.B. Du Bois was pondering in 1903.

To complicate matters further, the similarities in Matthews' position and traditional African and black American approaches to drama have, perhaps, onerous theoretical implications for those who would define Matthews' view as the exclusive by-product of "Euro-centric" culture. As will be discussed here later, a body of African American scholarship in the 1980s has shown that traditional African American aesthetic approaches lie much closer to Brander Matthews' unity of performance and the dramatic text than they do to Croce and Spingarn's "New Criticism."

The crosscurrents between black and what can be called mainstream

American dramatic theory, touched on here only briefly, are reason enough to justify a study of the history of African American dramatic theory. Moreover, events of history and race have placed African Americans at the very center of what is perhaps the most crucial American question: Can a heterogeneous culture attempting to define itself based on the "inalienable rights" of individuals rather than on racial, national, and gender identities fulfill its definition and survive and prosper in anything more than a purely material sense? If one feature of a culture is that it produces distinct art forms as well as handsome gross national products, then two of the three internationally known and appreciated American art products, the short story, "Jazz," and "The Blues," are art forms of African American origin, which, of course, underscores the centrality of African American culture in the American cultural landscape. All who have an interest in the history of American drama and theatre and in the general field of American cultural studies should have an abiding interest in a history of African American dramatic theory. No useful grasp of the historical contours of any aspect of American cultural studies can be gained without at least a working knowledge of its African American subfields. Without this knowledge, scholars in broader but related studies gain only an apartheid view of their fields, which is not only inadequate scholarship, but a step away from rather than to the uniquely American notion of the rights of all citizens in a multicultural, wholly democratic society.

Unlike Booker T. Washington before them, during the years leading up to World War I, a new Negro leadership, the product of Post-Slavery Classicism, was devoted to the non-conciliatory demands of immediate full citizenship for the Negro. Archibald Grimké (and his playwright daughter Angelina), Du Bois, Locke, Gregory, Johnson, Cole, and Cook all saw their classically-oriented, liberal educations as the true path to the American middle-class. This new leadership shaped the initial theoretical contours of African American drama.

I

The Dawn of Black Dramatic Theory and the Art or Propaganda Debate Goes Public, 1898–1916

Cole and Cook on Broadway

At the turn of century, Robert Cole and Will Marion Cook, following opposing philosophies of Negro drama, foreshadowed the art or propaganda debate destined to haunt black drama for most of the twentieth century. On Monday, 4 April 1898, Bob Cole's *A Trip to Coontown*, the first full-length musical comedy produced, directed, performed, and written by African Americans opened in the Third Avenue Theatre in New York City. About a year later, in the summer of 1899, Will Marion Cook's *Jes' Lak White Fo'ks* opened in the Casino Roof Garden Theatre on Broadway and 39th Streets, also in New York. Unlike *A Trip to Coontown*, Cook's *Jes' Lak White Fo'ks*, suffered what Allen Woll calls a "quick demise." But in this short musical play, Cook laid the foundation for his successful and better-documented "back-to-Africa musicals," *In Dahomey* (1903) and *Abyssinia* (1906). With this work he also began with Cole the then dimly articulated beginnings of the art or propaganda debate in black dramatic theory.[1]

Cook's approach to Negro musical comedy was in deep opposition to Cole's. James Weldon Johnson would later observe: "In everything he [Cole] did, he strove for the fine artistic effect, regardless of whether it had any direct relation to the Negro or not." Cook, on the other hand, believed that the Negro on stage ought to be a Negro, a "genuine" Negro, and that "the Negro should eschew 'white patterns,' and not employ his efforts in doing what 'the white artist could always do as well, generally better.'"[2] These philosophical differences caused "bitter clashes" between Cole and Cook, reports Johnson; they were the stage equivalents of the oppositions of being a Negro and an American in Du Bois' notion of "double consciousness," the forerunners of what would later become the struggle between Du Bois' "Outer Life" protest theory and Alain Locke's "Inner Life," art-theatre aesthetics. In short, Cole's philosophy of Negro theatre and drama had the Outer Life, propaganda objective of proving that Negro stage artists were as good as or better than their white counterparts, while Cook's primarily Inner Life, purely artistic objective was to explore and present what Du Bois called "Negro-ness" on the American stage. Energized by the opposing poles of Du Bois' double consciousness, Cole and Cook took the first steps away from the white Blackface minstrelsy into Negro musical comedy, and, in this process, they made more than one contribution to twentieth-century black dramatic theory.[3]

Whitefaced in *Coontown*: Cole's *Coontown* Contributions

In *A Trip to Coontown,* developed and performed with Billy Johnson (1858–1916), Cole imposed a slim but definite story line on the established performance traditions of the minstrelsy. Both the *Dramatic Mirror* (1898) and Johnson, in *Black Manhattan* (1930), reported that *A Trip to Coontown* had a "well-defined story." Johnson wrote that Cole's innovation of "having characters working out the story of a plot from beginning to end" ushered in "the first Negro Musical Comedy."[4] And Thomas Riis agrees that the addition of a more logical dramatic structure set the play "apart from many musicals of the day."[5] In terms of dramatic content and performance, Allen Woll observes that consistent with his philosophy that in the theatre "blacks should strive for excellence in artistic creation and must compete on an equal basis with whites," in *Coontown,* Cole first wrote, then cast himself in the role of a white New York "Bowery Boy," Willie Wayside; he also hired the then noted Negro impersonator Tom Brown to play, among other roles, an Italian, an Oriental and a Jew in the *Coontown* production. Cole played the Wayside role in whiteface, drawing from the presumably white reviewer at the *Dramatic Mirror* the observation that as Wayside, the tramp, he "was fully as good as any white comedian whose specialty is this style of eccentricity."[6] Cole had ventured into non-traditional territory for black theatre artists of the period. In *Coontown,* the old, "nostalgic" plantation images of the Negro minstrelsy were altogether banished.

Few critics and historians made much of the apparent historical reversals implied by Cole's use of whiteface make-up in the role of Wayside. David Krasner explains that Cole's whiteface performance went unnoted mostly because "nothing in the cultural system in America at the time prepared" mostly white audiences for

> the revolutionary trope initiated by Cole's appearance in whiteface ... the semiotic system of racial signifiers did not allow space for a reversal of racial

mimicry.... Cole was perceived as black no matter what make up he wore, while white actors in black-face claimed to represent "authentic" blackness.[7]

Other than Krasner, the omissions of contemporary critics on this issue suggests that postmodern semiotics, too, did not permit a space for Cole's "reversal of racial mimicry." Indeed, even the African American historian Mel Watkins in his work, *On the Real Side*, has apparently overlooked the theoretical implications of Cole's whiteface performance.[8]

Krasner makes the significant point that Cole's performance "was revolutionary because it emerged without preconceived signifiers." Cole's whiteface performance created a definite rupture in what Krasner calls the minstrelsy's "semiotic tradition." Quoting Eric Sundquist, Krasner characterizes Cole's whiteface performance as "imitation with a vengeance." But was it a parody of whites in the same sense that white minstrels, beginning with Thomas Dartmouth Rice in 1827, had parodied blacks? The anonymous reviewer in 1900 whom Krasner cites does not seem to think so:

> if there had ever been any superfluous or stupid lines or situations, they had long since been rooted out. The speeches of Bob Cole especially ... were uniformly rich, with touches of the nature which lies deeper than *pigment*, and the quick flashes came with an invariably irresistible quietness and unction.[9]

Similarly, Mel Watkins, too, privileges Cole's aesthetic achievements in his portrayal of Wayside as opposed to his "revolutionary," semiotic whiteface "reversal." Cole wrote and played Wayside as the "conspicuous" town drunk of many Northern, poor urban communities, and Watkins observes, without specifically noting Cole's whiteface makeup, that, as Wayside, Cole "slyly shifted the emphasis from the character's ethnic background to a conspicuous social problem."[10] The *Dramatic Mirror*'s reviewer, the anonymous reviewer, and Watkins offer an alternative to Krasner's reading of Cole's whiteface performance. Following them, Cole's performance seems to have reached beyond racial parody, signifying or referring to broader, more universal notions of what is commonly called the human condition. As Wayside, Cole seems not to have created a "stage" white man in the manner that, as Krasner correctly finds, white minstrels had created a "stage Negro," and in this deeper sense, his performance was beyond mere imitation. Watkins and the reviewers remind us that, despite his philosophy, Cole was primarily an artist involved in an art project and not a spokesman for his race. Cole's speeches as Wayside, "with the touches of nature which lies deeper than pigment," obviously mirror the humanist assumptions about art at the core of traditional African and black American beliefs and central to the Post-Slavery Classicism of which Cole was a direct product.

Further, in *Coontown*, the close "bond" of Cole's writing and performance point to that enduring theoretical issue of the relation of performance and the dramatic text. In tone and content, the review citing *Coontown*'s lack of "superfluous or stupid lines or situations" and its "rich speeches," written as well as performed by Cole, suggests that Cole's approach to dramatic art is nearer to Brander Matthews' notion of "the unbreakable bond" of performance and the text than it is to the Croce-Spingarn dichotomy discussed in the Introduction.[11]

Cole's Art and Philosophy

Yet, there is little doubt that *Coontown* was, at least in part, designed to demonstrate that black writers and performers could step beyond the constraints of the minstrelsy, and "compete with white performers on an equal basis." If the findings of his contemporary reviewers are accepted, Cole's whiteface creation of Wayside as a dramatist and performer must also be seen as a stunning execution of his philosophy. But Cole's apparent artistry and his overriding interest in "artistic effect" pushed him to and beyond the Du Boisian "Outer Life" goals of his philosophy. Borrowing Krasner's critical tool, it is not difficult to find that the semiotic system of Cole's achievement is virtually littered with a host of signs, symbols, and referents that point beyond negative and constricting mainstream views of the Negro theatre artists of his time to another set of theoretical assumptions about dramatic art that do not have their sole origin in slavery or in the "Jim Crow" system that followed it.

In "slyly shifting" Wayside from a stereotypic white drunk to an apparently sympathetic dramatic figure who could express himself with "quiet unction," Cole created a character that captured what could be termed performance aspects of the Blues. And the origin of the Blues is not the staggering trials and tribulations of slavery and Jim Crow. Long before their American experience, the humanist lessons of a cosmology that defined a universe full of dualities had been drummed into the collective African conscience. That precarious West African cosmos included anthropomorphic deities who, like ancient Egypt's Osiris and the more recent Nigerian trickster god *Eshu*, defined a pre–Christian, blues-like oneness of the standard Western oppositions: good and bad, joy and sorrow, spirituality and sexuality, life and death, etc. Significantly, *Eshu*, the Yoruba god of communication, is, among other things, a master of parodies that can both lead and mislead his supplicants, suggesting, as in the Vedic traditions, that opposites are merely a matter of appearances which in their opposition point to deeper, holistic assumptions about the nature of the cosmos. These synthesized opposites form fundamental aspects of the religious belief systems that not only created the Blues, but also were adapted into most forms of African American folklore and even into much of the traditional black Christian Church.[12] These belief systems were not the result of oppression; rather, they were the means by which African Americans survived oppression.

Cole's "revolutionary reversal" in the role of Wayside was at least as much the product of thousands of years of cultural history as it was the product of "resistance" to hundreds of years of oppression. His notion that he could put on whiteface makeup and depict the inner, duality-ridden workings of a white man's soul is certainly closer to the humanism of African beliefs than it is to the color-based assumptions of Colonialist or Jim Crow America.

Cook's *Jes' Lak White Fo'ks*: Classic Black Comedy and Thought

Will Marion Cook wrote the libretto, music, and most of the lyrics for what he called his "One Act Operetto [sic]," *Jes' Lak White Fo'ks*.[13] This nearly total authorship permitted Cook to advance the most complete statement of his philosophy to reach the stage. Thus, in a theoretical sense, *Jes' Lak White Fo'ks*, Cook's second short musical play, became as important in black dramatic theory as Cole's *Coontown*.

Cook was the adopted son of John Cook, the first dean of Howard University Law School. Cook and both his parents were educated at Oberlin College. Cook also studied at the *Hochschule für Musik* in Berlin, under the famous German violinist Joachim and at the National Conservatory in New York under Antonín Dvořák. He had been introduced to the world of black music and the violin at the age of ten when, because of his disruptiveness after his father's premature death, he was sent to live with his grandfather who played the violin and the clarinet. Under his grandfather's tutelage, Cook showed promise as a violinist, and his early mastery of the instrument helped him attain his exceptional education in music.[14] He was definitely a member of the Negro upper middle class of his day. But, in the effort to put his "genuine Negro" on stage, Cook examined and priviledged the traditional wisdom, culture, and political insights of ordinary Negroes.

In *Jes' Lak White Fo'ks*, Pompous Johnson (or Johnsing), an ordinary Negro, finds a pot of gold and, imitating the ways of "white fo'ks," he uses his newly found fortune to seek an African prince to wed his daughter Mandy:

> when white men gets rich dem don stay hyeah wha everybody knows 'em en knows dey ain' much. Dey go to Europe and by m [by and] by you readin' de

> papers en you say: "Huh! Heah Mr. Williams Vanderbilt Sunflower's daughter married a duke." But I ain't goin get no bargain counter duke for my daughter, huh-uh, honey. She is goin to marry a prince.

Mandy's true love is, however, an ordinary American-born Negro. Pompous eventually discovers that the prince is a "phony" and, following Cook's philosophy, he forsakes behaving "jes lak white fo'ks," marrying his daughter to Julius, her true love, and finding solace and comfort in his own Negro milieu.

Pompous' cloak of "stage Negro" dialect, carried over from the minstrelsy, covers the serious critique of the white American upper class and the Negro middle-class of the period. His decision to stop behaving "jes lak white fo'ks" and his ultimate acceptance of his daughter's working-class, but honest, suitor is here Cook's critique of the white *nouveaux riches* as well as the Negro middle class. The American industrial boom of the 1890s and early 1900s did, in fact, send many white, upper class families scurrying in search of "lineage" to legitimize their newly found wealth through identification with and often marriage to European nobility.[15]

In his valuable examination of *Jes' Lak White Fo'k*s, Krasner makes much of the class and color schisms in late nineteenth and early twentieth-century Negro life.[16] But Cook's satire of the American *nouveaux riches* as well as the Negro middle class of his day in *Jes' Lak White Fo'k*s, viewed from inside of Negro life and culture rather than primarily through the prism of American race relations, reveals the theoretically traditional, even classical comedic ground on which Cook erected his "One Act Negro Operetto."

In "Evah [Every] Niggah Is a King," a song that many would, no doubt, today find racially offensive and "politically incorrect," Cook expands his critique of the *nouveaux riches* using Pompous to coolly question the apparently much touted "yankee" devotion to democratic ideals:

> Dah's [There's] a mighty curus [curious] circumstance
> Dats a bother in all de nation.
> All de yankees is dissatisfied
> Wid [with] deir untitled station.
> Dey is huntin' after titles
> Wid a golden net to scare em.
> An' dese *democratic* people
> Dey most mighty glad to wear em.[17]

Pompous' cool yet crude critique of the American *nouveaux riches* is milder and less bawdy than the political attacks in Aristophanes' "old comedy," but its political and social implications, nevertheless, place it in the same family with the politically activist subject matter with which Aristophanes founded Classical Greek comedy. We must read Cook's critiques not only as vehicles of "resistance," but also as a statement of his aesthetic agreement with the classical tradition as to the nature of comedic drama.[18] The use of crude and seemingly superficial buffoonery to present social and political issues on stage which could not be broached in society's usual vehicles of discourse had been, by the time Cook wrote *Jes' Lak White Fo'ks*, a staple of the Western comedic tradition. But the parodic inversion of our expectations at the core of that tradition has what can be called transcultural theoretical roots.

Cook, Aristophanes, Eshu, Osiris, and Dionysus

In Aristophanes' comedy, the honest and democratic Athenian politician is revealed to be a corrupt potential tyrant. In West Africa the god *Eshu*, the means by which the Yoruba communicate with their other gods, is revealed to be a trickster deity who can mislead his followers and make them, among other things, the butt of general ridicule. These inversions or parodies of things as we expect them to be, good gods and honest politicians, are of the same theoretical cloth. Both inversions contain serious subject matter, yet both can be occasions for humor. It matters not that one inversion appears to have its origin in political reality and the other in religion or myth, or that one occurs in ancient Greece and the other in traditional Nigeria. The humor arises from an inversion or parody of persons or beings so that they are other than what those in these diverse cultures would usually expect them to be. Cook's satire in *Jes' Lak White Fo'ks* is consistent with the historical circumstance that stage comedy is most often made up of serious, real-world issues that rely on the inversion of our accustomed, real-world expectations. We expect and, indeed, we rely upon a world in which things are generally what they appear to be or what they are supposed to be. But, it is the prophetic assumption of the comedic tradition that a world of all honest politicians and gods who do not play tricks on us, is, regrettably, a dream world. Significantly, such a dream world bears a close relation to Nietzsche's "Apollonian dream world," a world of "individuation" in which "the contemplations and desires of the individual somehow stand apart from the rapture" and "oneness" of all things in an unpredictable and essentially chaotic "Dionysian" world. Nietzsche's Dionysian world of chaotic "oneness" is a fairly adequate description of the precarious and duality-filled world built within traditional African cosmologies.[19]

The affinities in the Dionysian world with much of the world of traditional African cosmology substantiates Herodotus' original report that Dionysus, Greek god of the theatre (Bacchus in Latin), and his cult practices were, in fact, a reworking or ancient Greek adaptation of Osiris, the Egyptian god of the underworld, and his cult practices. Herodotus writes:

Melampus, who was a wise man, and had acquired the art of divination, having become acquainted with the worship of Bacchus through knowledge derived from Egypt, introduced it into Greece, with a few slight changes, at the same time he brought in other practices [the Osiric "ceremonial of worship" and "the procession of the phallus"]. For I can by no means allow that it is by mere coincidence that the Bacchic ceremonies are so nearly the same as the Egyptian — they would have been more Greek in their character, and less recent in origin.[20]

In *Jes' Lak White Fo'ks*, purged of our contemporary "politically incorrect" sensibilities to Cook's dialect and blackface representations, we again come face to face with the ancient Osirian-Dionysian, yet widely unacknowledged, theoretical connection between "classical," African, and traditional black American aesthetic assumptions about dramatic art. Cook's philosophical commitment to put a "genuine Negro" on the stage and the elements of Post-slavery classicism in his education all but guaranteed that these cross-cultural affinities would be expressed in any work over which he had total control. Cook, like Cole, was a full-fledged member of Easton's "new emancipation literati."

Again, from that view from inside of Negro life and culture, in *Jes' Lak White Fo'ks* Cook's song the "Colored Girl from Vassar"'s most significant property is the running and enduring African American inside joke that whites, especially those of the upper class, are apparently too dumb to be able to tell one Negro from another. This joke, even in Cook's time, had reached folkloric proportions in Negro life. In the "Colored Girl from Vassar" song, Cook has Mandy sing:

> I am the first dark belle who ever went to Vassar.
> I played my part so well I came from Madagascar.
> They thought I was a swell and the boys they did adore.
> And if I gave a smile they quickly asked for more.
> They sent bouquets galore to the elegant brunette.
> I've got a stock in store of their *billet deux* as yet.
> They did not know sufficient to come in from out the wet.
> And now they're sore, they're sore you bet.

Having successfully played her trick on Vassar's students and faculty, Mandy gets her degree and produces her "dark papa" and then "bids them all tata." She continues:

> Oh the papers howled and said it was a shame...
> And they really thought that I was to blame...
> Thought I had played an awful game...
> Tho' they had to own that I got there just the same...
> And now they're sore.
> [Choral refrain] They're sore you bet.[21]

The "Colored Girl from Vassar" was a musical stage adaptation of an actual event, and it would be reprised as "The Vassar Girl" song in the librettos of *The Cannibal King* (1901) and *In Dahomey* (1903). The song's enduring critique of white misperceptions of blacks gave it special currency for African American audiences. In fact, throughout the whole of the late 1950s and 1960s period of "Integration," and the "Civil Rights Movement" there were jokes in the black community about ordinary Negroes posing as African dignitaries, regaled in traditional African dress and thereby gaining admittance to previously segregated Southern lunch counters. More than a half century after Cook's *Jes' Lak White Fo'ks*, at least in the realm of African American humor, white folks were still not smart enough to identify one Negro from another. This "genuine" African American humor was one result of Cook's attempt to create a "genuine" stage Negro.

Cook: Time and Possessions in Traditional Black Thought

Insightfully, Krasner points out that in *Jes' Lak White Fo'ks'* opening song, while there are references to the "chicken" and "possum" eating stereotypes of the minstrelsy, Cook's opening song is dominated by dialect-ridden lyrics, which covertly tell of an "eminent" deliverance from "white" oppression:

> Day am near when Zion gwine to lif its han
> It [in] de book [Bible] am written ob [of]
> ol' Zion's ban[d]. White folks no use
> tryin' fu [for] to do us ha'm [harm]...
> [Refrain]
> ...Ol' Egypt's people am comin. Comin
> up on high. Fum [from] de Valley...
> ob de darkness an' de day am nigh when
> he'll call us fum out dis wilderness ob
> trouble up into de sky.[22]

But, again, from a theoretical view internal to traditional black culture, the circumstance that "for blacks in the audience, Zion and God are intended not as mere references to the hereafter" is the result of belief systems which predate the Jim Crow era and therefore cannot be read, at least not in a deeper theoretical sense, only as a form of "resistance" to that era's oppression. In Cook's opening song we see almost at once the tendency of Christianized African slaves to regard themselves as the Lord's or Zion's chosen people in that peculiarly African American tradition of identifying the suffering of the exodus of the Jews and the trials of Jesus Christ with their personal experiences of oppression: "It [in] de book [the Bible] am written ob [of] ol' Zion's ban[d]." Here African slaves, not Biblical Jews, form old Zion's band. The same kinds of assumed identities can be found in the traditional black spiritual "Let My People Go": To North American slaves the lyric, "When Israel was in Egypt land" and its refrain, "Let my people go," meant African captivity in America; African slaves were the "people" to be "let go."

Cook's lyrics clearly remind us that in the minds of black slaves they were not like the Jews or like Jesus. They had, instead, become possessed of the very spirits and personas of these suffering religious entities.[23] That is, they were here-and-now earthly incarnations of these entities. Some years ago the noted African American writer James Baldwin pointed out to me that in the black Pentecostal church in which he was a fourteen-year-old minister, parishioners saw Jesus on the cross as themselves on the cross of American racism with all its debilitating and dehumanizing implications. In Baldwin's childhood storefront church, the singing of Christ's sufferings was indivisible from the personal sufferings of its black congregation. Vivid examples of religious "possessions" can still be found today in many small, traditional, and fundamentalist black churches. In such churches, like Baldwin's, it is not uncommon that entranced participants will suddenly begin "speaking in tongues," possessed of the spirit of the Christian "Holy Ghost." The cultural constructs that underlie these religious practices predate the experience of enslaved Africans; these practices were, in fact, tools borrowed from the old world which permitted in the new one the maintenance of one's humanity while managing the weight of racial oppression.[24]

In *Africa's Ogun*, and in *African Religions and Philosophies*, both Sandra Barnes and John Mbiti, respectively, give accounts of the "possession" religious practices of the *Ashanti, Baganda, Fon, Yoruba*, and of other West African peoples whose ancestors were the principal human cargo of the American slave trade. In both these studies, similarities between the general religious aura invoked in Cook's opening song, the "Holy Ghost possessions" in Baldwin's and other black Pentecostal churches, and the possession rituals of traditional West Africa are too great to be merely coincidental. In West Africa, too, entranced participants, or more precisely, human "mediums" possessed of powerful spirits, speak in tongues, becoming immediate earthly incarnations of spiritual entities.[25]

In Cook's lyrics, the whole notion of an "eminent future" throws into bold relief one of the purest elements of traditional African thought. Mbiti reports that in most of traditional Africa "time is a two-dimensional phenomenon, with a long past, a present and virtually no future. The linear concept of time in western thought, with an indefinite past, present and infinite future, is practically foreign to African thinking." Put another way: in traditional

African thought, time is not an inexorable universal force, devoid of human agency, which rushes us headlong to extinction. Extinction or death, in the western secular sense of finality, is, after all, an impossibility since the dead, as in ancient Egypt's Osirian drama, become not extinct beings, but rather members of an ancestral "living dead." These "living dead" are spiritual beings who (like Osiris) reside in an almost liminal space between the living and dead for as much as five generations; their earthly incarnations provide the foremost ground of communication between humanity and the *orisa* pantheon.

In much of African thought, time is created by human agency, that is, it is created and measured only in terms of the actions or events of humans and their humanized gods who govern all the elements of the natural and supernatural world. Thus, Mbiti continues, "the [distant] future is virtually absent because events which lie in it have not taken place."[26] Mbiti explains that this extremely humanist view of time dominates traditional African thought to the extent that most African languages contain no specific verb tenses that identify a distant future. All human action, political, social, or otherwise occurs within either a remote or recent past, elements of what is called *Zamani* time, or in the present and immediate future, elements of what is called *Sasa* time. In traditional Africa, the remote future, also a part of *Sasa* time, means a period of about two to six months.

The notion of an "eminent future" as Cook employed it in *Jes' Lak White Fo'ks'* opening song may, indeed, as Krasner and John Lovell suggest, represent a "battle tactic" in an "eminent future" in which African Americans planned for social and political gains."[27] But, divorced from the landscape of turn-of-the-century American race relations, the cultural construct of an "eminent future" is in the first instance an enduring, inherited old-world feature of black American culture, a clear case of what Joseph Holloway terms "Africanisms in American culture." The concept of an eminent future would have existed in black America with or without racial oppression. And, while valuable discourses based primarily on the historical socio-political nature of African American drama are, understandably, likely to omit this fact, theoretical examinations make clear this, for the most part, hidden African-American contribution to dramatic theory.

To return again to that penetrable African separation between the real and non-real worlds, the actual and the spirit worlds, discussed here briefly in the "Introduction," Pompous' discovery of the gold in *Jes' Lak White Fo'ks*, like the concept of an "eminent future," is yet another cultural element inherited and adapted from African cosmology. Pompous learns of the location of the gold that makes him "rich" in a dream, and the efficacy of that dream demonstrates the close relation between the real and non-real worlds that traditional black America has inherited from traditional West Africa. The belief in the portents of the dream world as they inevitably affect the real world is so much a cultural staple of traditional African American life that "dream books" were widely used in urban black America well into the 1960s and '70s. These books associated the contents of dreams with certain numbers facilitating the success of their readers' participation in the widespread, illegal lottery game known as the "policy" or "numbers" game. Cook, in his use of the "genuine Negroes" in his musical plays, may be the first to bring African American "number playing" and its relation to the dream world to a Broadway stage[28]:

> POMPOUS: I meet a man las' week dat say dey ain'nuttin' in dreams, I say, look heah, man you crazy, when I dream of a fun'al [funeral] you know what I do? I go right out an' play dead man's row.

Cook: Black Nationalism, Black Economics, and Democracy

In *Jes' Lak White Fo'ks*, Cook's special and early brand of Black Nationalism subtly informs his playwriting. For the period in the play that Pompous is purported to be behaving "jes lak white fo'ks," his specific objectives and therefore his cultural values are not precisely the same as the "white fo'ks" he imitates. Notably, he wants an African prince for his daughter, not a "bargain counter" European "duke," and, like the white *nouveaux riches* he criticizes, he, too, wants a family tree, but it must be an "Afro-American" family tree. And, here the term "Afro-American," with all of what is today frequently termed its social and political "Afrocentric" implications, is being employed for first time on a Broadway stage (1899) and likely for the first time in African American drama.

At the end of the play, Pompous decides that "he is happier as an ordinary darkey," and this decision can be read as a retreat from the unattainable and therefore superior accomplishments of whites, or as an early black nationalist cry for African American solidarity; whites in Cook's audience likely saw it as the former, while blacks most probably saw it as the latter. At any rate, the superior value that Cook covertly attributes to aspects of Negro life throughout this work indicates that the black solidarity reading is the one most consistent with his apparent intent. Cook presents Pompous as actually smarter and a better American than the upstart whites of whom he is critical; they have paper-thin notions of the ideals of American democracy. Pompous, on the other hand, finds his way back to the ethos and unpretentious superiority of the life of simple but democratic Negro folk. It seems that for Cook all social systems that validate the political primacy of a hereditary upper class are deeply suspect and intrinsically inferior. Yet, a strong case can be made that Cook almost religiously believed in the Negro aristocracy of intellect and artistic creativity in which he had spent his childhood, and he knew that such an aristocracy could not exist beyond the egalitarian ideals of American democracy.

The "suspicious, seedy and generally dilapidated [African] prince" whom Pompous rejects is evidence of Cook's democratic preferences, and the same may be said of the aborted African trip in *In Dahomey*, and Rastas Johnson's theme song in *Abyssinia*[29]:

> I'm just plain Rastus Johnson from U.S.A.
> I'm traveling 'round to see the sights and throw
> some coin away, I don't know my ancestry,
> I'se born down in Tennessee, thank you, just
> Rastus Johnson from U.S.A.

Yet, the essentially black nationalist and not altogether groundless belief that America's most likely royalty were, ironically, the descendants of African slaves is the main theme of *Jes' Lak White Fo'ks'* song "Evah Niggah Is a King":

> Once it used to be admitted
> Dat the colored man was fervant [sic]
> When he said dat he was Washington's
> Mos' loved and trusted servant.
> But you see that little story
> Got as stale as soldiers rations
> So now he builds his perpulation [population]
> On his African relations.
> An de very yaller people
> Dey don [done] get into de ring
> An' de only blood dats darkey
> Dey got native wid a king.[30]

But Pompous' romance with the enslaved kings and queens of his African heritage stops short at the acceptance of an aristocracy of any hue. Because of his background, Cook's special brand of nationalism is tied to his belief in the ideals of American democracy.

Riis writes that Cook's "musical accomplishments," mostly in the theatre, were "entirely eclipsed long before his death" chiefly because of his "personality ... his undisguised impatience, his fiery temper, and his occasionally overweening personal vanity."[31] This observation is corroborated by some of Johnson's remarks about the Cole-Cook rivalry: "Cook never hesitated to make belittling comments on Cole's limitations in musical and general education; he would even sneer at him on a fault in pronunciation." Cook also "never managed to achieve" the "stolid and non-threatening façades" that helped black theatre professionals "reach their goals in a white society threatened by the prospect of aggressive blacks," writes Riis. "Without evidence," Riis continues, Cook "accused his first publisher," Isidore Witmark, "of cheating him of" some of his "royalties for the songs in *Clorindy*." Thus, it is an expression of Cook's deeply held views when, in *Jes' Lak White Fo'ks*, the cast wants to tell everyone that Pompous has found the gold and Pompous replies:

> POMPOUS: Look hyeah now, don' be so fas; ain't you got sense enough to know if you go advertise dah gold all ovah town de white fo'ks grab it wid a skindicate?
> JUBE: What's a skindicate?
> POMPOUS: Ominously [obviously] you'll know time you get th'ar wid 'em, when wunner dem skindicates gits th'ar wid you, you mighty lucky if you got yo' skin still on.

Pompous' "skindicate" was in actuality "The Syndicate" of a handful of white theatre entrepreneurs, producers and booking agents, led by Marc Klaw and Abraham Erlanger, who effectively controlled theatres throughout the United States and therefore dominated major American theatrical production between 1896 and 1916.[32]

While Riis seems to insist that Cook's accusation against Witmark was an unfair one, Cook's seeming paranoia was certainly not unfounded. In money matters, the treatment of Negro performers of the period could be notoriously unfair.[33] Pompous' use of the malapropism "skindicate" was apparently correct if ungrammatical. In his theater memoir, the pioneer black filmmaker and theatre personality William Foster writes that

> when *Coontown* was ready to tour, the syndicate of white theatre managers dealt Cole another blow. They had already passed the word that any performer who signed up with the show would be boycotted for life. Now they informed [individual theatre] managers that any house booking "*A Trip to Coontown*" could not expect any other colored show.[34]

Cole's *Coontown* had the "distinction," wrote Lester Walton, black columnist of the *New York Age*, "of doing something unusual in show business — playing the worst houses in every city its first year and playing the best houses the next."

Cook's self-help message and the black economic determinism in Pompous' warnings about the "skindicate" are grounded in nationalist ideas that had currency among Negro intellectuals and the "new emancipation literati." Booker T. Washington, the most powerful black man in America at the time, as Du Bois would note (1903), had literally built his movement on the notion of black economic "self-help." Black economic determinism in the form of the "Back to Africa" Movement had been one of the ideas at the core of the Chicago Conference of 1893, and that Conference signaled the beginning of a Pan Africanist movement that would function in black America throughout the twentieth century.[35]

Descendants of Jes' Lak White Fo'ks: Cannibal King, In Dahomey, *and* Abyssinia

In Dahomey opened in the New York Theatre on Broadway in February of 1903, and *Abyssinia* opened on Broadway in the Majestic Theatre in February of 1906.[36] *The Cannibal King* (1901) was primarily a full-length treatment of *Jes' Lak White Fo'ks*.[37] Initially, Cook had asked Johnson to convince Paul Lawrence Dunbar, his first collaborator and Johnson's close friend, to write the book and lyrics for *The Cannibal King*. Cook accepted Johnson and later Cole as co-writers only after Johnson had failed to get Dunbar involved in the project. Nevertheless, it was *The Cannibal King* that began the process that steadily homogenized the insights and tuneful critiques of American social arrangements in *Jes' Lak White Fo'ks*.[38]

The Cannibal King added two new characters, Constance Still and Rastas Hotbones, to the *Jes' Lak White Fo'ks'* plot. As Krasner notes, the "text was enlarged ... in order to present lengthy vaudevillian comic exchanges" between Still and Hotbones, the two comic miscreants who try to steal Pompous' gold. But the biting Aristophian buffoonery of *Jes' Lak White Fo'ks* was softened in *The Cannibal King*. Pompous' sudden discovery of the gold through that traditional African American connection between dreams and the real world is gone. Gone, too, are Cook's black nationalist references to Africa, black pride, and black economic determinism. The Pompous of *Cannibal King* has no preferences for African princes. He is willing to marry his daughter to that "bargain counter duke" he found so objectionable in *Jes' Lak White Fo'ks:* "And I tell you for de las' time. You shall marry a lord, a duke, a prince, or if ders one on de market, a king."[39] The critique of the white *nouveaux riches* was totally expunged from *The Cannibal King, In Dahomey,* and *Abyssina*.

In Dahomey, from the book by Jesse Shipp, was Cook's first major success. The play reprises Cook's "Vassar Girl" song, and the satire of the Negro middle class in the songs "Society" and "Colored Aristocracy." But by omitting the general critique of the title seeking white *nouveaux riches* and the unifying, if romanticized, nationalist assertion of black pride, *In Dahomey* loses the moral and political high ground of *Jes' Lak White Fo'ks*. Clear examples of how this ground is lost can be seen in *In Dahomey*'s song "Evah Dahkey Is a

King," a rewrite of *Jes' Lak White Fo'ks'* "Evah Niggah Is a King." Immediately the substitution of the word "dahkey" for the word "nigger" signals the move away from pure aesthetics to more "politically correct" concerns. In the descending scale of pejoratives a "nigger" is even lower than a "dahkey," and thus, the power of the song's original ironic twist, the lowliest actually being the highest, is significantly diminished. In the original lyrics, this song's entire discussion of Negro lineage emerges out of what Cook obviously saw as the folly of so-called democratic yankees seeking non-democratic European titles. In Cook's carefully balanced comedic structure, the "yankees'" folly permits the Negro folly, that is, the Negro counter-claim that "evah niggah is a king." But this Negro sentiment, divorced from its catalyst of "curious yankee" political behavior, can be read as merely the claim of simple "dahkeys" that not only has no basis in fact, but also has no origin or counterpart in white American social history. It should be remembered, too, that in the original lyric, the honored position of George Washington's servant was no longer a matter of Negro pride. Taking pride in such a position had become as "stale as soldier rations." Even light-skinned, "yaller" blacks were "getting in the ring," that is, they were boasting about their African blood since it connected them to real royalty. But the rewrite of these lyrics in *In Dahomey* replaces this unifying message of black pride with a polite warning to white audience members: "White fo'ks what's got dahkey servants, try and get dem everything. You must never speak insulting, you may be talking to a king."[40] This shift from the internal concerns and circumstances in black life to a call for a modification of white thought and behavior is significant because it is early evidence of an objective which lies at the root of twentieth-century African American protest drama. It is also an early indication of that divide, as Samuel Hay suggests, between Du Bois' "Outer Life" drama and Alain Locke's "Inner Life," art-theatre drama mentioned earlier; this issue will be more closely examined later in this chapter.

Similarly, in *Abyssinia*, the omission of the white Americans seeking titles and family connections to European nobility effaces, by lack of comparison, Pompous Johnson's superior–American status and allows Rastas Johnson's theme song to be read as something close to black American jingo patriotism.[41] Unlike the Pompous of *Just Lak White Fo'ks*, Rastas can be easily read, especially by white audiences, as the Negro who takes no notice of his country's glaring social inequities and political contradictions. Further, the critique of the Negro middle class, which had survived in *In Dahomey*, is all but gone from *Abyssinia*. Indeed, Pompous, or rather Rastas and his traveling companions are, more or less, representatives of the Negro middle class. Rastas has won a lottery and, apparently not needing the money for the necessities of life, he takes his relatives and friends on a European tour and then to Abyssinia. The humor here does not center on a critique of the Negro middle class, but rather on a series of altercations and misunderstandings with the Abyssinian authorities. Although *Abyssinia* "depicted Africans ... as representatives of an ancient and praiseworthy culture,"[42] at the same time it moved even farther away than did *In Dahomey* from *Jes' Lak White Fo'ks'* close identity with the cultural, social, and political features of traditional Negro life. Both plays lost the original work's connection to the comedic drama of the classical stage.

But the "back-to-Africa" plays that followed *Jes' Lak White Fo'ks* do show us Cook's and the general response of African American theatre artists to the growing needs of black commercialization in the white controlled mainstream theatre. Johnson writes that while working on *Cannibal King*, ultimately the only thing that they (Cook, Cole, and Johnson) could totally agree on was the need to prove to the Syndicate that a Negro show could play successfully in "first-class" theaters.[43] Cook, as a playwright, became the first twentieth-century casualty of what Du Bois would later call "the embargo which white wealth lays on full Negro expression — and full picturing of the Negro soul."[44]

The "genuine" cultural elements of Negro life that Cook, given the appropriate reading, made clear in *Jes' Lak White Fo'ks* had to be expunged if success was to be had in mainstream theatre. For example, *Bandana Land*, variously reported to be the most successful of the Cook-Williams and Walker ventures, bears virtually no relation to *Jes' Lak White Fo'ks*. Skunton Bowser, as a former member of a traveling minstrel show, allowed *Bandana Land*, at least in part, to return to a minstrel-like "end-man interlocutor type dialogue" and a second act, cake-walk finale.[45] *Bandana Land* returns to a setting in the southern United States, and the story revolves entirely around the characters Bowser (Bert Williams, 1874–1922) and Bud Jenkins (George Walker, 1873–1911), who are involved in a land selling scheme.

Cook's dramatic philosophy as expressed in *Jes' Lak White Fo'ks* was, for the most part, set aside in *Abyssinia*. Cook's credo of putting "genuine" Negroes on stage seems to have been his guiding light; when commercial considerations caused that light to fade, so did his work in Negro musical comedy. All-black cast musicals returned to Broadway in the early 1920s. But after *Bandana Land* in 1908, although he outlived Cole by more than thirty years, Cook (with Alex Rogers) appears to have written the music for just one more all-black cast musical: *In the Jungles* (1911) produced by Black Patti's Troubadours.[46] Cook died in 1944.

The descendants of Cook's *Jes' Lak White Fo'ks*, *In Dahomey* and *Abyssinia*, and the unrelated *Bandana Land* were in reality showcases for the apparently prodigious performing talents of George Walker and Bert Williams. Like Bob Cole, both men were concerned with having their audiences see beyond the antics and blackface make-up of the minstrelsy to deeper, if comedic, aspects of humanity.[47] After *Jes' Lak White Fo'ks*, the staging of Cook's authentic Negro was left more and more to the performing talents of Williams and Walker. Such authenticity could no longer be expressed in Cook's philosophy of written drama. For example, Williams created a stage persona that so identified him with the vagaries of that blues-like, precarious African-trickster cosmos discussed earlier that his career extended beyond all-black cast shows into the Ziegfeld Follies.

Perfecting Negro Musical Comedy: The Shoo-Fly Regiment *and* The Red Moon

Bob Cole and composer J. Rosamund Johnson's (1873–1954) *Shoo-Fly Regiment* opened at the Grand Opera House on 3 June 1907 in New York, ran a week, then re-opened at the Bijou Theatre on Broadway on 6 August 1907. Two years later *The Red Moon* became Cole and Johnson's most financially successful play, opening on 3 May 1908 in the Majestic Theatre in New York, and then touring a number of cities, including Dayton, Ohio, Louisville, Chicago, and Indianapolis.[48] Both plays appear to have signaled Cole's continued departure from the minstrelsy and his transition to Negro musical comedy.

In the *Shoo-Fly Regiment*, Woll writes that Cole presented a cast of "brave, educated, and patriotic male leads" and a full-blown love story as central features of its plot. While the romantic leads in the play appear to be something new in 1907, in terms of dramatic content they are actually the more fully developed descendants of Mandy and Julius in *Jes' Lak White Fo'ks (1899)* and Parthenia and Jerry in *The Cannibal King* (1901). What was new in *Shoo-Fly Regiment* was Cole's attempt to successfully market to mainstream audiences a Negro musical comedy that featured a black romance and black military heroics. "While perfectly acceptable in white musical comedies," Woll writes, "love scenes were taboo in black shows." Even later, in the 1920s, Noble Sissle expected that the cast members of his and Eubie Blake's *Shuffle Along* (1921) would be pelted after singing the show's sensitive, romantic duet "Love Will Find a Way."[49] Sissle's cast members were cheered rather than pelted, but mainstream theatre's general injunction against black love stories remained in place throughout the twentieth century. Ironically, this fundamentally racist prohibition of white theatre managers, producers, and audiences would have, unwittingly, a strange bedfellow. Integration black drama of the late 1940s and 1950s would inherit the politically inspired "Outer Life" strategies of Du Bois' Protest drama. And, in the 1960s, "Outer Life" concerns would again be stressed in anti-integration, militant "Black Arts" drama. Thus, coupled with mainstream racism, politically oriented "Outer Life" strategies helped to insure the scarcity of black love stories in twentieth-century African American drama.[50]

Further, in *The Shoo-Fly Regiment*, the heroism of black soldiers was one of Cole's large steps away from the stereotypes of the minstrelsy. Images of Negro soldiers as "ludicrous" and "cowardly incompetents" had been carefully cultivated in the white blackface minstrelsy since the Civil War. Robert Toll writes that "during the war ... and reaching full development in the 1870's, minstrels created a series of popular farces centered on blacks who were ludicrously inept at 'playing soldier.'"[51]

Black American Cultural Diversity: *The Red Moon* and King Shotaway

After seeing a performance of *Red Moon*, Du Bois, writes Hay, "asked Cole to write Protest musicals." Cole, of course, declined, knowing that the conventions of musical comedy could not profitably encompass the likely important, but inevitably didactic messages that Du Bois wanted to impart.[52] But Du Bois' interest in *The Red Moon* tells us something important about this play for which we have no extant libretto.

In the nineteenth-century beginnings of African American drama, Native and African American intermixing is already a silent element of William Alexander Brown's *The Drama of King Shotaway* (1823). The play was about the actual 1795 revolt against the British of the Garifuna people on the Caribbean island of St. Vincent. The Garifuna people, the black Caribs of the Caribbean and Central America, are entirely the product of the kind of intermixing that, almost a century after Brown's play, was the catalytic story element in *The Red Moon*. Brown, founder of the African Grove theatre in New York City, may himself have been a black Carib. He had advertised *The Drama of King Shotaway*, claiming that he had been a participant in the revolt, and, as Hay points out, there is much circumstantial evidence to support this claim. The play is not extant, but from surviving handbills and other historical materials we know that Brown had put in his play the actual names of many of the Garifuna participants in the revolt. It is important to note here that nothing in the historical record emphasizes either Brown's possible Garifuna heritage or the fact that his Shotaway (Brown's anglicized name for the real Garifuna, paramount Chief

Joseph Chatoyer) was a black Native American.⁵³ It would seem that even in nineteenth-century Negro America, African and Native American racial intermixing was widespread enough to be taken for granted.⁵⁴

Thus, from an African American point of view, *The Red Moon*'s dramatic content of interracial relationships or "race-mixing" between an African American woman and Native American man raised the issue of the actual cultural diversity of Negro America, and it was likely this element of the play that had so interested Du Bois. Jack Forbes' rather conservative suggestion that blacks "intermixed more often with [Native] Americans than with Europeans in the formative period of colonialism" is an understatement in African American terms.⁵⁵ By Cole's time, it was common knowledge among African Americans that race mixing between Negroes and Native Americans had been so prevalent that a considerable segment of the North and South American black population could claim Native American ancestry. Negroes, in actuality, were something other than the popular, denigrating racial and cultural definitions that had been imposed on them. Lester Walton, in the *New York Age*, underscores this circumstance when he writes about *The Red Moon* that

> the white critics — at least some of them — are awakening to the fact that the Negro race is not what they believed it to be nor is it what they have been trying to make the white public believe it to be, but that it is much different. Truly this is a great awakening!⁵⁶

Although no extant librettos have yet been unearthed for *Shoo-Fly Regiment* or for *The Red Moon*, it seems obvious that it was Cole and Johnson's intent with *The Red Moon* to foreground the issue of black cultural diversity, but determining just how they accomplished this feat, without the benefit of an extant libretto, is largely a matter of conjecture. Yet, we have seen that Cole's primary concern was that of artistic excellence, and the various reports of the show's ultimate success may be an indicator of what Cole and Johnson were able to achieve.⁵⁷

The oppositions in Cole and Cook's philosophies, the "Outer Life vs. Inner Life" tensions that would crystallize in the soon to be publicly aired art or propaganda debate, formed the beginnings of twentieth-century black dramatic theory. Pursuing their differences, mostly on Broadway, Cole and Cook dealt with issues relating to universality, classical comedy, traditional black humor, West African cosmology, American democracy, black middle-class values and heroism, and black cultural diversity. Their musical plays, produced on Broadway and toured in Negro audience theatres, also raised the problem of writing for two audiences, one black and one white. This "double audience" problem that James Weldon Johnson would later call "The Dilemma of the Negro Author" was also at the center of the Art or Propaganda debate.

The Art or Propaganda Debate Goes Public

In 1916, Angelina Grimké's (1880–1958) play *Rachel* publically precipitated the theoretical battle, the Art or Propaganda debate, which thereafter remained at the center of twentieth-century black dramatic theory. The NAACP's Washington, D.C., branch selected and produced *Rachel*, making it what is believed to be the first extant twentieth-century black, full-length straight drama produced in the United States. Moreover, the controversial success of D.W. Griffith's film *Birth of Nation* (1915) had strongly influenced the NAACP's choice of *Rachel*. If Griffiths' seminal film had used drama to reach new heights of anti–Negro propaganda, then why not use stage drama for pro–Negro propaganda? A brief look at the history of African American approaches to straight drama up to 1916 should lend an informative background to the far-reaching theoretical debate that the selection of *Rachel* inspired.

The protest drama tradition in which *Rachel* was written had already been clearly established in the nineteenth century by *The Escape: or Leap to Freedom* (1858), written by the escaped slave William Wells Brown. Brown's preface to his play makes clear that the work was drawn from his personal experiences. James Hatch writes that *The Escape* was written for Northern abolitionists: "Brown read the play aloud to these white liberals, hoping — one must assume — to outrage their consciences."[58] Drama designed to "outrage the consciences of white liberals" passed from Brown to Pauline Elizabeth Hopkins (1859–1930), considered by a many a seminal mother of African American literature.[59] In the 1870s, Hopkins' essay "Evils of Intemperance and Their Remedies" won first prize in a William Wells Brown Contest. In Boston (1880), the Hopkins' Colored Troubadours produced Hopkins' *Slaves Escape; or The Underground Railroad* as a musical.

Brown's *Escape* was written for 1858s abolitionists, and Grimké's *Rachel* for 1916s liberal whites. The NAACP intended to use the play to "enlighten the American people" about the "lamentable condition of ten millions of Colored citizens" at home just after "some 737,626" of those same "Colored citizens" had been mobilized to "Save Civilization" abroad in World War I.[60] Significantly, in light of the "lovemaking taboo" issue, Brown, Hopkins, and Grimké all have romantic issues motivating their most noted protest dramas. In both Brown's and Hopkins' plays, it is the endangered romantic relationship that finally makes slavery unbearable and therefore the catalyst for escape. In *Rachel*, the aborted romance between Rachel and John Strong makes it clear that the lynching of her father and brother — in the antecedent action — has destroyed Rachel's almost beatific belief in motherhood.[61]

Before 1916, the notion that Negroes should create their own Negro drama was still in its infancy. Fannin Belcher reports that for two seasons (1907 and 1908) the Pekin Theatre stock company supplied its Negro audiences with "straight comedies" written by J. Edward Green, the Pekin's manager. "What the minstrelsy caricatured, Green satirized," writes Belcher, and adds that this "might have been profitably studied by succeeding theatre groups and Negro playwrights." But here Belcher's findings are based not on Green's play scripts but, apparently, on interviews with some of the then (1945) still surviving members of the Pekin stock company. The scripts of Green's weekly straight comedies at the Pekin have yet to be unearthed, which may explain why "succeeding Negro playwrights" were unable to use them "profitably." After 1908, the Pekin ended its experiment with comedy drama and returned to the more profitable presentation of vaudeville and musical comedy. Other than Green's missing comedies, the comedic drama produced at the Pekin was, according to Belcher, "white shows."[62]

Similarly, in 1915 Anita Bush's organization of the Negro stock company that was to carry her name at Harlem's old Lincoln Theatre did not lead to drama by Negroes for Negro audiences. After twenty-six weeks of performances, the Anita Bush All-Colored Dramatic Stock Company was combined with its rival company at Harlem's new Lafayette Theatre, becoming the historic Lafayette Players (1915–1932). Controlled by a white manager, Robert Levy, who hired three successive white stage directors over the next seven years, the Lafayette Players firmly built their performance successes on plays that "had first secured Broadway's approval," writes Belcher. This policy, of course, excluded plays written by Negroes.[63] Moreover, with the exception of the company's 1928 Los Angeles production of DuBose and Dorothy Heyward's *Porgy*, the Lafayette's "best of Broadway" policy also excluded the plays of Negro life written by white authors. Although they are beyond the central concerns here, Negro dramas after 1916 by white authors, like Ridgely Torrence, Eugene O'Neill, Paul Green, and others would become a new and vital part of American drama; but they did not become a part of the Lafayette Players' repertoire.

By 1916, Ambassador Archibald H. Grimké, Angelina Grimké's father and Du Bois' close ally, was the NAACP's Vice-President. Du Bois had already laid much of the practical and theoretical groundwork supporting the NAACP's decision to produce *Rachel*. Entering the theatrical arena in 1911, Du Bois began writing his race pageant *The Star of Ethiopia* "in order to teach the colored people the meanings of their history and of their rich emotional life." The pageant recounted the history of black Americans from West Africa to the Americas. Early in 1912, Du Bois appeared at special U.S. Senate

Committee hearings on a planned exposition to celebrate the fiftieth anniversary of the Emancipation Proclamation. He wanted the Committee to support *The Star of Ethiopia* as a permanent — "distinctly educational" — exhibit, which would "try to show the condition of the colored people throughout the United States."[64] The Committee rejected Du Bois' race pageant; he, nevertheless, staged it in New York (1913), Washington, D.C. (1915), Philadelphia (1916), and in Los Angeles (1924).

In 1913, Du Bois was already enunciating a connection between African, specifically Egyptian, and American Negro Art, a central assumption in this book:

> The Negro blood which flowed in the veins of many of the mightiest of pharaohs accounts for much of Egyptian art, and indeed, Egyptian civilization owes much in its origin to the development of the large strain of Negro blood which manifested itself in every grade of Egyptian society.[65]

In 1916, he would flatly state, "the Negro is essentially dramatic," and he expanded the origin of the Negro's artistic and dramatic heritage beyond ancient Egypt's boarders: "All through Africa pageantry and dramatic recital is close mingled with religious rites and in America the "Shout" of the church revival is in its essential pure drama." Beyond connecting what can be termed the African and black American drama imperative, Du Bois calls to mind the drama's ancient origin as a vehicle of religion in Africa, Asia, and in Europe.[66]

Du Bois dreamed of a "new theatre" that "on the one hand would teach colored people the meaning of their history and their rich, emotional life ... and on the other reveal the Negro to the white world as a human, feeling thing." He had reduced to writing the art or propaganda tensions first glimpsed in the philosophies of Cole and Cook. Du Bois may not have known that in this early sketch of black dramatic theory, in keeping with his notion of double consciousness, he was actually laying the foundation for two opposing ideas of black drama. With Cole and Cook the art or propaganda debate had been subtextual and unpolarized. Cole, the consummate artist, was also a propagandist in the sense that he aimed to prove to white audiences that the Negro could compete with white theatre artists on an equal basis. Cook's privileging of the "Inner Life" truths of Negro culture over all other presentational concerns took him into subject matter that could well be read as propaganda. But Du Bois' fledgling writings brought a certain clarity to the art or propaganda argument that would lead to — in the practitioner world of the theatre — a Negro Folk drama primarily aimed at revealing to black audiences the Negro's "rich, emotional life," and an opposing Negro Protest drama designed primarily to convince whites of the Negro's humanity.

Locke vs. the NAACP: The *Rachel* Controversy

Against the foregoing historical background of Negro straight drama, the Rhodes Scholar and Howard University professor Alain LeRoy Locke would quietly become a proponent of that tributary of Du Bois' thought that saw the Negro audience's need for the depiction of its "rich, emotional life" associated with the cultural specificity of Folk drama. Hay writes that Locke "was not among the many" who judged Du Bois' *Star of Ethiopia* pageant "the best thing since cornbread, fat-back, and millet syrup." In 1915, he began trying "to change the Du Bois School from within, to shift it from protest to art-theatre," writes Hay, "quietly pushing dramatists away from protest writing."[67] In 1916, Locke was chosen to serve on the NAACP's Drama Committee, and in his subsequent resignation from that body, because of its selection of *Rachel*, he wrote:

> It was my impression that the Committee was free to discuss the matter [of developing a theatre] as itself a problem, and that, ... it was to consider how best to further race drama. I expected to have an open and carefully planned competition which would include other types of race or folk plays ... along with the problem play.[68]

Locke thought the Committee should be more than a glorified panel of play contest judges. Apparently, he had an alternative vision of the future of Negro drama and theatre long before his brief tenure on the NAACP's Committee. Montgomery Gregory, also a Committee member and Director of Drama at Howard University, strongly supported Locke's position. However, Locke would not begin to publicly reveal his position until 1922; in 1916, he and Gregory saw the sacrifices that Negroes were about to make in World War I as an opportunity to solicit the help of blacks and well-meaning whites to build an endowed National Negro Theatre — a Negro Folk play would better serve this broader aim. Locke and Gregrory believed that a Folk play would introduce its audiences not only to the problems of Negro life but also to its seldom-depicted beauties. Grimké's "problem play" was, for Locke, a single piece of propaganda that could not lead to the furtherance of the kind of "race drama" that would help develop a national Negro Theatre. Locke would later write: "one play no more makes a theatre than one swallow a summer."[69]

Black Protest Drama's 20th Century Mother: Angelina Grimké's *Rachel*

William Storm captures the central element of *Rachel*'s dramatic structure that makes the play perhaps the essence of protest drama: "It is to a large extent the reactions of this 'highly-strung girl' that Grimké sets out to dramatize,"[70] which, of course, begs the question whether or not, in realist drama, a totally passive, reactive central dramatic figure can be effectively dramatized? As often happens with authors of first plays, Grimké seemingly ignores this vital issue of dramatic construction. *Rachel*, as Storm writes, is a character in "reaction," not in action, as the usual principles of dramatic construction would seem to suggest. In keeping with Grimké's protest agenda, Rachel is a victim rather than a heroine. Heroines, from Isis to Ibsen's Nora or Williams' Blanche DuBois, generally react to the vicissitudes of life from an inner psychological core, an individual configuration of personality traits that are ultimately beyond the influence of the external events to which they react, be they murdered or oppressive husbands, or the loss of genteel fortunes. Borrowing Schopenhauer's terms, heroines succeed or fail precisely because they cannot accept the usually oppressive common or universal will.[71]

Something in Blanche DuBois does not allow her to give up her unshakable, if unreasonable, dream of somehow recapturing the gentility of Belle Reeve, as would most women in her impoverished circumstances. The spouse-imposed dollhood of *A Doll's House* is ultimately incompatible with Nora's individual quest for her own womanhood. Yet any number of wives in Nora's comfortable, middle-class circumstances would (and did) choose to continue their plaything status in their late nineteenth century, male-dominated worlds. Even in ancient Egypt, Isis does not dissolve into tears and sit idly by consumed in grief when she learns of her husband's fratricidal murder. Instead, something in her character launches her on the gruesome search for Osiris' severed remains — an action that most women, understandably, would be unable to undertake.[72] In the heroine (and the hero), external events, however dire, generally serve as a catalyst for those powerful, conscious or unconscious, core personality traits that ultimately transform their owners from characters in "reaction" to characters in action against the common or universal will. However, it is precisely Grimké's point that there is nothing at Rachel's psychological core, not even the love of children and motherhood that she espouses, which stands beyond the external forces of racism. As Storm writes, Rachel "approaches an authentically tragic identity"[73] but without fully realizing such an identity. She is constrained by the perceived needs of protest drama; she can have no indomitable will to motherhood that, when broken by the external force of racism, leads her to suicide or, like Blanche DuBois, to pure madness rather than mere hysteria. Rachel is putty in the hands of racial prejudice; thus her "direct and impassioned arguments with God" have severely compromised tragic weight.

Rachel has grown up fatherless, a circumstance which, to be sure, entails a certain kind of deprivation. But the reason why she is fatherless is not part of her personal experience. Her mother tells her of her father's lynching early in the play. She does not marry John Strong and lose him to an eventual lynching; she does not bear and raise a child who is killed or even beaten by an angry white mob. Her sufferings are the real world, flesh and blood sufferings of others, which she intellectualizes into a kind of hysteria; her tragedy is, in fact, her mother's tragedy, that is, her tragedy is second-hand.

Characterizing Rachel's bouts with God over His failure to act on behalf of the oppressed, especially innocent children, Storm writes: "The play's central conflict, in fact, is not between its people, or even between Rachel and the outside world of racial prejudice; it is rather a battle this character [Rachel] wages in the arena of religious doubt and faith." But the drama's need for actors rather than mere readers seems to suggest that the very nature of dramatic conflict is to express and personify itself in terms of dramatic figures. If the only conflict is between Rachel and God, then what need have we of the play's four supporting roles? If Storm is correct here, and I believe he is, these roles are extraneous; their speeches are but parts of Rachel's discussion with God, and their actions in no way determine or even modify the terms of that discussion; in their absence, the off-stage events in *Rachel*'s antecedent action could still have ignited the Rachel/God conflict.

Grimké writes that *Rachel* was her attempt to reach the "hearts" of "white women," mothers and potential mothers, so that "a great power to affect public opinion would be set free and the battle [against prejudice] would be half won."[74] From a contemporary vantage point, it seems academic that a true tragic heroine, one whom developing events had personally forced to the abyss of racism and gender prejudice, had a better chance of "reaching" any human "heart" than had Grimké's surrogate victim. When we carefully consider Storm's observations on *Rachel*'s conflict, we must conclude that perhaps the story that Grimké tried to dramatize did not meet even the minimum requirements of dramatic literature. A strong case can be made that stories of protagonists whose principal conflicts lie within their own minds, stories in which motivating events are in a distant past, and stories that achieve life-altering meanings only in the protagonist's thoughts are, in fact, stories better told in biographical or fictional literature.

The NAACP's Drama Committee produced *Rachel* on March 3 and 4 of 1916 at the Myrtilla Miner Normal School in Washington, D.C. The play was again presented in the Neighborhood Playhouse in lower Manhattan in New York City (26 April 1917) and in Cambridge, Massachusetts, by St. Bartholomew's Church (24 May 1917). Gloria T. Hull reports that, "for the most part," the play seems to have received "favorable reactions" from what appears to have been small and, in some cases, integrated audiences of family and friends. According to Hull, Ralph Graves of the *Washington Post* reviewed *Rachel*'s first production and complimented Grimké on the "sincerity" of her work and suggested that *Rachel* be "published" so that "it would have a wide field of Missionary usefulness."[75]

Three years later "Grimké resorted to self-subsidized publication of her drama" and, writes Hull, the play "commanded considerably more attention as a book" — as the remarks here on *Rachel*'s suitability to literary forms other than staged drama suggest. "Like closet drama, *Rachel* reads better than it acts," Hull admits, and *Rachel*'s favorable reviews as a book, some of which Hull cites, emphasize its merits as fictional literature.

In his resignation letter to the Drama Committee, Locke had also written that "most of all I had anticipated, and regarded as fundamental, the careful consideration of work that has already been done in the field of drama with ourselves or our problem as the subject."[76] Locke's willingness to risk endangering his relationship with the hierarchy of America's most powerful Negro organization early in his career strongly suggests that in 1916 there was, indeed, a small but definite body of Negro dramas in which the goals of art took precedence over the goals of protest. Apparently, there were at that time others, besides Locke and Gregory, who may very well have preferred Folk or art-theatre drama to the "problem play." Locke concludes his letter of resignation writing that he had hoped "to enlist the influence and interest of men who are already fast becoming authorities on the matter of modern playwriting and presentation." The letter's final sentence is Locke's conciliatory warning that "of course" he would "be glad to see any effort [any kind of play] pushed until it has demonstrated conclusively its possibilities of success or failure."[77]

From Locke's point of view, *Rachel* had to have been the failure of which he had politely warned. With only three performances, the play could not have reached those audiences of white women for which it was intended. Hull, in fact, "wonders" about the "vulnerability" of that "segment of Grimké's audience to her message."[78] Hull writes that Meta Warrick Fuller, the noted sculptor and Grimké's friend, attended *Rachel*'s Cambridge performance. Fuller wrote to Grimké that "while the [mixed] audience was sympathetic ... some of the finest points failed to get across." Fuller consoles Grimké, adding: "this was due not to the play nor to the actors but to that part of the audience that failed to look beneath the surface." Hull and Fuller imply that whites in *Rachel*'s audience were too remote from Negro life or too prejudiced to understand Grimké's subtextual message. However, it is also possible that the deficiencies in *Rachel*'s dramatic structure, already discussed here, failed to "get across" the "finer points" in the play. May Childs Nerney, secretary of the

NAACP, seemingly a prototype of the liberal white woman that Grimké wanted to reach, read an early draft of the play and wrote to Grimké (19 January 1915) that she "had no doubt that many young colored women feel and act as Janet [Rachel] is depicted as doing — it is the great tragedy of the problem — but somehow your play doesn't convince me of this."

In her defense against the charge, which emerged mostly from the Negro community, that *Rachel* "preached race suicide,"[79] Grimké insisted that *Rachel* depicted but one "highly-strung girl"'s reaction to racial prejudice, and few who are aware of Grimké's background would deny that her central character is, at least in part, autobiographical. Like many effective fiction writers, Grimké wrote from her own emotional experience and, unless we view 1916 Negro America as a cultural monolith, this suggests that *Rachel* emerged from but one tenth of "the submerged tenth," which was Grimké's insightful characterization of America's Negro population. In 1916, it is doubtful that even a tenth of American blacks had backgrounds and educations comparable to Grimké's. Her mother, Sarah Stanley Grimké, was from a well-known, white Boston family. Grimké had been named after her father's white aunt Angelina Weld Grimké, a noted activist for abolition and women's rights, who had early on guided her brilliant nephew into important liberal circles in Massachusetts.[80] Grimké received a better education than most white women of her day, attending excellent primary and secondary schools and Harvard University; in these institutions she was either one of a few or the only Negro.

Grimké, Motherhood, Ithyphallic Gods, and the Rise of Protest Theory

The criticism that *Rachel* was preaching "race suicide," while patently unfair, is an indicator of the theoretical distance between the message in Grimké's play and the assumptions of Negro folk culture. For the other nine-tenths of Negro society, motherhood (and fatherhood) represented not only an affirmation of personal humanity in the face of dehumanizing racial prejudice, but, as already discussed here in Cook's work, it also formed an unbreakable bond with the West African–related notion of an "eminent future" in which all things would be put aright. Siring and bearing children were ways to defeat the racist opposition in an "eminent future." While it became useful in postmodern, feminist circles to discuss motherhood as an ideological construct of the "male-white-Anglo-Saxon hegemony," it must be remembered that long before the rise of that hegemony, in predominantly agricultural societies, motherhood was associated with fertility and fertility was the means by which those agricultural societies physically survived. In Pharaonic Egypt and traditional West Africa, ithyphallic deities celebrated male fertility, too — a celebration that has its descendants in ancient Greek and Roman erotic art. The circumstance that West Africa, colonial, and post-colonial America were principally agricultural societies had, in fact, reinforced the privileged position of motherhood that is still in force in most of black America today.[81]

Disparity between the ultimate message in *Rachel* and the prevailing view of motherhood in black American culture was perhaps the most important reason why Locke preferred Negro Folk drama and why he opposed Grimké's play. Folk drama, he believed, was not only more likely to reach the status of art, but it was also more representative of Negro culture than Grimké's "problem play." And Locke was not interested in "art for art's sake." Unlike Du Bois, he believed in racial integration for the whole of his career, and establishing a national awareness of the validity and value of purely Negro art was his way of fighting racial prejudice. If the white people to whom *Rachel* was addressed were to be moved to ally themselves with the Negro's political objectives, they would, Locke believed, be moved by art and, like the NAACP's Secretary May Nerny, they would not be moved by the rhetoric of sympathetic propaganda swathed in dramatic clothing. Locke's art-theatre project was also a social justice project.

In her defense and explanation of *Rachel*, Grimké wrote what likely explains why *Rachel* and its attendant history are prophetic and seminal: "Because of environment and certain inherent qualities each of us react correspondingly and logically to the various forces about us ... if these forces be of love, we react with love, and if of hate with hate."[82] If we follow this statement to its logical conclusion we will find that, like Grimké's Rachel, the sum of Negro culture and therefore Negro art is in its *reaction* to the external forces of the mainstream's "love or hate" and, given the inarguable existence of American racial prejudice, we must find that Negro culture and art are the products of racial oppression. Here, none of the assumptions about the Negro art, music, or folk culture, discussed above in the Introduction and in this chapter, apply.

Grimké's observations are closely related to Barbara and Carlton Molettes' sociological inquiry into black theatre theory, which leads to an examination of the field in the shadow of an oppressive Euro-American cultural hegemony (1986); Krasner's useful evaluation of turn-of-the-century black theatre in terms of its relation to Jim Crow era race relations (1997), and Michael Pinkney's finding of black theatre's origin in the forced exercise/dance of shipboard slaves (1999).[83] From these and many other contemporary extensions of Grimké's thought we can but glimpse the pervasiveness of her assumptions. Although *Rachel* was never intended for Negro audiences, and its message varied widely from traditional assumptions in Negro culture, Grimké's 1916 message and thought have had a potent and enduring affect on the theoretical strategies shaping black American protest drama.

In fact, whatever *Rachel*'s value as dramatic art, Grimké is the true mother of twentieth-century African American protest drama. *Rachel* is not only the first of a genre of American protest dramas about lynching, but with this play Grimké also translated the propaganda and protest elements of Du Bois' pageantry into the format of straight drama and, for the first time, publicly exposed, as pageantry never could, the art or propaganda debate.

Cole, Cook, Grimké, and Du Bois' Double Consciousness

In the years between 1898 and 1910, the "Outer Life vs. Inner Life tensions in Cole and Cook's opposing philosophies gave theatrical form to Du Bois' 1903 notion of Negro "double consciousness." Du Bois wrote:

> The Negro is ... born with a veil, and gifted with second-sight in this American world,—a world which yields him no true self-consciousness, but only lets him see himself through the revelation of the other world. It is a peculiar sensation, this double-consciousness, this sense of always looking at one's self through the eyes of others, of measuring one's soul by the tape of a world that looks on in amused contempt and pity. One ever feels his twoness,—an American, a Negro; two souls, two thoughts, two unreconciled strivings; two warring ideals in one dark body.[84]

Yet Cole, devoted to revealing to that "other world" the equality of Negro theatre artists with their white counterparts, was led by his penchant for artistic excellence to create Negro musical art-drama that explored Inner as well as Outer Life issues. Cook, on the other hand, in his "self-conscious," Inner Life quest to put the "genuine" Negro on stage, explored many Negro political and social Outer Life issues. Nevertheless, both men faced that "embargo" that white theatre producers, managers, and mainstream critics and audiences levy, even today, on what Du Bois called the "full picturing of the Negro soul."

Finally, the *Rachel* controversy codified the central Inner Life–Outer Life, art or propaganda issues raised in Cole and Cook's practice and thought. In 1916, it was, for the most part, Du Bois, Locke, and Angelina Grimké who advanced, polarized, and expanded the art or propaganda debate that shaped black theory in the "New Negro" period and in the "High" Harlem Renaissance.

II

"The New Negro" and the High Harlem Renaissance: Core of 20th Century Black Dramatic Theory, 1917–1929

The "New Negro" period (later called the Harlem Renaissance) reached its zenith with the drum beats of World War I. In 1917, much of Negro leadership, including W.E.B. Du Bois and Archibald Grimké, wanted "reasonable, minimal steps toward social equality" as a condition of Negro participation in the war. David Lewis reports that three months after America's declaration of war, "the worst race riot in American history swept ... East Saint Louis, Illinois." Three weeks later in New York City, Du Bois, James Weldon Johnson, and other NAACP officials led the famous "silent march" up Fifth Avenue in which the only comments were from huge signs; one read: "Mr. President, why not make America safe for democracy," and "a streamer behind the national flag" read "Your Hands are full of blood." Du Bois, editor of the NAACP's national magazine the *Crisis,* eventually used his considerable influence to convince Negroes to support the war. But his support would harbor the implicit caveat and warning that after the war America would have to face the issue of democracy at home: "But by the God of heaven, we are cowards and jackasses if now that the war is over we do not marshal every ounce of our brain and brawn to fight a sterner, longer, more unbending battle against the forces of hell in our own land."[1]

In African American drama, *Rachel* and the war secured the temporary dominance of the propaganda/problem play. In *Mine Eyes Have Seen* (1918), a one-act play, Alice Dunbar Nelson (1875–1935), widow of Paul Lawrence Dunbar, took up Du Bois' pro-war propaganda, but not without sounding his "new Negro" tone. Nelson catalogs a list of injustices that could no longer be endured before sending one of her central characters patriotically off to war. In 1919, Mary Burrill's (1884–1946) first play, *They That Sit in Darkness,* the first extant black drama on the problem of birth control, is about a young black woman whose mother's death causes her to give up her education. The mother's death, the result of bearing too many children, happens because women are legally denied birth control information. Burrill's second problem play, *Aftermath* (1919), took "new Negro" militancy a step further when a soldier returns from the war only to discover that in his absence his father has been lynched. The play ends with the soldier, gun in hand, exiting his Carolina home to find the white perpetrators. *Aftermath* anticipated the "Red Summer" of 1919 when from June to September an outbreak of race riots and lynchings in Omaha, Chicago, Charleston, Washington, and elsewhere greeted recently returned Negro troops. The following year (1920), the battlefield problem and irony of race prejudice was explored in Joseph Seamon Cotter, Jr.'s (1895–1918), *On the Fields of France*. Cotter's tiny one-acter makes an early, subtle case for racial integration.[2]

Art over Propaganda: Du Bois, Hubert Harrison, and Eugene O'Neill

Also, in 1920, Du Bois identified a "renaissance of American Negro Literature" and in the field of dramatic criticism that "renaissance" was perhaps best exemplified by Hubert Harrison's review of Eugene O'Neill's *The Emperor Jones* (1920). In June 1921, Harrison defended O'Neill's play against the protest of some Negroes that the play "should never be staged ... regardless of theories, because it portrays the worst traits of the bad element of both races" — Du Bois cited this in the *Crisis* that same month. Harrison reviewed *The Emperor Jones* in *The Negro World*. The *World*, too, "had previously published a letter from a William Bridges, which argued" that the play "slandered the Negro," reports Jeffrey Perry.[3] But Harrison considered O'Neill's play a "work of genius" and his review gives special attention to the psychological dimension of Emperor Jones' attempted escape through a forest haunted by "specters" from his own past. Harrison writes:

> The soul of the individual is a bud on the stem of ancestry; the base of the individual's mind is bedded in the roots of his race, which is moulded of that race's experience. And in the succeeding scenes the specters are the past horrors of racial experience, which rise from the roots of Jones's subconscious mind.

Harrison sent his review to O'Neill and in a letter dated 9 June 1921 the author gratefully replied:

> I have read it [Harrison's review] with the greatest interest and consider it one of the very few intelligent criticisms of the piece [*The Emperor Jones*] that have

come to my notice. You know what you are writing about. I wish I could say the same for many others who have praised it unwisely for what it is not.

Harrison concluded his review with a criticism of Negro writers who, he said, did not believe that "a study of the technique of drama" was "prerequisite to uttering opinions of things dramatic"; he added that among Negro writers there were "others with commendable racial pride, but unfortunate misunderstanding, [who] object that the play does not elevate the Negro." Harrison continues: "It is necessary to explain, therefore, that the drama is intended to mirror life, either in realistic outward terms, or ... the imaginative terms of inner experience." Strikingly, O'Neill replied to Harrison on this point with a characterization of propaganda in drama that Alain Locke could have written in his 1916 opposition to *Rachel*:

> I am glad to see you remonstrate with those ... who find fault with the play because it does not "elevate." Such folk do not realize that the only propaganda that ever strikes home is the truth about the human soul, black or white. Intentional uplift plays never amount to a damn — especially as uplift. To portray a human being that is all that counts ... the same criticism of "Jones" ... is a very common one made by a similar class of white people about my other plays — they don't "elevate" them.

And that same month, making what is perhaps his most prophetic, accurate application of his "double consciousness" notion to Negro drama authored by Negro writers, Du Bois was fully in agreement with Harrison and O'Neill:

> We are so used to seeing the truth distorted to our despite, that whenever we are portrayed on ... the stage, as simple humans with human frailties, we rebel. We want everything said about us to tell of the best and highest and noblest in us. We insist that our *Art and Propaganda be one*. This is wrong and the end is harmful. We have a right ... to insist that we produce something of the best in human character and that it is unfair to judge us by our criminals and prostitutes. This is justifiable propaganda. On the other hand we face the truth of Art. We have criminals and prostitutes, ignorant and debased elements, just as all folks have. When the artist paints us he has a right to paint us whole and not ignore everything which is not as perfect as we would wish it to be.... We fear that evil in us will be called racial, while in others it is viewed as individual. We fear that our shortcomings are not merely human but foreshadowings and threatenings of disaster and failure. The more highly trained we become the less we can laugh at Negro comedy — we will have it all tragedy and the triumph of dark Right over pale Villainy.... With a vast wealth of human material about us, our own writers and artists fear to paint the truth lest they criticize their own and be in turn criticized for it. They fail to see the Eternal Beauty that shines through all Truth, and try to portray a world of stilted artificial black folk such as never were on land or sea.[4]

This then, more fully developed, was that tributary of Du Bois' thought that by 1922 had carried Locke almost seven years into his career as an advocate for his Negro art-theatre.

A Negro Theatre: Locke, Gregory, the Howard Players, and De Reath Beausey

In "Steps toward a Negro Theatre," Locke finally went public in the *Crisis*, revealing that while he and Gregory may have been defeated in the NAACP's Drama Committee, they had taken their fight elsewhere: "Between the divided elements of the [Drama] committee, with a questionable paternity of minority radicalism, the idea of a Negro Theatre as distinguished from the idea of race drama was born." In 1919, Montgomery Gregory was appointed head of Howard University's speech department. Under Gregory's direction, assisted by Marie Moore–Forrest, Howard's "first department of dramatic art … was organized," writes Walter Dyson.[5] The new department offered academic credit for its courses, and it received the support and assistance of at least some of those "authorities on the matter of modern play writing and presentation" of whom Locke had written in his Drama Committee resignation letter: Clem Throckmorton, the technical director of the Provincetown Players, Charles Gilpin, Ridgely Torrence, and Eugene O'Neill. There would be an emphasis on playwriting in the new drama program. Locke believed that "the Negro actor without the Negro drama is a sporadic phenomenon, a chance wayside flower, at the mercy of wind and weed. He is precariously planted and still more precariously propagated." With Negro playwrights and actors who had flowered in their "own soil," Locke and Gregory intended to carefully build an "endowed," national Negro Theatre "which shall reveal us beyond all propaganda on the one side, and libel on the other, more deeply than self-praise and to the confusion of subsidized self-caricature and ridicule." And Locke was not unmindful of the dangers of commercialization and what today we would call commodification:

> The stock [playwrights and actors] must be cultivated beyond the demands and standards of the marketplace, or must be safe somewhere from the exploitation and ruthlessness of the commercial theatre and in the protected housing of the art-theatre.

Howard's "Dramatic Club of former years" and its new Drama department were "finally merged," writes Dyson, "into a group known as the Howard Players." Underscoring Locke and Gregory's interests in Negro Folk drama, "the players specialized in the production of plays of Negro life either written by students or others." By 1921, the Players had presented plays by Clyde

Fitch, Lord Dunsany, Ridgely Torrence, and Eugene O'Neill. In 1922, the Players presented Torrence's one-act play *Danse Calinda* and two one-act plays written by students: *The Yellow Tree* by De Reath Byrd Beausey, and *Genifriede* by Helen I. Webb.[6] Du Bois cited the Players' work "as one of the significant achievements of the race for the year 1922."

Of the student plays, perhaps Beausey's *Yellow Tree* best represented Locke's hope for the future of Negro drama. Set in 1919, in the "southern Ohio" household of "middle class" Negroes, the play steps away from the stereotypes still haunting Negro musical comedy. But Beausey makes an attempt to make all the characters sound like Negroes. She instructs: "All save Grace speak with some dialect." In fact, the character Lucy, "a neighbor," speaks in a rather heavy dialect, which is Beausey's attempt to make her short play representative of varied aspects of Negro life. Lending a strong folk element to the play, the yellow tree of Beausey's title is a dying tree, and it is emblematic of the waning life of Mary Hunley, one of the central characters. Beausey also captures "New Negro" sentiments in the rebellion of a wayward daughter (Eva Lou) against her mother's (Mary Hunley) middle-class morality. Eva Lou plans to marry an ordinary soldier who has just returned from the war rather than the "Washington professional man" her mother had long ago selected for her. Without Grimké's polished writing and attempting to do perhaps too much in a one-act play, Beausey, nevertheless, infuses her work with an immediacy that comes from the dramatic events and situations with which her characters are personally confronted. Mrs. Hunley is dying, and Eva Lou has been set up to marry the wrong man. But, unlike Rachel, Eva Lou's indomitable will cannot be broken by the external will of middle class Negro society. At play's end, Mrs. Hunley sees the dying yellow tree as a harbinger of Eva Lou's death; hallucinating in her illness, Hunley chops down the little tree; the tree falls towards her, she "holds out [her] arms, crying courageously: So you are the death Angel! But you shall not rush over me to get my baby." Thus, Mrs. Hunley dies. In *The Yellow Tree*, Locke's folk-inspired objectives become clear when we consider Beausey's critique of the Negro middle class and her privileging of elements of Negro folk culture.[7]

Gene Toomer, Willis Richardson, Locke and Max Reinhardt

In 1923 and 1924, respectively, the Howard Players' productions of works by Negro authors would maintain this theoretical position with the presentation of Jean Toomer's (1894–1967) *Balo* and Willis Richardson's (1889–1977) *Mortgaged*. *Balo* ignored the Negro middle class altogether. "Mr. Toomer does not burden his characters or himself with plot. He shows the country life of Georgia Black folks," writes James Hatch.[8] For the most part, *Balo* is not so much a play as it is a gifted fiction writer's literary meditation on the pure folk aspects of Negro religion, Negro music, and almost mystical, surrealistic aspects of Negro interpersonal relationships.

Richardson's *Mortgaged* is, ostensibly, another picture of middle class Negro life. But, at bottom, it is a critique of a "materialism" which can be the result of so-called middle class values. Like *Balo*, the play privileges folkloric assumptions, specifically, the "John Henry" notion of hard work, that is, work in which one's soul is involved, as a form of spiritual ascendancy. In Richardson's play and in the folk elements it captures, monetary remuneration for such work is a secondary, almost trivial result.

In *The Chip Woman's Fortune* (1923), Richardson had humorously demonstrated the moral superiority of the folk characters Aunt Nancy and Jim, her "jailbird" son, to the members of a nearly middle class family who invite Aunt Nancy into their home; she is given lodging in exchange for the healing powers she practices on Liza, the ailing mistress of the house. In 1919, in the *Crisis*, Richardson had called for a Negro drama that would go beyond Grimké's "propaganda play."[9] Five years later, the natural humanity of his characters helped to make *The Chip Woman's Fortune* the first straight drama by a Negro author produced on Broadway.

Locke and Charles Johnson, editor of *Opportunity Magazine*, interviewed stage director Max Reinhardt (1873–1943) in 1924, and the encounter may have been a turning point in Locke's dramatic theory. The German director championed then current Negro shows, like *Liza* (1922) and *Running Wild* (1923), as having "tremendous artistic possibilities," and "most modern, most American, most expressionistic." By 1924, the success of *Shuffle Along* (1921) had again, writes Woll, "legitimized Black musical comedy on Broadway."[10] But Locke and most Negro intellectuals of the period considered these shows little more than "coon shows." "Ah yes, I see," Reinhardt said, "you view these plays for what they are ... I view them for what they will become and I am more than right." He added:

> The drama must turn at every fresh period of creative development to an aspect which had been ... neglected ... in this day ... we come back to the ... most basic aspect of drama for a new starting point ... and revival of art ... that aspect is pantomime ... the use of the body to portray emotion ... your people have that art — it is ... their forte — it is their special genius.

After his interview with Reinhardt, Negro musical comedy became "the foundation of Locke's Art Theatre," writes Samuel Hay. But it may also have been clear to Locke that Cole and Will Marion Cook's philosophies and practice had deeply informed Negro musical comedy, and that his notion of the role of Negro Folk drama was, as we have seen, closely related to Bob Cole's art project aimed at demonstrating Negro equality to mainstream theatre audiences and Cook's attempt to put the "genuine Negro" on the American stage.

By 1924, Du Bois, Locke, Grimké's *Rachel,* and the renaissance of Negro literature, cited by Du Bois, had established the discourse on the nature of Black drama in terms of the progress of Negro straight drama — Locke had already moved to dominate the development of Negro straight drama in 1922. But from 1912 to 1924 it had been Du Bois, Locke, Angelina Grimké, and the rise of the "New Negro," that clarified and, in many ways, fortified the tensions in the continuing Art or Propaganda debate in which the "high" Harlem Renaissance would take shape.

Locke's Double-barrel Fusillade Against Propaganda

At the beginning of the High Harlem Renaissance, March of 1925, Alain Locke "unloaded a double-barrel" in the developing Art or Propaganda war. In the *Survey Graphic,* Locke's "Enter the New Negro" announced that "The Sociologist, The Philanthropist, and the Race-leader," the three "norns" that had been more or less in charge of "the Negro problem," now had "a changeling in their laps," the new Negro. And these norns, according to Locke, had mistakenly defined the Negro as a "formula — a something to be ... condemned or defended ... kept down or helped up ... a social bogey or a social burden." But, Locke suggests that the new Negro no longer saw himself as "a social problem"; the Negro was experiencing "a spiritual Coming of Age." Grimké's ideal audience of liberal white women for *Rachel* and Du Bois' protest goals, aimed at "pricking white consciences" and putting the Negro's "best face forward" were, apparently, strategies of the past. In "Youth Speaks," the second shot in Locke's "double-barrel" fusillade against propaganda in Negro art, he wrote: "Where formerly they [Negro writers] spoke to others and tried to interpret, they now speak to their own and try to express."

There is, in fact, little doubt that Du Bois was The Sociologist and Race Leader in Locke's "Enter the New Negro." Before 1925, Du Bois' "new theatre," writes Hay, "consisted of characters and situations that depicted the struggle of African Americans against racism, which Du Bois called 'Outer Life.'" But, in "Youth Speaks," Locke found that it was the "ideals of American democracy" that firmly made up the goals of the Negro's Outer Life. Locke had begun to see in Negro art what he described as efforts to "repair a damaged group psychology and reshape a warped social perspective," a process primarily unconcerned with "putting the best face forward" for white consumption. These Inner Life objectives, repairs of group psychology and the re-shaping of Negro social perspective, were, Locke found, already producing in Negro art a "lapse of sentimental appeal," and a "rise from social disillusionment to race pride."

Locke's public attack on the Outer Life, social and political objectives of Du Bois' drama had, in fact, begun in 1923. That year, in his review of Ernest Culbertson's *Goat Alley,* he insisted that "fine realistic [Negro] tragedy" would eventually appear when dramatists, Negro and white, learned to regard Negro life

> more with an eye of pity than of scorn, more from the point of view of interest than of problem-hunting or problem solving. [But] Such drama will leave the race problem precisely where it stood ... *it is not the business of plays to solve problems or to reform society.*

In 1923, Du Bois seems to have either ignored or overlooked this one-line salvo against propaganda plays.[13] But, a year later, what appears to have been a reply to Locke's characterization of drama's inability "to reform society" and his general stand against propaganda plays came from an unexpected quarter. Willis Richardson, in "The Negro and the Stage" (October 1924), suggested that the theatre was an "educational institution along with the school." Educational institutions certainly have at least the potential to reform society. In "Propaganda in the Theatre," published a month later, Richardson reduced the definition of the propaganda play to "a play written for some purpose other than the entertainment of an audience."[14] Although such a definition would seem to apply to most, if not all, dramatic works, Richardson cites, among other works, as examples of excellent propaganda plays, Shaw's *Mrs. Warren's Profession* (1894), Eugene Brieux's *The Red Robe* (1900), and Gerhart Hauptman's *The Weavers* (1892). And for Richardson, Shaw was "the most important person in the drama" and one of "the drama's leading propagandists." "*Mrs. Warren's Profession* is a harsh criticism of the system which compels a single woman to choose between the two evils of working for starvation wages and selling herself," writes Richardson, and "*The Red Robe* ... shows all the greed of the judges for greater power." *The Weavers,* a play about a group of exploited workers driven to revolt, was, Richardson continues, "another forceful document against capitalistic greed." These and all propaganda plays were written "for the [valid] purpose," he explains, "of waging war against certain evils existing among the people."

But Locke's "Enter the New Negro," and "Youth Speaks," deal, primarily, with Du Bois' notions and are not replies to Richardson's earlier, 1924, assertions. Locke's essays proceed as though the specifics of Richardson's positions on the educational uses of drama and the value of propaganda plays had never been made. He had either overlooked or ignored Richardson's arguments.

The distinction between plays that were "social documents" and "so-called Negro [propaganda] plays" was, two years later, made by Theophilus Lewis (1891–1974). In the 1920s, Lewis "produced," writes Theodore Kornweibel, "the most thoughtout [sic] and consistent commentary on black theatre ... during the Harlem Renaissance." Richardson made no distinction between Negro propaganda plays and Shaw, Brieux, and Hauptman's social dramas. Yet, it was Richardson himself who had, five years earlier, called for a Negro drama that would go beyond Grimké's propaganda play, *Rachel*.

Oddly enough, Richardson's seeming ambivalence on this point may have had much to do with the changing meanings of the word propaganda; the term's usages were apparently in flux early in the twentieth century. By all indications, Du Bois, a child of the nineteenth century, used the word in its original sense, which simply meant to propagate or spread ideas. Propaganda's original etymology has no references to the truth or the positive value of the ideas that it spreads. For Du Bois, propaganda could be true or untrue, negative or positive. But early in the twentieth century, the term became increasingly associated with the propagation of Socialist and Communist ideas. Hence, in the capitalist West, the word began to absorb its now familiar pejorative usages, describing the spread of lies or, at best, half-truths, for hidden political purposes which generally have little to do with the common social good. Locke, almost two decades younger than Du Bois, had begun to use the term in its twentieth century sense, and Richardson seemed to be theoretically trapped between the two. Richardson's dilemma concerning the term propaganda would not be his alone. As will be noted again in this study, later there will be a general misunderstanding of Du Bois' use of the term. Further, this misreading, at least in part, would become a theoretical support for the 1960s militant, Black Arts Movement.[15]

Early Renaissance Plays: George Schuyler on Eloise Thompson and Eulalie Spence

The presentation of one-act plays that seemed to signal a move away from earlier Negro protest drama had also preceded Locke's 1925 essays "Enter the New Negro" and "Youth Speaks." On an October evening in 1924, the National Ethiopian Art Theatre presented *On Being Forty* by Eulalie Spence (1894–1981) and *Cooped Up* by Eloise Bibb Thompson (1878–1927) at the Lafayette Theater in Harlem. Spence and Thompson were both students at the Ethiopian Art Theatre's school, and their plays had non-protest plots. In *On Being Forty*, a spinster is trapped in a small town; her vengeful elder brother has years before thwarted her marriage to a childhood sweetheart. The elder brother lost the woman he wanted to the father of his sister's sweetheart. Reaching her fortieth birthday, the spinster decides to leave her brother's house over his objections. In *Cooped Up*, the keeper of a rooming house not far from New Orleans falls in love with one of her tenants, a married man whom she attempts to separate from his young wife. *Bills*, a comedy about a debt-ridden married couple, completed the evening. A stuttering lawyer arrives at the couple's home bringing them news of an inheritance from a relative; but the couple mistakenly assumes that he is a bill collector. The lawyer struggles to give the couple the good news and, finally, exits leaving a letter that informs them of their good fortune.[16]

George S. Schuyler (1895–1977), critic, journalist, and satirist, reviewed these plays, providing us with all we presently know about the works. Extant copies of the plays have yet to be uncovered. Schuyler's review here is also significant because he would later be "considered the most prominent African American journalist and essayist of the early twentieth century." His favorable review of *Cooped Up* would be seconded when *Opportunity Magazine* sponsored a literature awards competition in which the play won "Honorable Mention."[17] Schuyler would also, the following year, try his hand at playwriting.

Thompson's *Cooped Up* was "a play written by one who knows life and the ingredients of real drama," writes Schuyler, and it was "much superior" to *On Being Forty* and *Bills*. Schuyler found that the characters in *On Being Forty* were not "true to Negro life," they did not "impress the audience with the feeling that they actually exist." And although "*Bills* was intended for comedy," writes Schuyler, "I did no laughing." The lack of play scripts for these works makes it difficult to comment on Schuyler's review. However, in 1925, Schuyler's review of Spence's play is intriguing because, while it is mostly negative, it does reveal elements of the potential depth of Spence's dramatic style. Those elements in her work would later make Spence's play *Undertow* (1927) one of the few Renaissance plays that can be successfully produced today. *Undertow* will be revisited later in this book.

Garveyism and Locke's "New Negro"

The foregoing discussion of Du Bois and Richardson's writings, the changing meanings of the term propaganda, and the presentation of non-protest plays form the immediate background to Locke's early 1925 arguments against propaganda in Negro art. But the meteoric rise (1919–1921) of Marcus Garvey's (1887–1940) Black Nationalist movement had formed a deeply cultural, and therefore potent theoretical impetus to Locke's 1925 assumptions about the changing nature of Negro art. E. David Cronon writes: "Within a few years after its inception Garvey's U.N.I.A [Universal Negro Improvement Association] had collected more money and claimed a larger membership than any other Negro group either before or since." By 1920, U.N.I.A. membership reached from "Africa to California, from Nova Scotia to South America." A charismatic leader and, apparently, an almost magical orator, Garvey had organized this extraordinary association based on an appeal for African and Negro pride, love, unity, and the ideals of self-help, an economic determinism borrowed from Booker T. Washington.[18] Garvey's program of "race redemption" intended to unite the world's Negroes and obtain for them a country of their own. These general features of the U.N.I.A.'s program came to be known as "Garveyism," and, "Garveyism" would have a number of rephrasings in African American life throughout the rest of the century. Tony Martin has devoted an entire study to the enduring influence that Garveyism has had on African American literature: *Literary Garveyism: Garvey, Black Arts and the Harlem Renaissance* (1983).

However, by 1925, the heyday of U.N.I.A. was well over. In February of that year, after the disastrous failure of his Black Star steamship line, Garvey lost his appeal of a lower court mail fraud conviction in the United States Court of Appeals.[19] Garvey's conviction had been, at best, dubious. The government had failed to prove that its one government witness, who had allegedly received fraudulent mail from the Black Star Line, had, in fact, received such mail. Garvey received a five-year sentence and was imprisoned in Atlanta Penitentiary. His arrest marked the beginning of the decline of the U.N.I.A.'s influence in the Negro world. On the other hand, even in early 1925 Garvey's message of Negro pride, "race consciousness," and self-help was beginning to be seen as a cultural watershed in African American life. Shortly after he lost his court battle, a Harlem newspaper opposed to Garvey and his movement admitted that he had

> awakened the race consciousness and race pride of the masses of Africans everywhere as no man ever did ... save Booker T. Washington.... He made them think, he made them cooperate, he organized and marshaled their forces. For these things his service will be historic and epoch-making.[20]

In fact, Locke's out of touch "norns" of 1925, the "Sociologist," "Race Leader," and "Philanthropist," were contemporary applications of Garvey's thought. In 1916, Garvey had met with "some of what he scornfully termed the so-called Negro leaders," reports Cronon. Garvey characterized these leaders as men who "had no program, but were opportunists living off their so-called leadership while the poor [Negro] people were groping in the dark."[21]

Many Negro leaders relied on white philanthropists for support, and Garvey saw such leaders as "the most dangerous member[s] of our society." This sort of leader, Garvey maintained, "would turn back the clock of progress when his benefactors ask him to do so."

Locke's clarion calls for Negro aesthetic independence in "Enter the New Negro" and "Youth Speaks" were the direct results of Garvey's impact on the Negro world. Perhaps more than any other contemporary cultural force, the spectacular phenomenon of Garveyism, with its overriding essentials of race consciousness and pride, allowed Locke to write: "now [the Negro] becomes a conscious contributor and lays aside the status of a beneficiary and ward for that of a collaborator and participant in American civilization."[22] Locke's new Negro artists, whom, in part, Garveyism had created, would win "cultural recognition" and "should ... prove [to be] the key to that revaluation of the Negro which must precede or accompany any considerable further betterment of race relations." Thus, early in 1925, Locke revealed his Negro art project for social justice; he had received a spectacular, if generally unacknowledged, helping hand from Marcus Aurelius Garvey.

Lewis, Owen, and Richardson and Black Drama's Negro Audience Problems

In the *Messenger* (January 1925), before Locke's *Survey Graphic* articles were published, Theophilus Lewis' "Same Old Blues," and Chandler Owen's (1889–1967) "New Ideas on Art" responded to Du Bois' notion of the "legitimate stage," and his Keatsian "Truth and Beauty" School of art.[23] "Same Old Blues," is mostly a refutation of Benjamin Brawley's (1882–1939) claim, writes Lewis, that "the Theatre is a field peculiarly adapted to the ability of the Negro race." Brawley, Lewis notes, expressed this view in his *The Negro in Literature and Art in the United States* (1921). But in 1925, "in most ... urban black belts," Lewis found "no groups of professional and amateur actors ... continuously presenting some form of the drama before appreciative ... audiences" to support Brawley's claim. In "Same Old Blues" Lewis also charged that Du Bois had "unconsciously," but perfectly, exemplified the notion that the "legitimate" stage was indivisible from the white stage and drama. Du Bois had written that Charles Gilpin "got his first chance on the legitimate stage playing the part of Curtis in Drinkwater's *Abraham Lincoln*" [1918] after training with Williams and Walker and other colored companies.[24] "The term 'legitimate stage,'" writes Lewis, "as employed by white writers, means the stage devoted to the serious portrayal of character (note I do not say the portrayal of serious characters).... When Gilpin appeared in "The Old Man's Boy" ... he was playing in legitimate drama."[25] For Lewis, Du Bois' unconscious "attitude" that the white stage was the legitimate stage and therefore produced the only legitimate drama was part and parcel of the Negro theatre's "same old blues." "In the mind of this foremost Negro scholar," writes Lewis, "a Negro actor has not played a legitimate role unless he has played it on Broadway." He continued:

> This attitude has been assumed by practically the whole body of Negroes with theatrical aspirations.... Hence the most useful factotum who has appeared early in ... almost every other group, ... the actor-dramatist, striving to express the group character ... esthetically, has never been evolved by the Negro Theatre. In his stead the Negro Theatre has produced the actor-showsmith who sought his material, not in Negro life, but on the Caucasian stage.

In Lewis' view, this "unconscious philosophy" on the part of Du Bois and others was the reason why Negro theatre had "practically no body of even mediocre drama." Lewis found that "the white American theatre, which the Aframerican actor-writer ... imitates, [had] not provided" Negro Theatre "with ... working models, either in the form of plays or characters."

In "New Ideas on Art," Chandler Owen obviously had Du Bois in mind (perhaps Locke, too) positing that "art may, or may not, be beautiful," and that "Truth is not an indispensable part of art.... The function of art is to emphasize by exaggerating." Here, Owen gives many examples of art that he judged ugly, untrue, and in no way good. For example, he writes: "*The Klansman* and *Birth of Nation* are certainly art products, yet both are vicious and mean." On the other hand, Owen writes: "The anti-slavery artists picture slavery in hideous horror. The uglier the art, the more effective ... ugliness was of the essence." To Owen, all art was untrue in the sense that it was unnatural: "So clearly is Art unnatural, that the very antipode of the word *natural* is *artificial*, meaning made by art." But Owen seems to tire of his own voluminous case against Du Bois' "Truth and Beauty" School: "To go on, quoting Art and comparing facts ... would consume much time and reams of paper." Owen, instead, ends his discussion returning to the dead-end questions about art that Keats begs us to avoid. He quotes Keats' "Truth is beauty, beauty is truth. That is all ye know and all ye need to know," then adds his own "—Art?" at the end of the quotation. Unlike Du Bois and Locke, Chandler Owen seemed to find the true nature of art unknowable.

In "The Negro Audience" (April 1925), Willis Richardson recounts the story of an English teacher who, after seeing the Howard Players' production of *The Emperor Jones*, found that Eugene O'Neill had "no standing as a playwright." This "respected" English teacher, Richardson reports, and many other

Negro audience members "wondered why the University would stoop to allow its students to give a performance of a play in which the leading character was a crapshooter and [an] escaped convict."[26] Richardson concludes that average Negro audiences "do not generally like dialect, they do not like unpleasant characters and endings, and the most important thing of all they forget, if they ever knew, the main business of the drama is the portrayal of human characters." Richardson's remarks on the Negro audience were related to the "increasing swarms of college educated preachers, school teachers, doctors, and university alumni" whom Lewis had addressed in "Same Old Blues" four months earlier. In his concluding comments on the Negro notion of the "legitimate" stage as synonymous with the white stage, Lewis called on educated Negroes to stop "crying for white folks to give them a chance on the 'legitimate' stage" and "turn their attention to producing Negro drama for Negro audiences." But it appears that, given Richardson's remarks, much of the audience on whom Lewis would rest the future of Negro drama wanted propaganda and not art. Du Bois had already identified this issue in broader, more theoretical terms in 1921:

> We are so used to seeing the truth distorted to our despite, that whenever we are portrayed on ... the stage, as simple humans with human frailties, we rebel. We want everything said about us to tell of the best and highest and noblest in us. We insist that our Art and Propaganda be one. This is wrong and the end is harmful.[27]

And many Negro intellectuals, like Chandler Owen, had, essentially, placed Art on the back burner of Negro needs and goals. Unlike Du Bois, Locke, Richardson and Lewis, these intellectuals had no real functional definition of Art and therefore no immediate place for it in an American Negro society beset by enormous social and political inequities: Art could be good, bad, ugly, or beautiful; but most of all it was the icing on a social and economic black American cake that had yet to be baked.

A month after Richardson's "The Negro Audience" appeared in *Opportunity*, Du Bois seemingly responded to both Richardson and Chandler Owen's "New Ideas On Art." In May, Du Bois announced the *Crisis*' new editorial policy: "We shall stress Beauty — all Beauty, but especially the beauty of Negro life and character; its dancing, its drawing and painting and the new birth of its literature."[28] Owen's "New Ideas on Art" had been ignored. But here Du Bois agreed with Richardson, restating his 1921 position on the Negro reader and audience's need for propaganda:

> We are seriously crippling Negro art and literature by refusing to contemplate any but handsome heroes, unblemished heroines ... we insist on being always

and everywhere all right and often we ruin our cause by claiming too much and admitting no faults.

Perhaps encouraged by Du Bois, Richardson continued his critique of Negro audiences in his essays "Characters," and "The Unpleasant Play."[29] In "Characters," Richardson wrote that everyone knew that Negro audiences accepted, "with wild applause," the black face comedian, "whether he be bootlegger, thief ... or criminal of whatever kind.... But for one moment wash the ... paint from his face and let him be a bootlegger planning seriously to become wealthy by this illegal practice and he is at once taboo." And Richardson wondered: "Has it narrowed down to the fact that as a fool a Negro character may do anything he wills and gain applause while one error on the part of a Negro character as a man will make the whole race throw up its hands in horror?"

Here, too, Richardson acknowledged the desire in a segment of the black audience "for Negro characters of refinement." But he asked, almost humorously, should such Negro characters be like Hamlet, refined, cultured, a "Prince of the blood, but harboring revenge in his heart?" A revenge, it should be noted, in part ignited by the sordid spectre of Hamlet's mother's possible infidelity and sexual betrayal with Claudius, her husband's brother. Richardson asked should the cultured Negro characters be like "the Macbeths committing murder," or like the noble Othello "listening to the ... lies of a scoundrel and strangling a faithful wife?" In the "The Unpleasant Play," Richardson laments the circumstance that "the crowd [Negro and white audiences] is wild about 'blood and thunder,' but at the end of the play, [it] will not be satisfied unless the characters forget all previous grievances, and fly to each other's arms." Richardson finds that unpleasant plays are among the "masterpieces" of nearly all the "great playwrights," and he cites a number of the appropriate works of Ibsen, Gorky, O'Neill, Strindberg, Ostrovsky, even Shaw and others to support that finding. Yet, "playwrights who have depicted unpleasant Negro characters," he notes, "have gotten very little encouragement from the Negro group." Nevertheless, he concludes: "The Negro writer, if he wishes his work to attain any permanence, must not be discouraged.... He must make his audience hear the truth or nothing." For Richardson, too, dramatic art was definitely a search for truth.

Du Bois: Origins of Negro Art

At year's end, 1925, in "The Social Origins of American Negro Art," Du Bois seemed to be attempting to sum up the background and meaning of the Negro art renaissance he had predicted in 1920.[30] He wrote that not all art executed by Negroes could be called Negro Art. The Negro painter Henry Tanner and writers William Braithwaite and Charles Chesnutt were artists who had done "fine work," but they "could hardly be classified as contributing to any particular [Negro] group expression." However, there had been a recent body of Negro produced art in novels, plays, painting, sculpture, and, of course, music that could be called Negro art. This new art's source was, Du Bois observed, "primarily individualistic ... the cry of some caged soul yearning for expression." But, also, in the new Negro art "a certain group compulsion" had combined with the "individual impulse" so "that the ... experience of thousands ... influence ... the message of the one...." Here, too, Du Bois — as many would do after him — attributed the "group compulsion" inspiring this new art to "the sorrow ... inherent in American slavery," and "the difficulties that sprang from emancipation." The African elements in Negro art, the religious "recitals" of African pageantry and the "Shout," in his earlier writings (1913 and 1916) were gone; most probably, these elements disappeared because Du Bois now viewed the Negro art renaissance in a popular Darwinian sense. African imperatives in Negro art were closely related to slavery and, for Du Bois,

> art expression in the day of slavery had to be very limited, a matter of wild ... strains of music with still wilder laughing and dancing.... But as the Negro rises more ... toward economic freedom he is going ... to say more clearly what he wants to say ... and realize what the ... methods of expression may be.[31]

Du Bois, admittedly, had little knowledge of Negro slave art, and, as Darwin Turner reminds us, he was a reserved "New-England-born, Harvard-trained" Negro, and therefore the "wildness," which he attributed to slave art, was not "essential to, or desirable in, Negro life and art."[32] To Du Bois, Negro art was on an evolutionary path to higher forms. Max Reinhardt's premise that for a "revival of art," art had to periodically return to its "basic aspects" was not part of Du Bois' thought at the end of 1925.

Schuyler's The Yellow Peril *and Anderson's* Appearances

In 1925, the discourse on Negro drama between Du Bois, Locke, Lewis, and Richardson, apparently, related to only a few Negro authored plays actually staged that year.[33] The two extant plays that we know reached the stage in 1925 were George Schuyler's *The Yellow Peril* and Garland Anderson's (1886–1939) *Appearances*, the first full-length, straight play by a Negro to be presented on Broadway.[34] Schuyler's play was a non-protest comedy built on the single idea of Negro light-skinned color preferences, and Anderson's *Appearances* seems a paean to Du Bois' notion of a socially serviceable Negro drama that "pricked white consciences."

Locke's "lapse of sentimental appeal" and "recovery from hyper-sensitiveness" is certainly observable in *The Yellow Peril*. Here, The Girl, Schulyer's main character, is a light-skinned or "high yellow" peril to the manners and morals of polite Harlem society. She is an unsentimental and unsympathetic prostitute who manipulates, for all she can get, the sexual desires of six suitors who individually pay her rent, buy her hats, dresses, shoes and jewelry. More a farce than a satire, in *The Yellow Peril* Schuyler stands a great, unsympathetic distance from the characters he creates. For this reason, his people here are of only two (sometimes just one) dimensions and thus not altogether "true to Negro life," which was, oddly enough, his criticism of Spence's *On Being Forty*.

In *Appearances*, a Negro bellhop, Carl, makes almost a religion of putting his "best face forward" in the belief that he can become a professional playwright, which means that any man "can do anything he believes he can." A presumably white female hotel patron wrongly accuses Carl of assault. But here a prologue tells us that all of the events in the play are but parts of Carl's "beautiful and realistic dream"—his play. In this dream, Carl is ultimately found innocent of the crime and, rather conveniently for Anderson's mostly white, Broadway audiences, Elsie Bennett, Carl's accuser, turns out to be a mulatto rather than a real white woman. The protest theme of the Negro man wrongly accused by a white woman is sufficiently compromised. *Appearances* seems to be carefully crafted not to offend prevailing white, 1925 sentiments about the Negro question. With only three Negro characters, like *Rachel*, the play was written primarily for white audiences. John Monroe reports that for most Negro critics "Anderson's theme, that truth and decency will always triumph, was considered naive."

Du Bois: Truth, Beauty, and the Depiction Problem

In the *Crisis*, Du Bois began 1926 giving Locke a somewhat backhanded compliment on Albert and Charles Boni's late 1925 publication of *The New Negro*, which Locke had edited. Du Bois noted that although Locke argues for "Beauty" in "Negro literature and art" as opposed to "Propaganda," *The New Negro* itself "proves the falseness of this thesis." The book was, according to Du Bois, simply "filled ... with [a] propaganda" that was "beautiful and painstakingly done." But Du Bois also warns that if Locke's thesis in this highly acclaimed book was too broadly applied it could lead "the Negro Renaissance into decadence." Du Bois insisted that the late nineteenth and early twentieth century New Negro struggle for "Life and Liberty" had been "the soul" of the new movement in Negro Arts and Letters. Most of all, he feared that if this struggle was forgotten and "the young Negro tries to do pretty things or things that catch the ... fancy of the really unimportant critics ... he will find that he has killed the soul of Beauty in art."

Locke, of course, was as devoted to the idea of Truth in Negro art as was Du Bois. Here, however, Du Bois, conveniently and strategically omits that fact from his characterization of Locke's position. In this *Crisis* issue, Du Bois continually expresses what Turner calls the "inherent contradictions that have deceived critics who unsuspectingly have fixed Du Bois at one or another of his positions." Du Bois wanted Negro authors to create what he called "beautiful things," but for him "Life and Truth" were the most important elements of serious literature and "Beauty," he writes, "comes to make their importance visible and tolerable." Du Bois seems to be saying here that important truths are hidden in the conventions and rush of everyday life, and that Beauty in art frames and illuminates these truths, recovering them from the mundane. Further, for Du Bois, beauty in art is also a palliative that makes tolerable life's often harsh and ugly truths. He begged Negro writers to write from their own experience and counseled them that "in the *Crisis* ... you do not have to confine your writings to the portrayal of beggars, scoundrels and prostitutes; you can write about ordinary decent colored people if you want." But he adds: "Do not fear the Truth.... If you want to paint Crime and Destitution and Evil, paint it.... Use propaganda if you want. Discard it and laugh if you will. But be ... sincere ... thorough ... do a beautiful job."

What Turner calls Du Bois' contradictions, complimenting Locke then warning of possible dire results from Locke's thesis, then calling for propaganda and artistic freedom in the same breath were, in fact, indications of Du Bois' fear of mainstream influence on Negro literature. Du Bois knew that Locke's position could be manipulated to justify an image of Negro life that had, in virtually all American media, conscientiously excluded realistic depictions of the Negro middle and upper-middle class. Locke's assumptions could supply a theoretical rationale allowing Negro writers to join the mainstream arts establishment in the continued exploitation of the lower class Negro stereotypes that had grievously distorted the Negro's popular image.

Du Bois' fears were certainly warranted. Even Willis Richardson felt that cultured, middle-class Negroes were so much like cultured, middle-class whites that such Negro dramatic figures were "seldom interestingly different enough to be typical of the whole Negro race." Writing a play about cultured Negroes would be, Richardson reasoned, "very nearly" the same thing as writing one about cultured whites. Such a "thing is not impossible to do," he admitted, but the resulting play "will not have the strength of those plays written around the peasant class of the Negro group." Interestingly, while Locke saw the folk traditions of the Negro lower class as the main source of a developing black aesthetic, Richardson felt, as did Du Bois, that good Negro drama also presented an opportunity for racial uplift: "I suppose those less fortunate among us ... sometimes called the lower class do form the weakest link in this chain of Negro life; but I imagine, though I may be wrong, that it is rather our duty to strengthen that weak link than to be ashamed of it." The honest and sympathetic depictions of Negro dramatic figures that were "typical of the whole Negro race" would, Richardson believed, help to strengthen that "weak link."

Despite Richardson's claim of the similarity of cultured, middle class whites and Negroes, there is little evidence that Du Bois or Locke, the *crème de la crème* of Negro middle-class society, ever thought that they were, to borrow Cook's phrase, "Jes' Lak White Fo'ks." Moreover, the history of the Grimkés, at the pinnacle of Negro society, was a virtual hotbed of public achievements and shattering psychological conflicts. Following the work of Anton Chekhov and the Moscow Art Theatre, the Grimké story, properly dramatized, could have been the source for more than one extraordinary modern Negro drama. Such a play (or plays) about Negro upper class life would not necessarily have been "non-racial," as Richardson suggests. In the Grimkés' case, for example, the American race question was everywhere in evidence: the sexual relationship of a slave girl and her master (Archibald Grimké's mother and father); the discovery of a brilliant young Negro (Grimké) by his white, abolitionist-feminist aunt; Archibald Grimké's failed interracial marriage; a white mother's apparent desertion of her Negro daughter (Angelina), and, perhaps as a result of that desertion, a gifted young Negro woman's obsessive search for the real nature of motherhood.

Angelina Grimké had been Richardson's high school English teacher, and Grimké and Richardson had, writes Christine Gray, "an informal relationship."[38] Seeing *Rachel* had inspired Richardson to write his first play. But, he either failed to see or was unaware of the dramatic potential in the Grimké story. Of course, that dramatic potential would only reveal itself if Du Bois' "Truth in Art" principles were applied to the Grimkés or other families in the Negro upper class who had similar personal histories. But plays built on such subject matter may have been seen to severely limit the public achievements of these Negro groups, which again raises Du Bois' "best face forward" propaganda question. How much truth in Negro art did Du Bois really want? Perhaps, fortunately for him, he never had to answer that question. Searing dramatic investigations of psychological conflicts in the Negro middle and upper class were not staged or published during the Renaissance and remained foreign to Negro drama until the 1960s.

The following month, February 1926, Locke published "The Negro and the American Stage" for *Theatre Arts Monthly*, which was his version of Du Bois' 1923 "Can the Negro Serve the Drama?"[39] Like Du Bois' piece, Locke's article is primarily about Negro acting, and it is germane to this discussion only in so far as it shows that Locke was willing to significantly adjust his positions for *Theatre Arts*' presumably mostly white readers. In the *Crisis* (1922), "the Negro actor without the Negro drama" had been a "sporadic phenomenon ... at the mercy of wind and weed," but for *Theatre Arts* readers in 1926 the Negro was now part of "a race of actors [who could] revolutionize the drama quite as definitely and perhaps more vitally than a coterie of dramatists."[40] In fact, writes Locke, "the most vital contribution" of Negroes to the American stage would come from the "unemancipated resources of the Negro actor." Locke may have spent the preceding decade struggling with Du Bois to become Negro drama's preeminent theoretical father, but he was unwilling to have those efforts endanger his other integration inspired goals, one of which was to have black performers become full participants on the mainstream American stage.

That same month, February 1926, Du Bois called for a symposium on Negro literature in the *Crisis*. He invited prominent authors to respond to a set of questions; among other things, he asked:

> Can publishers be criticized for failing to publish works about educated Negroes? What can Negroes do if they are continually painted at their worst? ... Isn't the literary emphasis upon sordid, foolish and criminal Negroes persuading readers that this is the truth and preventing authors from writing otherwise?

Du Bois' questions were indicative of his fear of the "literary world" enlisting Negro writers to continue, even expand, the distortion of the popular Negro image. As with Richardson, the responses to his questions from white, mainstream authors suggested that his fears were not unwarranted. Carl Van Vechten, author of *Nigger Heaven* (1926), felt that the "squalor and vice of Negro life would [necessarily] be overdone" in literature because they offered "a wealth of novel, exotic, picturesque material." Van Vechten, like Richardson, also rejected depictions of cultured, middle class Negroes because they were too much like whites to be interesting.[41] H.L. Mencken felt that Negroes should see the humor in Negro caricatures and "write works ridiculing whites." Sherwood Anderson felt that Negroes were being "too sensitive," and that "they had no more reason to complain about their portraits in literature than whites would have." Sinclair Lewis wanted to set up a conference to consider the issues. Julia Peterkin, who wrote on Negro subjects, "praised the 'Black Negro Mammy' and, writes Turner "chastised Negroes for protesting against a proposal in Congress to erect a monument to the Mammy."[42]

In June 1926, at the NAACP's Conference in Chicago, Du Bois made his most comprehensive statements, to date, on Beauty, Truth, and Propaganda in Negro art in his speech "Criteria of Negro Art." His comments, in part, had to have been inspired by two circumstances: the national attention that Locke's *New Negro* began receiving shortly after its publication, which confirmed the drift of younger artists to Locke's position (many of whom were published in *The New Negro*), and what Du Bois had to have seen as the disappointing results of his February symposium.[43]

In "Criteria of Negro Art," Du Bois summed up his discussion of Beauty, writing that Negro artists needed to employ the techniques and strategies of all the artists of the past "to [do] the ... work of the creation of Beauty." He suggested that historically artists had "used Truth," which was, he contended, "the highest handmaid of imagination," and a "vehicle of universal understanding." And for Du Bois, Truth was Beauty and Beauty was Truth because, in art, even truth that revealed ugliness also revealed Beauty. For example, in truthfully depicting what Chandler Owen called the "hideous horror" of slavery, Du Bois probably felt that abolitionist artists were pointing, inversely, to the beauty of freedom or to the beauty of indomitable human will clinging to life whatever the circumstances. The "goodness" which Owen could identify with no fundamental principle of art was, for Du Bois, "a tool that artists used as [a] method of gaining sympathy and human interest." Again, unlike Owen, to Du Bois Truth and Beauty were indivisible and the artist who honestly sought to depict one could not but help to depict the other. And this was so, Du Bois reasoned, because of an "inner and outer compulsion" that deeply influenced the true artist. Therefore, he writes, "all Art is propaganda ... despite the wailing of the purists." The Sociologist, Race Leader had finally responded to the principal wailing purist. That is, Du Bois had finally responded to Locke, author of "Enter the New Negro" and "Youth Speaks," the "double-barreled" attacks against propaganda in Negro art.

In "Criteria of Negro Art," Du Bois also cited the limitations that the reading and ticket-buying white majority imposed on white artists who dealt with Negro subject matter. He said that when the subject matter had anything to do with the Negro, the white majority insisted on a "racial prejudgment," from its white artists that "distorts Truth and Justice." But here, too, in his finding that a great many Negroes also required that Negro artists be "equally unfree," it can be seen that Du Bois' use of the term propaganda was not an advocacy for a system of lies, or even half-truths in Negro art. Du Bois complained that too much of the Negro public when evaluating the work of their artists were "bound by ... customs," that were, in effect, the "second-hand clothes of white patrons." According to Du Bois, too many Negroes were "ashamed of sex," and, "our religion," he adds, "holds us in superstition." He also argues that mainstream America had "so shamelessly emphasized" the Negro's faults that Negroes themselves were "denying" they "ever had" any faults. Two years later, James Weldon Johnson would make a similar argument in the pages of *American Mercury*.

In his concluding remarks, we can see the buds of the separatist strategies that would lead to Du Bois' complete break with the NAACP in the 1930s. Du Bois insisted that the Negro public had to be the "ultimate judge" of Negro literature, most especially plays. He writes that "if a colored man wants to publish a book, he has got to get a white publisher and a white newspaper to say it is great; and then you and I say so." The Negro was, he argues, "handing everything over to a white jury." Yet it was the Negro who could "afford the Truth," whereas "white folk today cannot," he writes. And true to both his advocacy of Negro art and his notions of racial equality, Du Bois sought an independent and "eternal" Negro judgment that would make the Negro "just of soul to all men."

Then, echoing Locke's art-project-for-social-justice program, Du Bois said that the Negro would not be judged entirely "human," until the art he produced "compels recognition." He concluded his address to the Conference finding that the ultimate black art would be "as new as it is old and as old as new." Here, Du Bois again stepped into those ancestor-based African/Asian assumptions about the cosmos and therefore about art which abhor notions of linear progression. He was (perhaps unconsciously) defining as a "criteria of Negro art" the distinctly African view of time as a wheel rather than a Euclidian line segment.

In the first half of 1926, Du Bois was not alone in dealing with the knotty theoretical question of appropriate Negro literature and art. In April, Theophilus Lewis, reviewing a stage version of F. Scott's Fitzgerald's *The Great Gatsby*, suggested that although the play had not "the remotest relation to Negro life," he was "half convinced that the thoughtful Aframerican who knows that sociology is not just a big word will find it a more interesting and diverting *social document* than any of the so-called Negro plays which have so far appeared on the American stage." Lewis, unlike Richardson, made a distinction between Negro propaganda plays and plays like *The Great Gatsby* and O'Neill's Negro dramas, which he considered "social documents."

Lewis gave a glowing review to O'Neill's *The Emperor Jones* in this same column.

Schulyer vs. Hughes: "Lamp-Blacked Anglo-Saxons" or Soul People?

Also, in June 1926, George Schulyer and Langston Hughes published in the *Nation* their opposing views on Negro art: Schuyler's "The Negro-Art Hokum" (16 June 1926), and Hughes' "The Negro Artist and the Racial Mountain" (23 June 1926).[45] Schuyler, apparently, heard nothing of Africa in Negro musical art forms, and he did not feel, as did Du Bois, that the Africanized rituals of much of the black church were, in essence, pure drama. For Schuyler, the Negro-invented Charleston was merely an "eccentric dance," having no relation to the stunningly similar ritual dances of traditional West Africa. The duality of humor and sorrow at the core of West African cosmology and virtually all American Negro music were, writes Schuyler, "contributions of a caste in a certain section of the country. They are foreign to Northern Negroes, West Indian Negroes, and African Negroes."[46] The development of all truly Negro art was, writes Schuyler, "among the numerous black nations of Africa." In his view, to suggest that such a development was taking place "among the ten million colored people" in the United States was "self-evident foolishness." The "Aframerican," Schuyler writes, was "merely a lamp-blacked Anglo-Saxon." Thus, the discourse on Negro art between Du Bois, Locke, Lewis, Richardson, and others constituted "The Negro-Art Hokum."

Hughes' rebuttal, "The Negro Artist and the Racial Mountain," took the form of a severe critique of the Negro middle and upper class. Hughes insisted that rather than being "lamp-blacked Anglo-Saxons," these Negro groups wished and pretended to be such, that is, they wanted to be white. And for Hughes, wanting to be white was the great tragedy of self-hatred in Negro life. Hughes writes that in the typical Negro middle class home

> one sees ... how difficult it would be for an artist born in such a home to interest himself in interpreting the beauty of his own people. He is never taught to see that beauty. He is taught rather not to see it, or ... to be ashamed of it....

And the "self-styled, high-class" Negroes, Hughes writes, will do "more aping of things white than the less cultured or less wealthy" Negroes; the "high-class" Negroes will "themselves draw a color line." Hughes continues:

> In the North they go to white theaters and white movies. And in the South they have at least two cars and a house "like white folks." Nordic manners ...

> Nordic art (if any), an Episcopal heaven. A very high mountain for the ... racial artist to climb ... to discover himself and his people.

But here, too, Hughes rejoices in what he calls "the so-called common element" who were "the majority—may the Lord be praised!" These people, writes Hughes, were not

> too learned to watch the lazy world go round ... and they do not particularly care whether they are like white folks ... [They] are not afraid of spirituals, as for a long time their more intellectual brethren were, and jazz is their child.... And they accept what beauty is their own without question.

The "racial mountain" that Negro artists had to climb had been, in fact, Hughes contends, co-constructed by the Negro upper class and the white majority. Whites, in their mountain building, implicitly and inevitably called on Negro artists to "be stereotyped, don't shatter our illusions about you, don't amuse us too seriously. We will pay you."

To Hughes, Schuyler's notion that Negroes, even given their internal differences, did not constitute a distinct social, political, and cultural group was, indeed, "self-evident foolishness," to borrow Schuyler's phrase. It would seem that Garvey's U.N.I.A. movement had, years before, settled the issue of the Negro's distinctive national character. But more than an effort to have Negroes considered white people in blackface, Schuyler's statements (or over-statements) on this issue were ultimately the result of his fear of white racism's historical use of Negro distinctiveness to justify color prejudice. "The Negro-art hokum" was gaining popularity, Schuyler concluded, because it was consistent with

> the last stand of the old myth palmed off by Negrophobists for all these many years, and recently rehashed by the sainted Harding, that there are "fundamental, eternal, and inescapable differences" between white and black Americans."

Racism could become the ultimate arbiter of any discourse on Negro art, even for a self-styled, H.L. Mencken–like intellectual like George S. Schuyler.

Du Bois and the Krigwa Players

In July, Du Bois reported that a new Harlem theatre company, The Krigwa Players Little Negro Theatre, had been organized in May.[47] Du Bois was himself one of the company's principal organizers, and its establishment seemed an answer to Lewis' 1925 suggestion that educated Negroes stop "crying for white folks to give them a chance on the 'legitimate' stage" and produce their own "Negro drama for Negro audiences." Sounding like Locke, in "Steps Toward a Negro Theatre," Du Bois asserted in July 1926 that "the best of the Negro actor and the ... Negro drama have not been called for. This could be evoked only by a Negro audience desiring to see its own life depicted by its own writers and actors."

Here, too, Du Bois contributed significantly to the discourse on black American drama, raising, for perhaps the first time, the issue of the uneasy relationship between pure Negro drama and the Negro Church. The strongest institutions in Negro life, the Baptist and Methodist churches, writes Du Bois, had "frowned upon drama ... the American Negro [had] been hindered in his natural dramatic impulses." This was (and remains) the Puritanic "mountain" that Negro artists, especially dramatists, had to climb.[48]

In setting up this new theatre company, Du Bois laid down four principles of African American drama and theatre that would become almost a battle cry of the later, militant, Black Arts movement:

> The plays of the Negro theatre must be: 1. *About us.* That is, they must have plots which reveal Negro life as it is. 2. *By us.* That is, they must be written by Negro authors who understand ... what it means to be a Negro today. 3. *For us.* That is, the theatre must cater ... to Negro audiences and be ... maintained by their entertainment and approval. 4. *Near us.* The theatre must be in a neighborhood near the mass of ordinary Negro people.

Then, sounding even more like Locke, Du Bois added, "only in this way can a real folk-play movement of American Negroes be built up."

Audience Class Distinctions and Needs

If the recurring pronoun "Us" in Du Bois' principles of Negro drama and theatre tended to wrap Negro audiences in a monolithic veil, Theophilus Lewis would have none of it. That same month, July 1926, in his "Theatre Column," Lewis divided the Negro audience into two groups: "the groundlings" and the "indifferent, better class" that "insists on the Negro theatre copying the conventions of the contemporary white American theatre."[49] This "better class" of Negroes was, Lewis continued, "unaware that the white stage reflects the racial experience of a people whose cultural background has never resembled ours...."

These observations were, of course, closely related to the wanting-to-be-white syndrome which Hughes had made the thematic core of his "Racial Mountain" essay. Lewis' "groundlings" were representatives of the majority, "low down, common folks" in whom Hughes rejoiced, and, as Richardson had observed, many of those "common folks" thoroughly enjoyed the stereotyped antics of the blackface comics in the Negro musical theatre. But the groundlings, writes Lewis, "pay the fiddler," that is, they supported the theatre with their "money, presence, and applause," while the better, educated class "stays away and favors the theatre with the boon of its criticism." The Negro theatre's predominantly lower class audience, Lewis observed, inevitably contained "unlettered and lewd folks, laborers and menials ... persons who are materially prosperous but spiritually bankrupt." Since the days of ancient Rome, the theatre has presented to its paying "clientele" entertainment that it could "comprehend and enjoy," writes Lewis. The theatre that caters to the predominantly lower class Negro audience, as with the ancient Roman audience, "must devote itself to ... buffoonery ... farce and ... dancing, supplemented with giants, midgets, acrobats, ... and mathematical jackasses." But, Lewis quickly added: "This does not mean that the audience ... is vicious. It is merely vulgar." In fact, he finds that "a low spiritual tone is not necessarily an unwholesome one. The important thing is that the spiritual expression of a people should be spontaneous and unaffected." And while lower class domination of the Negro audience was "unfortunate in some respects," it was, Lewis felt, better than the "indifference and affectation" that the Negro upper class had thus far offered the black theatre. He concludes: "Sincerity, however crudely expressed, is at the root of every true art." But Lewis' remarks also make clear that for some time there had been in the broad Negro audience a need for an educated, aesthetically informed segment bent on perpetuating black culture in the theatre arts: "The educated classes who, because of their higher standard of life, make more exacting demands on the theatre." The lack of such an element in the broad Negro audience defined a narrow path for the development of Negro drama. In 1926, Du Bois, with his Krigwa Players Little Negro Theatre, was exploring that narrow path.

The Problem of Writing Drama and a Word from Eulalie Spence

Nearing the end of the year, October 1926, in "The Drama of Negro Life," Locke seemed to be seeking reasons why his 1922 call for a flowering of Negro drama had not yet come to pass, even though, as many thought and Locke agreed, "Negro life [was] ... rich in dramatic values." According to Locke, foremost of the many reasons behind this paradox was the circumstance that "the drama" was the result of some measure of "cultural maturity," and, in 1926, Locke explains, Negro art was just beginning to consider the issue of "cultural self expression." Locke and Du Bois also agreed that a dramatist needed at least a minimum amount of economic security. But, as might be expected, for Locke, propaganda was still the main barrier to the development of Negro drama. He felt that playwrights who had followed Du Bois' problem play strategy had mistakenly "pushed forward their moralistic allegories ... melodramatic protests as ... correctives ... antidotes for race prejudice."

But here, too, Locke seemed to soften his stand against Du Bois' problem plays. He admitted that such plays were "immediately appealing." However, he also found that the Negro dramatist's "creativity" was trapped between a drama that seemingly limited itself to the depiction of polemics and "social analysis" and "the drama of expression and artistic interpretation." Expressive and artistically interpretive drama was, of course, none other than Locke's proposed Art-theatre drama. Locke insisted that the creation of viable Negro drama could not begin with the powerful problem plays that Du Bois sought until there had been among Negro dramatists a "development ... of the capacity for self criticism." He believed that the creation of a problem play that could reach the artistic heights of authentic tragedy and comedy would require "genius," and "the objectivity of great art." He also believed that the elements of authentic tragedy and comedy were right there in Negro life, waiting to be mined. He writes that the circumstances of "race hold tragedies and ironies as deep and keen as those of the ancient classics." Negro dramas by white authors, including plays by the Negro author Willis Richardson, needed, Locke writes, "more of the ... depth of pity and terror and ... the joy of life even when [it] flows tragically." Again, seemingly in deference to Du Bois, Locke agreed that an important objective of the new Negro drama was to attack the "false stereotypes" that had historically plagued the Negro. But, he argued that it was still more important "that drama should stimulate the group ... give it the spiritual quickening of native art." In other words, folk drama was more vital and important to black American life than propaganda plays.

As Du Bois had already implied, Locke, too, felt that African culture and art had a central role to play in the development of Negro drama, which could use, writes Locke, "adaptations of its [African] folk lore, art-idioms and symbols." Again, like Du Bois, he felt that the Negro's African "mimetic" tradition had been broken by the "inhibitions" of "Puritanism." That is, writes Locke, except when "the traces" of that tradition "flare up spectacularly when the touch of a serious dramatic motive once again touches them." But Locke warned that this return to African aesthetic sources could not be forced or specifically programmed; it would come, he concludes, "only [with] the play of the race spirit over its own heritage and tradition."

In 1927, in "Our Little Renaissance," Locke wrote: "The Negro Renaissance must be an integral phase of contemporary American art and literature; more and more we must divorce it in our minds from propaganda and politics. Otherwise, why call it a renaissance?" Locke felt that the offerings of white artists, working with Negro subject matter, such as, O'Neill, Torrence, Julia Peterkin, and others should also be judged part of the output of the Negro renaissance. "What is the issue," he asked, "sociology or art — a quality of spirit or complexions?" In 1927, Locke found, too, that "overt propaganda [was] as exceptional as it used to be typical." The younger Negro artists were "trekking back to their root-sources," and were beginning to recover from a "rhetorical acceptance of race." Race in the work of these younger artists was now "taken more instinctively for granted."

In his monthly "Theatre column," (February 1927) Lewis attacked what he called some of "the bogus ideas about art and artists" that kept "bobbing up ... to impede and embarrass sensible men and women engaged in creative work."[52] First on his list of "bogus ideas" was "the art for art's sake hokum." Art was not, writes Lewis, "hauled down out of airy nothingness," as the "art for art's sake" dictum seemed to suggest: "it is extracted from the very core of life. This is why the highest art, no matter how thoroughly it is refined and perfumed, never quite loses the odor of viscera and bowels.... The raw material of art is the way men live." Art's "function," Lewis added, "is to satisfy ... spiritual hunger," and "its final and efficient causes are immanent in the acts and wants of people." Therefore, Lewis reasoned, "it follows that genuine art can be produced only by men [and women] with a sound understanding of the nature and processes of life."

Reviewing *In Abraham's Bosom* by Paul Green, a white dramatist, Lewis revealed one of his fundamental principles of dramatic structure: "The basis of drama, as William Archer has pointed out, is character. Every worthwhile play is built around the way some distinctive man or woman struggles with some problem of life." In structuring, *In Abraham's Bosom*, Lewis felt that Green had "spliced two shorter plays together." These two "welded" plays had, according to Lewis, central characters of wholly "differing temperaments." Thus, Green had destroyed a unity of character in which Lewis firmly believed. Lewis' later review of Green's *Lonesome Road: Six Plays for a Negro Theatre*[53] elicited another of his views on the essence of dramatic structure: "The only kind of struggle suitable for dramatic treatment is the clash between desire so intense that it will sweep aside or destroy any ordinary obstacle and opposition so strong that it will crush any ordinary desire."[54]

That next month, March 1927, Du Bois, too, found fault in Green's Pulitzer Prize winning *In Abraham's Bosom*. It was, he declared, an "example" of "the defeatist genre of Negro art which is so common."[55] According to

Turner, Du Bois felt that even if a white writer, like Green, wrote honestly about "black people's refusal to accept failure, the publisher or producer would prohibit a portrayal of triumphant blacks."[56] Du Bois feared that "pathetic, inevitable defeat or exotic degeneracy ... would be the dominant images of black life unless black writers corrected the images," writes Turner. A month earlier, Lewis had been concerned with dramatic structure, but in March, Du Bois' focus was on the social and political implications of a negative Negro popular image.

In April 1927, Du Bois again reminded his readers of the Negro's African artistic roots; he discussed, Turner writes, "the impressive black heritage revealed in the fine arts of Ethiopia, Egypt, and the rest of Africa." Du Bois seemed to be taking a cue from Locke's similar, late 1926 comments in "The Drama of Negro Life." Turner adds that "in contemporary America," Du Bois insisted that the Negro's African artistic heritage "must be continued in the art of the spoken and written word." Here, too, he also insists, yet again, that the Negro artist "must have the freedom to wonder where he will, portray what he will, interpret whatever he may see according to the canons of beauty which the world through long experience has laid down."[57] Beyond Keats, Du Bois' (and Locke's) "canons of beauty" could also be found in the Negro's ancient African past.

In July 1927, in "Main Problems of the Negro Theater," Lewis found that the dramatist was "the only worker in the theater who contributes anything of permanent value."[58] Lewis then ranked what he called "the problems of theater" as follows: "Drama, Acting, Audience, and Production." Further, for Lewis, the problem of audience and drama were crucially interrelated in the Negro theatre. He estimated that in Harlem, "the center of dramatic activity," the total audience for the Negro theatre was not above ten thousand. But that number had to be reduced because, writes Lewis,

> the ... prosperous classes cannot be included in the potential audience until Negro playwrights become efficient craftsmen. While Negro drama is in ... experimental stages they will continue to patronize Broadway theaters.

"The demand for Negro drama," Lewis asserted, "reduced to a plain proposition, is a demand for plays written by Negro authors." This understood, he writes: "the next problem our theater must face is how to encourage colored playwrights in such a way that they may pass through ... apprenticeship ... produce mature plays as early as possible." To answer this problem, Lewis proposed that a "repertory system" be set up in the "large centers of population, leading to an exchange of companies which will knit the ... units together in a National Negro Theater"—Hay would make a similar proposal sixty-seven years later.[59] In such a national theatre, Lewis continues, consisting of compact organizations of actors and auxiliaries sensitive to the cultural demands of the race, the dramatist would be at home ... [and] able to work with comfort ... while he proceeds with the idealization of race character which ... is the real meaning of Negro drama.

By April 1928, in "Beauty Instead of Ashes," Locke wondered, rhetorically, if "the simple first products and ground flow" of the New Negro art would ever be producing "more mature products and bi-products [sic]?"[60] And would such an art "of Negro Life ... make its contribution to American culture and the ... materials of art?" Locke answered these questions, as might be expected, writing that the younger artists' mission was to produce more mature art products. He also found that white authors O'Neill, Torrence, and Green in the drama, and Vachel Lindsay and Carl Van Vechten in literature, were already "broadening out the main course" of American drama and literature with Negro materials. However, here Locke intended no blanket endorsement of white writers working with Negro subject matter. His 1923 criticism of Culbertson's *Goat Alley* and 1926 finding that Paul Green's *No 'Count Boy* was "over-studied" and therefore "lacking in spontaneity" were still in force.[61] Moreover, the most important "cultural influence," Locke insists, is "the Negro folk tradition and temperament" itself. Nevertheless, leaving behind "generations of comic, sentimental, and genre interest in Negro life, white American letters," Locke observed, "at last dug down to richer treasure." Then, apparently taking Du Bois in his sights, he continues:

> Negro intellectuals ... generally have complained of this artistically important development — some ... of the defeatist trend of most of the themes, others because of a "peasant, low life portrayal that misrepresents by omission the better element of Negro life." They mistake for color prejudice the ... love for a strong local color, and for condescension ... interest in folk life.

But, he insists, "as modernists," the younger Negro artists, had that same interest in folk life. Evidence of this was "unmistakably shown" in recently published novels by Jean Toomer and Eric Waldron and in Rudolph Fisher and Claude McKay's "pungent Harlem stories." What Locke calls "the group trend of *Fire*, a quarterly brought out ... devoted to younger Negro artists" was additional evidence of the modernist black interest in folk life.[62] Significantly, Locke adds that "the critics, Negro reformers, forget how protectively closed the upper levels of Negro society have been, and how stiffly posed ... before the sociologist's camera."[63] As the relationship between Angelina Grimké and Willis Richardson suggests, the Negro upper class was, indeed, beyond the reach of the younger Negro artist.

Locke felt that "Negro genius" had not yet attained its "full power in the domain of the novel and the drama." Yet much of what he has to say here concerning the younger artists, centers on fiction writing other than drama. However, we may reasonably assume that Locke's views on Negro literature were doubly applied to Negro drama; he was not unaware that because plays are mainly written for performance, they often have a more visceral effect on their audiences than do other forms of literature. Du Bois, too, was keenly aware of this special quality of the drama. His comments on Negro literature have even greater weight when they are applied to Negro drama. And Du Bois "considered [all] art," Turner writes, "a vehicle for enunciating and effecting social, political, and economic ideas."

In June 1928, Du Bois' praise of Nella Larsen's *Quicksand* and censure of Claude McKay's *Home to Harlem* would probably have been the same in content but magnified in intensity if these works had been plays rather than novels. In his *Crisis* column "The Browsing Reader," Du Bois judged that Larsen's "theme is not defeatist like the work of Peterkin and Green ... despite the lack of a happy ending." Larsen's heroine, writes Du Bois, "is typical of the new, honest, young Negro woman — the one on whom "race" sits negligibly and Life is always first and its wandering path is but darkened, not obliterated by the shadow of the Veil."[64] Du Bois longed for such a stage heroine. On the other hand, he would have, most probably, done everything in his power to keep from the stage what he felt was the untoward "drunkeness ... lascivious sexual promiscuity and utter absence of restraint" in the characters with which McKay had peopled *Home to Harlem*. But, even though the "dirtier parts" of McKay's book made Du Bois "feel distinctly like taking a bath," he could not bring himself to overlook its author's aesthetic gifts. "McKay is too great a poet to make any complete failure in writing," Du Bois writes. He also saw beauty in *Home to Harlem*:

> The continued changes upon the theme of the beauty of colored skins; the portrayal of the fascination of their new yearnings for each other which Negroes are developing. The chief character ... has something appealing, and the glimpses of the Haitian ... have all the materials of a great piece of fiction.

Nevertheless, Du Bois found that McKay had, for the most part, "set out" to "cater to that prurient demand on the part of white folk for a portrayal in Negroes of that utter licentiousness which conventional civilization holds white folk back from enjoying — if enjoyment it can be called." Du Bois concludes his critique of *Home to Harlem* writing that he is "sorry that the author [McKay] has stooped to this." Had the people of McKay's book been flesh and blood dramatic figures on a stage, Du Bois would have been more than "sorry"; he would have been enraged.

The potent effect that drama has on its audiences as compared to the novel's more cerebral and therefore less explosive influence on its reading public was taken up, albeit indirectly, in Eulalie Spence's "A Criticism of Negro Drama," also published in June 1928. Here, Spence found that "American drama" was two to three decades "behind the novel and short story." "There is," she writes, "almost no subject ... that cannot be discussed with the most revolting detail between the covers of a book." And Spence offers McKay's *Home to Harlem* as evidence of the barriers of the usual propriety that the novel had overcome.

However, in the drama, "we have elected to be squeamish," writes Spence. But despite its lack of subject matter development, the drama had, in recent years, she insists, "developed a ... new genius of mechanism and a new direction." The "forward-thinking" Negro dramatist instead of being "affronted" by the plays of O'Neill, Green, and DuBose Heyward, "will admit," Spence notes, that a number of white writers of Negro subject matter have "heralded a new dawn." But, like Hubert Harrison, Spence felt that most Negro writers knew little about writing drama. She had read, she reports, Negro authored plays with the written caveat: "To Be Read. Not Played!" to which she replied: "Why not the song to be read not sung?" Spence sincerely believed that most Negro playwrights of her day had been unable to attract an appreciative and substantial audience because they "labored like the architect who has no knowledge of geometry."

Spence also advised that Negro playwrights avoid propaganda plays because "the white man is ... unresponsive to the subject," and "the Negro ... is hurt and humiliated by it." However, "if we have a Shaw or a Galsworthy," she observes, "let him wander ... in the ... devious by paths of race dissection." But the writers of such plays can have "no eye for the box office," Spence warns. With propaganda out of the picture, Spence concludes that what was left to the Negro dramatist was nothing less than the portrayal of "the life of his people, their foibles ... ambitions ... defeats ... [and] all these, told with tenderness and skill and a knowledge of the theatre and the technique of the times."

At the end of 1928, November and December, Locke and James Weldon Johnson published writings that are a fitting conclusion to the Art or Propaganda debate as it developed throughout the Harlem Renaissance. Accordingly, Lewis' observations on the nature of Negro drama in his 1929 review of Wallace Thurman (1902–1934) and Jourdan Rapp's (1895–1942) *Harlem* will be taken up briefly; this chapter will then conclude with Locke and Johnson's essays.

In terms of dramatic structure, Lewis writes that excluding O'Neill and one or two others, white dramatists dealing with Negro material have gone to "exceptional pains to discover unusual and quaint types for dramatic presentation." For Lewis, *Harlem* had banished all such "quaint" and "picaresque" types. If *Harlem* becomes a "box office success," Lewis asserts, "its influence on the trend of Negro drama will be of far greater significance than its intrinsic merit." He continues:

> Dramatic types are far more vivid than human types. The world knows Hamlet, as George Brandes pointed out, better than it knows any actual Dane that ever lived. If the picaresque [Negro] is continually presented on the stage, the world will quickly gain the impression, and later the conviction, that he represents normal Negro character.

And that quaint and picaresque Negro character was most often, Lewis contends, "capricious and irresponsible," someone to be "tolerated or even pampered but never invested with a position of importance or authority." Lewis felt that Negro drama needed normalcy, and, like Du Bois, he feared that young Negro playwrights were being led astray by the apparent success of colorful and exotic Negro dramatic figures.

> The dramatized rogue exerts an even more pernicious influence on Negro playwrights. Young artists, except those possessing actual genius, inevitably choose established artists as models. Already Paul Green ... is the patron saint of a cult of young Negro writers whose plays of frustration, submission and sorrow teem with happy-go-lucky banjo players and conjure women.

"The danger," Lewis adds, "is that that these eccentric forms of character may become ... traditions and when the original Negro artist appears he will have to spend in breaking down these traditions the energy he ought to use in creative work."

Locke's "Art or Propaganda?" Equals Johnson's "Negro Author's Dilemma"

In November 1928, Locke simply asked: "Art or Propaganda? Which? Is this more the generation of the prophet or that of the poet; shall our intellectual and cultural leadership preach and exhort or sing?"[67] Locke's question, at the end of the last full year of the Harlem Renaissance, identified the core issue that had dominated the discourse on Negro drama since Du Bois first raised it in "The Drama Among Black Folk" in 1916. After a decade and a half, the art or propaganda issue was, writes Locke, "artistically ... the one fundamental question for us today." The Negro drama's predominant use of quaint and picaresque dramatic figures; the Negro writer's lack of preparation to write drama; the lower class dominance of the Negro audience, and the double consciousness of the Negro middle class were all issues related to the art or propaganda question. Similarly, the taboo nature of realistic story material drawn from the Negro middle class; the issue of the value of white contributions to Negro drama, and the suggested establishment of a national black repertory system were all clearly extensions of the art or propaganda debate. In fact, the issue of separatism, which Lewis indirectly raised in his call for a national black repertory system, fueled the 1997 Wilson-Brustein debate.

In *American Mercury*, edited by H.L. Mencken, James Weldon Johnson made clear in "The Dilemma of The Negro Author" that the Negro author was, in effect, trapped between two audiences, a white one and a black one, each insisting on its own form of propaganda. Johnson writes that to "white America" Negroes were "simple, indolent, docile, improvident peasants, or ... impulsive, irrational, passionate savages." And, probably as well read as Du Bois and Locke, he could confidently add that practically all the Negro subject matter published in this country "and read ... by white America" honored "one or more of these" Negro stereotypes. For example, Johnson suggests that it would take "supreme genius" to put "heroic language" in the mouths of "Crispus Attucks, Nat Turner, or Denmark Vesey and have white America accept the work as authentic." Johnson even doubted that thirty percent of the whites reading "The Dilemma of The Negro Author" knew anything about Attucks, Turner, or Vesey, whom he called three "tragic heroes" of American Negro history and therefore of American history. Johnson also felt that white propaganda about Negroes was so deeply entrenched that if a Negro author published a novel depicting the lives of the "wealthy class" of Negroes, "it would strain the credulity of white America beyond the breaking point."

But the Negro author had, Johnson writes, "no more ... absolute freedom ... addressing black America," which Hughes had suggested in "The Negro Artist and The Racial Mountain." There were areas of Negro life — mostly in the Negro upper-middle class — that the Negro author "dare not touch ... without incurring the wrath of the entire colored pulpit and press," writes Johnson. And this was so, he adds, because American Negroes were, in fact, an "antagonized minority ... unremittingly on the defensive.... Their faults are exploited to produce exaggerated effects," and thus "they have a strong feeling against exhibiting ... anything but their best points." Du Bois' "best face forward" was embedded into Negro America at the survival level, and his 1903 notion of "double consciousness" was, according to Johnson, yet another horn of the Negro author's dilemma: Johnson suggests that no Negro could completely escape the "influence" of ninety percent of his fellow-American population, which was, of course, almost wholly white.

Concluding his article, Johnson found that "a psychoanalysis of ... Negro authors of literature, written in strict conformity to the taboos of black America, would reveal that they were unconsciously addressing themselves mainly to white America."

This point returns us to Locke's essay and what is, perhaps, his most revealing statement about his opposition to propaganda in Negro Art:

> My chief objection to propaganda, apart from its besetting sin of monotony and disproportion, is that it perpetuates the position of group inferiority even in crying out against it. For it lives and speaks under the shadow of a dominant majority whom it harangues, cajoles, threatens or supplicates. It is too extroverted for balance or poise or inner dignity and self-respect. Art in the best sense is rooted in self-expression and whether naive or sophisticated is self-contained.

While Du Bois' greatest fear was of whites' ability to co-opt Negro art to perpetuate a deep-rooted system of color prejudice, Locke's greatest fear was of what propagandist Negro art was doing to the Negro. Johnson's finding that Negro authors, bound to "best face forward" propaganda, were unconsciously addressing themselves to whites, ignoring the beauties of their own race, was anathema to Locke. He believed that propaganda expanded and nurtured an already all too vivid Negro sense of inferiority: "Self-conviction must supplant self-justification and in the dignity of this attitude a convinced minority must confront a condescending majority. Art cannot completely accomplish this, but I believe it can lead the way."

Almost a decade before Locke published "Art or Propaganda?" the Harlem Renaissance had begun with an exuberance and vitality that solidified the "New Negro," or, more accurately, a new Negro image. But a post–World War I rebirth of Negro art needed more than the high spirits ignited by victoriously returning troops and the spectacular but brief black romanticism of Garveyism. The obstacles that barred the way to Negro creativity in the arts (internal and external) had to be examined. The discourse on Negro art in the High Harlem Renaissance (1925–29) made that examination. Moreover, as a consequence of the consistent clarity and quality of that discourse, on both sides of the art or propaganda issue, no other five-year period in the twentieth century would codify as far-reaching assumptions about the nature of African American drama.

III

Black Theory in the Great Depression and Beyond, 1930–1949, Part I

Du Bois' Revisionism: How and Why

In the first full year (May 1930) of the Great Depression, W.E.B. Du Bois quietly, and almost elegantly, reconciled his own thinking about the art or propaganda issue in Negro art that he had first raised in 1913. In a theoretical discussion contained in his glowing review of white author Marc Connelly's *The Green Pastures*, he found simply that "all art is propaganda ... but ... all propaganda is not art."[1] Most propaganda was, Du Bois added, "not at all artistically done" and "was not meant to be, no matter how true [it] may be." He continued:

> It is difficult for the Negro audience to judge a play for themselves.... What do we want in a play? A picture of ourselves as we would like to seem? ... Or a caricature of Negro life as today it is certainly not? Yet all these things can be portrayed upon the stage ... and if the result is artistic, the play has a right to be given.

Similarly, Du Bois writes, "if a person portrays ideal Negro life, the sole judgment of its success is whether the picture is a beautiful thing. He cannot be criticized simply because white folk think the facts untrue...." Indeed, here Du Bois' "white folk" possessed, at best, a very selective notion of the truth, which made them incapable of defining what was and was not art in Negro literature and drama. "The black world," he adds, "does rightly complain that white folk insist on judging art as truth and then refusing to accept or see or read any artistic work which does not portray the truth as they want it." At first glance, it would seem that by 1930, Du Bois was backing away from that first pillar of his Keatsian Truth and Beauty School of Negro art. He writes here that even if dramatists portrayed Negro life as "sordid and despicable, the critic's criterion is not whether the work is complete or true to life, but solely, is the idea well presented?" But here, too, he finds:

> The difficulty ... with the Negro on the American stage, is that the white audience ... demands caricatures ... and the Negro ... either cringes to the demand because he needs the pay, or ... condemns every Negro book or show [that] does not paint colored folks at their best. Their criticisms should be aimed ... at the embargo which white wealth lays on ... a full picturing of the Negro soul.

Reading these assertions in context with what Du Bois has already said, it seems clear that in 1930 he had not walked away from his truth criteria. Rather, for the first time in his writing, he suggests that he is looking for truth and "completeness" not in a single Negro artwork but in a body of Negro literature and in a canon of Negro drama. He also suggests that even if the Negro farces and caricatures demanded by white audiences are artistic, they represent but a fraction of a potential canon of Negro drama that, taken as a whole, would amount to the "full picturing of the Negro soul." But "white wealth" had "embargoed" Negro middle-class dramas, and social dramas about the Negro's struggle against the color line; these were propaganda materials to be sure, but, as had been proved by Shaw, Brieux, and Hauptman, propaganda could be elevated to the level of art.

Du Bois correctly saw that at least two thirds of the potential canon of Negro drama and literature was missing in action, so to speak. He saw, too, that Negroes themselves were not calling attention to this larger issue; they were still embroiled in the narrower concerns of what had been, at the beginning of the Renaissance, his "best face forward" notion of Negro art. The changes in Du Bois' thinking had not occurred in a vacuum. While he was, for the most part, guided by his own counsel, as a trained sociologist he was extremely sensitive to the flow of ideas and events around him.

Reverberations from the High Harlem Renaissance

From the beginning of the Renaissance others shared Alain Locke, Theophilus Lewis, and Eulalie Spence's opposition to Negro propaganda plays. In 1920, John Monroe reports that, like Spence, Lester Walton, of the *Age* and manager of Harlem's Lafayette Theatre, found that "blacks did not wish to be burdened with an examination of racial issues when they attended the theatre for entertainment."[2] Monroe also reports that the black periodicals, *Age* and *Amsterdam News* "welcomed" Frank Wilson's (1886–1956) *Pa Williams' Gal* (1923), "as a race play 'without preachment or propaganda'" when it opened in the Lafayette Theatre.

Later, in 1927, the Lafayette Theatre in Harlem presented Irvin Miller's musical "satire" *Gay Harlem*. Lewis' review of this show related to the issues of artistic caricature and positive-image propaganda that Du Bois later raised in his review of *The Green Pastures*. Lewis took to task Edgar Grey, staff writer for the *Amsterdam News*, for his negative review of *Gay Harlem*. Grey had "complained," writes Lewis, that the show "was a medley of loose morals and lasciviousness blended with a wanton display of female flesh."[3] But Lewis writes:

> *Gay Harlem* was an intelligent and highly entertaining lampoon of the more picaresque phases of life as it is in a community of rooming houses and hot-dog stands. The revue poked a good deal of ribald fun at the journalistic corruption and high pressure gold digging which exist in this and other big cities.

In *Gay Harlem*, Miller had, following Shakespeare, "held the mirror up to" real aspects of Harlem life, writes Lewis, and he had satirized them, "artistically." Lewis added: "If we do not like the social ugliness we see on the stage, the remedy is not to close the theatre or bawl the actors out, but to change our way of living." Du Bois was almost certainly aware of this critical dispute between Lewis and Grey. By 1930, he was, apparently, siding with Lewis' view that Negro caricature could attain the level of serviceable stage art, especially when it satirized or lampooned actual situations in Negro life.

The need for that complete canon of Negro drama that Du Bois seemed to be calling for in 1930 had been articulated as early as 1923. Lovett Fort-Whiteman, the *Messenger*'s early drama editor, noted that for Harlem audiences the popularity of "passé Broadway successes with Negro casts" had plummeted. Too many in the Negro community, along with "prostituted sections of the Negro press, had unwisely believed" that this "transplanted drama could be fastened on the feelings of the Negro," writes Fort-Whiteman. He added: "today the Negro stage can hardly be said to exist," which was "due almost wholly to a dearth of Negro playwrights." Fort-Whiteman felt that in 1923 the Negro was presented with "the ripest occasion, fraught with the most propitious circumstances for the establishing of a genuine Negro playhouse, and humble beginnings made toward imparting some Negro *spirituelle* to our growing American dramatic literature." But a few months after this rallying call for the development of native Negro drama, Wallace Jackson, another early writer for the *Messenger*, wrote:

> Drama does not spring spontaneously from the life of a people.... The great epics of the Greeks and Romans and early Anglo-Saxons were preceded by many years of the lyric. Thus time and technic [*sic*] are necessary before the Negro Stage will become dramatic.[4]

The original Negro authors for whom Locke, Lewis, Spence, Johnson and others waited may simply have not had enough time to develop in the decade between 1920 and 1930. As Jackson suggests, if we were to expect that a flowering canon of Negro drama would develop in the Harlem Renaissance as, for example, vernacular drama developed in the Italian Renaissance, then such a Negro canon could be expected to appear in about two hundred years. In music it had taken the Negro at least two centuries to completely synthesize Western harmonics into the distinctive African American musical forms of the 1930s.

In his praise for Connelly's *Green Pastures*, Du Bois seemed to acknowledge the necessarily slow pace of progress in the development of drama relative to the progress made in the sciences and other disciplines. He suggested that although the play was "an extraordinarily appealing and beautiful play based on the folk religion of Negroes," it was, essentially, the latest slow but inexorable footstep leading the "American public" to "the bitter but reviving waters of the life history of the American Negro." Darwin Turner writes that in "the waning moments of the Renaissance, Du Bois seemed increasingly reluctant to castigate any Afro-American writer."[5] Apparently, it was becoming clear to him that the development of Negro writers who could raise propaganda to the level of art would take more than a decade.

It can be argued that in 1930 Du Bois' modified position on Negro drama and literature amounted to support for black writers as the Great Depression began to reverse what some would have called the artistic gains made in the Harlem Renaissance. But there had been earlier signs of flexibility in Du Bois' position. As Turner notes, his "frequent attacks upon white authors' distortions of black life" did not mean that Du Bois felt that "white Americans could never portray blacks successfully." Despite what Turner calls Du Bois' inability "to comprehend that black men ... may differ in their visions of the Truth of Afro-American life," he could comprehend that there were aspects of Negro life beyond his own experience; he also understood that even a white writer, writing honestly, might portray areas of black life that he could not authenticate:

> I assume that the white stranger cannot write about black people. In nine cases out of ten I am right. In the tenth case, and Du Bose Heywood [*sic*] is the tenth case, the stranger can write about the colored people whom he knows; but those very people ... are sometimes so strange to me, that I cannot for the life of me make them authentic.[6]

The relatively few significant plays by Negro authors on black subject matter that actually reached the stage during the High Harlem Renaissance (1925–29) was to some extent evidence of the truth of Fort-Whiteman's 1923 comments concerning the "dearth" of Negro playwrights and Jackson's finding that "time and technique are necessary" before there could be a flowering of

Negro drama. In 1925, Romeo Dougherty, drama editor of Harlem's *New York Amsterdam News*, had begun a running battle with the Lafayette Theatre's management in an attempt to get more drama presented on the Lafayette stage. Monroe suggests that Dougherty advocated the presentation of serious drama written by whites at the Lafayette as a kind of holding action, "keeping drama alive while black playwrights developed."[7]

In the terms of the art or propaganda debate, the nature of the produced High Harlem Renaissance plays undoubtedly pressed Du Bois to modify his position. By 1930, there were few produced examples of the pure propaganda vehicles he initially advocated. Two plays by Negroes, on Negro subject matter, had full, Broadway productions during the High Harlem Renaissance: Frank Wilson's *Meek Mose* (1928) and Wallace Thurman and William J. Rapp's *Harlem* (1929).[8] Both these plays lacked the ideal Negro middle class subject matter that Du Bois desired; yet, following his 1930 view of the relation of art and propaganda, it would be difficult to claim that these works contained no dramatic art.

Frank Wilson's *Meek Mose*

In January 1928, Wilson's *Meek Mose* had "tried out" in Philadelphia in the black-owned Gibson theatre, it then officially opened at the Princess Theatre in New York City.[9] The play, set in Texas, presented the story of a community of poor Negroes who are asked to relocate to a marshland next to a garbage dump. Local white businessmen want to erect a cotton gin on the Negroes' land. Mose Johnston, the Negroes' spiritual leader, accepts the businessmen's proposal over the objections of a powerful faction in the Negro community. Mose relocates to the marsh. Most of the Negroes follow him and the unsanitary conditions cause sickness and even death in their community. Mose is blamed for these dire events, but, ultimately, it is discovered that the marsh has rich petroleum deposits and Mose's choice and meekness are vindicated.

While Mose's meekness and the last-minute discovery of oil in the Negro marsh can be considered, respectively, a non–Du Bosian propaganda element designed to please white audiences and an inartistic, coincidental ending, it could be argued, using Du Bois' 1930 assumptions, that *Meek Mose* retained enough truth and artistic merit to "have a right to be given." There were, in fact, Negroes who religiously subscribed to the biblical quotation by which Mose lives his life: "Blessed are the meek, for they shall inherit the earth." Moreover, the play also contained a subplot of developing romances between four of its supporting characters, challenging that taboo against black love stories that had haunted Negro drama since the days of the minstrelsy and early Negro musical comedy.

Wallace Thurman and Jourdan Rapp's *Harlem*

Like *Meek Mose*, Thurman and Rapp's *Harlem* deals primarily with the Negro lower class though the action of the latter work takes place in a more intense urban setting. *Harlem* was adapted from Thurman's short story, "Cordelia the Crude," published in *Fire*, the quarterly edited by Thurman, and the publication in which Locke saw (1928) the younger writers' interest in "folk materials." Thus, *Harlem*, a huge melodrama of some sixty characters, chronicles the life and family of Cordelia, its central dramatic figure. According to Thurman and Rapp, Cordelia is "selfish, lazy, sullen," and she leads a host of characters with equally flawed personalities.[10] In fact, Cordelia's older brother Jasper — she has four siblings in all — is the only reasonably balanced personality among the play's important characters. All the events in the play leave Cordelia unchanged at play's end: they include a raucous rent party; a murder; the framing of an innocent man for the murder (the real felon is Cordelia's new boyfriend); and the murderer's fatal fall from a window as he is pursued by policemen.

Nevertheless, beneath *Harlem*'s sensationalism is the seldom depicted and devastating social dilemma of the rural, southern Negro's attempt to adapt to a poverty-stricken, urban milieu. *Harlem* contains that strong element of social realism that Lewis had called for in 1926. As Lewis implied, the play does not have great "intrinsic merit" as dramatic art, but, in its social realism, it is, as Lewis also found, an important step away from the "quaint" and "picaresque" portrayals that had dominated much of Negro drama — especially Negro drama written by whites.

Meek Mose and *Harlem*, as Broadway productions, both heavily employed only those aspects of the black experience that would not destabilize mainstream views of Negro life in the 1920s. However, as has been noted above, by 1930, Du Bois appeared to be calling for an expression of the truth and "completeness" of Negro life in a canon of Negro drama rather than in single art works. Although neither work could claim to represent the entire Negro experience, *Meek Mose* and *Harlem* would have qualified as legitimate entries into that hoped-for canon of Negro drama. However, it may be safely assumed that two Broadway productions of Negro plays did not influence Du Bois' assumptions about appropriate black dramatic art as strongly as the plays presented by his own Little Theatre company, the Krigwa players. Krigwa's most produced playwrights were Eulalie Spence and Willis Richardson. Spence, as has been noted, was opposed to propaganda plays, and Richardson had little interest in the "ideal," middle-class Negro drama that Du Bois wanted to bring to the stage.

Freda Scott reports that on 14 August 1925 the Krigwa Players presented their first production at Harlem's Renaissance Casino, which was more a dance hall than a theatre. The group debuted with Richardson's *Broken Banjo*.[11] In May 1926, *Broken Banjo* was reprised when the group moved to its permanent home at the 135th Street branch of the New York Public Library. *Compromise* (1925), another Richardson play, was presented on the same bill, along with a comedy, Ruth Ada Gaines-Shelton's *Church Fight*. In October 1926, Spence's comedy *Foreign Mail* was performed at the awards event for the *Crisis* Prizes in Literature and Art at New York's International House. Then, early in 1927, the Krigwa Players presented *Foreign Mail* again and Spence's play *Her* in their second season at the 135th Street Public Library. "Spence," writes Scott, "was largely responsible for the honors the Krigwa Players received in the Fifth Annual International Little Theatre Tournament ... in May 1927." Spence's *Fool's Errand* was one of five tournament finalists and was awarded $200 as "one of the best unpublished plays."

Willis Richardson's *Broken Banjo* and *Compromise*

Richardson's *Broken Banjo* had won first prize in the *Crisis* Play Contest in 1925; it was later published in Locke and Gregory's *Plays of Negro Life: A Source Book of Native American Drama* (New York: Harper, 1927). In this work, Matt Turner, the banjo player, is ultimately arrested for the unpremeditated murder of "old man" Shelton. Matt, carrying his banjo, had accidentally stepped in Shelton's potato patch. Shelton then attacked Turner with his walking stick. One of Shelton's blows breaks Matt's banjo. Enraged at the breaking of his banjo and "before he knowed it," Matt picks up a rock and strikes Shelton on the head killing him. "Old man" Shelton is, presumably, a white landowner and herein is the propaganda element of the play. Also, Turner giving himself up to the law at play's end perhaps qualifies as a "best face forward" conclusion to the plot. But in *Broken Banjo*, these propaganda elements are but background to Richardson's study of black-on-black relationships. Matt is the proverbial outsider who relates more to his banjo than he does to human beings; he all but ignores Emma, his faithful wife, and has a violent relationship with Sam, Emma's ne'er-do-well brother, and Sam's equally worthless friend, Adam.

In the antecedent action of Richardson's *Compromise*, a white farmer, Carter, accidentally shoots his neighbor's elder son. The neighbor, Jim, a poor black farmer, accepts a $100 payment from Carter as compensation for his son's death. Jim agonizes over this "compromise" and drinks himself to death. As the play opens Carter has ostensibly repaired his friendship with the surviving members of Jim's family: the widow Jane Lee, her second son, Alec, and two daughters, Annie and Ruth. Richardson complicates the plot, introducing an off-stage, interracial romance between Annie and Carter's son Jack. Jack has impregnated Annie, and when this fact comes to light Carter makes clear to Jane Lee that marriage between Annie and Jack is not an option. When Alec learns that Jack has impregnated his sister, he attacks Jack, breaking his arm with one blow of a rifle butt. The play ends as the distraught Jane Lee prepares for her son Alec's escape from the county to avoid arrest.[12]

While *Compromise* brings Du Bois' protest elements to the foreground, the rigid dichotomies of pure propaganda, right and wrong, good and evil, are mitigated by Carter's friendly relationship with Jane Lee, and a subtle sharing of responsibility for the disasters that have befallen her family. Richardson opens the play with Carter enjoying a morning cup of coffee with Jane Lee. Shortly, it is revealed that Jane Lee's son was killed when Carter fired a shot into his fruit tree to scare away a group of skylarking boys whom he had warned about stealing fruit. Carter was unaware that Jane's son was in the tree busily pilfering fruit. The boy was, at least in part, responsible for the fatal accident. Jane Lee constantly refers to her deceased husband, Jim, as "good for nuthin'," and Jim is responsible for making the "compromise," valuing his son's life at a mere $100. Finally, it is made clear that Jack and Annie are equally responsible for the girl's pregnancy.

In 1927, both Theophilus Lewis and William Clark praised Spence's *Foreign Mail*, a comedy, and *Her*, a ghost story. *Foreign Mail* won second prize in the *Crisis* playwriting contest (1926), and Clark found that *Her* "was written with such skill that it rose to the heights of a three act tragedy that might have been written by a Eugene O'Neill."[13] Neither play was remotely related to Du Bois' initial propaganda goals.

Eulalie Spence's *Fool's Errand*

Spence's *Fool's Errand* (New York: Samuel French, Inc., 1927), a folk play, is set in the home of a poor, rural southern family in the 1920s; the drama is about the dilemma of a young woman, Maza, whom a group of pious neighbors accuse of being pregnant out of wedlock. The accusation is based on the evidence of baby clothing that Maza has allegedly made. At play's end, Maza's mother enters just as her daughter is about to be forced to marry the wrong man, Freddie, whom Maza's father (Doug) and the community have decided is the expected child's father. But Maza's mother has made the baby clothing; she is the expectant new mother. The community's accusations of impropriety, including those of Maza's father and her boyfriend (Jud), are completely unearned.

Devoid of propaganda elements, *Fool's Errand* won the Krigwa Players their highest honors, but its success proved to be the undoing of the company. A controversy developed over the distribution of the prize money ($200) when Du Bois used it to defray production expenses. Spence and other Krigwa members felt that the money should have been shared among the members who had, in fact, won the prize. Angered actors, who also blamed Spence, left the company. Du Bois disbanded the Krigwa Players.[14]

In selecting *Fool's Errand* for the Little Theatre Tournament, Du Bois told Spence that he would have preferred a propaganda play.[15] Scott suggests that "Du Bois may have put the idea of possibly winning a prize or prizes and proving the group before the general public in this manner ahead of ideology." More specifically, it is likely that, given what appears to have been Spence's relatively advanced skill, Du Bois recognized that *Fool's Errand* was the most artistic work the Krigwa Players had to offer. While *Fool's Errand* appears to be a simple folk comedy, Du Bois, too, may have seen that the play also contains what Scott calls "elements of domestic melodrama, and serio-comedic satire." It could not have escaped his notice that in a play contest the most artistic work rather than the most ideological one would have the best chance of success. Citing Spence, Scott writes that Du Bois' response to the breakup of his Krigwa Players was one of "bitter disappointment." It is not too difficult to see how this circumstance, along with his practical experience of the Krigwa Players' most important plays, at least in part, led Du Bois to his 1930 revisions on the relation of art and propaganda.

From 1924 to 1927, both *Crisis* (Du Bois) and *Opportunity* (Charles Johnson) magazines had sponsored play contests; most of the plays that won awards were never produced, but they are, in part, evidence of how approaches to drama were being shaped throughout the Harlem Renaissance. Addell Austin has set up the following categories for twenty-seven award-winning one-act plays (1924–1927): Race Dramas (four), Miscegenation Dramas (four), Complexion Plays (two), Domestic Plays (twelve), and Religious Plays (three). Three Domestic Plays, like *Broken Banjo*, about problems internal to Negro life and having few propaganda or protest elements, were first-prize winners, and three Race dramas, like *Compromise*, plays that at least superficially conformed to Du Bois' earlier propaganda goals, were also first-prize winners. But Marita Bonner's *Purple Flower* is the only one of the first-prize Race Dramas that qualifies as a pure propaganda vehicle. Among all the prize-winning plays, there are twice as many Domestic Plays as there are Race Dramas, and Domestic Plays far outnumber all other categories.[16]

By 1930, the Locke led preference for art over propaganda in Negro drama had resulted in an overwhelming dominance of Locke's "Inner Life" aesthetics in almost all produced black plays and a preponderance of those aesthetics in published Negro drama. As in Richardson's *Compromise*, George Lipscomb's *Frances* (1925), and Frank Wilson's *Sugar Cane* (1926), Locke's Inner Life elements even appeared in dramas that would otherwise be considered pure propaganda plays.[17] Throughout the Harlem Renaissance, serious theatre practitioners and thinkers, black and white, had preferred art over propaganda. Even at *The Crisis*, Du Bois was but one of a group of judges who were, for the most part, adherents to Locke's art-theatre philosophy concerning Negro drama. Among others, Eugene O'Neill, Lester Walton, Willis Richardson, and Charles Burroughs, stage director of the Krigwa Player's first productions, served as *Crisis* drama judges.[18] Despite his alleged stubbornness, Du Bois' 1930 revisions represented the integration of his ideas with those of Locke, Lewis, Spence and others in the discourse on African American dramatic theory.

Specifically, Du Bois' 1930 revisions meant that he was no longer at odds with Locke. Even in Locke's 1925 "double barrel" attack against propaganda in Negro art, he had not totally ruled out propaganda materials as a valid basis for black literature and drama. Locke wrote: "Not all the art is in the field of pure art values. There is poetry of sturdy social protest, and fiction of calm dispassionate social analysis. But reason and realism have cured us of sentimentality: instead of the wail and appeal, there is challenge and indictment."[19] Locke, in effect, had early on agreed with Du Bois' notion that propaganda could be raised to the level of art, and that Negro drama dealing with "the situations of race [held] tragedies and ironies as deep and keen as those of the ancient classics." But in 1926, Locke had also found that the "proper development of these social problem themes will require the objectivity of great art." It seemed that by 1930, Du Bois, too, was resigned to wait for that Negro dramatist who could bring "the objectivity of great art" to the propaganda themes that he thought necessary to help obliterate the American color line.

Locke's Crystal Ball and 1930s Black Theory

The disastrous economic and concurrent social effects of the Great Depression would almost completely overshadow Du Bois' 1930 revisionism severely limiting the further development of black dramatic theory. To address the class inequities of capitalism, which many believed was the root cause of the Depression, propaganda would become an acceptable and major component of American drama. Recalling the onset of the Great Depression, Lofton Mitchell writes: "The so-called propaganda play forged the dreams of black people for freedom and the dreams of white men for a decent living."[20]

Jeffrey Stewart reports that in January 1929, well before the stock market crash in October of that year, in his "1928: A Retrospective Review" of Negro literature,[21] Locke predicted the collapse of the Negro renaissance: He noted that in 1928 "more books have been published about Negro life ... than was the normal output of more than a decade in the past." Ominously, Locke saw in these numbers the statistical imprint of a "typical ... major American fad," and he believed that this fact would not be apparent until it was too late. He wrote that "the movement will lose thousands" who "would be equally hypnotized by the next craze."

By January of 1929, there was for Locke a great deal of chaff in the wheat of the Negro Renaissance; he looked forward to the circumstance that "as with ... another boom ... bubbles must burst." Locke believed that until the Negro fad was spent, the essence and importance of the new Negro movement in Arts and Letters would not be fully realized. Such a revelation, he observed, needed "an introspective calm, a spiritually poised approach, a deeply matured understanding," which, in 1928, had been obstructed by what he called a "vogue of Negro idioms."

Randolph Edmonds: The Negro College Solution

In October 1930, five months after Du Bois published his revised view of the relation of art and propaganda, Randolph Edmonds' (1900–1983) "Some Reflections on the Negro in American Drama" appeared in *Opportunity*. In the *Crisis* and in *Opportunity*, Edmonds' one-act plays had won "Honorable Mention" awards in playwriting contests that these publications sponsored (1926 and 1927). In 1930, however, Edmonds had come to the "conclusion that the so-called 'Negro Renaissance' has been almost a total failure in so far as the development of the drama is concerned."[22] Edmonds found that "Negro drama, as written by Negroes, is too stilted ... imitative of white authors, and as a rule inferior in craftsmanship with ... almost no theatric values." In 1926, Locke had concluded that Willis Richardson's drama and the work of two white playwrights, Ernest Culbertson and Paul Green, lacked "the joy of life even when life flows tragically" and "more of the emotional depth of pity and terror." In 1930, Edmonds echoed these sentiments, writing that Negro-authored drama had, in the main, failed to capture the "joyful and poetic side of life beyond the color line," and it had "no subtle suggestion of tragedy that rises in ominous overtones from black philosophy." Like Du Bois, Edmonds, too, praised Connelly's *Green Pastures*, and he hoped for "Negro plays by Negro authors" that would "reveal the soul of the black man."

Edmonds, like Spence, observed that Negro progress in the development of fiction, poetry, and the novel had far out-stripped the progress of Negro-authored drama. He concluded, as Wallace Jackson had in 1923, that "the verdict of history decrees a long ... apprenticeship both in tradition and accomplishment for ... success in ... the theatre." Edmonds suggests, as Spence, Lewis and others had before him, that most Negro playwrights were remote from the Negro stage. Eulalie Spence, Eloise Bibb Thompson, and Frank Wilson were part of that tiny minority of produced or published High Harlem Renaissance playwrights who were actually products of theatre companies. But, writes Edmonds:

> Most of the great playwrights have been closely connected with the stage. The truth of this can be easily seen if we look at ... Aeschylus and the Greeks, Shakespeare and the Elizabethans, and Ibsen and the Moderns. Most of them learned ... by actually working in the theatre.

In 1924, Willis Richardson had seen the theatre as "an educational institution," and in 1930, Edmonds saw educational theatre as the only effective means by which to develop professional Negro dramatists. Edmonds writes: "The colored schools of this country have ... not awakened to the educational and aesthetic values ... of real university theatres, and have ... done little to facilitate the writing of Negro plays." Concluding his 1930 *Opportunity* article, Edmonds advanced a plan for developing an intercollegiate Negro theatre. He believed that such an institution would result in more authors writing on "Negro life ... with such sincerity ... that universal sorrows ... and joys might be revealed through the medium of black folk." Edmonds was clearly an adherent to both Du Bois' Truth and Beauty School of Negro drama and Locke's art-theatre philosophy.

The Green Pastures: *Folk Play or White Put-down?*

Locke reviewed no Negro-authored plays in his annual 1930 evaluation of Negro literature, and his critique of *The Green Pastures* was far more mixed than Du Bois and Edmonds' reviews of the play. *The Green Pastures* "was too drably realistic, and not apocalyptic enough to be a true version of the Negro's religion," writes Locke. Yet, he insisted that "in spite of questionable detail and a generous injection of 'Black Zionism,'" the play "achieves spiritual represenativeness of the deepest and most moving kind." Du Bois, Edmonds, and Locke's appraisal of *Green Pastures* in no way represented the majority opinion of the play in the Negro community. Edmonds wrote: "Negroes who have never seen the play criticize it sharply. They cannot see how a fish fry could represent the Negro idea of heaven when they have been told all their lives about pearly gates and golden stairs."[23]

Lofton Mitchell would later write: "black blood flowed in those pastures as white knives ripped at the Negro image." Mitchell would also cite the outrage that the play had ignited in Dick Campbell, a leader of Harlem's Depression era theatre community: "I would be a traitor to the religion of my ancestors if I did not decry *The Green Pastures*." As the debilitating economic effects of the Great Depression took hold in black communities throughout the nation, Du Bois' earlier, "best face forward" philosophy seemed to exert an even stronger grip on notions of black dramatic theory.

Propaganda Returns with a Vengeance and Du Bois' Swan Song

In his review of Negro literature in 1931, Locke noted:

The problem has come back ... after an all too brief exile since its brave banishment by the blithe creative spirit of the Negro Renaissance. Negro and white authors alike are obsessed nowadays with the social seriousness of the racial situation, and seem convinced of an imperative need for sober inventory, analysis and appraisal.[24]

But Locke hoped there was "consolation in the fact that a new foundation of fundamental truth is being laid down rather rapidly, as a basis, we hope, for a superstructure of later humane and vital interpretation of Negro life."

A year later, in "Black Truth and Black Beauty, a Review of Negro Literature for 1932," Locke wrote: "It becomes more obvious as the years go by that in this matter of the portrayal of Negro life in American literature we must pay artistic penance for our social sins, and so must seek the sober, painful truth before we can find the beauty we set out to capture."[25] Only in the "rarest instances" could Locke find what he called "the sweetness and light of a Renaissance." The Negro literature of 1932 was, he wrote, dominated by "the bitter tang and tonic of the Reformation," and he lamented: "rarely, it seems can truth and beauty be found dwelling, as they should, together." Locke's art-theatre was apparently at an end; again, he reviewed no Negro-authored plays of 1932. But Locke maintained his belief, or perhaps hope, that a deepening of the "folk-school tradition" was still in progress, and, in 1932, a "rare instance" that was evidence of that progress was Sterling Brown's volume of verse, *Southern Road*. Locke judged that Brown's book had married Truth and Beauty, employing the "difficult combination of intimacy and detachment," and thus had "introduced a new dimension into Negro folk portraiture." Nevertheless, in this same writing, Locke was perhaps the first to note that the folk-school tradition was losing its "chief exponent." Hughes, Locke reported, "was turning ... in the direction of social protest and propaganda."

In August 1933, while Hughes was poetically calling on blacks to unite with the "red world," which was really another white dominated world of leftists, liberals, and communists, Du Bois sounded the first notes of his coming divorce from the NAACP and his seemingly sudden advocacy of an almost Garvey-like separatism. But, Du Bois had not changed his beliefs, he had changed his strategies; Turner writes that ultimately Du Bois still believed in an integrated American society — which is a rather obvious conclusion when one recalls, as Turner, reminds us, that Du Bois had previously fought for such a goal for more than a quarter of a century.[26]

But in 1933, Du Bois evaluated the role of black colleges in relation to mounting Negro economic and social losses and wrote: "We [Negroes] are ... hammered into a separate unity by spiritual intolerance and legal sanction backed by mob law." Du Bois believed that the Depression era wretched condition of American Negroes had, in fact, been consistently deteriorating for the past fifty years, and that this condition was so entrenched in the American social and economic system that it could not be materially altered "for centuries to come." While Edmonds wanted to place the fate of Negro drama and theatre in the hands of black colleges and universities, Du Bois was now convinced that the entire black project of racial and cultural equality could only survive and prosper in Negro institutions of higher learning. According to Du Bois, these institutions had been "founded on a knowledge of [Negro] history ... in Africa and in the United States," and with an organic understanding of the Negro's "present condition." Thus, they, and they alone, could find ways to "train" Negroes "to earn a living and live a life ... under the circumstances in which they find themselves."

For Du Bois, Turner explains, adhering to and fully exploiting these exclusively Negro concerns was "the only route to universality." Du Bois wrote that in Negro universities the investigation of all aspects of black life would inevitably lead to the study "of all life and matter in the universe." His separatism, it can be argued, was a long-term, alternative strategy designed to ultimately achieve complete equality for blacks within American society. Significantly, for the purposes of this discussion, his separatism also carried with it the goal of universality, an enduring theoretical element of traditional African cosmological design and the Post-Slavery Classicism of which Du Bois was an immediate product.

Having reconciled the art and propaganda oppositions at the core of the black discourse on the nature of appropriate Negro literature and drama, Du Bois began to withdraw from the debate. He reasoned, it may be assumed, that in Negro life, all such discourses, especially as concerned Negro drama, had been rendered useless by the distorting, calamitous external forces of the Great Depression. For Du Bois, such discourses could now only have meaning and efficacy in his proposed separate world of the Negro university. Locke, on the other hand, still believed that the Depression was helping to lay the "foundation of fundamental truth needed to unleash the potential power of the Negro renaissance."

In "The Saving Grace of Realism: Retrospective Review of the Negro Literature of 1933" (January 1934), Locke wrote:

> as the fad subsides, a sounder more artistic expression of Negro life and character takes its place.... the typical Negro author is no longer propagandist on the one hand or exhibitionist on the other; the average white author is now neither a hectic faddist nor a superficial or commercialized exploiter in his attitude toward Negro subject matter.[27]

Here, too, Locke found that "contemporary realism" had "almost completely achieved" the painful task of "reconstructing" the old "Negro stereotypes in fiction drama and sociology" into "truer, livelier, more representative substitutes." But, again, his 1933 review of Negro literature included no plays on Negro subject matter by black or by white authors.

In "What Good Are College Dramatics?" (August 1934), Edmonds was convinced that "the real drama of a people must root itself in their life, reveal their psychology and to a great extent receive their support."[28] He insisted that the "ultimate goals of Negro theatre were to produce worthwhile plays, to train workers in the crafts, to train playwrights, to train teachers, and to train our audiences in the importance, beauty, and significance of the drama." Edmonds' advocacy of the Negro university as the savior of black theatre and drama in 1930 had been almost wholly a revival of Gregory and Locke's goals at Howard University in 1921. Edmonds had, in fact, observed that "The Howard Players, under the direction of Professor Montgomery Gregory, made a very brilliant start in 1921, but the interest soon died out when he left."[29] Now, in 1934, Edmonds reported that in March 1930, representatives from Howard University, Morgan State College, Hampton Institute, Virginia State

College, and Virginia Union College had formed The Negro Intercollegiate Dramatic Association. After four years in operation, Edmonds boasted that the association had mounted some 204 productions. However, of those productions, Edmonds reports, twenty-six of the plays presented dealt with Negro subject matter and Negroes authored half of those works. With only six percent of its productions authored by Negroes in four years, it appears that even in the closed and protective environment of The Negro Intercollegiate Dramatic Association, relatively little could be done to hasten the development of professional Negro dramatists.[30]

Locke Resists Agitprop Fever

In 1935, while the Federal Theatre Project (FTP) was tooling up to become the United States' first experiment with a national theatre, Locke was, according to Jeffrey Stewart, "shedding his skin as an apologist for the writers of the Renaissance," and "becoming a leader of the more militant, politically charged art of the 1930s." But in his 1936 review of the Negro literature of 1935, Locke still seemed firmly, if more subtly, faithful to his art-theatre philosophy:

> The approaching proletarian phase is not the hoped-for sea but the inescapable delta. I even grant its practical role as a suddenly looming middle passage, but still these ... trying shoals of propagandist realism ... never can be the oceanic depths of universal art.[31]

In 1937, Sterling Brown, in *Negro Poetry and Drama and the Negro in American Fiction*, could still accurately attack Broadway's continued commercialization of Negro subject matter, and find that "the Negro audience [still] frequently wants flattery instead of representation, plaster saints instead of human beings.... And the typical white audience wants stereotypes."[32] Brown also wrote: "Escape from drudgery and insult by laughter is what the Negro theatre means to too many Negroes. Serious drama of their lives is neither wanted, nor understood." Brown's observations about Broadway and Negro audiences were revived elements of the discourse on Negro theatre and drama carried on throughout the Harlem Renaissance. His remarks here are evidence that the discourse on Negro art, including the central theoretical issue of the relation of art and propaganda, had, in many ways, turned back on itself, failing to incorporate Du Bois' 1930 revisions.

Hughes was not alone in his conversion to the fever of the Left. In 1938, John Davis, writer, activist and later a NAACP researcher, suggested that the "New Negro" movement had substituted cultural expression for a real push for economic and social change and had promoted an elitist isolation from the Negro masses. According to Davis, Locke's New Negro movement assumed that "racial prejudice would soon disappear before the altars of truth, art and intellectual achievement."[33] Davis had obviously overlooked Locke's enduring allegiance to the folk traditions of the Negro masses, and his early warning (1923) that it was "not the business of plays [or other Negro art] to solve problems or to reform society."

Citing passages from his own "Enter the New Negro" and *The New Negro* (1925), Locke, in his review of the Negro literature of 1938, defended the New Negro movement. He attacked "the *enfant terribles* of today's youth movement," suggesting that they had a "class action solution" to problems that contained cultural as well as economic dimensions.[34] Locke had written in 1925, "The Negro is radical on race matters, conservative on others.... Yet under further ... injustice," he predicted, "iconoclastic thought ... will inevitably increase." The Negro, he added, was a "forced radical," and he warned: "But this forced attempt to build his Americanism on race values is a unique social experiment, and its ultimate success is impossible except through the fullest sharing of American culture." For Locke, the Negro Depression era art of "social documentation and criticism" was an expected "development ... of the trends [he had] seen and analyzed in 1925." Thus, he supported much of what was considered leftist drama — by blacks and by whites — as that "practical middle passage" leading to the Negro, folk-inspired art that he had championed throughout the Harlem Renaissance.

In Paul Peters and George Sklar's *Stevedore* (1934), a militant Negro is saved from a racist mob by black and white dockhands, combining racial and proletarian themes. The play had not "scaled the dramatic heights," writes Locke, it had "burrowed under" them; "No matter where one stands on the issues," he added, "there is no denying the force and effect of *Stevedore*." Langston Hughes' *Angelo Herndon Jones* (1936) was, for Locke, "a good beginning," even if it was "too obviously dramatized propaganda." He felt that *Turpentine* (1936), J.A. Smith and Peter Morell's FTP labor play about southern loggers, "brought the thesis of labor and class struggle dramatically to life." Another FTP play with leftist leanings, Theodore Ward's *Big White Fog* (1938), Locke called a "hit," and he insisted that Hughes' *Don't You Want to Be Free?* (1937) had "vindicated the possibilities of a new dramatic approach." However, in 1939, Locke still insisted: "a really vital Negro drama must have as one of it taproots a genuine Negro folk theatre." He found that "the drama of Negro life still lacks vital continuity and true folk represenativeness"; Negro playwrights still had "a relatively superficial contact" with their "basic materials," and the Negro masses suffered from a "tragic separation from the serious theatre."³⁵ Throughout the 1930s Locke had remained fundamentally wedded to his folk-inspired art-theatre objectives.

Significant Black Plays of the 1930s

The establishment of The Federal Theatre Project (1935–1939) resulted in more Negro-authored plays reaching the stage in the 1930s than had been the case in the previous decade. What follows are examinations of some of the produced works which both characterize the Negro dramatic output of the 1930s and relate to issues of black dramatic theory. The drama of leftist agitation and propaganda, what John Gassner termed "agitprop" drama, did not "dominate" the 1930s American stage. Based on her examination of Morgan Himelstein's study of left-wing theatre in New York, Doris Abramson writes:

> The theatre of the thirties was at best only partially a theatre of revolt or even of social significance. Plays about Negro life, whether by white or Negro playwrights, continued to be attempts at honest representation but often ended, as had their predecessors, in commercial compromise.³⁶

Black-authored, non-propaganda plays of the thirties included George Norford's domestic comedy *Joy Exceeding Glory* (1938), Abram Hill's (1911–1986) farce-comedy *On Strivers Row* (1939), and even two verse plays by Owen Dodson (1914–1983), *Divine Comedy* (1938) and *Garden of Time* (1939). The latter work is an interracial reworking of the Jason and Medea legend, initially set in ancient Greece, followed by second and third modern retellings set in Athens, Georgia, and Haiti.³⁷ However, the 1930s began with productions of three plays that were almost quintessential examples of Locke's folk and art-theatre principles:

Andrew Burris' (1898-ca. 1977) *You Mus' Be Bo'n Ag'in*, Eulalie Spence's *Undertow*, and Francis Hall Johnson's (1888–1970) *Run Little Chillun*.

Andrew Burris' *You Mus' Be Bo'n Ag'in*

You Mus' Be Bo'n Ag'in,³⁸ a comedy-drama, was first produced at the Harlem Experimental Theatre (ca. 1929), and the Charles Gilpin Players of Cleveland's Karamu Theatre presented the play in 1931. The work is set in 1900, in Camdus, a rural Arkansas community, and tells the story of Clem Coleman, a farmer who has sired two children by his common-law wife, Eliza. Pressed by Camdus' leading citizens, the members of "Piney Grove Baptist Church," Clem consents to officially marry Eliza and join the church. But in

Act III, he reverses his decision when the leading members of the Piney Grove church prove to be hypocrites, and the church's much-revered Pastor, the Reverend Tukes, tries to seduce Eliza. *You Mus' Be Bo'n Ag'in* has music in the form of spirituals and shouts as a major component of its second act revival scene; James Hatch and Leo Hamalian note that this act presents one of the best of many such scenes written for the Negro stage.

Eulalie Spence's *Undertow*

Although Spence's *Undertow* had won third prize in the *Crisis* 1927 play contest, the Howard University Players staged it for the first time in 1932.[39] Despite its melodramatic ending, *Undertow*, is perhaps one of the first Negro-authored dramas to achieve a brooding, almost Chekhovian sense of what Locke would have undoubtedly termed "Inner Life" psychological realism. *Undertow* is a one-act play written from a woman's point of view and Spence's only surviving completely serious drama. It is set in a "private house," probably a brownstone, on a Harlem winter evening in the late 1920s. The play swiftly presents the story of a romantic triangle: a wife (Hattie), her husband (Dan), and the "other woman" (Clem). Spence gives life to this much-used theme in mainstream theatre by stepping away from the contemporary moral conventions of the 1920s. Hattie, the wife, is far from a faultless victim of marital infidelity, and Spence draws Clem, "the other woman," sympathetically and gives her somewhat heroic tendencies. In Spence's plot, Dan and Clem's relationship is part of the play's antecedent action. They met and fell in love years before, when Hattie and Clem were friends and Hattie was a young, pregnant bride. Spence's central characters here are intimate acquaintances whose personalities and desires have not changed. Thus, the play depicts the second and psychologically weightier confrontation of its central characters. This plot device heightens the dramatic tension and dilutes the "first time" melodrama of the much-used romantic triangle theme.

Undertow, like Angelina Grimké's *Rachel*, however we may judge its artistic merit, is a seminal work in twentieth-century African American drama. Its psychological realism clearly exemplifies Locke's art-theatre goals, making the play emblematic of the pro-art argument of the art or propaganda debate. Further, a central issue of that debate, the "double audience" question raised in James Weldon Johnson's "The Dilemma of the Negro Author," is illuminated by *Undertow*'s theme. It is understandable that mainstream audiences and critics most probably would have seen Spence's love triangle as a bit shopworn. Even by 1932, romantic triangles had been a centuries-old staple of Euro-American drama. But, for black audiences, and any critic who evaluates black drama in terms of its own historical development, Spence's theme in this work has to be judged as almost revolutionary. The old mainstream taboo against black romantic themes and Du Bois' influential "Outer Life" strategies insured that no plethora of black romantic plays had reached the stage such that Negro audiences could find Spence's theme overused.

Hall Johnson's *Run Little Chillun*

In 1933, Francis Hall Johnson coupled a romantic triangle with the stirring music of Negro spirituals to create *Run Little Chillun*. In the spring of 1933, the play ran for four months in Broadway's Lyric Theatre despite the devastating depression; it drew the unqualified praise of the white critic Kenneth Burke: "In '*Run, Little Chillun,*' one sees a Negro genius, an attractive positive ability, exemplified with a conviction, a liquidness, a sense of esthetic blossoming, and a gift of spontaneous organization."[40]

The play, often called a folk opera, was at once popular and theoretically intriguing since its action probes the question of the true nature of Negro religion. Set in a black southern community, Johnson's plot depicts the conflict between the so-called pagan (Africanized) New Day Pilgrims and the Christian congregation of Hope Baptist Church. The triangle that sets in motion the larger conflict between the opposing faiths consists of Jim Jones, son of the Pastor of the Baptist church, Jim's wife, Eliza, a much-respected member of Hope, and Sulamai, Jim's "sweetheart," a recent convert to the New Day Pilgrims.

Kenneth Burke also suggested that in *Run Little Chillun,* "audiences were seeing on stage" for the first time "the power that has made it possible for American Negroes to survive in a society that has continually kept them down."[41] The will and power to survive against the almost terrifying odds, which Burke discovered in the subtext of Johnson's play, is, in fact, the message of *Run Little Chillun*'s Africanized worshippers. In Act II, addressing a moon-worshiping gathering of the Pilgrims, Brother Moses intones:

> the very chains that once bound your feet so securely have also taught them how to dance the rhythm which sets the Universe in motion; and out of the deep-throated cries of your most bitter anguish you have created the song that makes articulate the soul.

Brother Moses is the New Day Pilgrims' leader and, we are told, he speaks the thoughts of the group's silent prophet, Elder Tongola. For the Pilgrims, "God and Nature and Joy Is One," which would seem to sanction love and sexual desire in all its forms. But when Brother Moses, betrothed to Tongola's granddaughter since childhood, falls in love with Sulamai, further plot complications make it clear that not only Christians disapprove of illicit romantic triangles. This question of duality in the psychology and religious beliefs of *Run Little Chillun*'s central dramatic figures points to issues of duality and parody in African cosmology, which are, it will be recalled, related to the theoretical assumptions supporting much of Will Marion Cook's *Jes' Lak White Fo'ks*.

Langston Hughes' *Mulatto* and *Don't You Want to Be Free?*

Hughes, too, made his contribution to the number of black-authored, 1930s non-propaganda plays. He wrote five plays that were produced by Karamu House Theatre in Cleveland: *When the Jack Hollars* (1936), co-written with Arna Bontemps, is a comedy about black and white sharecroppers. *Troubled Island* (1936) is Hughes' full-length nineteenth century history play about the rise and fall of the Haitian emperor Dessalines. *Joy to My Soul* (1937)[42] is a three-act farce-comedy about a wealthy bachelor who gains a fiancée through "lonely hearts" correspondence; the bachelor's intended is, in fact, twice his age and involved in a conspiracy to relieve him of his wealth. *The Front Porch* (1938) is an "Inner Life" drama that examines black-on-black class and color prejudices in the form of a Negro mother's attempt to separate herself and her family from the problems of the Negro working class. *The Front Porch* calls to mind Hughes Allison's *Trial of Dr. Beck* (1937), produced a year earlier, by the New Jersey Negro FTP unit. Allison's play is, ostensibly, about a murder trial, but it, too, raises issues of color prejudices within Negro life. *The Trial of Dr. Beck* ran for four weeks on Broadway at the Maxine Elliot Theatre after its Newark opening.[43]

By the mid-thirties, Hughes, too, had been to Broadway, but unlike *The Trial of Dr. Beck*, his *Mulatto* had become a bona fide "Broadway hit" in 1935. Hughes set *Mulatto* in the south of the 1930s. The owner and operator of an old plantation, Colonel Norford, and his live-in Negro mistress and servant, Cora Lewis, have had, years before, three children: William, Bert, and Sally. Norford has no other children. At Cora's request, Norford agreed to send Bert and Sally away to Northern schools, and, as the play opens, they are both home on vacation. The action centers on Bert, an eighteen year old college student who, against all the rules of the southern caste system, insists on behaving as if he is Norford's legal son and heir. Events lead to a principal confrontation scene in which Norford, holding a gun on Bert, threatens to kill his son but somehow cannot pull the trigger. Bert responds, choking his father to death. When he tries to flee the neighborhood through a local swamp, the inevitable white lynch mob pursues him. Bert returns to the plantation, where Cora has promised to hide him. Then, with the lynch mob in hot pursuit, Bert shoots himself, choosing suicide rather than facing death at the hands of a predictably rabid white mob.

Mulatto is particularly important in this discussion since, in both its original text and in its rewritten production script, it is almost a textbook of Du Bois and Locke's greatest fears. Locke found that the "magnificent potentialities" of *Mulatto*'s "theme" were "for the most part amateurishly smothered in talk and naïve melodrama." And, in his later evaluation of Hughes as a playwright, Turner writes that *Mulatto* is "weak artistically in plot, structure, language, and thought."[44] Locke's unheeded warnings about the dangers of propaganda appear to be the central problem in Hughes' original text. In Hughes' version of the play, Colonel Norford is little more than a stick-figure racist. There is no scene in the play that adequately depicts his concern for any of his children or for their mother, Cora. Hughes allows Norford very little humanity, apparently, so that the patricide in the play may gain some hint of justification. In this work, Hughes is an equal opportunity stereotypist. Bert, too, is a stick-figure mulatto, having no real concern for anyone but himself. He despises other Negroes and never once seriously considers how his behavior might affect his mother, Cora, whom he, presumably, loves.

Mulatto, after 373 performances at the Vanderbilt Theatre and despite a host of mixed and negative reviews in the mainstream press, became what was then the longest running "Negro-authored" play ever on Broadway.[45] But, as both James Hatch and Jay Plum report, Martin Jones, Hughes' white producer, had re-written significant portions of the original text. Jones created the character of Mary Lowell, "a visitor from New York who defends the concept of uplifting the African American race through education," writes Plum. Jones also expanded the roles of Sally, Bert's sister, and Talbot, the overseer, so that after Bert has killed Norford, Act III opens with Talbot's attempt to force a murder confession from Bert at gunpoint; Talbot rapes Sally later in the act. There is little doubt that the rape scene added to the sensational, and therefore commercial, appeal already inherent in Hughes' miscegenation play. Hughes had initially objected to the rape scene, but the need to pay for his mother's cancer treatments apparently severely limited his ability to protect the integrity of his original text.

In writing *Mulatto*, Hughes' need to make rhetorical points about the evils of racism prompted him to reduce his dramatic figures to little more than sociological abstracts, yet his realist drama seemed to call for the complexity of real human beings. Whatever its artistic value, in its failure to depict Du Bois' "full-picturing of the Negro soul," *Mulatto* became a stunning real-world example of that "embargo of white wealth" on Negro drama.

For Du Bois, the disparity between *Mulatto*'s critical failure and box-office success would hardly have been worth serious examination. Cole and Cook's Broadway period had, long before 1935, demonstrated that Negro shows on Broadway were subject to the severest commercialization and commodification. However, Plum's interest in this disparity is important since it raises the issue of the relation of performance to the dramatic text, a concern of any branch of dramatic theory. Plum asserts that what Marvin Carlson calls "message-bearing constructs" can help to determine the success of a play despite, or perhaps because of, the work's critical reviews. Carlson writes: "message-bearing constructs constitute for most audiences the most obvious first exposure to the possible world of the performance."[46] Plum suggests that when *Mulatto*'s mainstream reviewers began to see Colonel Norton as a kind of victim and his son Bert as a kind of villain, they were employing message-bearing constructs that shaped the world of the performance of the play for potential audiences: "These reviews, in effect, shifted sympathy from the socially marginalized mulatto son to the figure of [the] benevolent patriarch," writes Plum. *Mulatto*, according to Plum, became a warning to its mostly white audiences about "the race-polluting evils of miscegenation."[47]

But the "message-bearing constructs" of *Mulatto*'s reviewers may have had their origin in the text or in the performance of the play. The rewritten text of the play has yet to be uncovered. Changes in the missing script may also account for Norford's transformation from the near-villain of Hughes' original to the "sympathetic patriarch" of Martin Jones' rewrite. Even if Jones' revised script contained only those changes that Plum has uncovered, Abramson's claim that "Broadway audiences in 1935 were moved by the production more than they were by the script" cannot be wholly dismissed.[48] The chief production element on which Abramson based this claim was, as Plum notes, "the effectiveness of the acting ensemble led by Rose McClendon." The ability of performance to alter and even invert the meaning of text is, one would assume, an obvious given in the practical world of the theatre. For example, the "effectiveness" that some critics saw in McClendon's portrayal of Cora Lewis may have been the result of an actor's performance choices which then formed the basis for the messages critics and reviewers passed on to potential audiences.[49] The same would be true for Stuart Beebe's performance of Colonel Norford. Even in the realist theatre, performance, which may or may not agree with explicit or implicit textual meanings, can be the most potent originator of message-bearing constructs.

By 1937, Langston Hughes had all but completely defected to the "proletarian phase" that he had been, in Locke's words, "turning in the direction of" since 1932. Susan Duffy reports that in a 1936 letter to his close friend, the white writer Noel Sullivan, Hughes wrote:

> I have come to the conclusion that Fate never intended for me to have a full pocket of anything but manuscripts, so the only thing I can do is to string along with the Left until maybe someday all us poor folks will get enough to eat including rent, gas, light, and water — said bills being the bane of my life.[50]

From these remarks, it seems that Hughes' defection had more to do with, yet again, Du Bois' "embargo of white wealth" on Negro creativity than a sea change in Hughes' political beliefs or his artistic evolution from Negro folk traditions to leftist realism.

However, Hughes would make his unique contribution to the propaganda or "agitprop" drama that had already been effectively introduced by the white, leftist authors Frederick Schlick (*Bloodstream*, 1932), John Wexley (*They Shall Not Die*, 1934), and Paul Peters and George Sklar (*Stevedore*, 1934). As in other leftist plays, as Duffy notes, in Hughes' *Harvest* (1935) and *Angelo Herndon Jones* (1936), "the devil identified ... is American capitalism, and salvation from modern social problems comes with the color-blind brotherhood of trade unionism and Communism."[51] But Hughes informed much of his poetry and drama with his Negro folk traditions. "The music of the blues, jazz, swing and other popular forms is omnipresent in his lines of poetry and in several of his dramatic works," writes Duffy.

Don't You Want to Be Free?, essentially Hughes' reworking of Du Bois' pageant, *The Star of Ethiopia* (1913), is perhaps the best example of his contribution to agitprop drama. Hughes' work here is an intermingling of skits, poems, soliloquies, Blues and Jazz music that purport to be, in the words of the Hughes' narrator, "about what it means [and has meant] to be colored in America." The play concludes in song with a rousing agitprop ending, characteristically calling for the unity of working class blacks and whites. Hughes wrote this work for his Suitcase Theatre, founded in Harlem in 1937, and the play ran for 130 performances, playing on weekends for two years.

Hughes and Vsevolod Meyerhold

To create this work, Hughes borrowed and adapted ideas from Vsevolod Meyerhold (1874–1943) and Nikolai Okhlopov (1900–1966); both directors had invited Hughes to audit their rehearsals on his 1937 visit to the Soviet Union.[52] Hay writes that with *Don't You Want to Be Free?* Hughes "smudged the line of demarcation between Art theatre and Protest theatre."[53] But this "smudging" of the line between Art and Protest theatre was, in effect, a departure from core assumptions in both Locke and Du Bois' notions of black dramatic art. In this work, Hughes' aesthetic practice was not an effort to supply Negro drama with a foundation drawn from its own origins — as Locke and Du Bois had advised; it was, instead, a direct application of Soviet *avantgarde* assumptions about stage art to Negro theatre. Hughes attempted to marry Okhlopov and Meyerhold's formalist, anti-psychological, and anti-realist tendencies with the folk elements of Locke's art-theatre. But the Inner Life objectives of Locke's drama almost demand psychological investigation. On the other hand, Du Bois' Protest theatre seems to cry out for realist depictions of the "color line" question. Du Bois had almost surely seen his original pageant as the beginning of a Negro Theatre that would create realist Protest dramas. He had not gone to the trouble to found the Krigwa Players to present pageants.

It is difficult to discover the organic relationship of Meyerhold's tendency "to elevate form over content"[54] to the historically holistic presentation of form and content in the Blues, Jazz, and folk-inspired poetry that Hughes employed in *Don't You Want to Be Free?* One wonders how Meyerhold's comparison of "a theatre built on psychology" to "a house built on sand" applies to a Negro theatre of Hughes' poetry and "musical" literary lines embedded with Blues and Jazz idioms. The very core of the Blues is an expression of psychological states, and Jazz's "call and response" improvisational form, inherited from African percussive styles, is designed to capture at the instant of performance Meyerhold's "shifting sands" of psychological moods in both the performers and their audiences. Thus, it can be argued that while *Don't You Want to Be Free?* superficially follows the aims of Du Bois' Protest theatre and uses folk materials from Locke's art-theatre, the play may actually be an example of Du Bois' troubling 1903 notion of "Negro double consciousness." Ironically, the popularity of Hughes' theoretically questionable hybrid in Harlem ensured that in the name of heightened political consciousness and militant protest, European *avant-garde* aesthetics would inform the development of much African American protest drama well into the 1960s.

Theodore Ward and *Big White Fog*

In 1938, the FTP's Chicago Negro Unit produced Theodore Ward's (1902–1983) *Big White Fog*. The play opened at the Great Northern Theatre on 7 April 1938 and ran for thirty-seven performances, playing to mixed audiences. *Big White Fog* is the first of a trio of thematically related African American dramas set in Chicago that are significant in twentieth-century black drama: Richard Wright (1908–1960) and Paul Green's *Native Son* (1941) and

Lorraine Hansberry's *A Raisin in the Sun* (1958) complete that trio. Set in a period beginning in the 1920s and ending in the Depression years, *Big White Fog* examines the problems of a Negro family that had migrated from the South to Chicago. Issues of racism, Negro color consciousness, marital relations, prostitution, Garveyism, and Communism are all raised in Ward's play. In fact, a valid criticism of the work is that in his first major stage work, Ward takes on more problems than can be adequately dealt with in the dramatic form.

On the other hand, Ward, for the most part, achieved a humanity in his dramatic figures which began to approach the kind of Negro "social document" that Lewis had called for since 1926, and that, in keeping with Du Bois' 1930 comments, could raise propaganda to the level of art. Ward's hero, Victor Mason, is no faultless demagogue of Garveyism or Communism. At the end of Act I, he foolishly invests his family's meager savings in what is obviously the all but defunct Garvey movement. Unlike *Mulatto*, everywhere in this work there are touches of real-world human complexity. The deterioration of Victor's marriage proceeds, inexorably, beneath the action. Brooks, Victor's mother-in-law, filled with Negro color consciousness and pride in only the white part of her ancestry, is at odds with her dark-skinned son-in-law throughout most of the action. But in a third-act *rapprochement* with Victor, she is also sympathetically revealed as a helpless but honorable old woman. Even the tiny role of the bartering Jew, Marx, who has come to buy the Masons' furniture as the family sinks to the depths of the Depression, is balanced with the larger role of Nathan Pizer, "a Jewish student" and activist, who tries to help the Masons. In this way, Ward avoids the familiar stereotype of all Jews as Shylock, while depicting the Northern, inner-city reality that most merchants serving black communities during the period were, in fact, Jews.

Reviewing the 1940 Negro Playwrights Company's production of *Big White Fog*, Locke wrote that the play "holds a situation with first-class dramatic possibilities. But instead of holding to its excellently posed character conflicts, over money and race loyalty, Americanism and Garveyism, it swerves to a solution by way of radical social action for its denouement."[55] In the denouement to which Locke objects, the police mortally wound Victor in their attempt to evict the Masons from their home. Lester, Victor's eldest son, reveals to his dying father that he, too, is now a "Comrade," as workers, blacks and whites, prevent the police from removing the Masons' furniture. Lester confides to Victor that he no longer sees the world as a "big white fog." For Lester, recruited by Pizer, there is now a light of the white and black brotherhood of "radical social action." This agitprop conclusion appears to offer a solution to the Mason family's many problems. But Ward's ending is more likely a sign of the times than evidence of his political affiliations. Abramson notes that Clifford Odets, in *Waiting for Lefty* (1935), had also been influenced by the "labor clichés" and "Marxist" ideas of the period.[56] In any case, for the purposes of this discussion, the difficulties in *Big White Fog*, as Locke suggests, lie more in its dramatic structure than in its politics.

Ralph Ellison on *Big White Fog*

In his 1940 mixed review of *Big White Fog*, Ralph Ellison also seems to suggest that Ward may have been trying to deal with too many problems: "Ward has sought to illustrate his theme with that variety of incidents which is better suited to the novel. The play form does not allow for the successful development of these many aspects of his problem."[57] Ellison also felt that Ward's dialogue lacked the appropriate Negro "imagery," and, more importantly, Ward had failed to fully develop the character of Victor Mason's son, Lester. This, Ellison contends, leaves "the play's solution undramatized" since Lester, formed by a "different set of circumstances" than his father, is "presented as the solution to his father's problem." Ellison adds: "But Lester's transformation comes in the form of abstract speeches. Ward misses one of his most accessible dramatic opportunities: that of contrasting the father with the son, the illusory with the realistic, the utopian with the scientific." Interestingly, Ward's failure to fully develop Lester suggests that he was not consumed with the politics of the Left, as many have charged. Had this been the case, he almost certainly would have been more explicit and less rhetorical about Lester's transformation to a "Comrade." *Big White Fog* is dominated by Victor Mason's tragedy of lost hopes and the destruction of the Mason family at the hands of American racism.

Black Theory and Black Producing Theatres in the 1930s

During the 1930s, the Karamu House Theatre in Cleveland, Ohio presented more than twenty Negro-authored plays. Langston Hughes remarked as late as 1961 that "It is a cultural shame that a great country like America, with twenty million people of color, has no primarily serious colored theatre. There isn't. Karamu is the very nearest thing to it."[58] Karamu House, a neighborhood settlement founded (1915) by the white sociologists Russell and Rowena Jelliffe, organized the Karamu Theatre and its Gilpin Players in 1920. The Jelliffes established their settlement house in one of Cleveland's poor, minority neighborhoods. Rowena Jelliffe headed the Karamu Theatre, and concerning Negro drama, early on, she was firmly in the art camp of the art or propaganda debate:

> The primary consideration of the Negro dramatist ... should be for the art of the theatre. Sociological considerations should be secondary. Nor should the theatre be considered a medium for propaganda ... I believe that the Negro artist achieves in the ... drama in about the proportion to which he is able to escape the bonds of race consciousness. Then is he able, having acquired the necessary perspective, to portray and interpret the life and mood of his race beautifully and truly.[59]

Jelliffe writes that by 1928 Karamu's audiences were mixed, "half colored and half white." After eight years of efforts to present serious drama, her Negro audiences (and actors) no longer had an interest in Negro drama "only when it told a good joke," and were no longer "opposed to Negro plays" on the grounds that they were "highly degrading to their race."

In 1935, under the Works Progress Administration (WPA), President Roosevelt's answer to the Great Depression, the U.S. Congress created the Federal Theatre Project (FTP). The FTP was part of a twenty-seven million dollar national arts program set up for unemployed musicians, writers, artists, and actors. For the first time in the country's history, the federal government would "claim that artists and the arts were an integral part of a democratic people and a democratic culture," writes Rena Fraden.[60] In 1939, the U.S. Congress, driven by its fear of the Communist Party, would abolish the Federal Theatre Project, ending the United States government's singular experiment with a national theatre.

But in 1935, the FTP was headed by Hallie Flanagan. Flanagan, writes Fraden, was "the most outspoken of all the directors in her belief that art should represent and reflect America in all its diversity." The FTP established sixteen Negro units throughout the country, including theatres in New York, Chicago, Seattle, Newark, New Jersey, and Durham, North Carolina.[61] And, the kind of diversity that Flanagan hoped to achieve in the FTP's Negro units is perhaps best exemplified in a letter that William Farnsworth, an FTP official, sent to New York State governor Alfred E. Smith: "As you know, it is the desire of the Federal Theatre Project to establish the Negro unit in the Lafayette Theatre in New York as a Negro theatre for Negroes, rather than as a Harlem attraction for downtown whites."

While in its relatively short-lived history, the FTP did provide experience in the professional theatre for a number of Negro playwrights, its actual development of black dramatists did little to obviate the need for Randolph Edmonds' intercollegiate black drama or Du Bois' separatism. As Fraden reports, among other things, the "scarcity of time and money" had seriously limited the FTP's ability to develop Negro dramatists.[62]

The Chicago Federal Theatre and "Best Face Forward" Censorship

FTP Negro authors were subjected to a censorship stemming both from Congressional politics and the art or propaganda debate. In "Liberty Censored: Black Living Newspapers of the Federal Theatre Project," Paul Nadler reports that although the living newspaper was "a favorite genre" of Hallie Flanagan, and that although "three living newspapers about African Americans were completed" by the FTP, "not a single one was produced."[63] The living newspaper had "descended from the Soviet Red Army's *Zhivaya Gazeta* ('Alive' or 'Living Newspaper') and German and American agitprop troupes," writes Nadler; the form "used huge casts, spectacular sets, and film, vaudeville, and agitprop techniques to depict contemporary political and social issues in theatrical terms." The direct and hard-hitting aspects of the living newspapers, which "does not," Nadler writes, "hide its truths behind the mask of fiction," may have been the elements that prevented the FTP from actually producing a black living newspaper. At any rate, in the New York FTP Negro unit, *Liberty Deferred: A History of the Negro in the United States* (1938) became the FTP's last developed but unproduced black living newspaper. The Negro writers, Abram Hill and John Silvera, had authored this aborted stage work.

In Chicago, the FTP's Negro unit's production of *Big White Fog* was almost aborted when the work received only "grudging support" from Harry Minturn, the acting director of the Chicago Project, and familiar aspects of the art or propaganda debate endangered the support of the play among black, middle-class Chicagoans.[64] Fraden reports that at Minturn's request, Shirley Graham, a black director for the Negro unit, had arranged a reading of *Big White Fog* "to drum up support within the black community." Graham, a well-educated playwright, who later married Du Bois, was herself a member of the Negro middle class. Not surprisingly, she invited an audience to the reading that included representatives from the NAACP, the Urban League, black churches, funeral associations, black music clubs, and selected fraternities.

According to Graham's written report to Minturn, the initial response to the reading was "courteous" and even "showed intelligent interest." But then Kay Ewing, the white director whom Minturn had assigned to direct *Big White Fog*, remarked: "This play is so absolutely typical of the Negro in Chicago." Graham reported that after the reading, Ewing's remark was repeated and resented throughout the Negro community. People were saying that unlike the characters and situations in Ward's play, black men were respected in their homes in the black community; they were successful businessmen; perhaps most of all, their daughters did not have to sleep with white men for fifty dollars. Graham had initially approved of Ward's script, but after these developments she advised Minturn not to produce it.

Despite these difficulties, *Big White Fog* was produced when Mrs. Hale, an influential black woman from the South Side, "went downtown and said her people were eager to see *Big White Fog*," reports Fraden. Hale had not made Graham's list of middle-class invitees to the reading. She was obviously not a member of that statistically tiny group of middle-class Negroes, the "usual suspects," whom white controlled institutions have historically consulted to determine the views of a relatively vast working and lower class Negro majority. Oddly enough, the likelihood that Hale was a better representative of the generally ignored Negro urban majority in Chicago than the group Graham had assembled is revealed in one of Ward's characterizations of Hale's influence: "She could go down to any judge and get somebody out of jail."

If we are to believe Graham's account of the responses to the reading of Ward's play, the root of the difficulty was the relationship between Graham's black middle-class group and Kay Ewing, whom the Negroes inevitably saw as a representative of white opinion. Put another way: for the Negroes, what became of paramount importance about the play was not what they thought of it but what Ewing thought of it. As Hughes had suggested in 1926 and Du Bois in 1930, among much of the Negro middle-classes, the evaluation of ideas presented in literature, drama, or in the socio-political arena in terms of "what white people think" is a classic syndrome and result of American racial oppression. For the oppressed, whose lives are largely shaped by the economic and political power of the oppressive "other," paying strict attention to the opinions of that "other" is a matter of survival. This circumstance, of course, returns us to the underpinnings of the "best face forward" strategies supporting the propaganda side of the art or propaganda debate. In 1938, Du Bois' old "best face forward" strategies were clearly still prevalent in African American communities and playing a role in defining the way theatre institutions dealt with the development and presentation of African American drama.

Black Theory and Theatres in the Harlem Community

Lofton Mitchell reports that The Rose McClendon Players, founded by Dick Campbell at the Public Library on 124th Street in Harlem and officially opening in 1939, also produced a number of works by black authors. The group produced Norford's *Joy Exceeding Glory*, Hill's farce-comedy *On Strivers Row*, and William Ashby's *Booker T. Washington* (1940). A program from one of the McClendon Players' early Harlem performances announced, writes Mitchell, that the group had begun with the mission to "encourage Negro playwrights to fashion their unborn creations along the vein of contemporary Negro life."[65]

Other theatre companies of the period included the Negro People's Theatre, the Harlem Players, and, of course, Hughes' Suitcase Theatre. But, in terms of Negro drama, these actor-oriented companies did little to advance the development of African American dramatists. The short-lived Negro People's Theatre, founded by Rose McClendon and Dick Campbell, had opened in Harlem's Rockland Palace (1935). The company presented "a Negro version of Clifford Odets' *Waiting for Lefty*," writes Mitchell. But, also in 1935, McClendon's premature death broke up the company, and most of its members moved on to the ranks of the FTP.

Hughes' Suitcase Theatre was almost exclusively devoted to Hughes' stage work, and founded, Duffy reports, to create "working class plays to be given before labor organizations." Duffy writes: "While Hughes is credited with founding the Suitcase Theatre ... what is not generally known is that the group grew out of the John Reed Club in New York. Hughes was one of four directors of the newly formed company."[66] John Reed (1887–1920), a white American journalist and activist, had founded the American Communist Labor Party in 1919. But by the 1930s, the national association of leftists clubs that used Reed's name, writes Duffy, "received no institutional recognition from the Communist party." However, among other leftist strategies, the John Reed Clubs "promoted the use of art for social and class liberation."

In fact, Hughes shared the responsibility of running the Suitcase Theatre with three noted white leftists: "Jacob Burck of the *Daily Worker*, Paul Peters, author of *Stevedore;* and most surprisingly, Whittaker Chambers, who later turned state's evidence against Alger Hiss in one of the most celebrated spy trials in U.S. history." The Suitcase Theatre had certainly not been founded to encourage the development of Negro playwrights, especially those who, unlike Hughes, would not have found it easy to fall in with the company's leftist agenda.

IV

Black Theory in the Great Depression and Beyond, 1930–1949, Part II

Black Dramatic Theory in the 1940s

Langston Hughes' 1961 lamentation that for the black playwright the Karamu Theatre was, so to speak, "the only game in town," was certainly true in 1940. The demise of the Federal Theatre Project and the actor-oriented nature of most community-based, black Theatre companies left potential black dramatists with little hope of a true home in which to develop. Rowena Jelliffe's 1928 observation about the opposition of Negro actors and audiences to Negro plays had not lost its validity. In 1940, Harold Cruse joined a Harlem drama group, and in his book, *The Crisis of the Negro Intellectual: A Historical Analysis of the Failure of Black Leadership*, he writes: "The first thing about the group that struck me as highly curious was the fact that all the members were overwhelmingly in favor of doing white plays with Negro casts.... These amateur actors were not very favorable to the play about Negro life..."[1] Cruse's stated "preoccupation with aesthetic values" ultimately led him to the general thesis of his book, which is, in fact, a further expression of Du Bois' 1903 notion of "double consciousness." Beginning with the Harlem Renaissance, Cruse contends, black intellectuals failed to establish an aesthetic system that resolved the distance between what Du Bois called "Negro-ness and Ameri-can-ness," and thus they made essentially self-serving alliances with white liberals and leftists; these alliances, according to Cruse, supplanted the legitimate aesthetic approaches and political needs of the Harlem community with the artistic standards and political agenda of white leftists and liberals.

It is difficult not to see Cruse's charges as a chillingly accurate description of the theoretical implications of Hughes' political drama. Cruse's main thesis here could have been taken directly from Du Bois. In his 1933 effort to remove the discourse and development of all forms of Negro culture, most specifically literature, to Negro universities and colleges, Du Bois wrote that the Negro renaissance had failed because "it was a transplanted and exotic thing." It produced "literature written for the benefit of white people" and "at the behest of white readers" rather than arising from "the heart" and "experience of Negroes." And, for Du Bois, no authentic literature, and by implication no legitimate arts movement, could be created "on such an artificial basis."[2] Arguably, more than any other figure, Du Bois had been the progenitor of the "New Negro" renaissance and the bitterness of his personal failure is characteristically expressed here in the rhetoric of overstatement. Locke, too, had, a year later, attacked much of the Negro renaissance as "faddist" and "exhibitionist."

Turner confirms that by 1940, Du Bois had begun to practice his relatively new separatist theory and had all but withdrawn from the discourse on Negro art. He had exited the NAACP and, practicing what he preached about the potential of black universities to sustain and develop Negro culture, he again took up his post at Atlanta University.[3] However, in 1940, Du Bois suggested that the strong sense of community in Africa could be applied to Negro America; he wrote that "the nascent art in song, dance and drama" in the American Negro could "inspire" the Negro rather than merely entertain mainstream white audiences. Du Bois could imagine "no more magnificent ... promising crusade in modern times."

Moreover, Du Bois reported that a group of influential Negro intellectuals intended to resurrect African Art. They aimed to exploit, writes Du Bois, "the rich ... life of the Negro in America and elsewhere as a basis," for all Negro art forms. A group of new artists of African-inspired Negro American art would necessarily be the result of this plan. But Du Bois warned that if this new art was to be supported by Negroes, then that group "must be deliberately ... schooled in art appreciation," and it had to "accept new canons of art" and reject "the herd instinct of the nation."

In 1940, these observations established Du Bois, as Turner notes, as the original father of the Black Arts movement of the sixties and seventies; they also demonstrated the vast theoretical gulf between him and the previous decade's promoters of the drama of black and white proletarian unity.

Theodore Ward, the New Theatre League and Locke's View of Broadway

In many respects, the author of *Big White Fog*, Theodore Ward, shared Du Bois' belief that Negro art had to achieve oneness with Negro life and culture. In September of 1940, the New Theatre League gave a benefit, hosted by The Group Theatre's Morris Carnovsky (1898–1992), for the newly organized Negro Playwrights Company (NPC).[4] Ward, a central figure in the new company, began his address to the New Theatre League's members quoting what he said was one of Julius Bob's encyclopedia entries: "Every theatre in the true sense of the word is a unity, at the core of which is the living community finding some vital part of itself reflected in the creations of the dramatist and actor."[5] According to Ward, this was the kind of theatre that the NPC wanted to build in Harlem. Ward then discussed ancient aspects of dance as the origin of theatre: "The dance was a collective ritual descriptive of the ... process of securing a livelihood." Ward indicated that the cultural and social function of this early dance was to depict "the relation between man's ways of life, his work and art." He said that "participation in the dance [produced] an emotional compensation" and "motivated individual conduct," which, presumably, became conduct aimed at the economic survival of the group in these early village economies. Further, according to Ward, the dance in these early societies functioned, individually and collectively "as a spiritual and cultural award." For Ward, the economic needs (hunting, planting, etc.) of the tribe or group, were at the core of the early dancers' art form. And, he went on to suggest that "work and protest songs" had similar collective functions in traditional Negro America.

Inherited from primitive dance, the "collective" character of the theatre, Ward asserted, was so well established in ancient Greece that "whole communities knew and understood ... Sophocles and Euripides." But, he added that the eventual rise of "class structures" materially weakened the bond between the theatre and "the life of the ordinary man."

Like Du Bois, Ward realized, too, that the NPC would have the formidable task of "deliberately training" Harlem audiences to appreciate the kind of drama the new company was advocating. He acknowledged that much of the Harlem audience, comprised of "oppressed peoples," had bought into the notion of "the theatre as primarily a means of escape." But this view, he advised, was "the product of those who wish to keep ... people in ignorance, so that they may be more easily exploited." It was, Ward suggests, the self-serving "lie" that defined as "propaganda" all that was not in agreement with the "interests and opinions" of the ruling class. "It is an error," Ward warned, "to assume that," there is a meaningful difference "between a vital theatre and a theatre of amusement."

Playwrights, too, according to Ward, had to accept some responsibility for supporting the false notion "that vital theatre is boring." Ward found that too many playwrights had the "tendency to deal with problems which had ... no relation to ... ordinary citizen[s]," and too often mismanaged "the treatment of their subject matter." Lacking sufficient ability, another set of playwrights,

Ward charged, used mostly "reportage, polemics and ... naturalistic transference of the phenomena of life [to] ... the stage." As is often done today, Ward did not conflate the meanings of realism and naturalism.

Perhaps Ward's most important observation here is his citing of the relation of theatre to ancient village economies. Had he really been one of Du Bois' "Negro intelligentsia" who planned to foster a new African-inspired Negro art, he might have chosen the better-documented and more germane West African "talking drum" tradition to illustrate his point. It is widely known that the talking drum represents performance techniques with which traditional African musicians frequently raised the musical art of drumming to the level of language. There is little doubt that this drum language was initially devised and used to facilitate communications relating to issues of village economies, hunting parties, trade festivals, group crop harvestings, even war parties, etc.[6]

But in Africa, as well as in Ward's example of ancient Greece, there is little to support his contention that the rise of class distinctions alienated the common man from the collective character of nascent theatre art forms, which had been, in effect, a peoples' art. It is perhaps common knowledge that on the African continent royal families in the form of kingships and chieftainships appear to predate recorded history. There is no evidence that the talking drum tradition evolved in classless West African societies. In fact, the reverse seems to be true, that is, this musical tradition was needed to ensure communications between villages that were part of larger territories governed by ruling families. In Greece, too, "the whole communities," who "knew and understood Sophocles and Euripides," would have had little to know and understand had not a succession of ruling tyrants and members of the Greek upper class taken it upon themselves to sponsor the many drama festivals in which the people were introduced to the works of their "immortal dramatists."[7] The same might be said for Shakespeare and the drama of Elizabethan England, a society steeped in class distinctions.

Ward may have chosen his non-racially and non-culturally specific ancient dancers analogy precisely because he knew that any similar analogy using Africa would rush him headlong into the theoretical disparities between his leftist assumptions about class and the function of social hierarchies throughout traditional Africa. In the case of Greece, he may have simply hoped that his audience would overlook the powerful class structures that were, at least in part, responsible for the rise of classical Greek drama. In any case, Ward does not deny that although his dancers' art may have been derived from village economics, their dance had the power to "spiritually" and "culturally" reward, for a hard day's work, the dancers as well as their celebrants.

But at what point did the dancers' performance cease being merely a chronicle of the harvest and the hunt and become a cultural and spiritual vehicle, in other words, an art form with which performers and audience could be rewarded? The answer to this question may well be that for Ward's ancient dancers and their followers, village economics, the cultural, and the spiritual were one, that is, these seemingly separate constructs were but aspects of their singular relationship to a godhead and to the cosmos. From the cave paintings at Lascaux in Europe to the Pharaonic Nile and the Buffalo gods of the Native American West, history and pre-history abound with examples of traditional peoples who deified the basic elements of their economic survival, raising them to the realm of art and philosophy.

However, it is precisely the holistic nature of these cultural constructs that make them incompatible with Ward's leftist assumptions. For one thing, class distinctions in culturally homogeneous societies that construct a holism of religion and economics cannot have the same meanings and outcomes as such distinctions have in the heterogeneous, often dichotomous cultural system that Ward and we inhabit. The distinctiveness and primacy of economics over religious beliefs is perhaps the one supposition on which ardent capitalists and communists, alike, can agree.

Ward himself was evidence of the tensions raised by the opposing assumptions in his and others' attempts to meld Negro culture into leftist thought. He had attempted that difficult process in *Big White Fog's* final scene and, as Ellison notes, his play had suffered because of it. However, as in his play, in his address, despite its lacings of leftist assumptions, Ward could not help privileging issues peculiar to Negro dramatic art: the problems and responsibilities of the Negro dramatist, and the need for "training" Negro audiences. At the end of his talk he even employed what sounded like an invocation of Du Bois' Truth and Beauty School: "We know that Harlem can possess such a theatre that reflects all the grace and the beauty and the historical truth of our daily life."

But the notion of the spiritual in art and Ward's acceptance of it did raise certain problems. In strict leftist thought, that notion, with its implication of religious beliefs and practices, was at best tenuous and, for the most part, disposable as merely an aspect of a controlling ideological tool of the ruling class, an "opiate of the masses." Yet, no canon of drama that hoped to capture the historical truth of daily African American life could avoid that opiate. The spiritual dimensions of art, Christian or otherwise, had thus far been a central feature of both African and African American culture. As Cruse would later suggest and, by 1940, Langston Hughes and Ward demonstrated, the attempted reconciliation of the notions of the Left with historical black cultural constructs was perhaps an all too vivid example of "the crisis of the Negro intellectual."

In "Broadway and the Negro Drama" (1941), Locke attempted to evaluate the Negro drama that had reached Broadway since the 1920s. His list of fourteen plays included only three by Negro authors, and one of them, *Native Son*, had been co-authored by Paul Green, a Southern white dramatist. Although Locke acknowledged the intermittent success of Negro drama on Broadway over the previous two decades, he was quick to point to the ill effects of Broadway's "sporadic" presentation of Negro plays:

> Good, even great actors have gone to seed, and forward-looking precedents have closed in again as timorous lapses have followed some of the boldest innovations. With the courage of its own successes, Broadway could have extended at least a half dozen ... [Negro] plays into a sustained tradition of original and typically American drama.[8]

Concerning Broadway's "choice of Negro plays, Locke acknowledged that much of the drama of the Negro little theatre groups was "amateurish in conception and execution," but, he noted that Broadway had always found ways of "professionally remodelling [sic] the themes that it wants," that is, except in the case of Negro drama:

> In the Negro field the tyranny of what the public is supposed to want has stood in the way of the development of some of the most obviously original and significant strains of Negro drama, particularly the social problem play based on one or another aspect of the racial situation.

Locke's "Broadway and the Negro Drama" is, of course, at bottom, a retread of issues treated in the High Renaissance, especially Johnson's "The Dilemma of the Negro Author," and, yet again, Du Bois' "embargo of white wealth" syndrome. Locke's suggestion that Broadway could and should "remodel" Negro themes had already proved to be aesthetically dangerous, as he himself had noted in the case of Hughes' *Mulatto*. By 1941, Locke's need to integrate the Negro into the American mainstream appeared to begin to play havoc with his art-theatre aesthetics. On the other hand, it is possible, too, that, by 1941, for both budding and mature black theatre artists, Locke saw integration as that proverbial "only game in town." If this view of the state of the Negro theatre was, for Locke, too bleak to essay publicly, such was not the case for Theophilus Lewis.

Theophilus Lewis: "The Frustration of Negro Art"

In April 1942, five months after Pearl Harbor, in "The Frustration of Negro Art," Lewis begins by posing the issue which kind of "race prejudice" is most "pernicious": prejudice that severely limits the economic "interest of a race" or prejudice that "injures" its "soul?" Lewis admitted that though other forms of prejudice were "more bitter," the "diabolically effective repression of Negro art" would constitute, over time, an evil not to be underestimated. And this was so because, in Lewis' view, "the highest expressions of the soul are religion and art."[9]

Yet, this repression of Negro art, Lewis insisted, was not due to a "sinister" plot hatched by American whites. In fact, the reverse was true. Lewis observed that a great many Negro artists received support from whites and white-controlled foundations, and he found that white "critics sometimes lean over backward to praise the works of Negro [artists] far beyond their ... merits." The "frustration of Negro art," Lewis concluded, was largely due to "the nature of art itself" and the circumstances needed for its creation. Examining those circumstances, Lewis found that both "Greek drama," and "Negro Spirituals" were initially "produced for ... local audience[s]." He notes, for example, that Classical Greek theatre had first been established solely for "the citizens of Athens," and, much later, Negro Spirituals had been initially performed "in plantation meeting houses." Ancient Greek dramatists and the "black bards" of slavery were able, Lewis asserts, to achieve "a universal human note" by diving "into the souls of their own ... races."

Negro artists, if they wanted to create durable art, would again have to cater to Negro audiences, Lewis contends, and not to "Broadway first-nighters." But, tragically, the economic oppression of Negroes had seen to it that no appreciable Negro audience existed to which Negro artists could cater. Lewis surmised that the well-educated, relatively small number of Negroes with adequate "leisure" and "enough money" to partake of Negro art was practically non-existent. For example, in 1942, he estimated that there were not more than thirty thousand Negro college graduates. "Many of them," he notes, were employed at menial jobs, and very few of these well-educated menials earned enough money to consistently attend the theatre. In short, Lewis found that the economic prejudice that Negroes almost universally encountered functioned as "a definite brake on the Negro's cultural progress." Of course, for the Negro artist who, more or less, condoned "Marxian theory" there was, Lewis noted, some newly established support from the Communist Party. But that kind of assistance would not help the "conscientious artist" who was "too sensitive to ... subscribe to an ideology as a short cut to recognition," writes Lewis. Such an artist, he lamented, was likely to be overlooked "while third-raters and charlatans jockey themselves into the limelight, where they ... calumniate Negro art."

Lewis concluded his article, writing that a generally anemic Negro theatre had, in fact, created a "galaxy of superior actors," and "Negroes are producing symphonies without symphony orchestras," but, he added: "There is a limit to our ingenuity." Lewis's observations on the state of Negro art and, more specifically, on the state of Negro drama in the early months of World War II had a ring of finality. Unlike Locke, he was willing to, almost ruthlessly, relate Negro art to the Negro's economic and social standing in 1942, and his conclusions seem incontrovertible. While Ward had not completely interrogated the implications of the connections between art and economy, he correctly found that economies, even in simple village forms, not to mention mega capitalist systems, are, at least in part, at the core of the how and why of the production of art.

Edmonds: College Drama and Community Theatre — Hope for the Future

After the war, in 1947, both Randolph Edmonds and George Norford looked again to Negro colleges and universities for signs of hope in future black drama and theatre. Norford had become *Opportunity*'s "Theatrical Editor," and, much as Edmonds had done in 1930, he enthusiastically reported on developments in the member colleges and universities of the Southern Association of Dramatic and Speech Arts (SADSA) and the Inter-Collegiate Drama Association.[10] Edmonds, however, in "Towards Community Drama," began to think that graduates of collegiate theatre programs could be used to strengthen what had largely been a failed Negro little theatre movement. That movement had failed, according to Edmonds, because "few, if any of the organizers" of the Negro community theatres "had any technical training in the theatre," and "community groups had no experienced reservoir of actors and technicians."[11]

Intercollegiate Negro theatre had not, as Edmonds had hoped, resulted in a meaningful increase of Negro authors writing exceptional plays on Negro subject matter. But Edmonds' plan to have Negro community theatres work closely with the Negro educational theatre might achieve that goal and was, in effect, a strategy to attain that still elusive "real American Negro theatre." In his October 1948 address to the Thirty-third Annual Meeting of the Association for the Study of Negro Life, Edmonds stated:

> Despite the popularity and spectacular successes of a few Broadway plays dealing with Negro life ... it is thought by many that hope for a real Negro American theatre lies in the Little Theatre Movement. This idea is prevalent because everything involved in the production of a play from the writing or selection of the script to the close of the final curtain is under the control of Negroes.[12]

Calling to mind Lewis' injunction about the Negro artist first serving the Negro audience, Edmonds continued: "And since the audiences, for the most part, are made up of Negroes those things which are really characteristic of the race and present a true picture of their aims and ideals can always be presented without hindrance." Hopefully, this "true picture" of Negro "aims and ideals," would, eventually, constitute that local, superior art that Lewis had found in ancient Athens and in Negro slave songs.

In 1949, it seemed clear that the day of Negro-authored native drama had still not arrived, and that Broadway would have little to do with the dawning of such a day. Ward, Norford, and Edmonds looked to the Negro little theatre movement to both develop Negro drama and to "train the Negro audience." And, in the matter of audience training, Edmonds had correctly observed: "Theatre audiences are built on a multiplicity of productions rather than a few excellent ones. Infrequent productions, however good they are, cannot develop a theatre-going habit."[13] According to Rowena Jelliffe, Karamu's Gilpin Players had thus far been the only Negro theatre group that we know of to successfully accomplish this kind of audience training.

Even before the beginning of the forties, Du Bois had almost summarily rejected Broadway and all mainstream venues; Locke later took Broadway to task for what it had not done; Lewis had not only supplied a disturbing explanation for the moribund state of black drama and theatre in the 1940s but, at least for Negro artists, reduced Cruse's "crisis of the Negro intellectual" to practical, economic dimensions.

Significant Black Plays of the 1940s

Yet even the Great Depression and a world war could not completely defeat what can be termed the African American drama imperative. Not many Negro dramas reached the stage during and just after the war years. But a few produced works bore evidence of shifts in the art or propaganda debate which, after a half century, still defined the parameters of black dramatic theory. Ward's *Big White Fog*, which has already been treated here, Abram Hill's *On Strivers Row*, and Ted Browne's *Natural Man*, plays first produced in the late 1930s, were all staged in the early 1940s. The latter works and Richard Wright and Paul Green's *Native Son*, like *Big White Fog*, moved black drama closer to the social document and propaganda raised to the level of dramatic art called for by Lewis and Du Bois.

Abram Hill's On Strivers Row and Will Marion Cook Revisited

On Strivers Row was produced by the Rose McClendon Players in January of 1940, and staged again in September by the newly organized American Negro Theatre (ANT) in the 135th Street branch of the New York Public Library, ANT's new Harlem home.[14] The play is set in a stylish, Stanford White designed home on West 139th Street, which is today an actual Harlem street of brownstone homes still called "Strivers' Row." The work is, for the most part, a satirical critique of the upper class Negroes that E. Franklin Frazier termed the "black bourgeoisie."[15] A Negro family, the Van Strivens, now inhabits the chic 139th Street home, and the action and comedy in the play center on a debutante ball planned by Dolly, mother of the family, for her daughter Cobina. Despite appearances, the Van Strivens are heavily in debt. So, to secure a business deal, Oscar Van Striven, head of the family, must commit the social *faux pas* of inviting Ruby Jackson to his daughter's "coming out" ball. Jackson is a former cook, a social climbing Negro who has won the lottery, and she has offered to buy some of Van Striven's unproductive Brooklyn real estate.

Doris Abramson finds "Hill's attempt to dramatize the black bourgeoisie only superficially convincing." ANT revived the play in 1946, and Abramson cites Louis Kronenberger's summing up of what he then saw as the play's major problem: the play needed to contain "either the good-humored exuberance of a spoof, or the sobriety of real criticism."[16] Kronenberger found that Hill's play provided both satirical strategies and that they "did not mix well." Lofton Mitchell later records Kronenberger's critique but writes only that "despite Mr. Kronenberger's objections, *On Strivers Row* drew large audiences from the community." Locke had called the play "a good ground-breaking excursion into social comedy," and his worry that Negro audiences, "who have yet to become conditioned to dramatic self-criticism," would not support the work was apparently unwarranted.[17]

On Strivers Row is Hill's attempt to write a realistic and poignant comedy which both exploits and accepts the human foibles in both upper and lower class Negro life. Ruby Jackson foolishly wants to be a member of Negro society, and Dolly Van Striven thoughtlessly courts the friendship of Tillie Petunia though she has every reason to suspect that Petunia is little more than a pretentious social viper. But Hill seems to build his characters from invention rather than from observation, a strategy appropriate to farce-comedy, but not to the comedic realism that he seems to have been trying to write. His characters too often do not sound like real people. The Negro upper class of the

1940s had language patterns, syntaxes, and allusions expressive of their peculiar place in the American architecture of race relations. This circumstance would seem to be especially true for Hill's Van Strivens, since in their ultimate acceptance of Ruby Jackson and Chuck, Cobina's lower class beau, they demonstrate that they are, after all, really just Negroes. Even Hill's lower class Negroes, once their "jive" talk desists, do not quite sound like ordinary 1940s Negroes.

Subtitled "A Satire," Hill's play, for the most part, lacks the biting wit and droll humor that satire would seem to require. Instead, throughout Act I, Hill's writing seems to rely on the broad playing and almost nonsensical performing techniques usually associated with farce. Yet, also in Act I, Hill's jokes are mostly a matter of dialogue and not one of physical comedy, as also would be expected in a farce-comedy. For example, we must be told that Dolly Van Striven has spent her family into debt. We see none of her outlandish buying sprees, or possible bouts with irate tradesman when all the bills come due. Similarly, the calculated sloth of her maid, Sophie, results in no real household difficulties, like scorched linens, cold tea, mismatched table settings, etc. Instead, Sophie, in Act I, ii, carefully counts roses as she places them in vases in preparation for Cobina's debutante party. Character flaws in Hill's dramatic figures rarely become comedic objectives or actions. Moreover, the Van Strivens, Dolly, Oscar, and Oscar's venerable mother-in-law, Mrs. Pace, are not quite the same people in Act I as they are in Act II. The humanity that belatedly springs forth in their characters in Act II, Scene ii, apparently to aid Hill's happy ending, is almost non-existent in Act I — hence Kronenberger's perception of two different kinds of satire.

James Hatch and Ted Shine agree with Mitchell that *On Strivers Row* was a Harlem hit, writing that ANT's first production of the play ran 101 performances and "became so popular that ANT revived it twice, once as a musical."[18] Hatch and Shine also make a perceptive analogy of *On Strivers Row* to Will Marion Cook and Jesse Shipp's *In Dahomey*:

> The Van Striven family members ... are dramatically "kissing cousins" to the Lightfoot family of *In Dahomey*. They both live in a chichi neighborhood; they both have a daughter they wish to place in high society; they both are surrounded by a greedy entourage; and both party-crashing Joe Smothers of *On Strivers* Row and jive-talking Hustling Charlie of *In Dahomey* embarrass the families by their low-class behavior. Finally, in both plays, young, true love wins out over family pretense.

On Strivers Row returns us to Cook's turn-of-the-century dramatic ideas. The critique of the black upper class had been an important theme in Cook's *Jes' Lak White Fo'ks* (1899), which later found its way into Cook and Shipp's *In Dahomey* (1902). In fact, after *In Dahomey*, themes that critiqued the Negro middle and upper class became rare in the twentieth-century black drama, which may account for *On Striver Row*'s Harlem successes. It had been almost forty years since Negro audiences had the opportunity to collectively laugh at what was widely known in the black community to be the historic and farcical social pretensions lurking among the black bourgeoisie.

Richard Wright and Paul Green's *Native Son*

At the end of March 1941, *Native Son*, directed by Orson Welles, opened in the St. James Theatre, becoming another one of Broadway's intermittent productions of Negro subject matter. *Native Son* is based on Richard Wright's popular novel of the same title, which had been a Book-of-the-Month-Club selection in 1940. The *New York Times* years later reported that Wright had partially based the novel on "the case of Robert Nixon, a Chicago Negro who was put to death in the electric chair in 1938 for the murder of a white girl."[19] Thus, the novel and play tell the story of Bigger Thomas, an inner-city Negro youth of about twenty who accidentally kills his employer's daughter, tries to conceal the deed, and is tried and executed for the girl's murder. Bigger, hired as a chauffeur to a wealthy white Chicago family, is no mild-mannered, falsely accused Negro hero; he is, according to Wright, a bundle of fears and hatreds, all related to his experience of racial and economic oppression in Chicago's "Black belt":

> He hated his family because he knew that they were suffering and that he was powerless to help them. He knew that the moment he allowed himself to feel to its fullness how they lived, the shame and misery of their lives, he would be swept out of himself in fear and despair. So he held toward them an attitude of iron reserve; he lived with them, but behind a wall.... And toward himself he was even more exacting. He knew that the moment he allowed what his life meant to enter fully into his consciousness, he would either kill himself or someone else. So he denied himself and acted tough.[20]

Wright's Bigger is emotionally deformed, and he is a direct descendant of earlier American literature's "brute Negro." As Sterling Brown had indicated, the abolition of slavery and the history of Reconstruction had prompted white authors like Thomas Nelson Page and Thomas Dixon to introduce to American literature the stereotype of the "brute Negro" or Negro monster. Dixon, it will be recalled, wrote the novel *The Clansman*, on which D.W. Griffith based *The Birth of a Nation*. This groundbreaking film, in addition to its cinematic achievements, introduced Dixon's Negro monster to a much wider audience than had his novel. But unlike Page and Dixon, Wright's "genius," Hatch insists, "was to take this monster and present him for what he was — a creation of the white world."[21]

In his novel, Wright, as omnipotent narrator, brilliantly establishes what motivates and even justifies Bigger's behavior, and this produces a new and powerfully human view of Bigger that all but severs his relation to Page and Dixon's "brute Negro." But, without an omnipotent narration, the play appears not to have humanized Bigger's motivations as effectively as had the novel. To achieve Bigger's status as victim of society in Act I, iv,[22] in which he kills Mary, his employer's daughter, Wright and Green rely, perhaps too much, on Bigger's fear of whites. In fear, Bigger escorts the drunken Mary safely into her room; he is both afraid to be caught in a white woman's bedroom and afraid to disobey a white woman's wishes. Mary wants to talk and she begins with a speech about being a member of the "penitent rich" and ends with what can be described as, among other things, her repressed sexual desires: "I wish I was black — Honest, I do — Black like you ... to start all over again, a new life," and "she puts out her hand toward him; he shivers and stands helplessly paralyzed. She touches his hair."

At this point, we must assume that Bigger is paralyzed with fear, not sexual desire. But the scene's sexual implications, at least on Mary's part, take a more explicit turn when she "touches his cheek" and he, "in a whispering scream" replies: "Naw — Naw." Mary begins to "weep noiselessly," and Bigger "gasps" the words "lemme go." There is no indication in the stage directions that Mary is still physically touching Bigger; he is, apparently, still paralyzed with fear, like a frog before a snake, or Mary's tears have aided her seduction attempt and now Bigger's desire is beginning to rise. At any rate, Mary seems to take Bigger's agonizing request to be let go as a confirmation of mutual desire; she says, "Yes, that's what I want — to break through and find you." Mary then falls and Bigger lifts her into his arms muttering a refrain that he has had throughout the scene: "Ain't my job — ain't my job." Mary now begins to talk drunkenly about the hardness and safety of Bigger's arms. She wants him to make her feel safe — "and hurt," she says, "I want to suffer — begin all over again."

At this moment, what could have been Mary's seduction scene rather than Bigger's murder scene would be complete except that Mary begins singing "Swing Low Sweet Chariot" and says, "That's my mother's favorite song"; then, "with a cry," she says, "Mother!" and demands that Bigger let her go. "But still his arms, as if against his will, hold her," the stage directions instruct. Here, Bigger's inability to let Mary go is the first sign of his own desire and his realization that he is the one in control of this situation. After "staring at him coldly" and "shrieking, stop — stop it," Mary collapses in Bigger's arms. He "gazes in fascination" at her face, "his lips open and breathless." To censure his rising desire, Bigger must "jerk his face away from" Mary's. He puts her down and struggles to get her limp body onto her bed. When Mary's mother, the conveniently blind Mrs. Dalton, enters the bedroom, Bigger again has opportunities to escape the room but now he is paralyzed by his fear of what he imagines is the "blinding condemnation" of Mrs. Dalton's, "sightless face." It is the fear that his presence will be revealed, not murderous intent that makes Bigger "instinctively" cover Mary's face with a pillow when she awakes from her faint and begins mumbling. This, of course, leads to Mary's death when she struggles under the pillow and Bigger "heedless of her struggle," watches Mrs. Dalton until Mary's "white hands have fallen limp," and Mrs. Dalton leaves the room.

The sexual nature of this scene, mostly on Mary's part, is obvious. It is only the jolt of accidentally remembering her mother that renders her seduction incomplete. Mary's memory of her mother reminds her that white women do not seduce and go to bed with black men, no matter how hard and comforting such men's arms may be. Bigger's fear of being accused of either raping or trying to rape a white woman is the prime motivator of his actions throughout the scene. Yet his fear never quite reaches a pitch that would force him to take advantage of his many opportunities to exit the scene before killing Mary and sealing his fate. And it is here that the play, without the benefit of omnipotent narration, reduces Bigger from the deeply but plausibly flawed human being that he appeared to be in previous scenes to Wright's polemic about the American racial and economic system's creation of Negro monsters. Bigger's fear of whites, in all its forms, which, in this scene, becomes almost a one-note redundancy, cannot be taken to the logical conclusion of escape if Wright's didactic point is to be made.

The dramatic structure of *Native Son* is built on Act I, iv. In the purest dramatic sense, if this scene does not work, then the plausibility and force of the entire work fall into question. Not surprisingly, the play did suffer criticisms that the book seems to have avoided. Both Abramson and Hatch note that while most mainstream reviewers "praised" Canada Lee in the role of Bigger Thomas, they doubted that the play had the power and insights of the novel. Hatch notes, too, that the reviewers' comments raised certain other questions; he writes: "Was the script merely a vehicle for Communist propaganda? Had Orson Welles gimmicked the production and sensationalized the story? Was the audience let off the hook or accused in the murder of Bigger Thomas?"[23] To cover the flaws in the critical Act I, iv, Welles, as director, may very well have gone to his plentiful bag of theatrical tricks. His casting of Canada Lee as Bigger was almost certainly a masterstroke aimed at dealing with camouflaging what could be seen as Wright's Communist inspired thesis. Lee's entire performance career was based on his pervasive, yet delicate sensitivity and his compelling psychological vulnerability, both qualities that in performance tend to obscure textual polemics of any kind, communist or otherwise.[24] Some critics, however, apparently saw through all of this to the basic flaws in Wright and Green's play script.

Native Son ran on Broadway for ninety-seven performances in 1941, went on tour, and opened again on Broadway in 1942 and ran for eighty-four more performances. But, pursuing Hatch's last question, whether the audience was "let off the hook" or made to feel implicated in Bigger's downfall, gives rise to competing answers. Edith Issacs felt that "*Native Son* had a very real effect on the social conscience of its audience." James Baldwin, on the other hand, found that what appeared to be the attempt to present Bigger Thomas to mainstream audiences as a "warning" was futile. Baldwin writes: "To present Bigger as a warning is simply to reinforce the American guilt and fear concerning him, it is most forcefully to limit him to that ... social arena in which he has no human validity, it is simply to condemn him to death." Did much of *Native Son*'s mostly white Broadway audience see Bigger as an affirmation of its greatest fears, thereby reinforcing its lack of social consciousness as Baldwin suggests and Jay Plum actually found in his examination of *Mulatto*? Abramson writes that "there were stories circulated about members of the audience who went home and fired their Negro chauffeurs."[25] Perhaps, *Native Son*, too, awaits the kind of "accounting for the audience" reconstruction that Plum applied to Hughes' *Mulatto*; that is, if we want to better understand how a seemingly radical play received unexpected and relatively strong mainstream audience support.

However, pursuing the central concerns of this book, it seems fairly clear that Wright's primary concern with his polemic did, in the play, leave Bigger theoretically linked to Negro stereotypes designed by Dixon and others. Because the drama relies on performance to tell its story, in the pivotal scene Wright and Green were forced to choose for Bigger either plausible behavior, or to manipulate his actions to suit Wright's thesis. The writers opted to adjust his behavior to suit the thesis. On the other hand, in Wright and Green's unapologetic depiction of Bigger Thomas, and their respectful dramatization of Negro lower class urban life, Negro drama did move closer to that longed-for black social document raised to the level of dramatic art.

Ted Browne's *Natural Man* and Other Plays

Six weeks after *Native Son* opened on Broadway, Theodore Browne's (1910–1979) *Natural Man*[26] opened uptown in Harlem, becoming the American Negro Theatre's second major production. In 1937, the FTP's Seattle,

Washington, Negro unit had produced *Natural Man* as a folk opera. ANT staged it as a play with music in May 1941. Browne built the work on the story of John Henry, the well-known figure of Negro folklore. In Browne's play, as in the legend, John Henry competes in a contest with a steam engine clearing rock from a railway tunnel. He wins the contest but loses his life in the process. Browne is reported to have said: "I've always felt strongly about a Negro Peoples' Theatre that emphasizes the heroic aspects of the black experience in America — the Exemplars who triumphed over the odds." Consequently, *Natural Man*, with only a veneer of Locke's Inner Life folk elements, pursues the propaganda of race pride and black nationalism in its re-telling of the John Henry story. The play's eight rather sparse episodes seem to rely heavily on music and staging for their effect. Episodes one, two, and eight cover the present action of the contest; the other episodes cover the problems in John Henry's past: his encounter with a "Beale Street" prostitute; his imprisonment as a result of that encounter and his removal to a chain gang; his escape from the chain gang after killing a white guard who flogged a dead prisoner; his brief stay with a "camp-meeting" of Negro Revivalists; and his stay with a group of white hoboes.

Significantly, Abramson's reconstruction of *Natural Man* reports that the play had nine episodes rather than the eight that appear in Hatch's reprint of the work as ANT performed it in 1941.[27] The episode in question is one in which John Henry goes North and becomes a "scab" worker, "accused by white men of stealing their jobs," writes Abramson, and she cites the following encounter between John Henry and white workers:

> FIRST: We white workers can't get a living wage scale, for you goddamned niggers!
> JOHN HEN.: Colored folks entitled to live the same as you whites.
> SECOND: They ain't entitled to buck no union.
> JOHN HEN.: We ain't aiming to buck no union.
> FIRST: No, you ain't! Not much!
> JOHN HEN.: We just doing what we got a right to do — work. If you white folks had awanted us in your union, you'd asked us.
> FIRST: We don't allow any niggers in our union.[28]

The episode, as Abramson reconstructs it, reveals racial tensions between the Negro and white working class and, as such, is a departure from the utopian message of black-white proletarian unity in much of Hughes' work in the thirties and in the final scene of Ward's *Big White Fog*. Apparently, the alliance between Harlem's intelligentsia and the Left, about which Cruse would later complain, had excised Browne's anti-union scene from ANT's presentation of *Natural Man*, and consequently, from all editions of the script used in that production.

In the final episode in the play, Browne makes John Henry's death a Negro triumph over racial prejudice and, to a lesser extent, a symbol of the survival of the human spirit in a mechanized world. In terms of Lewis' hoped-for social document, *Natural Man* is the least impressive of the plays that had been initially produced in the thirties and revived in the early forties. Character relationships in *Natural Man* are, for the most part, abbreviated and the entire work is largely symbolic.

The early 1940s also saw Karamu's Gilpin Players and the Yale School of Drama produce plays by Shirley Graham (1906–1977). Graham is the same Graham who was the black director at Chicago's FTP Negro unit that almost rejected Theodore Ward's *Big White Fog*. In 1940, Graham's one act play, *It's a Morning*,[29] about a Negro woman who murders her daughter to prevent her from being sold into slavery, was a race problem play, pure and simple. The play was produced at Yale and directed by the Hollywood film director Otto Preminger, then a member of Yale's faculty. Karamu's Gilpin Players and Yale produced versions of Graham's *Dust to Earth*, a full-length Negro labor tragedy set in the West Virginia coal mines; The Gilpin Players premiered the play in 1938, and it was rewritten and staged at Yale and again at Karamu in 1941.[30]

After the war, Mitchell reports that the 115th Street People's Theatre in Harlem presented Oliver Pitcher's poetic drama *Spring Beginning* (ca. 1947), featuring, among other then unknowns, Clarice Taylor, Maxwell Glanville and Ruby Dee; the same company also produced Harold Holifield's fantasy *Cow in the Apartment* (ca. 1948). Mitchell notes, too, that Gertrude Jeannette's autobiographical drama set in rural Arkansas, *This Way Forward* (1948), was also produced at the Elks Community Theatre in Harlem. Jeannette had been an ANT member since the early 1940s, and *This Way Forward* was initially staged as an ANT workshop production (1949).[31] Pitcher's *Spring Beginning* and Holifield's *Cow in the Apartment* also appear to be no longer extant, but Jeannette's Harlem theatre company, The H.A.D.L.E.Y. Players, has staged *This Way Forward* a number of times over the past two decades. Jeannette's play is also significant because it is evidence of what appeared to be a re-emerging strategy that married overt propaganda with Locke's Inner Life, folk-inspired art-theatre aesthetics. Willis Richardson had fathered this technique early in the Harlem Renaissance but, two (or three) years before Jeannette's play was staged, Theodore Ward had perfected the technique in *Our Lan'*.

Theodore Ward's *Our Lan'*

In April 1947, Ward's *Our Lan': An Historical Negro Drama* (1946) was produced at the Henry Street Playhouse in New York City. In September, the play opened at the Royale Theatre on Broadway and ran for fifty-one performances.[32] Ward had written the final draft of *Our Lan'* in a playwriting seminar conducted by Kenneth Rowe and sponsored by the New York Theatre Guild. Rowe insisted that *Our Lan'* "had a respectable rather than a hit run," because it was one of those "not infrequent examples" demonstrating "that length of run and the quality of a play do not always correspond." At any rate, for a number of mainstream reviewers, including, Brooks Atkinson and George Jean Nathan, that completely human document of an aspect of Negro life had finally reached the American stage.

Ward set his historical drama, for the most part, in the Reconstruction era, though it begins in the closing moments of the Civil War. Tain, Ward's heroic, central dramatic figure, leads his fellow Freedmen to land that has been set aside for them in the State of Georgia by order of the victorious General Sherman. However, after Lincoln is assassinated and Andrew Johnson, a Tennessee-born southern sympathizer, becomes President, the Federal government reverses Sherman's order. Now the government directs that the land be returned to Burkhardt, a former slaveholding planter. The play concludes with Tain leading his followers in a futile skirmish with Federal troops who have been sent to remove the Freedmen from the land.

The historical background in *Our Lan'* is flawlessly written. In the beginning of the play's published text, Ward's "acknowledgements" include Manuel Gottlieb's "The Land Question in Georgia during Reconstruction" and works of Elisabeth Lawson, James Allen, and Du Bois as his "major sources" for the play. Yet, Ward does not allow what can be the more mundane aspects of history to interfere with the needs of his drama. As Lofton Mitchell writes, Ward told his story "in moving and dramatic terms."[33] Those terms included a delicately revealed, star-crossed romance between Tain and a young woman, Delphine, and Ward's characteristic tendency of avoiding depictions of whites as stick-figure racists. Ward includes a depiction of sympathetic Confederate soldiers in his play. He privileges the simple folk wisdom of his newly freed slaves, but he is careful to include their flaws as well. Even Delphine, Tain's romantic interest, becomes pregnant by Ollie, "a young pre–Civil War Mulatto Freedman." Her pregnancy may be the result of Ollie's nefarious use of "love powders." Tain, too, is not without failings. He is much older than Delphine, and although he eventually accepts her and her expected child as his own, he does so only after nearly ending their relationship with a torrent of jealousy and chauvinist moralizing.

Mitchell and a number of reviewers "were more favorable to" the Henry Street production of the play than they were to its Broadway mounting.[34] Mitchell writes: "Anyone who could see and understand Mr. Ward's play and still believed that Broadway would welcome it ... must have been suffering from naïveté—or expecting to create income tax exemptions." Mitchell adds that on Broadway the many Negro spirituals in the play "were far from revolutionary in presentation." Years later, in a personal interview, Ward is reported to have told Abramson that he allowed "a scene of compromise to be cut" and thereby "sacrificed the belly of the play for Broadway." And, in the same interview, in keeping with Mitchell's view of the music in the play, Ward complained: "the director had a tenor sing offstage before the curtain and everyone expected a musical."[35] *Our Lan'* seems to be a case of what Locke called, in 1941, Broadway's "tyranny of what the public is supposed to want." With *Our Lan'* Broadway appears to have, paraphrasing Locke, severely compromised an "obviously original and significant strain of Negro drama."

But, despite Broadway's commercial manipulations, in terms of the progress of black drama, a close reading of Ward's play reveals that he had, for the most part, achieved that marriage of dramatic art and propaganda that Du Bois had called for in 1930. Moreover, in raising propaganda to the level of stage art he had removed what Locke had called, in 1929, propaganda's tendency to "harangue" or supplicate to an oppressive majority. Yet, Ward did not give up his ideas about race and economics to write *Our Lan'*. The core theme in the play is the black struggle for political and economic equality. Further, Ward's depiction of the vast gulf between Burkhardt and the sympathetic Confederate soldiers (Act II, iv, 396) is a frontal attack on a capitalist system that places white men of wealth in control of the lives of both poor blacks and whites. Finally, it was a prominent white reviewer, George Jean Nathan, who perhaps best summed up what the play meant in the Art or Propaganda debate that had defined black dramatic theory for almost a half century. Sounding as if Theophilus Lewis had tutored him, Nathan wrote: "The Natural tragic force of the theme is immeasurably greater and much more impressive than the artificial soapbox force of all the recent Negro Propaganda rolled into one."[36]

The Struggle Continues—Theatres Influencing Black Drama of the 1940s

In 1947, Ward's difficulties with the Broadway production of *Our Lan'* underscored, yet again, that Broadway was a commercial venue that occasionally exploited Negro drama but not one, as Du Bois had warned, that would nurture and develop it. Ward almost certainly found his 1947 Broadway experience particularly bitter since seven years earlier, in 1940, he had been one of the principal founders of the short-lived Negro Playwrights Company (NPC). Set up to be the home of emerging Negro dramatists, NPC appears to have been the century's first major American playwright-oriented Negro theatre company. NPC was a not-for-profit corporation; Paul Robeson, Richard Wright, and Alain Locke were among its board members; the company's membership included Ward's fellow playwrights Abram Hill, Owen Dodson, Theodore Browne, Langston Hughes and George Norford.[37]

In NPC's brochure, *A Professional Theatre with an Idea*, a section entitled "Perspective" found that "the lack of a Negro literature of the drama comparable with reality or truth" had resulted in "the absence of a healthy and competent Negro theatre."[38] Consequently, the playwrights of NPC would, the Perspective states, "recognize that they live in a real society where there are no ivory towers."

As NPC's inaugural production, Ward's *Big White Fog* opened in October of 1940 in the Lincoln Theatre in Harlem. Given NPC's goals and, perhaps more importantly, its political and artistic prerequisites for NPC playwrights, the selection of Ward's play seemed more than appropriate. *Big White Fog* ran nearly twice as long as it had run in its original Chicago production. Rowe, it will be recalled, would later consider the fifty-one Broadway performances of *Our Lan'* a "respectable" run. And the *Pittsburgh Courier*, of the black press, agreed, seeing NPC's sixty-four performances of *Big White Fog* as an NPC triumph; the paper headlined its story on NPC boasting about the "64 Performances" that the company had "chalked up"; then the *Courier* announced NPC's preparations for its next production, an "intimate revue."[39]

But after *Big White Fog* closed on 14 December 1940, the NPC died almost as quickly as it had been born. That the company's first play was not a smash hit seems an incomplete explanation of its demise. But *Big White Fog* does point to what may have been an important reason for NPC's premature end. Ward is reported to have claimed that a deepening split in the American Left, precipitated by Stalin's 1939 pact with Hitler, and the United States' impending entry into the war, had drawn public support away from anything that could be considered Communist or Communist inspired.[40] In 1938, *Big White Fog* had been branded as a Communist play, mostly because of its ending; two years later, it had not out-lived that reputation. Moreover, the prerequisites for NPC playwrights, as stated in its "Perspective," could be read as Communist inspired propaganda:

> And if they as playwrights do not in any way have to be active political workers, they will be writers worthy of the name only if they remain independent of the forces which have reduced brains to a commodity and driven weaklings and panderers to the practice of falsifying truth in order to make it conform

to accepted beliefs and the tastes of those who tend to regard the Negro people as children of slaves placed in the world for their own exploitation and amusement.[41]

If Ward's view is accepted, the country's quixotic, pre–World War II political atmosphere prevented *Big White Fog* from becoming NPC's much needed inaugural hit; and that atmosphere also dried up what seemed, only six months earlier, the company's broad and unflagging support. The first major company primarily devoted to the development of black drama and, by implication, a concerted development of black dramatic theory was quickly at an end.

That same year, 1940, saw the birth of the American Negro Theatre. Unlike the NPC, the company was an actor-oriented institution. In 1943, Abram Hill, ANT's principal founder, remarked: "We're trying to discover something that could be called the art of Negro acting." This attempt to discover the essence of Negro performance resulted in an eleven-year history (1940–1951), which, arguably, remains matchless in its twentieth-century contribution to African American performance.[42]

But, in terms of black-authored dramas, ANT has a rather sketchy record of achievement. Between 1940 and 1949, more than half of ANT's reported nineteen productions appear to have been authored by white writers. Hill's *On Strivers Row*, *Anna Lucasta* (1944), *Walk Hard* (1944), *A Long Way Home* (1948); Browne's *Natural Man* (1941), Dodson's *Garden of Time* (1945), and Flournoy Miller and Aubrey Lyles' *Sugar Hill* (1947) account for only seven of ANT's nineteen productions.[43] And three of Hill's four plays were adaptations of works by white authors. Apparently, a price was paid for this reliance on the works of white writers. After 1945, when, according to Ethel Pitts, most of the white-authored plays were staged, "the company produced a series of mediocre plays and received a series of mediocre reviews."[44]

But ANT's looking to white writers for material for adaptations and for original play scripts was most certainly due to the historical lack of serviceable Negro-authored plays, an issue that black theatre thinkers had discussed since the early days of the Harlem Renaissance. In fact, as early as 1917, the Broadway production of white playwright Ridgley Torrence's *Three Plays for a Negro Theatre* had fully demonstrated that the development of the Negro performer had, even then, far outstripped that of the Negro dramatist. Perhaps it is too much to suggest that ANT could have done for African American drama what it had almost miraculously accomplished for African American performance. Yet, given that Hill was also, at least initially, one of the principal founders of NPC, it is perhaps one of the great tragedies in twentieth-century African American theatre history that *Art or Propaganda* ideological differences prevented the reconstitution of NPC as one of ANT's workshop units.

Hill later reported that in 1940 he had called together Hughes Allison (*The Trial of Dr. Beck*), Ward, Hughes, Browne, Powell Lindsay, and Norford to "discuss the plight of black theatre, which was nonexistent since the Federal Theater went out." Hill continued:

> As a result we decided to organize the Negro Playwrights Company ... Though I was the initiator of the movement, I was only able to stay with the group for about six months. I resigned because the feeling of the majority of the members was that the theatre had a great social message to deliver — at the expense of what I considered to be artistic potential. The majority of the members could not see a play unless it had a certain political leaning.[45]

By 1948, as has been mentioned, Randolph Edmonds had started to look to the Community theatre to save professional Negro theatre rather than to the Negro College and University as he had done in 1930. In 1949, he reported that black community theatres had been founded in Dallas, New Orleans, Washington, D.C., Atlantic City, Detroit, Columbus, Ohio, Boston, Pittsburgh, and in other cities around the country.[46] At the close of the decade, New York's Negro community theatres included Harlem's 115th Street People's Theatre and the Elks Community Theatre, The Negro Drama Group, and The American Negro Repertory Players. But Edmonds does not tell us which of these companies had become a true home for the developing Negro dramatist. It seems clear that even the Community theatres that produced available Negro plays did not have the stability needed to develop Negro drama. In the 1940s, even Karamu Theatre's Gilpin Players faced severe limitations, having no major productions in the war years, 1942 to 1945.[47]

In 1930, Du Bois' "All art is propaganda, but all propaganda is not art," had all but resolved the art or propaganda debate, but a decade of soup lines and nearly five years of world war had all but obliterated his cryptic message. In the onslaught of the Great Depression, the propaganda of the proletariat superseded Negro propaganda about the color line; attempts to meld the two, in some cases naïve, in others self-serving, overlooked the imperatives and depth of both traditional black culture and American apartheid. Yet, in theory at least, leftist thought had raised the issue of the relation of art and economics. Du Bois' "white wealth embargo of Negro art" observation seemed more vivid and ubiquitous than it had ever been.

By the late 1940s, the push to remove the Negro art project to black colleges and universities had proved unworkable, and building a "real" Negro drama and theatre became the province of an essentially fledgling "Negro Little Theatre Movement." Yet, Negro drama in Hill's *On Strivers Row* had, in many ways, returned to its traditional roots of self-criticism, and Wright and Green's *Native Son* had cut a path to viable Negro social drama that Ward's *Our Lan'* completely traversed. Beset by worldwide depression and a world war, it had taken black drama seventeen years to discover that "All art is propaganda, but all propaganda is not art.

V

Civil Rights vs. Integration and the Persistence of Art-Theatre Drama, 1950–1959

The 1947 aesthetic strategies that had raised *Our Lan'* to the dramatized Negro "social document" that Theophilus Lewis had been looking for did not have a devastating impact on Negro theatre. In 1950 Lewis wrote that after a half-century there were still too few Negroes who could be reasonably called dramatists: "While our actors have come a long way since the beginning of the century, we have produced less than a handful of really good playwrights."[1]

In the 1950s, the proletarian propaganda of "black and white togetherness" of the thirties flowered into the propaganda of a fully blown civil rights movement. Paul Nadler reports that "because the war [had been] fought against the racist empires of Germany and Japan, racism at home came to seem more insupportable than ever." In 1945, when African American troops returned home yet again as less than equal citizens from another world war, "thousands of people from dozens of organizations," writes Nadler, began a twenty-year struggle to eliminate American apartheid.[2] Propaganda, artistic or inartistic, received a new and seemingly irresistible impetus and was again very much in vogue.

John Adams: "A Nation of Laws and Not of Men"

The national struggle against segregation became popularly known as the "Civil Rights" or "Integration Movement." However, in the theoretical terms of this discussion, it must be noted that in black communities throughout the United States, especially among Negro artists, the terms "civil rights" and "integration" were not synonymous. In fact, the now historic Supreme Court case *Brown v. The Board of Education* did not begin as a suit for school desegregation. The *Briggs v. Clarendon County* case (1950) was "the most important of the five school desegregation cases that had been collectively brought before the Supreme Court as *Brown v. Board*," Nadler reports, and the Briggs case, he continues, "had been a classic example of a separate but unequal funding. The county's white schools received over sixty percent of school funds, even though whites made up only a quarter of the student population." The *Briggs*' suit "asked not for desegregation *per se*," but only for black schools to be given funding equal to white schools." *Briggs*, in other words, initially followed the doctrine of "separate-but-equal." However, in 1954, ruling on Briggs and the other four *Brown* cases, the Supreme Court found that segregation in public schools was unconstitutional. Thurgood Marshall and the NAACP's legal staff representing *Brown* had effectively argued that "separate-but-equal" was "unconstitutional under the Fourteenth Amendment," and that "the only way to equalize school and other public facilities was to integrate them."

The integration of public facilities for most Negroes was a civil rights issue; it did not mean "completely identifying the Negro with the American image," as the noted Negro writer Julian Mayfield (1928–1985) would state in 1959. Mayfield wrote that the concentration on integration had been largely "the singular push [of Negro] church, civic and political leaders." Such a push, Mayfield agreed, should be "applauded" and "encouraged," but only with the following proviso:

> so long as integration is interpreted to mean the attainment of full citizenship rights in such areas as voting, housing, education, employment, and the like. But if, as the writers have reason to suspect, integration means completely identifying the Negro with the American image — that great-power face that the world knows and the Negro knows better — then the writer must not be judged too harshly for balking at the prospect.[3]

Mayfield characterizes the distinction between civil rights and integration that had prevailed in most of black America since the end of the war. His interpretation of the meaning of integration exclusively in terms of actual civil rights had been the goal of Du Bois, Locke, and other Harlem Renaissance figures, and it would later apply even to the militant and separatist Black Arts movement. It had taken the nation more than a century and a half to get round to John Adams' notion of "a government of laws and not of men."[4] In Black America this principle had almost universally formed the core of all political thinking since the end of the Civil War. It had been a core belief motivating the New Negro movement, and, whatever its separatist claims, the 1960s Black Arts movement would certainly assume that blacks were entitled to equal treatment under law. But melding black American culture into the white American mainstream would have meant the obliteration of

Locke's folk-inspired art-theatre, and an end to the cultural, often African related, distinctions that both Du Bois and Locke had championed in Negro art — such an identification with white America, of course, later became anathema to the rising Black Arts movement.

The Negroes among the "thousands" who actively participated in the civil rights movement were actually a tiny fraction of the Negro population. The push for "integration" as opposed to "civil rights," was not the product of a groundswell of Negro public opinion. Rather, as Mayfield notes and Doris Abramson suggests, it was the creature of a post-war and early 1950s Negro leadership. The proposition that this leadership would protect black culture and art through the new rigors of integration seemed to Mayfield and most of the black artistic community highly "suspect." After all, this leadership was, for the most part, not unlike the leadership from which Du Bois had withdrawn twenty years earlier, largely on cultural grounds; it was composed of a small contingent of liberal whites and, it could be reasonably argued, dominated by that same class of Negroes whom Lewis had criticized for failing to support the Negro theatre. It could also be argued that among its members were the same kind of middle class Negroes who in Chicago had cared more about a white woman's opinion (Kay Ewing) than their own feelings about a black writer's (Ted Ward) play. In short, Mayfield, black artists, and much of ordinary black America feared that too many in the faction that was promoting integration were that same group of middle class Negroes whom Langston Hughes had once considered, to use George Schuyler's term, little more than "lamp-blacked Anglo-Saxons."

Abramson correctly observes that in the 1950s, "there [were] those, of course, who are not persuaded that integration is the whole answer, who wonder about the value of the society Negroes are trying so desperately to enter." Mayfield was an example of the unpersuaded; he wondered about the artistic value of the American mainstream literary establishment into which he and other Negro writers were supposed to integrate:

> The phenomenon of our era is the seeming lack of concern shown by American creative writers for the great questions facing the peoples of the world.... the American writer has turned his back on them. He deals with the foibles of suburban living, the junior executive, dope addiction, homosexuality, incest and divorce.[5]

Throughout Negro America there were real questions about the relative value of what can be called cultural and social integration as distinguished from Adams' "government of laws" that blindly bestowed on all its citizens equal civil rights, whatever their differing measures of wit, wealth, or beauty.

Locke, James Baldwin, William Couch, and 1950s Black Theory

In 1954, after a prolonged illness, Alain Leroy Locke died.[6] The voice that had made for almost thirty years the most consistent contribution to the twentieth-century discourse on African American literature, fiction, poetry, and drama was gone. But Locke's work had not been in vain. The core of the discourse on black art, the Art or Propaganda debate, did not die with him. In fact, Mayfield's 1959 comments about retaining the cultural distinctiveness of Negro writing had come as a result of what many Negro writers had come to see, with the advent of the integration movement, as the increasingly less viable tradition of Negro protest writing.[7]

In "Everybody's Protest Novel," James Baldwin had a decade earlier appeared to be assuming Locke's old anti-propagandist role. Baldwin's ideas about fiction are significant in twentieth-century black drama and therefore to this discussion since most of them would be expressed in his major plays, *The Amen Corner* (1954) and *Blues for Mister Charlie* (1964); the first work is almost a primer of Locke's Inner Life, art-theatre goals, and the latter play is an Inner Life examination of both white and black dramatic figures that masqueraded as a civil rights protest play.

In 1949, Baldwin had launched a thoroughgoing and convincing attack on what had historically been, arguably, America's most popular protest novel, Harriet Beecher Stowe's *Uncle Tom's Cabin* (1852). But his real target was not Mrs. Stowe's book. He considered *Uncle Tom's Cabin* the "cornerstone of American social protest fiction," and that far too many Negro writers had built their literary houses on that foundation.[8] If he could dislodge Mrs. Stowe's cornerstone, Baldwin seems to say, then the Negro protest literature that it supported could soon be disassembled. To begin this task, he recalled an encounter between Stowe's characters St. Clare and his cousin Miss Ophelia:

> St. Clare, the kindly master, remarks to his coldly disapproving Yankee cousin, Miss Ophelia, that, ... the blacks have been turned over to the devil for the benefit of the whites in this world — however, he adds thoughtfully, it may turn out in the next. Miss Ophelia's reaction is ... vehemently right-minded: "This is perfectly horrible!" she exclaims. "You ought to be ashamed of yourselves!"[9]

Neither character, Baldwin observes, "questions the medieval morality from which their dialogue springs." Baldwin was convinced that like Miss Ophelia, Stowe's "virtuous rage was motivated ... merely by a panic of ... being caught in traffic with the devil." For Stowe, Baldwin writes,

Black equates with evil and white with grace; if being mindful of the necessity of good works, she could not cast out the black — a wretched, huddled mass, apparently, claiming ... her inner eye — she could not embrace them either without purifying them of sin.... Tom, therefore ... has been robbed of his humanity and divested of his sex. It is the price for that darkness for which he has been branded.

Baldwin proposes that "medieval morality" was a reality for Stowe as well as her characters; he adds:

they spurned and were terrified of the darkness and considered from this aspect, Miss Ophelia's exclamation, like Mrs. Stowe's novel, achieves ... almost a lurid significance, like the light from a fire which consumes a witch.

Stowe's "cornerstone" of protest literature was obviously no fit foundation for a Negro writer. Sounding more like Locke than Locke, Baldwin writes that "novels of oppression written by Negroes ... actually reinforce ... the principles which activate the oppression they decry." Baldwin also found that the contemporary protest novel, "far from being disturbing," had become "an accepted and comforting aspect of the American scene":

Whatever unsettling questions are raised are ... remote, for this has nothing to do with us ... indeed, it has nothing to do with anyone, so that finally we receive a ... thrill of virtue from the fact that we are reading such a book at all. This report from the pit reassures us of its reality and its darkness and of our own salvation.

In "Many Thousands Gone" (1951), Baldwin would continue to develop this theme of the white majority's need to safely abstract the Negro into a social problem, a need that propaganda and protest writing so adequately serviced. Baldwin suggests that the Negro as a social problem helped to obscure "the many ways in which [the Negro] has affected American psychology." But that fact was betrayed not only in American popular culture, but also in American morality:

In our estrangement from him [the Negro] is the depth of our estrangement from ourselves. We cannot ask: what do we really feel about him? — such a question merely opens the gates on chaos. What we really feel about him is involved with all that we feel about everything, about everyone, about ourselves.[10]

The Negro, Baldwin seems to say, had been consigned to an abstract, shadowy sociological existence to prevent mainstream America from, as it were, looking too deeply into the moral ambiguities in its own soul. "The story of the Negro in America is the story of America — or, more precisely, it is the story of Americans," writes Baldwin.

The Negro protest novel that best served this American subterranean matrix of Negro oppression allied with the suppression of mainstream guilt was, according to Baldwin, Richard Wright's *Native Son*. In 1951, *Native Son* was still "the most powerful and celebrated statement we have yet had of what it means to be a Negro in America," Baldwin asserts. And he observes that Wright's book, "at the time of its publication," was generally received as "bitter, uncompromising, shocking"; the novel's "very existence gave proof of what strides might be taken in a free democracy; and its indisputable success, proof that Americans were now able to look full in the face without flinching the dreadful facts." But, Baldwin adds:

> Americans, unhappily have the most remarkable ability to alchemize all bitter truths into an innocuous but piquant confection and to transform moral contradictions, or public discussion of such contradictions into a proud decoration such as are given for heroism on the field of battle.

But beyond the public discussion, in the privacy of their souls, Baldwin suggests that most white Americans recognize that, as in the case of Bigger Thomas, they are in some way responsible for the bitter injustices revealed in the protest novel. However, Baldwin contends, they recognize their responsibility for these agonizing truths in the same way they recognize it for Bigger, "not only with hatred and fear and guilt and the resulting fury of the self-righteous but also with that morbid fullness of pride mixed with [the] horror with which one regards the extent and power of one's wickedness." This mixture of fear, pride, and horror can be sensed in Stowe's kindly master St. Clare when he says that in this life blacks have been given over to the devil for the purposes of whites and in the death sentence that Bigger receives from his white judge and jury in *Native Son*. In Bigger's case, no "piquant confection" can be made of the injustices that have helped to set him on his path. He must be quickly destroyed so that the telltale evidence of the collective guilt that his life personifies may return again to that hidden place where, as Baldwin writes, estrangement from Bigger guarantees estrangement from our American selves.

Thus, in the waning years of Locke's life, Baldwin would not only become his major disciple, but he would extend Locke's Inner Life, art-theatre assumptions to include all Americans, not just Negroes. Bigger deludes himself, "accepting a theology [Stowe's] that denies him life," writes Baldwin, and "he admits to the possibility of his being sub-human." Similarly, those who dehumanized him end in dehumanizing themselves; Baldwin writes: "The loss of their identity is the price paid for their annulment of his." In Baldwin's schema, it is the failure or the mismanagement of the ultimate Inner Life issue, the relationship with self, which is at the root of humanity's problem; this is the real stuff of novels and drama.

In 1950, a year after Baldwin's "Everybody's Protest Novel," and the year before his "Many Thousands Gone," William Couch, Jr., demonstrated that Baldwin was not Locke's only disciple. In "The Problem of Negro Character and Dramatic Incident," Couch questioned the artistic merit of some of what Nadler calls the "postwar boom" in civil rights drama. Couch admits that Negro characters in these postwar novels and plays generally exhibited more "intelligence" than prewar Negro characters, and that they inhabited story structures that had mostly removed what he calls the "low comic ... maudlin elements of the past." Yet, Couch felt that a more careful and extended examination of the subject could reveal that quite a bit of "inferior literature has ... passed unchallenged," and this circumstance, Couch warned, "may promote more social and artistic confusion than previously existed."[11] For Couch, the new Negro characters were seldom what are called "characters in action," and when they took action, it was usually "a caricature of sane cognitive response," ultimately inconsistent "with the ... stature of the character," writes Couch, and "our ... knowledge of human nature." And he found that this problem existed in stage drama, novels, and the cinema, all mediums that used Negro characters in what Couch calls "dramatic incidents."

Couch believed that the problem of dramatic incident concerning Negro characters had its origin in the circumstance that the drama required "consequential action" executed "by a protagonist with whom we can sympathize." But he observes that the sentiments of white America were obviously not agreeable to "emphatic and uncompromising" Negroes, on stage or anywhere else, and these were the very elements needed for an effective central character. Couch writes that for example, in Arnaud d'Usseau and James Gow's *Deep Are the Roots* (1945) Brett Charles, an educated Negro war hero lacks the competency to even perceive the true nature of his problems, let alone resolve them. In fact, Charles appears to fail in all his dramatic objectives, which is, as Couch notes, totally inconsistent with his education and his given experience of the world. And in this play Couch finds that reconciliation, usually a significant part of dramatic structure, grows out of the way events have expanded the consciences of white characters, not Charles'; thus the result of this so-called new civil rights drama is, fundamentally, the same as in the old drama. Charles, like the Negro characters of old, is, Couch notes, deprived of "purpose" and "self-will"; he is left to seek the answer to his problems in the "awakening of white conscience," and, Couch adds, "there can be [no] ... success for him," not even "the 'success' of tragic failure."

Couch also charges that in the film adaptation (1949) of Arthur Laurents' stage play, *Home of the Brave* (1946), "the considerable accomplishments" of the central dramatic figure Moss, a young Negro soldier, are not used to develop his character. He is "a high school graduate ... has [had] special ... training" and "has volunteered for a dangerous mission." But these facts are merely expository elements; visually, they are virtually undramatized in the film. Instead, Moss' character is developed, as Couch notes, mainly through his "mute suffering, which ... increases to hysteria."

Negro protagonists who strangely had no "competency" for their own problems were, in Couch's view, legion in much of civil rights literature. Moreover, for Couch there were at least four major affirmations of the popularity of Negro characters who, in violation of dramatic logic, lacked the usual responses of human nature: the 1940s Hollywood re-release of the original film version (1934) of Fannie Hurst's novel *Imitation of Life* (1933), and the Broadway staging (1945) of Lillian Smith's novel *Strange Fruit* (1944) in New York's Royale Theatre.[12]

Couch also found that most integration or protest literature had the special feature of "at least one strong speech [about] ... racial discrimination." These sequences, most often come near the end of the work, and are normally explicated by "a white spokesman [having] no ... connection ... with the main action," writes Couch. As examples of this prevalent technique, Couch cites the white lawyer in the stage adaptation of *Native Son*, the white psychiatrist in *Home of the Brave*, and the white doctor in *Strange Fruit*. Couch suggests that these speeches take the place of "retribution," which is, for him, an important and usual feature of the drama. Perhaps more importantly for Couch, these speeches also replace "punitive justice," an element of retribution in the regular drama that is almost never the fate of white miscreants and antagonists in civil rights literature.

On the whole, Couch judged that the Negro characters in the new civil rights drama understood very clearly but one thing: "they must suffer." And he found that this "submissive suffering," is not the "Suffering of Tragedy" because it is almost always "without reference to an excess of causes" structured into the specific work. Above all, it is a suffering, Couch affirms, that the Negro sufferer does not "resist or investigate." And, perhaps following Baldwin's lead, Couch, too, finds that the protest literature strategies set so firmly in place by Stowe's *Uncle Tom's Cabin* are the likely cause of this seemingly causeless suffering. Like Baldwin, he finds that in too much protest literature, ultimately, the sin for which the Negro suffers, following Stowe, is the blackness of his skin. Concluding his discussion, Couch advises that if the new efforts to deal with Negro subject matter are to be fruitful "we must strive ... towards a complete assimilation of racial experience to basic human experience and sound dramatic principles."[13]

Alice Childress on Civil Rights vs. Cultural Integration

In February of 1951, the noted actor-director-playwright Alice Childress (1920–1994) in "For a Negro Theatre" wrote of her own struggle with the differences between civil rights and cultural integration. Childress begins, writing of a "heated though friendly discussion" between herself and Theodore Ward in which Ward claimed that there was still "a definite need" for a Negro Theatre.[14] Childress, however, "held to the idea that a Negro theatre sounded as though it might be a Jim Crow institution." Childress reports that she pondered everything Ward had said for "several months" before she could come to "an understanding of what he meant." In hindsight, it seems extraordinary that Childress, a member of The American Negro Theatre, the company that James Hatch has called "the most renowned theatre group of the forties,"[15] should need to be convinced in the early fifties of the need for a Negro theatre. Childress' initial reaction to Ward's remarks likely offers us a picture of the fever pitch that the integration movement had reached only six short years after World War II. Ward's mere mention that Negroes should organize among themselves, for any purpose, at first seemed to Childress like tacit support of the segregationist policies that many blacks and liberal whites were struggling to defeat.

On the other hand, Childress was apparently too sensitive and too much herself a creative artist not to ultimately understand the cultural needs of the Negro artist. When her integration stupor faded, she wrote that, as in the public schools of the period, "the Negro actor attends drama schools which ... take little interest in the cultural or historical background of the Negro people." Apparently, she realized, too, as did Theophilus Lewis, that depriving a people of their culture was but another form of racism. She observed that in these drama schools, "Negroes ... were learning only the technique developed by whites." To be sure, Childress had a deep appreciation of the techniques taught in the better drama schools of the day. But she was convinced that instruction that would "advance the white as well as the Negro actor and playwright in [the] knowledge of the Negro people's culture" should be an integral part of any serious study of American drama.

In this writing, Childress demonstrates that she was very much in touch with what Locke would have called the folkways of the Negro people. In lines that read more like poetry than sentences in an expository essay, she sets for herself the task of observation, the much needed skill of the mature theatre artist; her gaze as a Negro artist delving into her own culture is directed at what she calls "my people," a people that she closely observes "in railroad stations ... fields ... tenements, at the factory wheels, in the stores." Her observations reveal her people's essential Blues-like quality of duality that, as has been discussed earlier, reaches back into African cosmology: Childress' people both "smile and think of death," and "frown and think of life."

Childress, in almost poetic detail, describes her people on the subway "weary... [from] scrubbing ... carrying, lifting, cooking ... shining ... polishing ... ironing." But they "fight drowsiness. No one must say that they are lazy or sleepy or slow." Then she asks: "What could be a more fruitful study in the craft of acting than to reproduce one of these weary people?"

Concluding her brief essay in a manifesto-like statement, Childress calls for a Negro people's theatre that would help to attain "the liberation of all oppressed people." This new Negro theatre, she writes, needed to study the theatres of all cultures, including the "oppressed groups which have no formal theatre as we know it, but we must discover theatre as they know it." In theory, Childress' Negro theatre was not all that different from Du Bois' Negro universities (1940) in which "the examination of black life, history, social development, science, and humanities" would lead to the study "of all life and matter in the universe."

Couch and Childress' comments relating specifically to theatre and drama are significant for their rarity if for nothing else. William Branch and Phillip Hayes Dean had plays produced in the 1950s, and they have both confirmed that the fifties lacked authoritative voices probing issues that related specifically to the nature of black dramatic art.[16] It must be remembered that for all his eloquence interpreting and perhaps even reinterpreting Locke's position, in the early 1950s, at the beginning of his career, Baldwin was primarily concerned with the art of the novel; his comments would have considerably less weight in this discussion had he not also contributed two important works to the twentieth-century canon of black drama.

The First Conference of Negro Writers, 1959

On the other hand, the question of the continued viability of Negro protest literature in the face of "integration" pertained to all forms of Negro literature, including drama. This issue, as Mayfield's comments above suggest, dominated the discussion and resulting papers of the First Conference of Negro Writers in 1959. The noted black literary critic and writer, Saunders Redding (1906–1988) functioned, more or less, as the dean of that conference. And in one of the resulting conference papers, "The Negro Writer and His Relationship to His Roots," Redding finds that the protest element in Negro literature is at the very core of the American Negro experience:

> Dishonor, bigotry, hatred, degradation, injustice, arrogance and obscenity do flourish in American life, and especially in the prescribed and proscriptive American Negro life; and it is the right and the duty of the Negro writer to say so — to complain.[17]

Arthur P. Davis also produced a conference paper, "Integration and Race Literature." Davis would later co-edit with Redding the 1971 anthology *Calvacade: Negro American Writing from 1760 to the Present*. In his conference paper Davis, finds that the "climate" of integration has dealt the Negro writer a "crushing blow":

> Ironical though it may be, we [Negro writers] have capitalized on oppression (I mean, of course, in a literary sense). Although we may deplore ... the cause, there is great creative motivation in a movement which brings all members of a group together and cements them in a common bond. That is ... what segregation did for the Negro, especially during the twenties and thirties when full segregation was ... tacitly condoned by the whole nation.

"The possibility of imminent integration," Davis continues, "has tended to destroy the protest element in Negro writing." Yet, he writes, "the para-dox" that has to be kept in mind is that "we do not have actual integration anywhere ... life for the overwhelming majority of Negroes is unchanged." Nevertheless, according to Davis, integration had already forced a number of Negro writers "to find new themes within the racial framework." And to make his point, he cites, among other examples, Chester Himes' *Third Generation* (1954), Owen Dodson's *Boy at the Window* (1951), Gwendolyn Brooks' *Maud Martha* (1953), and Langston Hughes' *Sweet Flypaper of Life* (1955); in all these novels, writes Davis, "the main stress is on life within the group, not on conflict with outside forces." Himes had authored *If He Hollers Let Him Go* (1945), a book Davis calls "the typical protest novel," and, though Davis does not mention it, Hughes had apparently completely left behind his proletarian phase. Concluding his paper, Davis writes:

> And when we finally reach that stage in which we can look at segregation in the same way that historians now regard ... the Hitler era or any other evil period of the past, we shall then do naturally ... what the Joyces and Dostoevskys of the world have always done.

That is, according to Davis, Negro authors will then be able to "write intimately and objectively of our own people in universal human terms."

For Samuel W. Allen and John Henrik Clarke (1915–1998), who also wrote papers for the conference, any intimate examination of what Davis calls "our own people" had to include, respectively, the notion of Négritude, and an understanding of the American Negro's African heritage. Allen is a noted African American poet and lawyer; his poetry is published in French and German, and he was the editor of the Parisian journal *Présence Africaine* in the late forties and early fifties; he would later serve as chief counsel in the U.S. Community Relations Service (1965-1968). Clarke, in 1959, was in the process of becoming one of the most influential chroniclers and teachers of African history in the United States, becoming a pioneer in the development of African Heritage and Black Studies programs throughout the United States.[18]

In "Négritude and Its Relevance to the American Negro Writer," Allen suggests that Négritude, in one sense, can be defined as "an effort toward a renewal of [a] lost organic vision of the universe." This definition is "revealed," Allen reports, "in the creative efforts" of a number of French-speaking Caribbean writers of African descent, including Aimé Césaire, Jacques Roumain, René Dépestre, and in a number of African writers, including Leopold Senghor, David Diop, Birago Diop, and Efua Morgue. Allen writes that in his "excellent preface to Senghor's 1947 anthology of African poetry in the French language," Jean Paul Sarte "likened negritude to an African Eurydice, recovered by the song of Orpheus from Pluto."[19] Allen concludes that the concept of Negritude is important to the American Negro because

> like the African, he has an imposing interest in the development of his image of the universe, in the correction of the distorted image of himself in this society, and in an exploration and fuller expression of his particular talents, whatever the subject matter with which he deals.

Following Allen's conclusion, Clarke, in his conference paper, "Reclaiming the Lost African Heritage," takes up the popular distortion of Africa "as a savage and backward land with little history and no golden age." Despite "voluminous documents in European libraries proving the contrary," writes Clarke, "imperialists who needed moral justification for their rape, pillage, and destruction of African cultural patterns and ways of life," created this distortion. In this paper, Clarke cites the works of the Caribbean-born Dr. Edward Wilmot Blyden (1832-1912), George Williams, W.E.B. Du Bois, Carter Woodson, and the white Africanists John W. Vandercook and Arthur Brisbane; he uses these authors to create a brief but tantalizing view of significant events in African history before and during the European colonization. Citing Vandercook, Clarke concludes his discussion, giving what he feels is the central reason why the American Negro, like the African, has to reclaim his heritage: "A Race is like a man. Until it uses its own talents, takes pride in its own history, and loves its own memories, it can never fulfill itself completely."

Curiously, while insisting that protest literature was native to the Negro writer, Redding, in the conference's first paper, had concluded his findings citing what he considered a masterful passage written by Baldwin, the anti-protest Lockeian. To make his final point, Redding read the following from Baldwin's *Notes of a Native Son* (1955):

> Since I no longer felt that I could stay in this cell forever, I was beginning to be able to make peace with it for a time ... The story of the *Drap De Lit*, ... caused great merriment in the courtroom.... I was chilled by their merriment, even though it was meant to warm me. It could only remind me of the laughter I had often heard at home.... This laughter is the laughter of those who consider themselves to be at a safe remove from all the wretched.... I had heard it so often in my native land that I resolved to find a place where I would never hear it anymore. In some deep, black stony and liberating way, my life ... began during that first year in Paris, when it was borne in on me that this laughter is universal and never can be stilled.[20]

This was, writes Redding, "the human condition, the discovery of self. Community. Identity. Surely this must be achieved before it can be seen that a particular identity has a relationship to a common identity commonly described as human." Redding's last remark here seems to be critical of the notion of a unity among Negro writers based alone on race and their mutual protest literature heritage. For Redding "the writer's ultimate purpose" was to "develop man's awareness of himself so that he, man, can become a better instrument for living together with other men." The "sense of identity" writes Redding, was "the root by which all honest creative effort is fed, and the writer's relation to it is the relation of the infant to the breast of the mother."

In citing Baldwin, Redding seemed to be saying that some protest literature was art and some was not, and that art depended on the revelation of self and identity as related to some community of persons. His observations are, in a sense, Du Bois in 1930 all over again: "all art is propaganda, but all propaganda is not art." Baldwin's characterization of the laughter in the Paris courtroom was certainly a protest of a sort, but by virtue of its revelation and discovery of self and its expression of the human condition within two human communities, France and America, it was, for Redding, the highest of literary art. If the 1959 First Conference of Negro Writers can be used as a judge, it seems that the silent assumptions of Du Bois and Locke were again taking hold. The "new themes within a racial framework" that integration had forced Negro writers to turn to, according to Arthur Davis, were, in fact, a return to the Inner Life assumptions of Locke's 1922 folk-inspired art-theatre. This circumstance, coupled with Davis' hope that Negro authors would eventually "write intimately and objectively of our own people in universal human terms"—as Redding found Baldwin already doing—suggests that by 1959, in the enduring Art or Propaganda debate, pure propaganda was again, theoretically at least, on the defensive.

Significant 1950s Plays: Civil Rights or Integration?

While the redbaiting, anti-communist McCarthy era reduced the number of protest plays authored by white writers, the 1950s experienced a relative boom in produced plays written by Negro authors.[21] This boom reflected the tensions between civil rights and cultural integration — tensions that had ignited the "heated" discussion between Childress and Ward in 1951 and were still haunting The First Conference of Negro Writers in 1959. Certain works of the period, like Lofton Mitchell's *A Land Beyond the River* (1957) and Lorraine Hansberry's (1930–1965) *A Raisin in the Sun* (1959), which will be more fully treated shortly, must be considered integration plays. Other works of the period are mainly protestations of those civil inequities to which Mayfield referred: education, employment, voting rights, etc. Examples of this second category would most likely include Ted Ward's *John Brown* (1950), Ossie Davis' *Alice in Wonder* (1952), William Branch's *In Splendid Error* (1954) and Hughes' *Ballot and Me* (1958).[22] There are also plays produced in the period that called for a redress of social as well as civil inequities yet backed away from blatant calls for integration. In fact, in these works the indictment of civil and social injustices are so comprehensive that the plays implicitly, perhaps unconsciously, signal the rise of the subsequent militant and separatist Black Arts movement; the best examples of such works are likely William Branch's *A Medal for Willie* (1951), produced by The Committee for the Negro in the Arts (CNA) at the Club Baron in Harlem, and Childress' *Trouble in Mind* (1955), produced by The Greenwich Mews Theatre in Greenwich Village, New York City's, lower Manhattan arts-oriented community.

William Branch's *A Medal for Willie*

In this, Branch's first play, a Negro mother must accept a medal posthumously awarded to her son, Willie, for extraordinary valor in the military. Set in a small southern town, the play begins in "the Colored" high school, Booker T. Washington, where preparations are being made for the presentation ceremony that will honor Willie for sacrificing his life to save his fellow infantrymen. The ceremony is perhaps one of the most important ever to be held in the small town; a general flies in from Washington, D.C., to present Willie's medal, and the town's white public officials, including its mayor, are in attendance.

A Medal for Willie is a textbook on the relation of style and content. The structure and tone of Branch's play bear a close relationship to the documentary style, living newspaper productions pioneered by the Federal Theatre in the 1930s. Branch uses prologue, epilogue, and a seven-scene no-act-break structure to carefully arrive at the moment (Act I, vii)[23] when Willie's mother, Mrs. Jackson, rejects the medal. The first scene is between Mrs. Jackson and her daughter Lucie Mae; they are getting ready to attend the presentation ceremony. We learn that Willie was a ne'er-do-well who had been expelled from high school, and who had trouble finding a job. Lucie Mae is elated at the prospect of attending the ceremony and her new status as the sister of a war hero. Mrs. Jackson, however, has second thoughts about the affair, which, according to her, is honoring Willie now that he is dead, when no one in town helped him when he was alive (Act I, i). This scene is followed by scenes that depict the racism of the general and white officials who will attend the ceremony; the inequity of the draft system that allows, even in war time, white young men of influence to avoid military service; the racism of the town's local press; the unwanted sexual attentions that black women can suffer, without redress, at the hands of white men; and the ineffectiveness of white-appointed Negro public officials as demonstrated by the obsequious principal of the Negro High School.

Mrs. Jackson's act of rejecting Willie's medal and its accompanying stirring speech are, in effect, a reply to the preceding array of depictions of civil and social injustices; thus her seemingly anti–American speech, nevertheless, takes on the air of irrefutability. Branch's understated, non-histrionic listing of the injustices that the ordinary Negroes in his play routinely suffer give these inequities the ring of unvarnished truth and therefore make them all the more egregious. So egregious, in fact, that Branch's mostly Negro audiences almost certainly questioned the social and cultural integration into a society that required people to fight and die to maintain the very systems that oppressed them.

In Branch's epilogue, a school custodian finds Willie's discarded medal and asks Mr. Taylor, the young Negro teacher who also serves as Branch's narrator, what she should do with the medal. Taylor replies that he is not sure what should be done with it. He holds the medal, "muses," and finally asks the audience as well as the janitor: "But what do you say — shall we try it? Shall we? Shall we make this medal worthy of Willie —?" The stage directions instruct that Taylor "holds aloft the medal as the curtain falls." Are Taylor's questions a call to Branch's Harlem audience to fight for equal justice under law so that no more Negro soldiers will die as second-class citizens, or a call to fight for integration to that same end? Taylor's questions are sufficiently vague on this point, permitting audience members, depending on their individual views, to make their own choices. But if Branch means Taylor's question as a call for integration, then his one-page epilogue seriously departs from the dramatic weight and thrust of the preceding action; for seven scenes Branch has almost relentlessly depicted the Negro's need for equal civil rights and equal justice under the law, chiefly in the areas of public policy, education, and employment. But for the epilogue, in this play Branch seems to call for immediate and militant political action before another Negro dies for his country. Taylor's eleventh hour call for integration, if that is indeed what it is, in theme and in content has little to do with the rest of Branch's play.

Alice Childress' *Trouble in Mind: A Comedy Drama*

Set in the 1950s in a New York theatre, Childress' *Trouble in Mind* (1955)[24] is particularly noteworthy since it takes place in a world that is, at least in Childress' play, an integrated one. Consequently, *Trouble in Mind* functions as a practical, microcosmic example of the larger, hoped-for world of integration that many, blacks and whites, were proposing at the time. Whereas Branch in *A Medal for Willie*, for the most part, avoids the specific issue of integration, Childress' dramatic structure allows her to evaluate it.

In *Trouble in Mind* Childress' central dramatic figure is Wiletta Mayer, a middle-aged Negro actress who has apparently spent the better part of her life in the theatre. Childress employs a play-within-a-play structure to tell Wiletta's story. Wiletta and her fellow actors are in rehearsal for a "civil rights" play, *Chaos in Belleville*, set in a southern town in the 1950s and written by Ted Bronson, a white author. Bronson's play is rife with Negro characters who, as Couch found in 1950, have no "competency" for their own problems, who "seem capable of comprehending only one fact: a malevolent fate pursues them and they must suffer."

As rehearsals begin, mostly to hold on to their rarely found jobs, Wiletta and the other Negro actors are prepared to overlook the Negro conventions and stereotypes plaguing Bronson's play. But Al Manners, the company's white director, almost immediately insists that Wiletta and the other Negro actors interpret their roles based on honest behavior and their own personal truths. This circumstance eventually leads to Childress' denouement. Doggedly following Manners' instructions, the outspoken and somewhat volatile Wiletta can find no honest behavior or personal truth in her role when the script requires her character (Ruby) to send her son to an almost certain death. In the play-within-a-play, Ruby encourages her son, who has been active in a voting rights campaign, to be guided by Mr. Renard, Bronson's obligatory white hero, a man who treats his Negro sharecroppers with some sensitivity. Renard suggests that the boy be placed into protective custody in the local jail. As might be expected, that is, by everyone except Ruby — a Negro character who has no competence in the dimensions of her own problem — a white mob breaks into the jail and lynches Ruby's son.

Again, in keeping with Couch's observations on the characterization problems in protest plays, Judge Willis and his daughter's consciences are expanded by this Negro tragedy. The seemingly obvious truth that *Chaos in Belleville* has to impart is that lynching is wrong in the same way, as Baldwin noted, that *Uncle Tom's Cabin* (1852) had, in essence, said little more than that slavery was wrong. In an angry outburst, Wiletta demands to know why the young Negro's "own people" do not help him; the play is a "lie," she exclaims, and she confronts Manners, asking if he would send his son to an almost certain death? The cast members attempt to quiet Wiletta, but Manners stops them. "He loves the challenge of this conflict and is determined to win the battle. He must win," reports Childress' directions.

> MANNERS: Why this great fear of death? Christ died for something....
> WILETTA: Sure, they came and got him and hauled him off to jail. His mother didn't turn him in, in fact, the one who did it was one of them so-called friends.
> MANNERS: His death proved something. Job's [Ruby's son] death brings him the lesson.
> WILETTA: That they should stop lynchin' *innocent* men! Fine thing! Lynch the guilty, is that the idea? The dark-skinned Oliver Twist. (Points to John [the, young, well-educated actor playing Job]) That's you. Yeah, I mean you got to go to school to justify this!

Manners finally says "I heard you out and even though you think you know more than the author ..." Wiletta interrupts: "You don't want to hear. You are a prejudiced man, a prejudiced racist." This gets a "gasp from the company" and launches Manners into what is almost a tirade about what he feels are the truths concerning race relations and the American theatre. Manners says that he knows that Wiletta thinks that all white people are in some kind of "club," then tells her about the white-on-white exploitations that go on in that club. The rule is that "you get nothin' for nothin' but nothin'!" he says. "Get wise, he continues, "there's damned few of us interested in putting on a colored show ... much less one that's going to say anything." It is, he contends, impossible to raise a hundred thousand dollars to tell the "unvarnished" truth about Negroes. So, maybe it's a lie," Manners continues, "but it's one of the finest lies you'll come across for a damned long time!" Moreover, he adds: "The American public is not ready to see you the way you want to be seen because, one, they don't believe it, two, they don't want to believe it, and three, they're convinced they're superior." Wiletta, throughout Manner's speech, has continued to interrupt him with a simple question, which he avoids: "Would you send your son out to be murdered?" Finally, Manners is "so wound up," Childress instructs, "he answers the question without thinking": "Don't compare yourself to me! What goes for my son doesn't necessarily go for yours! Don't compare him (Points to John) ... with three strikes against him, don't compare him with my son, they've nothing in common ... not a Goddamn thing!" Manners suddenly realizes what he has said; he has "lost the Company's sympathy" and is, "confused and embarrassed by his own statement," the stage directions report. He utters a final comment: "I tried to make it clear," and John, the young Negro actor whom he could not compare to his son, replies: "It is clear," and "Manners quickly exits to dressing room," writes Childress.

While Manners's remarks about comparing John to his son seem to brand him as exactly what Wiletta has charged, a "prejudiced man," there is much more here than the racism of one white man. For Childress, Manners seems to be a representative of that society into which many, if not most, Negroes were trying integrate. In the beginning of rehearsal she depicts Manners as friendly, open, and even somewhat generous. Even the ill-fated speech, which seemingly reveals him as a bigot, if put into the mouth of, say, a Negro father, warning his son of the dangers of assuming that the white world will treat him as it treats young white men, would be accepted for its ring of truth rather than evidence of racism. In fact, Childress makes sure that at least one character notes the large measure of truth in all that Manners has said. After his untimely exit, Millie, who plays the role of Petunia in *Chaos in Belleville*, remarks: "He was dead right about some things but I didn't appreciate that last remark." Millie does not "appreciate" the remark, but she does not characterize it as untrue. Manners' feelings of superiority, which he may, following Baldwin, experience with the "pride mixed with horror with which one regards the extent and power of one's wickedness," are for him new found and embarrassing things. They have taken him by surprise. Childress is careful to make clear that his dialogue revealing that superiority is uttered "without thinking." Manners is not of that relatively small population who can be easily identified as bigots. He reminds one of Baldwin's white Americans whose "estrangement from the Negro is the depth of their estrangement from themselves." Wiletta's accusation forces Manners to discover what he really feels about prejudice and the Negro, opening, as Baldwin warns, "the gates of chaos." In his tirade, Manners recalls how in his mid–Western upbringing he learned to say "nigger, kike, sheeny, spick, dago, wop and chink." He recalls the "sweet kind old aunt" who raised him and "spent her time gathering funds for missionaries" but who also "almost turned our town upside down when Mexicans moved in our block." Manners bitterly reports that in his early career he was exploited by more powerful men; he supplied the ideas, took the money, but never got the credit.

Through Manners, an ostensibly liberal member of the white middle class, Childress paints a picture of a duplicitous, materialistic American mainstream without integrity, full of bitternesses and resentments, class and ethnic prejudices, and with no more opportunities for individual contentment than resides in the Negro world. And Childress' other white characters help to complete this disturbing portrait. Judy Sears, in the play-with-in-a-play, has been cast in the role of Carrie, the daughter of Renard, the kindly segregationist. Carrie is sympathetic to the needs of her father's sharecroppers. At the beginning of rehearsals, Sears, an upper middle-class liberal, tries to play Carrie with an honest concern for Negroes under her father's control; but Manners objects to Judy's approach to the part, and, after a private meeting with him, Sears adds the required condescension to her portrayal. Bill O'Wray plays Renard, Carrie's father, and Childress explicitly describes his personal angst:

> When Bill drops out of character we see that he is very different from the strong Renard. He appears to be worried at all times... . Bill O'Wray is but a shadow of a man — by some miracle he turns into a dynamic figure as Renard. As Bill — he sees dragons in every corner and worries about each one.

In many ways, Henry, the sympathetic "elderly" Irish doorman, is Childress' personification of the results of mainstream, white-on-white ethnic and class prejudices, coupled with a general disregard for the aged. Childress finds moments in her script to have Henry expose all of these defects in Manners. With Henry, too, Childress reminds her mixed, Greenwich Village audience that there are issues of oppression beyond the color line question:

> HENRY: Ah, yes, we was fightin' for the home rule! Ah, there was some great men!
> WILETTA: I know it.
> HENRY: There was Parnell! Charles Stewart Parnell!
> WILETTA : All right!
> HENRY : A figure of a man! The highest! Fightin' hard for the home rule! A parliamentarian! And they clapped him in the blasted jailhouse for six months!
> WILETTA : Yes, my Lord!
> HENRY : And Gladstone introduced the bill ... and later on you had Dillon and John Redmond ... and then when the home rule was almost put through, what do you think happened? World War One! That killed the whole business!
> WILETTA: (Very indignant) Oh, if it ain't one thing it's another!

Using her white characters, Childress designs a mainstream which makes Du Bois' separatism seem constructive and judicious, a world from which most reasonable white people should be as desperate to escape as integrating Negroes were to enter. By 1955, for Childress, too, equal justice under law obviously was one thing, and integration was quite another — if it meant, as Mayfield would later write, "identifying the Negro with the American image, that great-power face that the world knows and the Negro knows better."

Lofton Mitchell's *A Land Beyond the River*

In 1957, The Greenwich Mews Theatre produced Lofton Mitchell's three-act play, *A Land Beyond the River*, which, according to Nadler, was "the first postwar civil rights play to thoroughly blur the distinction between contemporary history and fiction." Mitchell's blend is based on the *Briggs v. Clarendon* case, the strongest of the five suits making up *Brown v. Board of Education*. After he saw Ossie Davis' *The People of Clarendon County*,[25] Mitchell suggested to Davis that he expand the work to a full-length play. Davis' play is a short work that was performed in 1955 as a dramatic reading for Local 1199's Negro History Week celebration. Davis, Mitchell reports, was too busy with his acting to rewrite the work, and suggested that Mitchell pursue the project.

At the grassroots level, the Rev. Dr. Joseph A. DeLaine had been the leader and organizer of *Briggs v. Clarendon County* in South Carolina (1950). So Mitchell interviewed DeLaine as a first step to writing the play.[26] Mitchell's play, the result of the interview with DeLaine, for the most part, leaves intact the background and events of the actual case. The play is set in a small southern county. The Reverend DeLaine becomes the Rev. Joseph Layne. The first of the legal actions taken up by the Reverend Layne's group is an attempt to get school buses for the county's Negro students, which is how the DeLaine group began its activities. In the play, as in the actual case, the legal fight for school buses leads to a suit demanding equal funding for the county's Negro schools. Layne and the Negro farmers win this initial suit, as DeLaine and his group had won the actual case. However, beyond this point, Mitchell finds it necessary to fictionalize one significant fact. In the play, it is Layne and his followers who decide to alter their suit so that it is a demand for public school integration, an attack on the Supreme Court's 1896 *Plessy v. Ferguson* "separate but equal" ruling.[27] Mitchell, however, was well aware that the NAACP's legal team, led by Thurgood Marshall (1908–1993), had been responsible for this shift in legal tactics, not DeLaine or his group. Mitchell writes:

> Thurgood Marshall saw this as an excellent opportunity to attack the "separate but equal" doctrine. The Negroes agreed to change their petition and ... Glenn Ragin was one of the youngsters involved in the test case. And this test

was to be changed in Charleston to an attack on segregation in the public schools.[28]

Mitchell depicts the fight for public school integration as a Negro grassroots movement, which, as Mayfield suggests and Mitchell acknowledges, it was not. The battle against the Supreme Court's "separate but equal" doctrine had gone on for decades before the Court's 1954 school desegregation decision. But, far from a grassroots movement, it was a behind-closed-doors battle executed by a relatively small cadre of attorneys associated with the NAACP. Mitchell himself indicates that Marshall had won or helped to win cases that chipped away at *Plessy v. Ferguson* since 1935.

But Mitchell clearly believed that the political impact of his play would be greater if integration was perceived as a people's movement. To help accomplish this goal Mitchell gives the Reverend Layne's wife, Martha, heart disease. At the end of Act II, Martha, Layne, and Layne's congregation take refuge inside his church as outside the church, in reprisal for the group's activities, segregationists fire guns from a moving car. From the church, the group sees Layne's home burning to the ground; Martha is stricken and dies of a heart attack.[29] Martha's death engulfs Layne in a long period of grief in which he is initially against school integration. When he is told that one of the lawyers working with the group considers their court victory a loss, presumably because they still have not shaken the "separated but equal" clause, he "bitterly" responds: "Well, we don't want that part, anyway! We don't want our kids going to school with their kids, where they can learn how to make bombs and burn homes and lynch folks! We don't want to be with them and their crucifying souls!" But when two white men taunt and slap the son of one of Layne's followers, and the boy pleads with his father not to seek retribution, Layne sees the light; he sits the father down, looks at the boy, then speaks: "'A little Child Shall Lead Them.' The voice of God has roared in my ears this terrible day, charging us with the duty of saving the souls of white children that they may grow up to be our brothers — or saving the souls of all those who have been taught hate instead of love!" Layne is now a full-fledged integrationist. "For there's no such thing as being separate and equal! The only thing a man learns by being separate is that he's not equal," he says. Layne recalls that his wife, Martha, would have wanted him to fight for school integration, which is odd, since in the play, before she expired, Martha had not uttered one word to this effect.

Layne's transformation from grassroots civil rights leader to integrationist is strained and happens in the eleventh hour, making it stand out as something imposed on the work rather than organic to it; it is in the same politically motivated camp with the sudden communism of the eldest son in *Big White*

Fog, and Bigger's inability to escape the clutches of one drunken woman and another blind one before committing murder in *Native Son*. On the other hand, it is easy to see why *A Land Beyond the River* was, in fact, a successful piece of theatre.[30] It had been written in the spirit of the times and it played before the Mews' integrated audiences. Mitchell had gone to considerable trouble to make the play, in the terms of this discussion, more about integration than about civil rights, and that circumstance may have had a great deal to do with its unexpected success.

Lorraine Hansberry's *A Raisin in the Sun* and the Walter Lee Problem

Concluding his preface to *The American Negro Writer and His Roots*, John A. Williams writes:

> The conference was addressed at its final session by Miss Lorraine Hansberry, author of the successful play, *A Raisin in the Sun*. Miss Hansberry's play is social protest, but is such a consummate work of art that the objects of the protest applaud it vigorously each night on Broadway.

Getting the objects of the protest in a play to "applaud" the play is no mean feat, but that appears to be precisely what happened when *A Raisin in the Sun* opened on Broadway early in March of 1959 in the Ethel Barrymore Theatre. The play ran for 530 performances, becoming the longest running drama written by an African American on Broadway and Hansberry became the first black playwright to win the prestigious New York Drama Critics Circle Award.[31] Because of this extraordinary success, Hansberry's first play, even today, is, as Nadler notes, arguably black drama's most widely produced play.[32] Nadler adds that "so much attention has been showered upon [it] that in popular reputation — and unfortunately, even for some scholars — it remains the first major African American play." The play has been extensively staged, anthologized, and produced as a Columbia Pictures film in 1961[33]; hopefully, it has graced enough stages and been seen in enough movie houses to permit this discussion to move quickly to the many issues in the work that relate to the distinctions between integration and civil rights plays, and the propaganda versus art debate at the core of this book.

The action in *A Raisin in the Sun* centers on a conflict between Walter Lee Younger and his mother Lena, the matriarch of the Younger family. As the play opens, the family is expecting a $10,000 check in the mail, the proceeds of Walter Lee's deceased father's life insurance policy. Lena Younger intends to put some of this money aside for her daughter Beneatha's education and make a down payment on a "little old two-story somewhere." But Walter

Lee wants to invest the money in a liquor store. Ruth and Travis, Walter Lee's wife and ten-year old son, complete the list of central dramatic figures in the play. Other supporting roles in the play are Joseph Asagai, George Murchison, and Karl Linder. Asagai is one of Beneatha's suitors, a young African student; Murchison is a very middle class Negro college man who is also romantically interested in Beneatha. Linder is a representative of the all white "Clybourne Park Improvement Association."

Lena or Mama, as she is called in the play, makes the down payment on the house when internal family conflicts reach a fever pitch in the Younger household. Walter Lee's dream of becoming a businessman has been, according to him, "butchered" by Mama's actions. Mama relents and gives her son the rest of the insurance money to manage on the family's behalf. Walter Lee promptly gives the money to one of his partners in his liquor store venture; it will be used, he is told, to pay-off a few politicians, expediting the process of obtaining a liquor license. At the end of Act II, it is revealed that the partner (Willy) has absconded with the money; the Younger family's spirit reaches its lowest ebb.

Meanwhile, to keep them from integrating their all-white neighborhood, Mr. Linder has told the Youngers that his association will buy back, at a handsome price, the house on which Mama made the down payment. Earlier, the family had rejected Linder's offer, seeing it as the height of racism. But, in Act III, Walter Lee decides to accept the offer in order to recoup some of the family's losses, even if it means humiliating himself. However, when Linder arrives, Walter Lee, having a change of heart, rejects Linder's offer for a second time, regaling the white man (and the audience) with a stirring speech of familial and racial pride. The play ends with the Youngers en route to their new home.

The stunning success of Hansberry's first play overshadowed its lineage. As has been noted earlier, it is the last of a triumvirate of black Chicago Southside plays depicting the inner-city struggles of a lower class Negro family; it is a direct descendant of Ward's *Big White Fog* and Wright and Paul Green's *Native Son*. Scholars, at least the few who are concerned with such genealogies, have, in fact, made these connections. Vanita Vactor argues that although Ward never attained the status as a playwright that Hansberry achieved, it was Ward's Mason family in 1938 (and again in 1940), not Hansberry's 1959 Younger family, who first introduced the theatre-going public to an inner-city Chicago black family.[34] Abramson links the play to *Native Son* even more precisely:

> But neither the critics nor Miss Hansberry ever acknowledged her debt to Richard Wright's *Native Son* (novel or play), although surely one existed. Both

plays are set in Chicago's Southside. Bigger Thomas and Walter Younger are both chauffeurs, black men who feel caged in a white society. And they both "explode" because of a "dream deferred."

Abramson adds that Walter Lee Younger's explosion "is not so fatal as Bigger's, but it erupts from the same frustration and confusion," and "Walter is no more the 'head of a household' than a much younger Bigger Thomas." This issue of black male social and economic impotence within Negro life, though Abramson does not mention it, is also a central feature in *Big White Fog*. It should be remembered that Victor Mason's failure to provide economic security for his family leads to, among other things, his daughter's prostitution and the permanent breakdown of relations between himself and his wife.

According to Abramson, this socio-economic impotence of the male figure also occurs in poor white families (Betty Smith's 1943 novel *A Tree Grows in Brooklyn* comes to mind). But for the Negro male, Abramson writes, it is reinforced "by a white dominant society that would keep him a 'boy,' keep him harmless and 'in his place.'" Perhaps Abramson's phrase "white dominant society" at least from Walter Lee and Bigger's point of view, needs to be amended to read "a white male dominant society." Long before the term "white male Anglo-Saxon hegemony" was coined, Negro men deeply suspected that a hierarchy of white males designed and controlled all important aspects of American society, ideological and practical; this knowledge was one of the crueler lessons of chattel slavery. The notion of "keeping the Negro harmless and in his place" inevitably carried with it gender and, more specifically, sexual implications, as well as a fear of what was unconsciously recognized as justifiable retaliatory Negro violence. When Hansberry borrowed Walter Lee from Wright, if that is indeed what she did, it is not clear that she knew exactly what she was getting into. The triangular construct of the sanctity of white womanhood and the threat of black male sexuality, in all its alleged potent bestiality, as posited by a white male hierarchy, is nowhere in evidence in Hansberry's play. Yet that construct is one of the central psychological assumptions shaping the actions and reactions of the world's Walter Lee Youngers and Bigger Thomases.

Indeed, as employed by Wright, Bigger's knowledge of the threat of his sexuality, as perceived by dominant white males, is the one psychological element strong enough to humanize Wrights' polemic about Bigger's creation by white society. In Wright and Green's pivotal scene iv, Bigger's fear of Mary is actually limited to the fact that he knows, or deeply suspects, that she will characterize any uncovered sexual encounter between them as a rape or assault. Thus, it is not so much Mary that Bigger fears; rather it is the all-consuming power of white males, like Mary's father, that arouses his deepest fears; he knows that these dominant white men severely punish Negroes who are even suspected of such sexual transgressions. Mary, on the other hand, is frightened, even astonished, by her own sexuality. But for her, too, it is the reprobation of a society exclusively controlled by a select group of white males that underlies her fear of her mother's disapproval should she have sex with a black man.

Even if Hansberry were aware of the centrality of all of the above to Walter Lee's character, she could not explore its dramatic implications and at the same time maintain an unfettered integration agenda. Walter Lee's (or Bigger's) fears along these lines, if justified, raise serious questions about the efficacy and even the possibility of the Negro's social and cultural integration into mainstream society. Mainstream society was, after all, an almost 200-year-old democracy that had only forty years earlier finally given more than half its population the right to vote. And, even by 1959, as most feminist critics could quite convincingly argue, the 1920 recipients of that very much belated right to vote were still regarded by their male benefactors as frivolous second-class citizens needing protection from, among other things, the potent and, apparently, addictive dangers of black male sexuality.

In *A Raisin in the Sun*, the face of the white male hierarchy with which Walter Lee has to contend is given to John Fiedler, who later became Hollywood's number one elfin, squeaky-voiced and supremely asexual actor. Fiedler, the one white actor in the play, performs the role of Karl Linder. However many prejudices Linder quietly utters, if, as the ancient Greeks assumed, the theatre is "a place to see," we cannot imagine Linder as Walter Lee's sexual rival or suppressing women's right to vote. But Linder, or rather Fiedler as Linder, appears to have been appropriate to Hansberry's purposes. With Linder as Walter Lee's white male foil, Wright's notion of issues of sexuality as a core feature of black-white race relations is obliterated or at least trivialized, and, perhaps more importantly, centuries-old racial antipathies are, apparently, by 1959, reduced to little more than a misunderstanding. We cannot believe that once Mr. Linder really gets to know the Younger family he will be able to hold onto his prejudices. With little men like Linder its only opposition, integration had to be a destination that was, if not just around the corner, then at least plainly in sight in the near future. And, traveling to that destination, there would be no ghastly sacrifices that could make one question the value of the goal, no burnings of freedom buses and Negro homes, no blowing up of little girls in churches, no murders of black and white civil rights workers. Men like Linder were obviously incapable of such acts. Hansberry skillfully establishes Travis as the Younger family's much beloved, even spoiled, adorable ten-year old; thus, it is rather startling that in the Younger household no word of apprehension is uttered concerning the child's safety in a neighborhood that has to be filled with racists.

It may seem one-sided to examine Hansberry's play primarily through the lens, so to speak, of Walter Lee. With perhaps the exception of some of the roles in Ward's *Our Lan'*, Hansberry's Beneatha, Ruth, and Travis are crafted with a skill and charm that has been seen in no other Negro authored social dramas. As for Lena Younger, Abramson correctly finds that she "is the old-fashioned Negro mother that we have already seen in *Harlem*, in *Native Son* and in *A Medal for Willie*."[35] In fact, Lena Younger is a direct descendant of the 1916 mother, Mrs. Loving, in Angelina Grimké's *Rachel*. But in none of these works is this type of Negro mother so completely fleshed out as she is in Hansberry's play. For example, Mrs. Loving is a far more sentimental woman than Lena Younger; Mrs. Thomas in *Native Son* is a fairly humorless creature; Wright and Green seemed to have written her only as background for Bigger. And in *A Medal for Willie*, the singular focus of Branch's dramatic structure rightfully prevents us from seeing more than one side of Mrs. Jackson. But Hansberry infuses her standard Negro stage mother with such humanity that she becomes a fulfillment of the type rather than merely a repetition of it.

Nevertheless, it is, ironically, the deftness of Hansberry's realist dramaturgy that forces Walter Lee onto the attentions of the observant reader or audience member — as is obviously the case with Abramson. Hansberry either instinctively knows or has learned one of the most difficult lessons in realist playwriting: Plays must have exposition, but exposition must be told through action or the explication of dramatic objective. On page two of Act I, i, Walter Lee's third line in the play is the question to his wife: "Check coming today?" The check is the proceeds of his father's life insurance policy, and this line therefore establishes his dramatic objective for the next two acts. Similarly, in this beginning scene, all the important things we need to know about the Youngers' financial situation are told through small actions or objectives. Ruth has a hard time waking Travis; the little boy has no bedroom of his own, and he sleeps on a makeshift bed in the livingroom where his father's late-night guests have kept him awake. The Youngers' apartment has no bathroom, so Ruth must rush the sleepy child into a common toilet used by other tenants before someone from another family gets into the facility. Walter Lee, too, is worried about getting into this toilet on time so that he is not late for work. These small objectives show, rather than tell about, the Youngers' poverty, as does Ruth's annoyed, early morning weariness. Walter Lee's question about "the check" elicits the following exchange:

RUTH: They said Saturday and this is just Friday and I hopes to God you ain't goin' go get up here first thing this morning and start talking to me 'bout no money —'cause I 'bout don't want to hear it.
WALT.: Something the matter with you this morning?
RUTH: No, I'm just sleepy as the devil. What kind of eggs you want?[36]

Again, still only on the second page, Ruth's reply to Walter Lee's question about "the check" underscores the issue that will form the central conflict in the play and sets up what the noted American Absurdist playwright Arthur Kopit calls a "ticking clock," a heightening of audience expectations. Ruth's dialogue lets the audience know that her husband has been continually discussing the expected money and that it is coming the following day — "They said Saturday and this is just Friday." Moreover, all the business involving the little boy's sleepiness because he has no bedroom and the community toilet have firmly established the importance of money to Walter Lee's family. With a few lines and with behavior prompted by small objectives: waking up, fixing breakfast, getting into the bathroom, getting to work on time, Hansberry has taken us into the heart of her dramatic structure. And, in doing so, she has established Walter Lee both as the catalyst for and the first of one of two participants in the central conflict in the play.

Hansberry crafts Walter Lee's desire to become a successful businessman so that it is intimately involved with his manhood, his opinion of his own self worth, his role as husband and father. That this is no mistake and is, in fact, Hansberry's intent can be inferred from the title of the play, which is taken from Langston Hughes' short poem, *A Dream Deferred*. In the poem, Hughes begins by asking

> What happens to a dream deferred?
> Does it dry up like *a raisin in the sun*?"

In 1951, when it was published, *Dream Deferred* was both Hughes' amazingly concise metaphor for Negro America's still unrealized quest for political and social equality, and a rather stunning prophecy of the race-related riots that would "explode" in a number of American cities in the 1960s.

In Hansberry's play the "dream deferred" is Walter Lee's liquor store, which, as in Hughes' poem, is a metaphor for everything that Walter Lee hopes to become as a man, father, and husband. In tying his character and motivations to the title of the play and all that title implies, Hansberry makes Walter Lee, not his mother, the central focus of her work. Lena Younger's dream is not "deferred"; she gets her "little two-story" with a yard where her grandson can play. *A Raisin in the Sun* is really about the *agon* of Walter Lee Younger — or at least, as will be taken up shortly, that is what it started out to be before the play was headed for Broadway.

With Walter Lee as the central focus in the play, the work begins to reach the proportions of modern tragedy. Nowhere is this fact more evident than at the end of Act II, i, when Lena Younger agonizingly reveals to Walter Lee, Ruth, and her grandson what should be the happy news that she has bought a new home for the family. Ruth is overjoyed at the news, but after she and Travis exit, Walter Lee and his mother are left alone in a long and heavy silence. Earlier, Ruth's pregnancy and her plans to have an abortion because she and Walter cannot afford another child precipitated an ugly family confrontation (Act I, i). Lena demanded that Walter Lee tell his wife that the Youngers are about giving life to children, not about "killing" them; Walter Lee, overwhelmed with his family's financial circumstances, was unable to utter the words his mother wanted him to say. This incident, Lena now explains, made her feel that her family was "falling apart." She continues:

> MAMA: We was going backwards 'stead of forwards — talking 'bout killing babies and wishing each other was dead ... When it gets like that in life — you just got to do something different, push on out and do some thing bigger ... (she waits) I wish you say something, son ... I wish you say how deep inside you think I done the right thing —
> WALT.: (crossing slowly to his bedroom door and finally turning there and speaking measuredly) What you need me to say you done right for? You the head of this family. You run our lives like you want to. It was your money and you did what you wanted with it. So what you need me to say it was all right for? ... So you butchered up a dream of mine — you — who always talking 'bout your children's dreams ...
> MAMA: Walter Lee —
> (He just closes the door behind him. Mama sits alone, thinking heavily.
> (Curtain)

Consistent with modern tragedy, there are real psychological losses here. Not only does Walter Lee lose his liquor store, but also he must face the fact that he is in the untenable position of being a grown man whose mother "runs" his life. And Lena has to acknowledge that her actions, however much she justifies them, have crushed her son's spirit. In a very real sense, Hansberry has accomplished in this scene the Hegelian definition of tragedy posited by Amos Oz, the noted Israeli author: tragedy is a "clash between right and right."[38]

Comparing Walter Lee with an earlier modern tragic hero, Hatch and Ted Shine write:

> Like Willie Loman, the tragic protagonist in Arthur Miller's *Death of a Salesman*, Walter Lee believes in and pursues the American dream. Both men want to become capitalists, believing that wealth will solve their problems and bring them happiness. When they realize too late that these values are false ones,

Willie commits suicide, but Walter Lee retrieves his dignity and becomes the man that he always wanted to be.[39]

On the other hand, home-ownership is one of the bedrocks of the American dream from which American capitalists reap extraordinary profits. Is Mama also a victim of the American dream? Are her values "false ones"? Is Harold Cruse correct in characterizing Hansberry's play as "the most cleverly written soap opera I, personally, have ever seen on the stage?"[40] It seems undeniable that *A Raisin in the Sun* is full of middle class values about business, abortion, education, God, premarital sex, etc. But how could it be otherwise? Hansberry was a young middle-class black woman; in fact, in black economic and social terms she was upper middle class. Charles Gordone, the first black dramatist to win the Pulitzer Prize for his play *No Place to be Somebody* (1969), would later write: "A man [or woman] writes about what he comes from."[41] The only question of class that can reasonably bear upon the plausibility of Hansberry's realist characters is: are there actual working class Negroes in communities like Chicago's Southside or New York's Harlem who, like the Youngers, have middle-class aspirations? The answer, of course, is a resounding yes. By 1959, the American advertising industry had convinced almost everyone in urban and suburban America, regardless of race, creed, or color, that the material comforts of the middle class, automobiles, homes, dishwashers, televisions, telephones, etc., were not only accessible but also necessary to a decent life. And long before 1959, countless working class Negroes had absorbed the virtues of Christian middle-class morality concerning abortion, education, and premarital sex. Almost thirty-five years earlier, in *The New Negro*, Locke had warned: "the Negro is radical on race matters, conservative on others."

For Walter Lee and Willie Loman, the terms "manhood" and family "breadwinner" are synonymous. This, of course, would still be true if they were heads of General Motors or First Secretaries in John Reed's American Communist Labor Party. If their notion of male as breadwinner is mistaken, it is a mistake created by centuries of socialization and gender prejudice in the American work force. The difference between Walter Lee and Willie is, obviously, that Willie commits suicide and Walter wins back his dignity, or so we are told. But how does Walter Lee retrieve his dignity, and what causes his change from would-be liquor storeowner to a mature, dignified thirty-five year old chauffeur? A series of skillfully written, crowd-pleasing but, essentially, melodramatic events accomplish this task. In fact, these effects are so well written that only the closest scrutiny will reveal them as pure integration propaganda.

To begin with, that Walter Lee gives his father's insurance money to one of his bar-hopping friends whom he intends to go into business with has a decided ring of implausibilty (Act II, iii). We cannot imagine, for example, Bigger Thomas doing such a thing, though he is younger, less educated, and much more emotionally unstable than is Walter Lee. Walter Lee appears to have an extraordinary gullibility for one who has grown up on Chicago's Southside, if indeed he has. It is never quite clear how long the Youngers have been in Chicago. Walter and Beneatha have little of the South about them. So one assumes that they have been raised in Chicago.

When Mama learns that Walter Lee has lost the money, she intones a heart-rending speech about how the senior Mr. Younger had to "work night and day" to be able to have a $10,000 insurance policy. One wonders why it is that Walter Lee seems to have disregarded his father's sacrifice? There is a vagueness of detail in the play concerning the senior Mr. Younger. For example, we do not know when he died. The business of the life insurance indicates that his death must be in the recent past but, as the play opens, it does not seem that the family is still in mourning. While Lena refers to her husband a number of times in the play, Beneatha and Walter Lee almost never mention him. It is as if Lena is the only one who really knew the man. Yet, according to Lena, her husband loved his children and family so much that he worked himself to death for them. If this were true, it seems that the elder Mr. Younger would merit at least an occasional mention from his children. When Walter Lee discovers that his partner has stolen the money, he cries out: "that money is made out of my father's flesh." But if he really believes this, what kept him from paying off the politicians himself, or at least accompanying his partner on the alleged trip to take care of that matter? How could he have entrusted "the money made of his father's flesh" to anyone but himself?

The remoteness of Walter Lee and Beneatha from their father is emblematic of the Younger family's, except for Walter Lee, general remoteness from the Chicago Southside community. Ruth has no woman of her own age and circumstances to talk to about her unwanted pregnancy. Travis does not play with any other Southside little boys. Beneatha has no friends from the neighborhood. Her suitors, Asagai and Murchison, are not from her community. She is not involved with other bright young people from the community who are trying to get an education. Though Mama insists that there will always be "God in her house" (Act I. i), she appears never to be in the house of God. Mama has no fellow church members, no lady's altar guild friends, or pastor with whom she can share her troubles or seek spiritual guidance. Through Walter Lee, the Younger family (and its audiences) deals only with the bar hoppers and con men of Chicago's Southside. The significant reference to black music in the play is to a quasi-African music. Blues, Jazz, or even Spirituals are not a part of this play. But for the Youngers themselves, all the artifacts of African American culture have been wiped clean from the play, which will, no doubt, allow the Youngers to be more easily integrated into mainstream American society.

The next two emotionally stirring moments in the play are Walter Lee's decision to accept Linder's offer to buy back the house and his reversal of that decision in Act III. In the first instance, Walter Lee's decision is understandably motivated by the fact that his partner has duped him. He has "figured out" that "life is divided up between the takers" and what he calls "the tooken." He has called Linder and he will grovel, if necessary, to recoup some of his family's losses. The women are, of course, against this, and their opposition is primarily based on Du Bois' old Outer Life concerns of Negroes putting their best face forward and not the Inner Life concerns of how much will the mortgage be, how will the family, with a new baby coming, raise the money for Beneatha's education, etc. These Inner Life problems that have motivated the action in the play for two full acts are no longer of primary importance. Walter makes an agonizing speech about how he is going to grovel before Linder, if necessary, imitating every stereotype associated with Negro subservience. The speech, if one can get past its emotionalism, is a demonstration that Walter is far less concerned with whether or not his family actually needs the money than he is with the fact that Linder will likely see him, if he takes the deal, as an "Uncle Tom," old-fashioned darkie; the need to grovel to make the deal is in Walter Lee's head and not Linder's requirement.

The agony of Walter Lee's rehearsal speech to Linder telegraphs the fact that he is going to reverse his decision, which is precisely what he does when Linder arrives at the Younger apartment. In a speech that masterfully captures the political tenor of the times and actually has little to do with Linder or the drama at hand, Walter Lee delivers a halting, almost magnificent oration whose theme is of familial and racial pride. In essence, Walter Lee retrieves his dignity by telling a little white man, who simply could not care less, what a proud black man he has become. Ultimately, this is almost nonsensical, and why Cruse's charge that *A Raisin in the Sun* was the "cleverest soap opera" that he had ever seen on the stage, despite its vitriolic tinge, cannot be wholly dismissed. After Walter Lee's speech, Linder appeals to Mama as an older, wiser person, and she dutifully plays the role of the nice old colored lady, telling him that the decision is up to her son and adding: "You know how these young folks is nowadays, mister. Can't do a thing with 'em." Walter Lee is finally the head of the household, that is, now that he has come around to Mama's way of thinking. This ending, of course, is the final step in a subtle shift of focus from Walter Lee to his mother that began when Walter discovered that his partner had duped him.

Apparently, this shifting of focus from Walter Lee to Mama began while the play was still in rehearsal. Sidney Poitier, who created the role of Walter Lee on Broadway, reports that the play got excellent reviews in Philadelphia and the management (Philip Rose) "wanted to go directly into New York." Poitier continues: "I, alas, didn't think the play was being performed as effectively as it could have been, which got me into a lot of trouble with Lorraine, Phil [Rose] and [the director] Lloyd Richards, who were happy with the production the way it was."[42] Poitier writes that by the time the show got to Chicago he "was no longer on speaking terms with Lorraine, who was understandably happy because her play was doing so well and couldn't grasp why I was dissatisfied." Poitier was dissatisfied because in rehearsal Lena Younger had become the central focus in the play rather than Walter Lee, as has been argued here. Poitier writes:

> I believed from the first day I went into rehearsal that the play should not unfold from the mother's point of view ... I think that for maximum effect, *A Raisin in the Sun* should unfold from the point of view of the son, Walter Lee Younger (Yes, I played Walter Lee).

Poitier adds his parenthetic remark, apparently still sensitive to the fact that he was, of course, "accused of 'star' behavior" because he insisted that Walter Lee, not the mother, should be the focus of the play. He continues: "The simple truth of the matter was that if the play is told from the point of view of the mother, and you don't have an actor playing the part of Walter Lee strongly, then the end result may very well be a negative comment on the black male."

When he opened in *A Raisin in the Sun*, Poitier had not been on the stage for a decade, and he was returning to it with more than a little trepidation. He writes: "A camera hums softly while it's watching you; an audience breathes, it coughs, it shifts about in its seat and whispers to itself while it is watching you. I had forgotten how unpredictable that one-on-one between audience and performer can be." It is extremely doubtful that Poitier would have risked returning to the stage after so long a hiatus to perform a second lead role, by an unknown dramatist, that had, if he faltered, the danger of using his rising film stardom to make what he thought was "a negative comment on the black male." Such an undertaking would have had a decidedly negative effect on a ten-year film career in which he had specifically sought to improve the popular image of black men. The play that Hansberry had initially written and that Poitier had read and agreed to do was one thing, and the production that opened on Broadway in 1959 was obviously quite another. Nadler writes:

[Lloyd] Richards worked intensely with Hansberry on rewrites during the rehearsal process. Together they changed the play's focus from Lena to Walter Lee, cut out a character (an upstairs neighbor), removed an act (in which the aftermath of the move had been explored), and shortened the running time by forty-five minutes.[43]

A Raisin in the Sun, it appears, was more extensively rewritten for the Broadway stage than Hughes' *Mulatto* (1935), which, until Hansberry's play, had been the longest running Negro authored play on Broadway. Nadler's primary source for his report on rewrites of the play is the show's director, Lloyd Richards. However, Poitier, in 1980, directly contradicts Richards' 1975 report that "the play's focus" was changed from Lena to Walter Lee. Poitier writes that his only "ally" in the focus debate was Ruby Dee, who performed the role of Ruth. If there were script changes to support his point of view, Poitier seems to have been unaware of them; he writes that he and Dee

> decided on an approach, and conspired to keep the strength in the character of Walter Lee Younger, which meant playing against Claudia McNeil [who played Lena], who is a tower of strength as a stage personality. I had to change the whole performance to prevent the mother character from so dominating the stage it would cast a negative focus on the black male.[44]

Poitier writes that he and Ruby Dee were still dealing with the Walter Lee problem the night before the show closed in Chicago and headed for its New York opening. They "sat over drinks and analyzed the way the Walter Lee character should appear to the audience," writes Poitier. "The play opened in New York," Poitier continues, "with me playing it the way I wanted to play it, and it was an enormous success." Poitier was never aware that Hansberry and Richards had come round to his position. In fact, the Walter Lee problem appears to have engendered an enmity between Hansberry and Poitier that went far beyond the show's Broadway run: "Lorraine and I barely spoke for years after, until, with her health failing, the time came for us to put aside petty things," writes Poitier.

The rewrites appear to have shifted "the play's focus" from Walter Lee to his mother, not the other way round. Given the structure of the play that actually reached the stage, Poitier's version of the Walter Lee problem is far more compelling than Richards'. In fact, Richards' reports on the rewrites tend to strengthen Poitier's contentions. It is difficult to believe that the removal of an entire act had no effect on the central focus in the play, especially when that act, as Richards reports, "explored the aftermath" of the Youngers' integration into the white Chicago suburb. As a child, Hansberry herself had almost been seriously injured in a brick-throwing incident when her family integrated a Chicago suburb.[45] If she had exploited that kind of incident to write the edited act (she almost certainly did), one would have to have second thoughts about Walter Lee's initial plan to accept Linder's offer. If Walter Lee, for example, had to lead his family through a period of racist attacks, the focus in the play would have again returned to his character. Such an event and Walter Lee's response to it would have provided a concrete dramatic incident to depict his rise to manhood, rather than his crowd-pleasing, but nevertheless questionable, change of heart as in the produced script. In fact, the edited act may well have returned Hansberry to the original Negro social drama that she seemed to be writing in Act I and in most of Act II rather than converting the play to the integration propaganda vehicle that it becomes in Act III.

The popularity of the play with black audiences, even today, is based on the large measure of honesty that Hansberry gives to her characters, and the seldom seen sheer theatrical delight of having a black man tell off a white man on the American stage. For the mainstream white audience, the play, at least at the time, was both an affirmation of its superiority and proof of, as Baldwin wrote of *Native Son*, "what strides might be taken in a free democracy." Unlike Childress' *Trouble in Mind*, the play shines no critical light on the mainstream society that the Youngers are about to integrate, and the fact that they seem to be struggling to enter that society is proof of its superiority. What Poitier calls "the whiff of gold in the air" came with the success of the play with out-of-town, integrated audiences. No one but Ruby Dee had time for his seemingly egocentric quibbling with success. Hansberry, like Hughes and Ward before her, submitted her work to a commercial, Broadway process that Locke had taken to task and Du Bois, twenty years earlier, had found incapable of "the full picturing of the Negro soul."

The Persistence of Art-Theatre Drama, 1950–1959

During the period of integration and civil rights drama, plays dominated by Inner Life themes in keeping with Locke's art-theatre ideas continued to be staged. In 1950, the Theatre Guild of New York produced George Norford's 1938 domestic comedy *Joy Exceeding Glory* under the title *Head of the Family*.[46] In September of 1953, Louis Peterson's *Take a Giant Step*, a black coming of age drama, opened on Broadway in the Lyceum Theatre. The year 1954 saw the production of James Baldwin's *The Amen Corner* at Howard University; the play was produced again in Los Angeles in the early 1960s, where it ran for a year; then it opened in the Ethel Barrymore Theatre on Broadway in 1965.[47] In 1957, Hughes' *Simply Heavenly* opened in May in the 85th Street

Playhouse in New York City; the work centered on the life of Jessie B. Simple, Hughes' well-known fictional character. The following year, Ernestine McClendon's Harlem Workshop produced Philip Hayes Dean's one act play, *Noah's Dove* (later titled *The Owl Killer*). Hughes attended the Harlem opening and encouraged Dean. Dean would become one of the leading art-theatre dramatists of the seventies and eighties.[48]

Louis Peterson's *Take a Giant Step* and James Baldwin's *The Amen Corner*

Nadler writes that Peterson's *Take a Giant Step* "is largely biographical." The author "was raised in a mostly white neighborhood of Hartford, Connecticut."[49] Thus, in 1952, pursuing the Inner Life themes so dear to Locke, Peterson wrote a play that also touched on the Outer Life, post World War II race relations issue that was fueling the burgeoning American Civil Rights movement. As the play opens, Spencer Scott ("Spence"), an intelligent young middle class Negro of sixteen, is a friend of many of the boys in his mostly white neighborhood; but as the boys and Spence become interested in girls, Spence's friendship is subtly rejected. Spence's loneliness is heightened by the absence of his older brother, who is away at college. Spence gets into trouble in school, has a fruitless encounter with a black prostitute in the town's Negro section, and finally has a meaningful relationship with an older black woman. Ultimately, Spence grows up, as we all must, and is able to face the ills of the world, one of them being racial prejudice.

But Peterson's subtle play is also a not so subtle critique of integration. In *Take a Giant Step*, Peterson poses the serious question that Hansberry failed to address in *A Raisin in the Sun*: is the loss of our children's emotional health an equitable price to pay for integration? There can be little doubt that Negro adolescents trapped in environments filled with racial prejudice can be adversely affected, and that one must "take a giant step" to negotiate such an ordeal. Largely with the help and later the memory of his grandmother, Spence survives this special trial of the black adolescent emotionally intact. But do all Negro adolescents have wise grandmothers and enough intellect and sensitivity to make use of grandmotherly wisdom?

Baldwin, like Peterson, writing only of what he knew and had experienced, set *The Amen Corner* in the confining and restricted world of a Harlem storefront Pentecostal church — Baldwin had been a boy minister in just such a church. In the play, Margaret Alexander, pastor of the church, struggles to keep control of her congregation as her eighteen-year-old son, David, begins to find friends of his own age "out in the world," and Margaret's estranged husband Luke, a noted Jazz musician, suddenly reappears.[50] *The Amen Corner* is a virtual primer for Locke's folk inspired, Inner Life philosophy of Negro dramatic art. Baldwin is entirely consumed with the difficult issues of the reunion of star-crossed lovers, sexual repression released as Christian devotion, parenting, and an internecine battle for leadership of a church. And in the power-play that eventually deposes Margaret from leadership of the church, Baldwin, using Locke's mode of mature self-criticism, reminds us that sometimes "the fault lies within ourselves" and "not within" our white folks. For Baldwin, within the human breast there is a will to power and therefore to injustice and evil, even when the stakes are as small as the leadership of a Harlem storefront church. Baldwin's assumptions about the artistic viability of Negro music do not remain neatly tucked away in his theory; they become an integral part of the action in his play. Both in his plot, and in a patina of affection and simple human dignity in which he suffuses his dramatic figures, Baldwin avoids "holy-roller" stereotypes, giving added meaning to the Spirituals that are sung in the play. Modern Jazz, though it is not performed in the play, is inscribed in the character and behavior of Margaret's husband, Luke. Both awed and inspired by the musical accomplishments of his estranged father, David, too, wants to become a Jazz musician. Luke and Jazz represent the forces of the world beyond the church, the world drawing David beyond Margaret's protection. This means that what Du Bois calls Outer Life concerns do loom large in the play. Margaret knows that the world beyond the church is filled with the dangers of racial prejudice and all its economic and social implications, which is why she so desperately wants "to keep David home."

For Margaret, Luke is a living testament of the prejudice and social ills that await David beyond the church. As an exceptionally gifted musician, Luke has received critical acclaim but none of the financial rewards that should accompany such an achievement — an almost usual occurrence for an untold number of gifted Jazz musicians. Luke has led what Margaret considers a "worldly" life of nightclubs, drinking, smoking, cheap hotels and even cheaper women. In fact, Luke is stricken with a terminal case of tuberculosis, presumably contracted from a life of physical dissipation; he has suddenly reappeared because he wants to see his son before he dies.

Thus, racial prejudice and other external social problems do, in fact, play a significant role in Baldwin's dramaturgy, but he develops these elements employing a relentless pursuit of Inner Life conflicts. In this way, themes of social injustice do not stand outside the work as sociological generalizations applying to the "Negro group" rather than to black individuals; for this reason these social ills are all the more poignantly registered and felt. The audience is permitted to see the human losses that social inequalities engender rather than merely witnessing a discussion of these problems. In *The Amen Corner*, racism, poverty, the mainstream commodification of African American music, and Judeo-Christian fears of human sexuality are indivisible from the personal tragedy of Margaret and Luke Alexander.

Langston Hughes' *Simply Heavenly* and Philip Hayes Dean's *The Owl Killer*

Simply Heavenly is, more or less, Hughes' stage adaptation with music of his novel *Simple Takes a Wife*. The play is essentially a romance set in the Harlem community, with much of the action taking place in a local bar (Paddy's) of which Simple is a frequent patron. Hughes' depiction of everyday Harlem characters and their conversations in the local bar make the Harlem community another character in the play. In the slight plot, Simple, who is about to marry Joyce, a respectable young woman, becomes temporarily involved with Zarita. She is "a lively bar-stool girl wearing life like a loose garment, but she is not a prostitute," Hughes instructs.[51] But the difficulties with Joyce over his involvement with Zarita are soon repaired, and Simple marries Joyce.

As might be expected in a play largely set in a Harlem bar, issues of race are often subjects of discussion. In one scene, (Act I, iii) there is a heated discussion of "stereotypes" when one of the bar's patrons, Miss Mamie, extols the virtues of watermelon and black-eye peas and another patron labels her a stereotype. In a later scene (Act II, ix), Simple predicts that in "World War III" he will be a black General, "leading white Mississippi troops into action." In no way as significant a dramatic work as *The Amen Corner*, *Simply Heavenly* is a light confection of what Locke would have termed Harlem folk life and almost totally divorced from the propaganda that he so adamantly opposed.

Dean sets *The Owl Killer* "in a small city in the Midwest called Moloch," in the home of Noah and Emma Hamilton. Noah works in a nearby automotive plant. Emma is a housewife. As the play opens, the police are looking for the Hamiltons' son, Lamar, who is wanted for robbery and murder. Lamar is never seen in the play. Their oldest child, Stella Mae, arrives at the Hamilton home and begs her father to assist her brother should he return home looking for help. But Noah refuses. Dean describes Noah as "a little man with a cast iron face." He is what is called a hard man, who is "set in his ways." Concerning his family Noah says, "I've done my part," which means he has supported them, given them food, clothing, and shelter. However, for Noah, the price of that support has been a life of hard labor in an automotive plant and the loss of his self-respect. While he is a taskmaster and absolute ruler in his home, in a telephone conversation with his white boss, Noah reveals that at work he is something just short of an obsequious, accommodating "Uncle Tom."

Noah complains that his repayment for all of this effort is an apparently criminally insane son — Lamar also castrated the man he murdered — and a daughter who is a "slut" and a policy numbers banker. Stella Mae has five children, "all of them with different fathers," and is presently living with another woman's husband. Stella Mae, however, reminds Noah of the many beatings that she and her brother suffered at his hands, and that they both grew up deathly afraid of him; this, she suggests, is the probable reason for the condition of his children's lives.

Lamar, whose hobby it is to kill and stuff owls, does finally arrive at the Hamilton home. Off stage, he calls to his mother from the walkway just outside the house. When, against Noah's warnings, Emma opens the door, a dead owl hangs in the open doorway. Badly shaken, Noah cuts down the bird and goes to the cellar, ostensibly to burn the dead animal in his furnace. But the play ends as Noah's "screams and moans" are heard from the cellar, and Emma shouts into the telephone: "Stella Mae! Stella Mae! Come over here quick. Your daddy, your daddy! He stuck his head in the furnace. Call a doctor! Quick—."

Arguably, since Eulalie Spence's *Undertow* in 1927 no dramatist dealing with Negro subject matter had achieved the depths of Chekhovian psychological realism that Dean realizes in *The Owl Killer*. Dean even surpasses Spence in this regard, since his dramatic figures are more extensively developed. Primarily a writer of comedies, Spence herself recalls that writing *Undertow* had taken her by surprise; she was not in the habit of writing tragic dramas.[52] Nevertheless, it is undoubtedly more than coincidence that Spence and Dean are members of that relatively small club that Locke and Lewis had hoped for: African American dramatists who actually came of age in the theatre.

Again, as in *The Amen Corner*, in Dean's adherence to Locke's art-theatre, Inner Life strategies, without propaganda, he points to the ever-present forces of the outside world of racial prejudice that has helped to create the Hamiltons' bleak and loss-ridden lives. It is obvious that Noah's family have been the recipients of his rage and resentment because he dared not vent such feelings on those responsible for the injustices and everyday humiliations that have produced his implacable bitterness. In this way, tragically, Noah has played a major role in the destruction of his family.

The Paths of Black Dramatic Theory, 1950–1959

By the early 1950s, the postwar push for equal rights was well on its way to developing into a national Civil Rights movement. The coalition of liberal and leftist whites and Negro leaders that had come together before the war formed the core of this new movement. But now the emphasis was on civil rights and integration rather than the economically based proletarian propaganda of the Depression years. However, in the broad Negro public there remained a distinction between civil rights and integration, especially among Negro artists and intellectuals. In the mid-1950s, Negro America lost one of its most prominent intellectuals: Alain LeRoy Locke died in 1954, and Negro drama had lost its only recognized theorist. But James Baldwin had taken up Locke's ideas in 1949 and began expanding them in 1951. In the theatre, plays by Branch, Peterson, and Childress prophesized a new militantcy in the Negro community and seriously questioned integration.

By 1959, even while Lorraine Hansberry's integration play, *A Raisin in the Sun*, was having a phenomenal success on Broadway, other Negro writers were interrogating the cultural implications of integration. Negro literature began to turn away from its usual protest role and to reevaluate the Inner Life strategies of Locke's Negro literary theory. Moreover, Hansberry's emergence in 1959 signaled the coming of age of a young Negro intelligentsia; this new generation had only glimpsed Locke and the Harlem Renaissance through the refractions of World War II and the Great Depression. And, keeping the Art or Propaganda debate alive, throughout the 1950s there was the persistence of art-theatre drama.

VI

The Rise of Black Arts Theory and the Persistence of Art-Theatre Drama, 1960–1965

The black theory of the early 1960s was, in the main, advanced by a "new generation" of young black intellectuals born in the mid to late 1930s and the early 1940s. But, according to Harold Cruse, this new generation suffered from a vast and deep "historical discontinuity." Cruse writes:

> Marxist Communism (aided by the Great Depression), the Jewish Left and liberal seductions of the 1930s, the Jewish-Christian liberal paternalism of the 1940s and 1950s have all combined to eradicate the living threads between young Negro generations of the late 1950s and the 60s and their predecessors of the 1920s.[1]

Cruse's parenthetical placement of the Great Depression is revealing. In this instance, historical events seem to be, for Cruse, only of secondary importance when contemplating the ills of the Negro middle class, Communism, and the "Jewish Left." Just as with Hansberry's middle class status, Cruse seems to have a special axe to grind against Communists and leftist Jews. That the Negro middle class, American Communism, and the Jewish Left are all, in one way or another, by-products of American capitalism seems beyond Cruse's thinking. It is difficult to imagine that the communist or the leftist ideas of Jews or any other group could have become a potent political force for whites or blacks in the United States without the historical event of the Great Depression. Similarly, it seems clear that in the wake of that event the non–Jewish leftist also had a role in enlisting Negroes to the proletarian cause. But Cruse's finding that the leftist "seductions" of the thirties and the Left and "Christian paternalisms" of the forties and fifties cut the "living threads" between young Negro intellectuals and their "predecessors" in the Harlem Renaissance seems incontrovertible. In fact, it was not only the "new generation" that suffered from "historical discontinuity." Later in his study, Cruse admits that his own generation, born in the 1920s and veterans of World War

II, were separated from their prewar "American provincialism," and from "whatever tenuous moorings [they] might have had with [their] own historical past."

Of course, the historical discontinuity that, by the early 1960s, had been experienced in vast segments of Negro life created a discontinuity in African American aesthetic thought. The Depression, leftist politics, and World War II had obliterated or severely distorted whatever connection the "new generation" had to the Harlem Renaissance. For example, although Du Bois' "all art is propaganda" (1926) would become one of the more quotable phrases in the Black Nationalist movement of the 1960s, his "all propaganda is not art" (1930) enjoyed no such quotability. As for Locke, by 1968, Jeffrey Stewart writes, "few of the new generation of young blacks knew of the ... black philosopher," who had edited *The New Negro* and who "produced numerous articles, anthologies, and speeches documenting the African presence in the world."[2] It should be noted, too, that Theophilus Lewis, the man who arguably made the greatest day-to-day contribution to the discourse on black dramatic art, for the most part, even today remains virtually unknown beyond the smallest circle of mostly African American scholars. In short, the High Harlem Renaissance discourse on Negro art and its participants with all of its many theoretical implications, had become all but invisible by the 1960s.

"Historical Discontinuity": Lorraine Hansberry and LeRoi Jones

Lorraine Hansberry and LeRoi Jones (later Imamu Amiri Baraka), perhaps the two most prominent figures in black drama of the early and midsixties, were members of that "new generation" of black intellectuals who had been relieved of their aesthetic heritage by the cataclysmic events of the Great Depression and World War II. Hansberry was four years older than Jones, and the circumstance that her integrationist propaganda preceded and probably helped to precipitate his militant separatist propaganda tends to obscure the fact (even for Cruse apparently) that they were both young members of the Negro middle class intelligentsia. Cruse finds that historic aesthetic discontinuity "called upon the new generation to make up for lost time — about forty-five years of it." But a half-century of aesthetic history cannot in actuality be "made up for." Hansberry, Jones, and most of their generation, integrationists or separatists, did what most artists do when they are operating without an aesthetic past; they dealt with what they had at hand and became engaged in the dubious process of redesigning the wheel. In Hansberry's case what was at hand was the Liberal-Left alliances of an important group of Negro artists, and Jones' at-hand material was the Euro-American aesthetics of the "Beat Generation." With these tools, which did not have their origin in black culture, they brilliantly re-treaded bits and pieces of ideas from the 1920s that they had heard or read about briefly and most likely perceived through the anti–Harlem Renaissance proletarian lens of the 1930s; their exceptional gifts as writers, coupled with what was by the early 1960s a general public ignorance of the seriousness and complexity of the High Harlem Renaissance discourse on Negro art, made their observations seem fresh and, in Jones' case, even revolutionary.

In Hansberry's case, her early attack on Richard Wright's novel *The Outsider* (1953), and her 1960 call for what seems to amount to "positive images," though the term had not yet been coined, clearly demonstrates that she had little in-depth understanding of the complexity of thought — and the historical moment in which that thought was created — of at least three of her major predecessors. Wright's *The Outsider* was, according to Hansberry, a tale of "sheer violence, death ... a disgusting spectacle ... by a man who has seemingly come to despise humanity."[3]

Wright was certainly no stranger to violence; that fact had already been demonstrated in his autobiographical novel *Black Boy* (1945). And violence and death had a palpable existence in that Southside Chicago community in which Hansberry set *A Raisin in the Sun*. The fact that she chose not to write about it did not mean that the subject was off limits to other black writers. *The Outsider* was, as Cruse suggests, Wright's exploration of existentialism using Negro subject matter. Hansberry, the artist, surely could have understood this, that is, had she considered Wright in his own historical moment and appreciated his complexity as a man, a Negro, and an artist. Hansberry had to know that Negro life contained not only violence but also a black anguish in an almost Kafkaesque, white dominated world that in many ways was supremely suited to Wright's existentialist investigation. But apparently, for Hansberry, these "negative" Inner Life depictions, however true they were, had been historically part of the arsenal of those who "oppressed" the Negro and therefore should not be employed by a respectable Negro writer; in 1960 she writes that, in the main, white writers' depiction of the Negro "has never existed on land or sea." Those depictions, she charges, have rarely been of human beings; they were only a decidedly "romantic portrait of a concept." And this, according to Hansberry, was because "the very nature [of] white supremacy longed for the contentment of the Negro with 'his place'; one is always eager to believe somebody else is exhilarated by "plenty of nuttin'."[4]

Hansberry's "Negro who has never existed on land or sea" is, as has been cited earlier in this book, an appropriation of Du Bois' "black folk such as never were on land or sea." But Hansberry has consciously or subconsciously subverted and reversed the context in which Du Bois used this phrase. Du Bois addresses it not to white writers, but to Negro writers who were attempting to depict the 1921 version of Hansberry's 1960 "positive images":

> With a vast wealth of human material about us, our own writers and artists fear to paint the truth lest they criticize their own and be in turn criticized for it. They fail to see the Eternal Beauty that shines through all Truth, and try to portray a world of stilted artificial black folk such as never were on land or sea.

Given her own historical moment, almost forty years removed from the beginnings of the Harlem Renaissance, Hansberry had every right to disagree with the assumptions of Du Bois' Keatsian Truth and Beauty school of Negro art. One only wishes that she had either the knowledge or the critical integrity to say so rather than subvert Du Bois' meanings to her own purposes.

Continuing her misapplication of Du Bois' statement to white writers rather than to black ones, Hansberry writes that white writers did not exploit "the real life Negroes, with their history of insurrection, 'underground railways,' mass enlistments in the Union, press and literature and even music of protest." Instead, she writes that, primarily, these writers, populated their works with Negro characters that seemed unaware that "slavery was intolerable, or that subsequent and lingering oppression was a form of hell on earth." Illustrating her point with another reference to DuBose Heyward's *Porgy and Bess,* she continues:

> Thus in the make-believe domains of Porgy and Brutus Jones only the foibles of other Negroes are assaulted ... the heady passions of this ... happy breed are committed only to sex, liquor and a mysteriously motivated ultra violence, usually over "dis or dat womans."

The fact that mainstream American theatre had a penchant for producing Inner Life Negro subject matter that would not disrupt the prejudicial views of mainstream ticket buyers is undeniable. It was a circumstance that Du Bois had identified almost thirty years earlier and Locke had duly noted somewhat later. That white writers, working with Negro subject matter, who wanted to be produced, conformed to this system was nothing new. By 1960, this form of Du Bois' "embargo of white wealth on the full-picturing of the Negro soul" had been for the whole of the twentieth century a hallmark of the mainstream American theatre into which Hansberry was trying to integrate.

In fact, Hansberry, like Langston Hughes and Ted Ward, had experienced a somewhat milder form of this "embargo" when an entire act of her play, presumably depicting the problems of integration, was excised and its central focus shifted from an angry black man to a more comforting, less threatening traditional black mother. But in this article, Hansberry prefers to blame white writers, like Eugene O'Neill and Du Bose Heyward, for the historic and systemically circumscribed presentation of Negro subject matter practiced by mainstream theatre organizations that, in effect, hired all writers, whites and blacks. This is a curious position for the playwright whom Nadler insists "was among the most politically radical theatre artists of the civil rights period."[5] But in 1960, radical politics aside, Hansberry was profitably involved with the theatrical system that had historically limited "the full-picturing of the Negro soul." It is interesting, too, that Hansberry, unlike Ted Ward, did not appear to have at the top of her writing agenda a play about "the real life Negroes, their history of insurrection, 'underground railways,'" etc., that she said was lacking in the white writers' "Negro World." Following *A Raisin in the Sun*, her next major completed play project, *The Sign in Sidney Brustein's Window*, which opened in October of 1964 in the Longacre Theatre on Broadway, was not an exploration of any such Negro subject matter.

Again, keeping in mind Cruse's issue of "historical discontinuity," did Hansberry know that O'Neill's Brutus Jones had been based on Marcus Garvey? Did she know that Hubert Harrison had heartily approved of O'Neill's metaphorical characterization of Garvey (1921), and that Harrison was a Negro writer, critic, and activist with socialist and radical credentials that far exceeded her own and who seemingly knew as much as she did about dramatic structure? Did she know that although Du Bois' middle-class background prevented him from "authenticating" the people of Heyward's Catfish Row, he had the critical acumen and integrity to admit that Heyward was, in fact, writing about "the colored people whom he knows"?[6] Did Hansberry hear the critique of Mama Younger's middle class Christian morality in the lyrics of Ira Gershwin's aria, "It Ain't Necessarily So"? Did she see Porgy's insistence on a life of independence and self-respect as a Negro cripple as something unworthy of dramatic depiction? Did Hansberry miss the character Crown's biblical wrestling with God like Jacob with the Angel? Did she miss his John Henry-Paul Bunyan mythical heroics when he attempts to save a woman who will surely perish in a horrendous storm and, again wrestling with God, he survives the ordeal? And finally on this issue, why is the love of a black woman not worth fighting and dying for when Paris and Menelaus disrupted two ancient civilizations for the love of a white one? Would Hansberry call for a "larger scale of dreams and anguish" for Paris, Menelaus, and Agamemnon as she does for Porgy and Crown? Should the epic of the Trojan War be excised from the classical canon because, as in *Porgy and Bess*, its catalytic agent boils down to a struggle between Paris and the sons of Atreus over "dis or dat womans"?

In all fairness to Hansberry, her 1960 references to *Porgy and Bess* may derive from her 1959 review of the Columbia Pictures film production of the opera.[7] Unfortunately, in her 1960 *Theatre Arts* article, Hansberry makes no distinction between the film and the stage production of the opera, which she may have never seen. At any rate, the film production of the work was judged so devoid of artistic merit that the Gershwin and Heyward estates have until this day blocked the re-release of the film to motion picture distributors and television's broadcast, cable, and satellite networks.[8]

In March of 1962, LeRoi Jones (Emamu Amiri Baraka) addressed the American Society for African Culture. By that time, he had become a prominent figure among the group of contemporary *avant-garde* American artists who, more or less, had their own conclave in New York City's Greenwich Village and who were popularly known as the "Beat Generation." Jones had already been the co-editor of the journal *Yugen*, designed primarily to publish the works of East Village writers, and he had been co-founder of the American Theater for Poets, an experimental theatre company. His play, *Dante* (later produced under the titled *The Eighth Ditch*), had opened 29 October 1961 in the Off-Bowery Theatre in lower Manhattan; it ran for sixteen performances. He had also been the co-editor of *Floating Bear*, an underground literary newspaper in Greenwich Village.

Jones' talk, "The Myth of Negro Literature," was primarily an attack on middle-class Negro values that had, for the most part, he said, resulted in a Negro literature submerged in "mediocrity." But more than a precisely and deftly presented broadside against the debilitating effects of the Negro middle class on Negro art, Jones' speech seems to be a sterling example of the historical discontinuity that Cruse had identified in the "younger generation." Virtually all of Jones' address is built on ideas about the black middle class and related issues developed, in some cases extensively, by his historical predecessors. Jones' almost startling lack of references to these Negro predecessors gives the distinct impression that he was, as Cruse suggests, "making up for" forty-five years of black aesthetic history. Negroes who were in the financial position to pursue an art, "especially literature," were almost always, Jones asserts,

> members of the Negro middle class, a group that has always gone out of its way to cultivate any mediocrity, as long as that mediocrity was guaranteed to prove ... to the world at large, that they were not really who they were, i.e., Negroes.[9]

The June 1926 debate in the pages of the *Nation* between George Schuyler and Hughes over the true nature and origin of Negro art elicited from Hughes an attack on the Negro middle class. In many ways, the details of Hughes' attack were more acerbic and more thorough-going than anything Jones said in 1962. Perhaps Hughes' 1930s romance with the Left and World War II had relegated this noted 1926 attack on the Negro middle class to the dusty archives of the New York Public Library, beyond the reach of the new generation.

In his address, Jones also seems to be unaware of Theophilus Lewis' (1926) "better class" of Negroes who were "unaware that the white stage reflects the racial experience of a people whose cultural background has never resembled ours since the beginning of history." Jones also makes no reference to Willis Richardson's absolute dismay with that 1925 middle class segment of the Negro readers and theatre audiences who insisted on "Negro characters of refinement and culture," the "plaster saints" that Sterling Brown had noted in 1930. These desired "refined" Negro characters were the same folks that Du Bois "had never seen on land or sea" in 1921.

Continuing with his theme of the middle-class mediocrity of Negro literature, Jones found that this middle class ethic had dominated black America. "Negro music alone," he said, "had been able to survive the constant willful dilutions of the black middle-class." Negro music had survived "because it drew its strengths ... out of the depth of the black man's soul, and because ... its traditions could be carried on by the lowest class of Negroes." Here, too, at the beginning of World War II, Theophilus Lewis had made a less poetic, but more careful and extensive treatment of the issue of the survival of Negro music in "The Frustration of Negro Art." Lewis concluded that Negro musical artists could depend on Negro "churches, schools, and social groups" for support. "Negro music is," he added, "firmly rooted in the cultural life of the race and keeps pace with its progress"; he continued:

> Within the relative security of their own society colored musicians are free to experiment and improvise, and even free to be stilted and artificial. Because they are free to be artificial when they want to, most of them prefer to be original, making a conscientious effort to interpret the reverent, gay, and humorous emotions of the race as they understand them.[10]

Lewis' important issue of the relative economic security that allows artistic experimentation is missing from Jones' brief comments on this matter. James Baldwin, too, in "Many Thousands Gone" (1951), began his theme of the white majority's need to safely abstract the Negro into a social problem with the assertion that "it was only with his music ... that the Negro in America has been able to tell his story."[11] If Jones was aware of any of this, he did not refer to it.

However, Jones, a Howard University graduate, does make reference to Baldwin to illustrate the Negro middle class pretensions that he felt preoccupied much of the Howard faculty. When Baldwin's *The Amen Corner* "appeared at the Howard Players Theatre" (1954), Jones reports that an English professor "groaned" that the play had "set the speech department back ten years." But again, this story takes one back to the High Harlem Renaissance; it is almost identical to Willis Richardson's experience, over thirty-five years earlier, with a Howard Don. When Eugene O'Neill's *The Emperor Jones* was presented at Howard (1925), Richardson reported, as has been cited earlier, that a Howard professor "wondered why the University would stoop to allow its students to give a performance of a play in which the leading character was a crapshooter and [an] escaped convict."

On the subject of Negro music, Jones appears to slightly advance the discussion beyond Lewis' 1942 observations. He observes:

The "Coon Shout" proposed one version of the American Negro — and of America; Ornette Coleman proposes another.... Both these versions are ... informed with a legitimacy of emotional concern nowhere available in what is called "Negro literature," and ... not in the middlebrow literature of the white American.

That middle-class Negro literature and middlebrow white literature could not match Negro music in its expression of Negro life seems undeniable. But the fact that Jones appears not to be able to clearly connect the dots between Ornette Coleman, "the Coon Shout," and the Negro's African heritage is an early sign of his inability to foster a coherent black aesthetic that accounted for the traditional theoretical elements in Negro art derived from West African cosmology. Jones' observation that "Africanisms do exist in Negro culture, but they have been so ... transmuted by the American experience that they have become integral parts of that experience" is too general to be of use for the construction of a black aesthetic. Surely the cultural constructs that have "persisted" for almost four centuries in the United States, arguably the world's most powerful purveyor of Western culture, would of necessity have the distinctiveness and the vitality to keep them distinguishable within the "American experience."

Ornette Coleman, as a Negro Jazz musician, is functioning in a musical tradition that has a seemingly unbreakable aesthetic connection to the "Coon Shout." Jazz and the "Coon Shout" are derivatives of "call and response," improvisational West African music forms. African communicative ideas about musical percussion (i.e., the talking drum), including the piano, which is technically a percussive instrument, are essential to the "call and response" improvisational form. Traditional American Negro music, Jazz, Blues, and Spirituals, all employ to varying degrees combinations of these African derived performance strategies. In theoretical terms, black music on two continents, for over six thousand years, is the product of a set of assumptions that in our post-postmodern terms may seem almost violently humanist. The African "call and response" is a musical motif that underscores the cultural preeminence of both local human communication and an existential conversation with the forces of the cosmos — and those cosmic forces, as might be expected, are dealt with as humanized deities. It is, of course, the very vagaries of human existence, both for temporal beings and for deities, that make improvisation absolutely mandatory. For the American Negro, slavery and the Jim Crow period that followed it actually reinforced rather than obliterated the inherited notion of an unstable cosmos. Moreover, cultural constructs that celebrate the exigencies of human existence rather than responding to them with a set of calcified and simplistic dichotomies are by design and in the long run extraordinarily durable. While such cultural constructs may lack the easy *quid pro quo* answers to the problems of the human condition, they are, by their very nature, embedded with human resilience. These are at least some of the reasons that what Jones calls "abstract" Africanisms have "persisted" in black American culture over the centuries.

To improvise correctly, that is, to respond instantaneously to the myriad of human calls or statements that arise from the infinite unpredictability of the human condition, one needs a Zen-like mastery of the instruments of communication.[12] The instruments of communication in traditional black music are, of course, musical ones; in the drama they are physicalized modes of behavior as well as language, as Hansberry so ably demonstrates in the opening scene of *A Raisin in the Sun*. Jones makes the point that "the Negro remains an integral part of society, but is continually outside of it.... He is ... an invisible strength within it, an observer." This observation recalls Julian Mayfield's cryptic statement about the "American image, that great-power face that the world knows and the Negro knows better," and Baldwin's detailed treatment of the Negro relationship to the larger society in "Everybody's Protest Novel" (1949) and "Many Thousands Gone" (1951). In *Trouble in Mind* (1955), Childress designs her character Wiletta to vividly depict the Negro outsider, yet integral observer, that Jones describes.

Jones' 1962 finding that "the Negro as a writer, was always a social object, whether glorifying the concept of white superiority ... or in crying out against it," had been part of Locke's 1925 battle cry. In "Enter the New Negro," Locke had asserted, it will be recalled, that the Negro has been mistakenly defined as a "formula — a something to be argued about, condemned or defended, to be 'kept down' ... or 'helped up,' to be worried with or worried over, harassed or patronized, a social bogey or a social burden." Locke had begun this writing with the salvo that "the three norns, the Sociologist [Du Bois], the Race Leader and the Philanthropist," who "had traditionally presided over the Negro Problem" were collectively guilty of defining the Negro as a social problem. That the "stock 'protest' literature of the thirties" was in direct opposition to Locke's earlier call to free the Negro from the onus of being a social problem, and the fact that Locke's attempt was, at least in part, defeated by the social propaganda of the thirties is a fine point which Jones does not undertake. However, it can be convincingly argued, that the dominance of political, Outer Life ideas in the Black Arts movement, which Jones was to father in a few short years, would, as had the propaganda of the thirties, reinforce the image of Negro as a social problem.

Jones, for the most part, correctly finds that the Negro writer "as a social object never moved into the position where he could ... erect his own personal myths, as any great literature must." It would seem, too, that the philosophical material needed for Negro symbols and myth making already existed in the manner in which West African cosmology had been expressed in traditional American Negro thought and art. But, at least in 1962, Jones did not seem prepared to specifically define the existing connection between traditional West African and American Negro art.

Ossie Davis: Middle-Classism, Manhood, Laughter, and the Audience

Later in the spring of 1962, in *Freedomways,* Ossie Davis touched on the issue of the black middle class that Jones and others before him had discussed with such urgency. Also forming a core element of Davis' writing is the related issue of Negro manhood, which, as we have seen, is a central concern in black drama's Chicago triumvirate, *Big White Fog, Native Son,* and *A Raisin in the Sun.* Davis was, in 1962, fresh from the Broadway success of his play *Purlie Victorious* (1961), which was presented in the Cort Theatre by Philip Rose, the producer of *A Raisin in the Sun.* For Davis, the process of writing and performing in *Purlie Victorious,* and the audience response to the work, marked in his life a point of clarification about Negro middle class and manhood issues; he writes:

> Had not Purlie come along when he did ... I would by now have sidestepped completely the Negro Question (which is, to the best of my knowledge, "when the hell are we gonna be free?!"); I would have safely escaped into the Negro Middle Class ... and would probably have become ... an Honorary White man myself.[13]

The play, Davis contends, "is, in essence, the adventures of Negro manhood in search of itself in a world for whitefolks only." This search, of course, was most assuredly the search of Victor Mason (*Big White Fog*), Bigger Thomas (*Native Son*), and Walter Lee Younger (*A Raisin in the Sun*). That Davis chooses to present this search in comedic form obscures the fact that *Purlie Victorious* was, in many ways, a precursor of the ideas that were to form the militant and separatist movement in Negro life that Jones was about to lead. Davis reports that in his struggles to write his play he had to come to terms with the reality that:

> I would never ease my way into the bosom of American acceptance by pretending like Jacob, that I was Esau; by pretending that ... equality could be practiced between whites and blacks purely on a personal basis....

Jones' observation that the Negro writer, had to deal with his Negro-ness, so to speak, in order to avoid creating mediocre middle class literature seems to have been Davis' *modus operandi*. Davis asserts: "I would never find my manhood by asking the white man to define it for me."

Recalling that Davis was, in fact, one of Alain Locke's highly intelligent protégés, we understand that his statement here is not only a fairly militant one about black manhood, like Jones,' it is also an aesthetic contention that to create art, in this case dramatic art, one needs to first get in touch with one's own reality. Davis insists that before writing *Purlie* he "had never before been forced to admit even to myself, that, *in the context of American Society today; the term Negro and the term Man must mutually exclude each other!*" He had accepted that context as his reality before he assumed the challenge of writing *Purlie Victorious*. But persons who define themselves by the evaluations of others cannot create art, or in Jones' terms, art that is not inundated with mediocrity; this aesthetic assumption goes beyond the specifics of race and gender. Defining one's own manhood would become one of the battle cries of the Black Arts movement.

Davis characterizes the laughter that his play provokes as "black laughter"; like "all laughter" at "something disturbing," this "black laughter" takes us to a moment in which we are, Davis writes, "free to behold the universe ... from the same point of view," whether we are black or white. This Blues-like laughter, engendered by tragic human problems pushed to the point of absurdity, is built on the assumption that we all inhabit an often duality-ridden and precarious world, and that laughter is the only human antidote to this situation and an acceptance, even a celebration, of the absurdity of the human condition. As has been noted earlier in this book, this ancient assumption is African (*Eshu*) and Greek (Dionysus); therefore the laughter it produces is necessarily cross-cultural. While Davis was keenly aware of his work's debt to traditional Negro humor, apparently he also knew of its connection to classical comedic literature. He reports that the play received mostly favorable reviews but he was "disappointed that they [the critics] did not comment on Purlie ... as *literature*."

The process of creating and presenting *Purlie Victorius* also illuminated for Davis what he felt were "revolutionary" issues concerning the Negro audience. Davis reports that *Purlie Victorius* "[had] never been a 'big hit' with ... the 'expense account crowd'; and though we had some early support from theatre parties, it was not enough to really see us through." The play would have failed had it been "forced to rely on the normal avenue of Broadway patronage," writes Davis. Sylvester Leaks, a Harlem activist and writer, and John Henrik Clarke (the same Clarke of the First Conference of Negro Writers, 1959) saw the play on opening night, Davis reports, and decided that it "belonged to the Negro people," and "that decision made the difference." Leaks and Clarke publicized the play in the Negro community, and [it] got the message," writes Davis. If large numbers of Negroes supported their own theatre, then it meant that the Negro artists would be free to create without being "forced into artistic prostitution and ... the mad scramble to ... belong to some other people." Davis concludes this writing with a ringing plea to the black intelligentsia of the early 1960s: "It is time for us ... to rejoin the people from which we came. We shall then ... be free to tell the truth about our people, and that truth shall make us free!" And, moving back to his opening theme of manhood, Davis continues:

> Only then can we begin to take a truly independent position within ... American culture ... And from that position, walk, talk ... create, like men. Respectful of all ... but beholden to none save our own.

Jim Williams: Community Theatre, Politics, Economics and Black Dramatists

A year later, 1963, again in *Freedomways*, Jim Williams hailed Davis' concluding statement in "What Purlie Told Me!" but found his plea to Negro artists to rejoin the Negro people a bit vague. Williams writes that he has read many articles on the Negro theatre, and that he supported all the recent political action, picketing, Congressional hearings, "on the part of Negro actors to force their natural inclusion in theatre productions"; however, he continued: "But nowhere, do we read the obvious ... conclusion to be drawn from all the foregoing. The only realistic way for theatre workers and buffs to turn home is to build a Negro Community Theatre Now!"[14] Sounding like a slightly more militant version of Randolph Edmonds in 1948, Williams recounted "Broadway's" sins concerning Negro drama, and the benefits that would accrue to Negro theatre artists and the Negro theatre if black artists worked in their own theatre. According to Williams, Stanislavsky had lectured his students on the power of the modern theatre. He had told them, Williams contends, that the theatre "was more powerful than the school or pulpit could ever be." And Williams speculated that this was the reason why the Negro had "not been able to sustain a theatre, for if there are forces that would deny us our freedom, would they not deny us such a powerful weapon?"

Also in this writing, Williams gives his rather tortured explanation of the relation of art, politics, and economics; it is worth repeating in its entirety since it is precisely this relationship, or rather the perceived meaning of the relationship by black theatre thinkers and artists, that has helped to define the history of the art or propaganda debate; he writes:

> I'm of the school of thought that believes that politics and economics are the basis and foundation of our lives and that art and literature are the superstructure; that the superstructure reflects the base — that the base is specific and concrete. However once the superstructure comes into being it does not play merely a supine role or remain indifferent to the base. Exactly the opposite obtains; the superstructure plays a vital and dynamic role, aiding and buttressing the old base or helping to destroy an old moribund base in preparation for new conditions and new social forces. No longer can Negro writers rely on spontaneity or simple willy-nilly expediency.

In keeping with this view of politics and economics as the basis of art, the community theatre that Williams was calling for was a revolutionary one. He wondered:

> How can our creative writers ignore the freedom movements and the police, fire hoses, dogs, bombs, jailings, etc., used to oppose them? In the qualitative worldwide change represented by the dissolution of classic colonialism and the concomitant national liberation struggles of our own people, lies the richest of mines awaiting the creative Negro writer's golden touch.

Williams cites Esther Merle Jackson's "The American Negro and the Image of the Absurd" (*Phylon*, Winter 1962) in which Jackson makes the convincing argument that the Negro, in fact, "has served as a prototype of that contemporary, philosophic species, the absurd." Williams, however, finds it interesting

> that though the American Negro may very well be an objective prototype for the absurd having lived in a world from which he is alien, estranged, unsheltered, threatened, opaque; a world that has been desolate for over three hundred years, we have not succumbed subjectively to it nor have we in any numbers embraced the white man's currently popular nihilistic philosophy.

Williams suggests that the reason Negroes lack nihilistic views

> is that the capitalist world is not ours or of our making and therefore its dissolution is not of such grave concern to us. On the contrary, if we Negroes are ever going to be able to share in the fruits ... of mass production, industrial society, it is my belief that the capitalist system will have to be modified so as to be almost unrecognizable.

In the drama, Williams wanted for Negro theatre an alternative to the absurdist plays that he felt were the product of white nihilist philosophy. He cites Jean Anouilh's Tony award-winning play *Becket* (1960), Archibald MacLeish's Pulitzer prize-winning *JB* (1959), and Robert Bolt's *A Man for All Seasons* (1960) — all white authors — as "providing some of the answers" that black writers may need to depict "the sense and soul of the Negro." These dramatists, Williams contends, see man "whole, recognizing the strengths that exist within him, side by side with weaknesses."

Williams closed his article with a bit of current black theatre history that made it clear precisely why it was so difficult to get a professional theatre organized in Harlem. He reports that in 1958 he had been one of twenty Negro theatre artists who had come together to establish, in Harlem, a group called the Manhattan Art Theatre. The group's founding members included Godfrey Cambridge and Beah Richards, who had already appeared on Broadway in Davis' *Purlie Victorious*. Diana Sands, Douglas Turner (Ward), Lou Gossett, Lincoln Kilpatrick, and Frances Foster were also members of the group. Williams writes that when *A Raisin in the Sun* began casting, most of the group's most capable actors were cast and had long runs in the Broadway show; and the Manhattan Art Theatre "became a victim of infant mortality."

That same year, also in the pages of *Freedomways*, Lofton Mitchell, in "The Negro Theatre and the Harlem Community" concluded:

> Whether it is possible to build a Harlem community theatre in an era when community theatres are almost non-existent remains a tantalizing question. However, people like Maxwell Glanville, Jay Brooks and other tireless workers continue their efforts in Harlem. They fight eternally rising costs, the omnipotence of Broadway, cheap movie and television fare and a changing community.

The following year, 1964, Clebert Ford, in "Toward a Black Community Theatre,"[15] finds that "it is quite easy to understand why most attempts to establish a Negro theatre fail." Ford goes on to describe a humorous and hypothetical set of circumstances that mirror almost precisely the actual events that brought down Williams' Manhattan Art Theatre the year before. Ford concluded this account with what was by then the old but factual story of the American Negro Theatre's production of *Anna Lucasta*, in which Negro actors slowly escaped to the promise of Broadway, forsaking black community theatre. By the early 1960s, as the civil rights movement was reaching its zenith, there was, of course, another obstacle to establishing a professional black theatre in Harlem. Ford writes:

> With all the Negro's energies devoted to "integrationist" causes, it is no small wonder that the present situation with regard to Negro community theatrical activity is woefully lacking. This coupled with the "token" integration of the legitimate theatre makes for a trying predicament for the budding Negro playwright, actor or technician.

Ford's mention of "the budding Negro playwright" calls to mind that attempts at building a Negro theatre in Harlem had been approached almost wholly in terms of actors. Similarly, progress in the Negro theatre, such as it was, had been historically evaluated by the progress of its actors. The Negro theatre was, in fact, a theatre primarily created and controlled by actors. But professional actors, through no fault of their own, are essentially hired people; thus a theatre built on actors is essentially a theatre that is also for hire; hence, the history of the American Negro Theatre and the destruction of Williams' Manhattan Art Theatre, and so many others. It is as if no one who wanted to build a professional Negro community theatre had read Theophilus Lewis when, in 1927, he wrote that the dramatist is "*the only worker in the theater who contributes anything of permanent value.*"[16] The failure of the Negro Play wrights Company in 1940 was a far more devastating blow to those who wanted to create a professional Negro theatre than anyone at the time had judged and anyone in the 1960s knew. The importance of developing Negro dramatists was still not the primary goal of those who wanted to create a black community theatre.

The Rise of Black Arts Theory

By the early 1960s a rising militancy could be sensed in the American Negro community. For one thing, beginning in the mid– to late–1950s the cracks in the interracial coalition that had built the postwar civil rights movement were becoming craters. The 1950s postwar economic boom started a home-owning frenzy that led to a largely white-flight from the inner city to the suburbs. Travis Demsey writes that in Chicago, for example, the Federal Housing Administration refused loans to Negroes planning to move into white areas, and the Veterans Administration, although "it made funds available through the G.I. Bill to educate black minds," used the bill "to exclude Blacks from needed housing, most spectacularly in the suburbs."[17] There is no reason to believe that this was not a federal policy in most of the country's major urban centers. Moreover, it seems that the Supreme Court's 1954 instructions that integration had to be accomplished with "all deliberate speed," in practice, turned out to be more about "deliberateness" than it was about "speed."

By 1962, a little over two percent of Texas' Negro children were attending integrated schools, reports Jim Williams in the *Liberator*. Alabama, South Carolina and Mississippi, according to Williams, had, by 1962, integrated no Negro children into their white schools. Williams also cites the Negro journalist Carl T. Rowan; in 1963, Rowan noted in the *Crisis* that the State of North Carolina had only integrated 901 of its 339,840 Negro children into all-white schools.[18] This pace of integration infuriated large segments of the Negro community such that a growing militancy began to take hold in the late 1950s and early 1960s. Many Negroes who had been part of the post-war alliance of whites and blacks that formed the civil rights movement would see separatism as the only solution to the race problem. But this new separatism was, for the most part, not the "constructive" separatism that Du Bois had proposed in 1940; it was, understandably, a separatism filled with resentment, rage, and, because of the flight of former white allies to the suburbs, it was filled with a sense of betrayal and, therefore, hatred. These historical forces were, of course, bound to find their expression in art; they were, in fact, the main forces that led to the rise of the militant Black Arts movement and its drama.

In April of 1965, the black writer and critic Clayton Riley announced in the *Liberator* the organization of a new theatre group, The Black Arts, headed by LeRoi Jones.[19] "The Black Arts repertory theatre school, as its name indicates, will be a repertory theatre in Harlem, as well as a school," reports Riley. He also reports that the group had presented a benefit performance a month earlier at the St. Marks Playhouse in New York City's Greenwich Village. Though Riley refrains from a complete review of the plays presented at the St. Marks' benefit, he does mention that Jones' *The Toilet*, one of the plays on the benefit bill, "is a stunning piece of theatre that everyone should see." The play was "currently showing," Riley writes parenthetically, "on a regular off Broadway basis at the St. Marks."

Also, in April of 1965, Larry Neal, the Harlem writer and activist destined to become, more or less, the spokesman for the Black Arts movement, covered for the *Liberator* a "Youth Conference on Afro-American Culture." The Afro-American Cultural Association and The Squires sponsored the conference, reports Neal, and it was held "at Kappa Alpha Psi fraternity house in Harlem on April 9th, 10th, and 11th."[20] Neal was far from unaware of the need to reconcile black art with black politics, and he felt that Jones, as an artist who appreciated black music, was in a special position to accomplish this difficult task. Neal writes that Jones, in his *Blues People: Negro Music in White America*,[21] "comes closest to using ... music — to understand who the Afro-American is and who he desires to be."

Neal reports that the conference featured a number of panel discussions and the panelists included Jones, Cruse, Clayton Riley, and Dr. Ben Jochannen, the black historian who would later work closely with John Henrik Clarke. The discussions were aimed at two central issues, writes Neal: "Can an art that genuinely meets the needs of black people be evolved in the community? What has prevented the black artists from being more responsive to the needs of the community? The answers did not come easy," writes Neal. In hindsight, it is no wonder that the "answers did not come easy," since the panels' questions were so ill formed. Had black people actually existed in America for over three hundred years with no art that "serviced their needs"? If so, it had to be the first time such a thing occurred in the annals of human history. And which "needs" of black people were the discussions addressing? Spiritual and philosophical needs? Or would seeing a good black play or hearing excellent black music get one's rent paid or help one to find a job? The old adage that "sometimes the questions are more important than the answers" seems to have eluded the planners of the conference's discussions. In fact, the questions assume Williams' definition of the relation of politics, economics and art, with art as the result of the former two disciplines. Following this logic, more than three centuries of Negro folk tales, poetry, literature, Spirituals, Blues, Jazz had not given black people political or economic equality, and therefore black people had no art that "serviced their needs," such needs apparently existing only in the realms of politics and economics — another first in humanity's long history.

Neal, however, had begun this writing seeming to preserve some distinction for Negro art and culture: "The liberation of the Black Man is directly tied to his cultural liberation." However, the question was — and had been for the whole of the twentieth century — would the black man's culture, or more specifically, the art his culture produced, inform his politics? Or would the black man try to shape his art to suit his politics? This, of course, was the old issue that ignited the Art or Propaganda wars that Du Bois and Locke had fought during the Harlem Renaissance and that Du Bois had, for the most part, resolved in 1930. But as proof of the accuracy of Cruse's notion of "historical discontinuity," the "new generation" proceeded as if no such thing had ever happened.

In July 1965, the *Liberator* published Jones' "The Revolutionary Theatre." Jones had written the article for the *New York Times* in 1964. But the *Times* editorial staff rejected the piece, claiming that they "could not understand it."[22]

Jones' essay was, among other things, a mixture of sometimes rather obscure poetic phrases and very clear attacks on whites and white-controlled institutions. It seems the only reason Jones could have imagined that the *Times* would publish such a writing is that he had, with the success of his play *Dutchman* (1964), become, so to speak, the Negro darling of New York's *avant-garde* white theatre arts establishment. "White men," he writes, "will cower before this [new] theatre because it hates them ... The Revolutionary Theatre must hate them for hating." For Jones, the white West had declared the superiority of its "technology" over what he called "World Spirit." This new theatre, Jones continues, should be used to "slaughter ... dimwitted fat-bellied white guys who ... believe that ... the world is here for them to slobber on."

And, this revolutionary theatre, according to Jones, would also be "political," while at the same time it would "isolate the ritual and historical cycles of reality." It was a social theatre, too, because "all theatre is social," Jones insists. Moreover, he was prepared to use whatever theatrical tactics necessary to gain the public's attention: "Scream ... murder ... if it means some soul will be moved to actual understanding of what the world is," he writes, "and what the world ought to be."

Earlier in the essay, Jones acknowledged his new revolutionary theatre's link to Western culture and it's *advant-garde* ideas about theatre: "Even if it is Western, [it] must be anti-Western." Jones pointedly suggested that this new theatre had to show the disintegration of Euro/American culture as that disintegration had been "designed" in Artaud's *The Conquest of Mexico*.

Jones also writes: "Wittgenstein said ethics and aesthetics are one" and here agrees with this Austrian philosopher. And, in what sounds like an attack on the apolitical white artists of his own "Beat generation," he emphasizes the need for black art to be political: he felt that, for the most part, "white, Western artists," consciously or unconsciously, were "in sympathy with the world's most repressive forces" and therefore "do not need to be political." For blacks, he concludes, the drama "that will split the heavens ... will be ... THE DESTRUCTION OF AMERICA." Jones then names a number of historical, non-white "heroes" and adds that "most of you who are reading this," are the "enemies" of these "new heroes."

In all of this, Jones makes the Western heritage of his Revolutionary Theatre quite clear. The proposed theatrical bloodletting and violence of this new theatre, instituted in the hopes of emotionally dislodging the spectator's conventional complacency, can be traced directly to Antonin Artaud's (1895–1948) "Theatre of Cruelty."[23] And Jones' citation of Ludwig Wittgenstein's

(1889–1951) position on ethics and aesthetics is particularly interesting, since Wittgenstein's position seems to have grown out of a lifelong interest in religion, which Jones does not share. Jones' new theatre would "kill any God any one names except Common Sense." It should be noted, too, that Wittgenstein's thought had inspired at least two of Jones' white contemporaries, Peter Handke in Germany and Richard Foreman in the United States; both were avidly against the notion of political theatre.[24] Presumably, Jones judged Handke and Foreman to be among those apolitical white artists in agreement with the world's oppressive forces.

Arthur Schopenhauer's (1788–1860) *The World as Will and Idea* (1818) seems also to have a familiar inverted ring in Jones' repeated reference to a World Spirit. For Jones, in a typically American "pursuit of happiness" mode, the world spirit seems to represent the ultimate force, which will re-dress all issues of individual injustices allowing the individual to find peace. Schopenhauer, on the other hand, finds that the very fabric of world spirit or will is so tightly woven with the warring elements of justice and injustice that the individual can only find peace by relinquishing all personal objectives, even the will to live.[25]

At the end of 1965, Jones' Black Arts Repertory Theatre and School became embroiled in a federal investigation of the mismanagement of funds. Along with more than ninety other Harlem community organizations, Jones' group was supported by the Haryou Act, a federally funded umbrella organization. In the *Liberator*, Eddie Ellis reports that Jones was made the scapegoat in the New York press for "the alleged mismanagement of anti-poverty funds." According to Ellis, "the Black Arts had been separated from the other 97 or so participating agencies and attacked so maliciously," with Jones receiving the brunt of the assault.[26] Whatever the accuracy or inaccuracy of the federal government's charges, and whether or not Jones' group was in fact one of the groups mismanaging public funds, the financial scandal brought down the Black Arts Repertory Theatre and School. Ellis acknowledged that the Black Arts movement did not have "mass support" among black people. If such were the case, he writes, "we would be able to organize and finance our own programs." The Black Arts leadership needed to, according to Ellis, "reevaluate our position and our programs." Thus, only about a year into the rise of the Black Arts movement, Ellis would ask the question that, perhaps, should have been asked earlier: "Is Revolutionary Theatre in tune with the people?" Of course, it was not.

In 1965, Jones had done precisely what Hughes had done in *Don't You Want to be Free* in 1937. He had imposed on Negro dramatic art the current assumptions of the European *avant-garde*. Specifically, the fact that Jones could not connect the aesthetic dots in black American music rendered him incapable of designing a set of aesthetics for a theatre actually based on African American culture. Like Ted Ward in 1940, Jones' "God problem," so to speak, was a major obstacle in his establishing a usable black aesthetic. If his theatre had to "kill any God" that anyone proposed, that meant demolishing the Africanized Christianity of the traditional black church and wiping out the West African *orisa* pantheon that had formed the philosophic and aesthetic foundation of virtually all Negro music. It would seem that under Jones' rubric, the Shout and Negro Spirituals, and all of the Blues and Jazz that African and black American spiritual belief systems had so deeply informed, would have to be expunged from Negro life. Louis Armstrong, Mahalia Jackson, Ray Charles, Duke Ellington and Count Basie, if not out altogether, would be of only secondary importance to Ornette Coleman and Archie Shepp in Jones' new system of black aesthetics. To paraphrase Ellis, black people were definitely not in tune with this kind of "Revolutionary Theatre." As with Hansberry's character Beneatha, the atheism or agnosticism of an almost insignificant segment of the young, Negro middle-class intelligentsia, drawn mainly from an older set of middle class white intelligentsia, had no foundation in Negro culture — in Africa or America. In "The Revolutionary Theatre" Jones' assumptions about the nature of black dramatic art are, theoretically speaking, no less middle class and no less out of tune with Negro life than were Angelina Grimké's 1916 assumptions about the futility of Negro motherhood in a racist world.

Moreover, there was in Grimké, Jones, Hansberry, and in many of the 1960s "new generation" the historic and absolute conviction that "the system" they abhorred could be overthrown or radically changed from within. Total middle-class converts to the latest white Euro-American assumptions about the nature of politics and art in their given eras, they were unable to mine the vast and deep current of Negro culture to either perpetuate or create a usable black aesthetic. This circumstance is evident in Grimké's writing of *Rachel* as an address to white women; in Hansberry's integration propaganda; and in Jones' imagining that his "Revolutionary Theatre," by his own admission a "Western" theatre, could help destroy "Western" institutions; and then Jones' sending this message to be published in the *New York Times*, a periodical generally thought to be one of the bastions of Western journalism.

For the purposes of this discussion, perhaps the fundamental and most important assumption that the Negro middle-class intelligentsia had unconsciously (or consciously) absorbed from its older, white counterparts was the nature of the relationship between art and politics. Understandably, since the Great Depression of the 1930s, the view of that relationship, among a number of Negro intellectuals, had become increasingly materialist. Evidence of this is Ted Ward's 1940 definition of the origins of dramatic art in which he emphasizes economics, never quite deals with politics, and wholly excludes myth and religion. Jim Williams' speculation that "politics and economics are the basis and foundation of our lives and that art and literature are the superstructure" is telling, in that the politics precedes economics in Williams' thought. The vast political systems in modern, industrialized economies tend to obscure the fact that politics is merely the way a given society distributes its economic resources. Members of economically and socially deprived minorities, who are contained by, yet normally have little power in, such mega political systems most often miss the fact that politics is merely the handmaiden of economics. Members of such deprived groups, almost as a matter of form, generally spend considerably more energy in an effort to attain political influence than they expend in the pursuit of economic power.

In small, hunter-gatherer or slightly more advanced planter-harvester societies, we see immediately that the resources necessary to human survival, food, clothing, and shelter, are the first order of business in all human communities and that economy is therefore the parent of polity. In fact, in such societies, it usually follows that those who are most responsible for — or have the most control over — obtaining the resources necessary to human survival will most often be the same persons who decide, rightly or wrongly, justly or unjustly, how those resources are distributed; these are the people who get to design the politics of the given system. But the systems of economy that make political systems necessary, whatever their nature, are primarily responses to circumstances beyond human control. We did not decide to be organisms that need food in order to live, or clothing and shelter because of the vagaries of climate.

It is therefore the universal human tendency to interrogate the origin and meaning of those external, non-human forces, which require us to set up systems of economy and their attendant polities in order to survive. Who am I and who is my neighbor in relation to an external world that makes very specific demands on me is an inevitable and eternal human question. Of course, at the core of this question is the equally universal, biological issue of death; it has always been perfectly obvious to the human mind that something must die in order that something else may live, and that no amount of resources (economy) or the effectiveness of their distribution (polity) will enable us to avoid death; that is, the system, because of forces beyond human control, will, at least for the individual, inevitably fail. This means that in the interrogation of the meanings and origins of forces beyond our control, forces that, in many ways, control us, death has an overwhelming significance, and so, too, does its opposite: birth or life. Herein begins the depth of that existential conversation with the cosmos found in all human societies; it is a conversation which includes yet goes beyond issues of economics and politics, whatever their form — capitalism, communism, socialism; it is an existential conversation that questions the very efficacy of all human systems, since they are the results of mortal endeavors and therefore doomed to the extinctions of time; in other words, herein begins myth, religion, philosophy, and art.

In our contemporary world, major corporate entities do our killing and deliver the corpses (vegetable and animal) to the other corporate entities (supermarkets) where we, unlike our prehistoric ancestors, can obtain and consume organic matter without once thinking about the relationship between life and death. But in ancient hunter-gatherer or small planter-harvester societies the relation between life and death and its philosophical implications were inescapable. The fact that Western civilization has produced legions of modernists and postmodernists, artists and theorists alike, who imagine that they create and promote an art that far surpasses human biological imperatives — while they continue to trundle down to the supermarket — is glaring evidence of how contemporary society has sought to escape the admittedly vexing and mysterious problem of what it actually means to be human.

Ensconced in modern, industrialized economies, we are remote from human biological imperatives and their philosophical implications. Eating and even human sexuality, biological systems that allow us to live, breathe, and contemplate the nature of the cosmos, have been reduced to mechanical functions having no non-material implications. Moreover, modernist and postmodernist thought of the sixties and seventies have engendered a dismissive evaluation of the biological, of nature, of, in effect, the physical laws of the universe; this view, for the most part, is presented as an evaluation of the world which is far in advance of the understandings of the ancients; but, in fact, in this author's opinion, it is an unconscious contemporary rephrasing of biblical New Testament and medieval assumptions about the spiritual and opposing animal nature of the mind and body. In some modernist ideas of our contemporary world, this medieval dichotomy is inflected through and melded with more recently inherited Futurists' notions of the perfect machine, rather than nature, as the ideal of contemporary thinking and art.[27]

The point is that art, most especially for an oppressed people, is a system or practice that includes, yet goes beyond, the practical issues of economy and politics; art is a place from which we can evaluate these disciplines and our participation in them. It is the philosophical and spiritual space that fortifies us for the exigencies and often the horrors experienced in the realms of politics and economy. Without art we begin to identify ourselves with only our economic function in the world, which is probably not advisable even if one is the head of IBM, but hardly acceptable if one is the dishwasher at Mable's Soulfood Eatery. This, of course, was exactly the kind of non-political art that American Negroes had for the preceding 350 years and that their ancestors possessed for six millennia before that. That Jones was unable to use his celebrity to design a black aesthetic based on traditional African American assumptions about art was, in 1965, not only evidence of the validity of Cruse's notion of historical discontinuity, but also of Du Bois' 1903, yet seemingly ever-present, concept of "Negro double consciousness."

The Beginnings of Militancy: Early 1960s Civil Rights Drama

In early sixties civil rights drama, there seems to have been a subtle shift to plays that emphasized equal justice under the law rather than integration. C. Bernard Jackson and James Hatch's *Fly Blackbird* (1960), Hal DeWindt and Reni Santoni's *Raising Hell in the Son* (1961), and Ossie Davis' *Purlie Victorious* (1961) give evidence of this trend—*Purlie Victorious* will be given a closer examination shortly.

Fly Blackbird, a musical drama, is one of the first plays to center its action on the youth movement that formed an integral part of the struggle for civil rights. In a certain sense the play assumes that integration is a reality, at least for a younger set of informed Americans. In the play, the action centers on the Blackbirds, an integrated group of high school and college students who are picketing for civil rights.[28] *Raisin' Hell in the Son* is a spoof of *A Raisin in the Sun* in which a black family moves into a white neighborhood, hires a black butler and a white maid and, as might be expected, encounters various difficulties with their white neighbors.[29] This sendup of *A Raisin in the Sun* is, beneath its hilarity and nonsense, a deep critique of Hansberry's notion of integration; it is a critique that goes to the serious issue of the omission of that pivotal act in which Hansberry's Younger family decided to integrate into a white world which is, in fact, not overrun with harmless little white men like John Fiedler.

In 1964, Hughes' *Jerico–Jim-Crow* opened in January in the Greenwich Mews Playhouse in Lower Manhattan.[30] The play is subtitled *A Song Play,* and its structure was, more or less, a reworking of Hughes *Don't You Want to be Free?* (1937). As in the former work, Hughes employs songs and short scenes to tell the history of segregation. The emphasis in this work is not on integration, but on black people taking every step, short of violence, to rise from second-class citizenship. The demon-like figure of Jim Crow is the only role played by a white actor.

In 1965, Lofton Mitchell's *Star of the Morning*, a biographical drama on the life of the early twentieth-century Negro comedian, Bert Williams, opened in Cleveland, Ohio.[31] This work recounts the trials and tribulations of Williams' life, and is a kind of testament to achievement despite the ills of segregation. Promoting integration, of necessity, is given little emphasis in this work.

Douglas Turner Ward's *Happy Ending* and *Day of Absence*

In November 1965, Douglas Turner Ward's comedies, *Happy Ending* and *Day of Absence*, opened in the St. Marks Playhouse in New York City. The plays ran for 504 performances, closing in January 1967. Rather than promoting integration, Ward's comedies stressed the idea of black and white communities as two distinct but interdependent entities.

In *Happy Ending*, a politically conscious young man who lives with his aunts, two domestics, is shocked when he discovers them shattered and weeping over the imminent divorce of the Harrisons, their white employers. Initially, the young man chastises his aunts for behaving like a pair of "Uncle Toms." But when he learns that the women are actually distraught at the prospect of losing their jobs and therefore losing the clothing, food, furniture, and even money that they have purloined from the Harrisons over the years, he, too, becomes dissolved in tears. In an eleventh-hour telephone call from Mr. Harrison, the black family learns that the Harrisons have decided to stay together. The aunts and their nephew rejoice at the news, opening a bottle of purloined Harrison champagne. There is no integration here, only, beneath the laughter, a black economic dependency on white society.

In *Day of Absence*,[32] Ward hilariously examines white dependency on black society. Employing a blacks-in-whiteface performance technique, black actors play the roles of whites in a sleepy southern town that discovers that all the "Negras" have suddenly and mysteriously disappeared. There are no maids, no butlers, and no laborers. In this emergency, nearby towns refuse to lend the ailing community any of their Negroes, and black convicts that are brought in to relieve the shortage mysteriously disappear upon reaching the town limits. Panic sets in and there are riots in the streets, requiring the National Guard to be called in. The next day all the Negroes suddenly reappear as if nothing had happened, and life in the small town returns to what it "used to be." Or does it? This is the question that Ward leaves dangling and unanswered at the final curtain.

Written from a strictly Negro point of view, Ward's plays gradually found success playing before mixed audiences in the St. Marks Playhouse in New York City. The success of *Happy Ending* and *Day of Absence* eventually led to the formation of the Negro Ensemble Theatre Company, which was to have a decade run as the premier Negro theatre company of the United States.

Ossie Davis' *Purlie Victorious*

Purlie Victorious[33] had laid the groundwork for Ward's success and also deftly handled the shift from integration to civil rights in a period of rising Negro militancy. Davis' play opened in September of 1961 in the Cort Theatre on Broadway and ran for 261 performances. The play is set in "the recent past" in a fictional farming community in "South Georgia," Cotchipee County. Purlie Victorious Judson (Ossie Davis), an erstwhile black preacher, has hatched a scheme to rebuild Big Bethel (really a huge barn), the community's black church. A recently deceased relative, cousin Bee Judson, inherited $500 before her death from another deceased relative; cousin Bee has not lived in the county for many years. As the play opens, Purlie has secured the services of Lutiebelle Gussie Mae Jenkins (Ruby Dee), a very beautiful but not very bright Alabama domestic. Jenkins will pose as cousin Bee to claim the money, which will be used to rebuild Big Bethel. The funds, however, are in the hands of Ol' Cap'n Cotchipee (Sorrell Booke), the owner of the county's only plantation and the villain of the piece. As the sole ruler and despot of the county that carries his name, Cotchipee took charge of the money in cousin Bee's absence. He is, of course, unaware that cousin Bee has recently died.

Charlie (Alan Alda), Cotchipee's son, is the object of integration in the play. In the concluding scene (Act, III, i) he asks to become a member of Big Bethel's black congregation. Davis has crafted Charlie as what can be termed an "honorary Negro." Much of the humor in the work comes from scenes between Charlie and Idella (Beah Richards), Cotchipee's lifelong Negro servant. Idella, for all intents and purposes, is Charlie's mother. Charlie's biological mother died when he was a small boy, and Idella has raised him to manhood; he is, as might be expected, absolutely devoted to her and, in his way, a civil rights activist. Charlie has been beaten up for giving equal rights speeches in the local bar. He takes the $500 from his father's General Store and gives it to Purlie. Moreover, Cotchipee, a man who likes "everything done legal," instructs his son to buy Big Bethel and burn it down; Charlie, instead, buys the huge barn in Purlie's name and gives him the deed to the property. When Cotchipee discovers Purlie's name on the deed, he freezes and dies standing up — later he will be buried in a vertical coffin. All of this makes the point that Charlie is white in pigment only, and even then it is still Charlie who must ask to join a part of Negro society. But after Cotchipee's hilarious death, there is no groundswell of Negro sentiment aimed at integrating Cotichipee County's segregated institutions. In the epilogue, in which the reconstitution of Big Bethel is celebrated along with Ol' Cap'n Cotchipee's funeral services, the focus remains on the reconstitution of Big Bethel, a Negro institution.

Repeated references in the play to the current civil rights struggle obscure the fact that Davis has told his satirical tale using, primarily, Negro Inner Life concerns. Purlie's very personal need to become a bona fide preacher is the Inner Life dramatic objective that drives all of the political themes and motives in the work. Davis has followed almost religiously the concepts of Locke's folk inspired art-theatre drama, and, in Lewis' terms, created a play of social satire. Thus, as with Ward's later comedies, Davis suffuses his work with a totally Negro point of view. Like *Happy Ending* and *Day of Absence*, Davis' play is recognition of two separate societies, one black, the other white, but unlike in Ward's plays, he does not emphasize the interdependence of these two groups. *Purlie Victorious* is, instead, a satirical demand for equal justice under the law. In the terms of the play, anything less is absolutely ludicrous. Davis depicts the militancy of this demand in the incident in the play when Purlie "marches up the hill" to Cotchipee's plantation house to defend Lutiebelle's "honor" (Act II, ii). Earlier, Cotchipee had hired Lutiebelle to work in his home, where the young woman narrowly escapes an onslaught of his rude advances (Act II, ii). In fact, it was Charlie who saved Cotchipee from harm. He gave Purlie the long sought after $500 inheritance to assuage Purlie's rage. Purlie's militant defense of black womanhood in 1961 was a political sign of the times. But Davis, adhering to Locke's Inner Life principles, has Purlie fall hopelessly and uncontrollably in love with Lutiebelle before he "marches up the hill," reducing a political generality to a specific and entirely personal dramatic objective. It is love that sends Purlie up the hill, not a political generalization about the defense of black womanhood.

Significant Early 1960s Black Arts Drama

The separatist, militant, and Black Nationalist concerns traditionally identified with the rise of the Black Arts movement actually began with Louis Farrakhan's plays, *Orgena* and *The Trial* produced in 1956. Farrakhan is now the nationally known, principal leader of the Nation of Islam, the most widely known Black Muslim organization in the United States. Nadler has uncovered evidence of the existence of Farrakhan's plays in reviews and theatre programs; they were written when Farrakhan was known as Louis X in The Nation of Islam.[34] *Orgena* (a Negro spelled backwards) appears to be a more militant and separatist version of Du Bois' pageant *Star of Ethiopia* (1913). *The Trial* "enacts the indictment and prosecution of a symbolic white man for his 'crimes' against Black people in general and the Nation of Islam in particular," Nadler writes. Both plays were first produced in 1956 "as motivational pieces for the Nation of Islam" and, Nadler adds, "presented at Unity Parties, relatively informal Tuesday-night affairs held at Muslim Temples." In 1960, they were presented twice to predominantly black audiences in Carnegie Hall, the noted midtown concert venue in New York City.

In 1963, the Actors Studio in New York is reported to have presented as a workshop production Paul Carter Harrison's *Pavane for a Dead-Pan Minstrel*, a play about a white-faced black man and black-faced white man who compete in a sexual contest. Tellingly, a white woman, rather than a black one, is the contest prize. The work used the format of the American minstrelsy. The white man wins the contest using black dance techniques, and is killed by the white-faced black man, using the standard racist argument of the corruption of white womanhood. The work is an ironic explication of the Black Nationalism and separatism in Farrakhan's plays and the rage and hatred that would support many of the works of the Black Arts movement. The year 1964 saw the production of Jones' *Dutchman*, *The Baptism*, *The Toilet*, and *The Slave*. *Dutchman* and *The Slave* were the most definitive expressions of what would become Black Arts theory.[35]

LeRoi Jones' (Emamu Amiri Baraka's) *The Toilet*, *Dutchman*, and *The Slave*

Jones' *The Toilet* opened with his *The Slave* in December 1964 and ran to April 1965 in the St. Marks Playhouse in Greenwich Village in New York. Edward Albee's group, Theatre 1964 Playwrights Unit, first produced *Dutchman* in the Village South Theatre on 12 January 1964; the play was moved to the Cherry Lane Theatre, also in Greenwich Village, on 24 March 1964, where it ran 232 performances until February 1965.

However, *The Toilet* appears to be the earliest of Jones' plays produced in 1964; it was copyrighted in 1963 and it seems to be a reworking of his earlier play, *The Eighth Ditch* (1961). The middle class Negro Boy Scout who is raped and beaten in the first play becomes a white-skinned Hispanic in *The Toilet*; the Boy Scout's black, lower income, youthful assailant becomes, in

The Toilet, a gang of streetwise Negro youths. In *The Toilet*, the Hispanic youth is not raped, but he is beaten severely. He is a homosexual and he has sent a love letter to Foots, the leader of the black gang. Foots' cohorts have discovered this letter and arranged for him and the Hispanic youth to "fight it out," as it were, in the boys' bathroom of their school. By the time Foots arrives for the gathering in the toilet, the gang has already beaten Karolis, the Hispanic youth. It is obvious that Foots does not want to fight, but the gang finally forces the confrontation between the two boys. As the fight begins, Foots is still hesitant and Karolis gets the upper hand, getting Foots in a chokehold. The gang immediately intercedes, and they beat Karolis almost into unconsciousness. They all exit, leaving Karolis' crumpled body on the toilet floor. But Foots returns, writes Jones, "stares at Karolis' body for a second, looks quickly over his shoulder, then kneels before the body weeping and cradling the head in his arms."

Foots is either a great humanitarian or this is a play about a homosexual love affair, with one of the lovers "in the closet," so to speak, and the other "out." Foots' weeping at the end, coupled with the exchange between him and Karolis as the fight begins, makes it rather obvious that the two boys have a close relationship. Most telling is the fact that it is Karolis who repeatedly insists that they fight, leaving the inescapable impression that fighting between them is an unforgivable violation of their relationship. Karolis' mantra of "let's fight" rises to an "I want to Kill you" with the unspoken words "for not being man enough to admit that we are lovers" lingering in the air.

Curiously, these events and their seemingly obvious meaning eluded reviewers Langston Hughes, Larry Neal, and Waters Turpin, who included a review of the play in his "The Contemporary American Negro Playwright" in *CLAJ*. As might be expected, the cursing in the play and "bad taste"— characters frequently use the toilet facilities — overwhelmed Hughes. Turpin finds that "the Negro boy returns to comfort the victim."[36] It would seem that a victim could be comforted without one "weeping" and "cradling" the victim in one's arms. In a period when, in black militant circles, one did not openly discuss homosexuality — except as an aberration of white society — Neal comes closest to the truth of Jones' meaning; he writes: "This play is about the search for love under conditions that militate against it ever surviving past the destructive elements that crop up and block it."

The *Dutchman* is written in two scenes and has been described as an absurdist drama. Clay, a young, educated, middle-class Negro, rides a subway train in which he meets Lula, a bohemian white woman whose aim it is to seduce him. But throughout the play Lula taunts Clay about his middle class demeanor, suggesting that he is not a "true" black man. At play's end, Lula's taunts have grown to a vicious attack, and Clay, finally enraged, strikes back. As his anger dissipates and Clay prepares to move to another seat away from Lula, she stabs him, twice, and fellow passengers help her throw his body from the moving train.[37]

James Hatch writes that Lula must first make Clay into "the stereotypical Black figure whom whites create and demand." According to Hatch, the stereotype that Lula needs Clay to fulfill before she can have sex with him is "the white myth of Black Male sexuality"—which means, of course, black male sexual superiority. Clay, however, Hatch continues, uses this myth "to expose the systematic and deliberate annihilation of African Americans." Hatch cites a number of newspaper headlines reporting the lynchings of innocent black males, mostly precipitated by alleged sexual indiscretions that these ill-fated men were accused of imposing on white women.

There is little doubt that in *Dutchman*, Jones takes up the issue of white perceptions of black male sexuality, just as Wright had done in *Native Son* in 1941. But the symbolism in *Dutchman* and the middle-class nature of Clay's character supply an alternative reading, which does not easily reduce to the "black versus white" issues that still dominate interpretations of the play. Both Hatch and Bernard Peterson acknowledge that Clay and Lula are, to some extent, symbols of Adam and Eve. In the first scene, Lula incessantly devours apples. But, more importantly, Lula functions in the play as the traditional temptress, the role that a white, Western, and decidedly male ideology had assigned to women. Is Jones' use of this biblically derived symbolism a criticism of white male ideology or an affirmation of it? If it is the former, then one must look to sources other than *Dutchman* to substantiate that fact. In the play Lula acts in accordance with the biblical story and its attendant ideological assumptions about woman's role as temptress and seducer. This, of course, means that in the world of the play, Lula is first a woman and only secondarily a white woman.

Looked at in this way, the sexual conflict between Lula and Clay is more about male sexual inadequacy in the face of prodigious female desire than about Lula molding Clay into her image of a black male sexuality. It can be successfully argued that Lula's attack is, in fact, an attempt to divest Clay of his white-inspired, middle-class assumptions, such assumptions having sapped his vitality as a man and therefore as a sexual partner. Lula could mount the same case of sexual inadequacy against a white male middle-class intellectual. And Clay's racial rhetoric aside for the moment, his ultimate response to Lula's attack can also be read as the rage of a heterosexual male whose sexual prowess has been impugned by an attractive woman.

If one does look to sources beyond the play to judge its meaning, Jones' almost relentless 1962 attack on the Negro middle class in "The Myth of Negro Literature"[38] alone will give adequate support to this reading of *Dutchman*. The "mediocrity" of the Negro middle class, of which Clay is an obvious member, is a truism in Jones' universe. Moreover, in that 1962 speech, Jones' assault on Negro middle class mediocrity was so thorough-going that it is difficult to imagine that he does not believe, as does his Lula, that mediocrity can deplete a man's vitality and therefore his sexuality. To assert that this is not so, one must adhere to the notion of the division of the mind and body, another Western, male, biblically inspired assumption, closely related to the notion of Woman as temptress. If men can live in their minds, so to speak, they will no longer be prisoners of their body's seemingly relentless desire for women. The cultural construct of woman as temptress both explains the internal male struggle with desire and relieves males of responsibility for that desire, should they lose the apparently Olympian Judeo-Christian battle to keep themselves pure. Clay's middle class orientation makes him a definite convert to this particular cultural construct.

Perhaps even stronger evidence of Clay's immersion in an essentially white, middle class view of the world are the reasons he gives for why Charlie Parker plays the saxophone and Bessie Smith sings the Blues. At the top of his rage (Scene ii) Clay intones: "Bird [Charlie Parker] would've played not one note of music if he just walked up to East Sixty-seventh Street and killed the first ten white people he saw." He adds:

> If Bessie Smith had killed some white people she wouldn't have needed that music. She could have talked very straight and plain about the world. No metaphors. No grunts. No wiggles in the dark of her soul. Just straight two and two are four. Money. Power. Luxury.

With these utterances Clay takes African American dramatic theory back almost a half-century to 1920 and to Angelina Grimké's simple but prophetic assumptions: "Because of environment and certain inherent qualities each of us react correspondingly and logically to the various forces about us ... if these forces be of love, we react with love, and if of hate with hate." Following Grimké and Jones, Parker and Smith's music is a Negro art form assembled in response to the white mainstream. Without white oppression and its resultant black hatred, Parker and Smith's art would be non-existent.

Hughes had made the point in 1926 that most of the Negro middle class had no interest in, and therefore knew very little about, traditional Negro culture and the art it produced. That members of this Negro middle class most often dominated the ranks of Negro leadership in politics and in the arts is one reason for the relatively low visibility of traditional Negro and African art throughout the twentieth century. Had Hughes, for example, received the strong financial support of the Negro middle class in the 1920s, he would not have had to turn to the Left in the 1930s. This middle class, dismissive attitude to Negro art constitutes the historical background of Clay's seemingly radically black utterances in *Dutchman*. Contrary to Grimké's far-reaching protest theory and Clay's estimation of their art, Smith and Parker's music was created in that almost liminal space that the broad African-American populace had to create to survive as human beings, with all that term implies. Yet, Parker and Smith's music, or some form of it, would have been created with or without American oppression. And, this is so simply because the philosophical properties and the resulting aesthetic strategies that define the space in which they created their music is, at bottom, derived from an African humanist cosmology that existed thousands of years before the United States became a nation-state.

But for the Negro middle class, in large part remote from traditional Negro culture, no such space existed. Closer to the white middle class than nine-tenths of their brethren, it was, for the most part, inconceivable to middle class blacks that anything of value existed beyond white middle class assumptions. Therefore Clay, and all like him, cannot entertain the notion of an art created, in Du Bois' terms, "by" and "for" Negroes. Similarly, it is also inconceivable to Clay that Parker and Smith's primary interests are not the "money, power, and Luxury" that are iconic desires of his middle class existence. Clay's middle class limitations as concerns his evaluation of Negro art are, of course, Jones's deficiencies in the same area. Not only is Clay autobiographical, but Jones has also already sufficiently demonstrated, in his observations on Negro music and in the European *avant-garde* nature of his "The Revolutionary Theatre," that he, too, fundamentally, had very middle class notions about the nature of Negro art.

On the other hand, Jones has to be admired for telling the truth about himself in *Dutchman* and having the extraordinary courage to carry this process of emotionally disrobing before his audience even further in *The Slave*. Almost certainly a fictional and theatrical exploration of the real-life break up of his interracial marriage, *The Slave* tells the story of Walker Vessels. In this play, which Jones has subtitled *a fable*, Vessels returns to his former wife's home amid a war between whites and blacks. Vessels is the leader of the black revolutionary army prosecuting the war, and his purpose for "dropping in" on his ex-wife and her new (white) husband is, ostensibly, to retrieve his two children. *The Slave* has a poetically written prologue that seems to negate or illuminate all of Vessels' later assertions to his ex-wife, Grace, and to her husband, Easley. In the prologue Vessels appears as an elderly man, presumably after the war, and his monologue seems to be primarily a kind of apology that acknowledges Vessels' personal "deceit" and loss. His first lines in the play are:

> Whatever the core of our lives. Whatever the deceit. We live where we are, and seek nothing but ourselves. We are liars, and we are murderers. We invent death for others. Stop their pulses publicly. Stone possible lovers with heavy worlds we think are ideas.[39]

After this, in the main body of the play, Walker will shoot and kill Easley, watch Grace die after the house they are in receives a direct artillery hit, and leave his children to die in the burning building. Hatch warns that the "naturalism [in the play] is of little importance. It is merely ... an excuse for the real drama — the ritual of the drama of decolonization wherein not only is the colonizer killed, but his powerful spirit that possessed the colonized is ripped out and destroyed." Hatch is correct. In most of Jones' major plays, at least up to 1965, his characters are not human beings at all, but political abstractions behind which are the human problems of male fears of sexual inadequacy, marriage, divorce, parenting, etc. In the prologue, what Jones/Vessels seems to be telling us is that all efforts on behalf of others, wives, children, friends, etc., are "deceits." We are, at bottom, "liars and murderers" who are only concerned with ourselves and who kill the things we say we love. Coming from his own knowledge as it does, this is perhaps a brave and darkly poetic statement; but, since the theatre is the domain of flesh and blood beings, it may be a statement better expressed in a collection of dark and brooding poetry.

In 1965, Jones' Black Arts Repertory Theatre in Harlem presented his comedy *J-e-l-l-o* and *Experimental Death Unit #1*. In the theatre, these productions marked the official beginning of the Black Arts movement. In *J-e-l-l-o*, Jones' sendup of Jack Benny's 1950s television show, it is Rochester, Benny's servant, who, for the most part, eventually makes silly and decadent servants of Jack Benny, Mary Livingston, and Dennis Day. In *Experimental Death Unit*, blacks become a kind of military police, out to exterminate decadent whites and their black collaborators.[40]

It is difficult to disagree with Werner Sollors' finding that Jones essentially "inverts elements of American popular culture."[41] *The Slave*, too has, a similar inversion; Vessels allows his mulatto children to die much as a racist white father might allow his half-white offspring to perish. In fact, it is Jones' "inversion of elements of popular culture," as Sollors would have it, that ultimately places most of his drama in the field of protest literature. The violence and often shock value of his plays (following Artaud), and Jones' considerable powers as a poet tend to obscure this fact. But, as has been shown, Locke would have had as much to fear from Jones as he had to fear from Grimké.

Jones' drama up to 1965, perhaps more than any twentieth-century Negro-authored drama, seems to, in Locke's terms, "perpetuate the position of group inferiority even in crying out against it." In *Dutchman*, Clay rages about the villainy of whites and blacks' hatred of them, then casually reaches over Lula to retrieve his jacket, and the so-called white demon he's just berated stabs him to death. The very nature and energy of his "crying out" against his oppressor makes him a victim, an example of the superior power of his foe. The spirit of the oppressors that Walker Vessels fights is so superior that even after his armies have caused their deaths that spirit has so twisted Walker's mind that he leaves his children to perish in the building his army bombed because, presumably, through no fault of their own, the children are half white. In 1964, white society had apparently retained such superior power that it could still create Negro monsters as Wright had argued in *Native Son* almost a quarter century earlier.

The Persistence of Art-Theatre Drama, 1960–1965

The mid-1960s saw the production of Adrienne Kennedy's *Funnyhouse of a Negro* in East End Theatre, off-Broadway, in January of 1964. James Baldwin's *Blues for Mister Charlie* opened on Broadway in the ANTA Theatre in April 1964, and the Firehouse Repertory Theatre in San Francisco produced Ed Bullins *Clara's Ole Man* in 1965. Bullins' new play depicted the lives of the youngest segment of the "new generation," the group that Cruse called the "lost generation."

Adrienne Kennedy's *Funnyhouse of a Negro* and James Baldwin's *Blues for Mister Charlie*

Like Jones' *Dutchman*, Kennedy's *Funnyhouse of a Negro* was developed in Edward Albee's Theatre 1964 Playwrights Unit. Using the aesthetic strategies of symbolist and absurd theatre, masks, whiteface makeup, detached "ball heads," "falling hair," and abstract sets and lighting design, Kennedy investigates the Inner Life conflicts of Negro-Sarah, a young, middle class black woman. Peterson's *Take a Giant Step* (1954), and *Funnyhouse of a Negro* are likely the most significant black-authored dramatic works to present a serious critique of middle class Negro life before 1965. Negro-Sarah's crisis is that she is psychologically trapped between the Negro and white worlds. As Margaret Wilkerson writes, Kennedy "externalized the psychological confusion of a young Negro woman who struggles unsuccessfully to reconcile her African and European selves."[42] To depict this conflict between Negro-Sarah's "African and European selves," Kennedy designs dramatic figures that personify Sarah's opposing selves: the Duchess of Hapsburg, Queen Victoria Regina, Jesus, and Patrice Lumumba.[43] In fact, the play has but two characters, Funnyhouse Lady and Funnyhouse Man, who are not extensions of Negro-Sarah's psyche.

In this work, Kennedy depicts Du Bois' now sixty-one year old conundrum of Negro "double consciousness." Kennedy's observation that "autobiographical work is the only thing that interests me, apparently because that is what I do best,"[44] reveals that she is a religious, if unconscious, follower of Locke's Inner Life strategies. What may be even more significant about much of Kennedy's drama is that her mixture of *avant-garde* strategies, most especially her sometimes almost alogical dialogue, governed by her inner life as a Negro woman, may have unconsciously released, as Max Reinhardt had told Locke (1924), the dramatic power of "the body to portray emotion"; this was, according to Reinhardt, the "special genius" of Negro performance. Recalling that Reinhardt also identified "the use of the body to portray emotion" (pantomime) as "the most basic [and ancient] aspect of drama," it may be surmised that Kennedy, in dramatizing her own "double consciousness," may have found and vividly depicted an aesthetic unity between dramatic art and an enduring psychological syndrome in African American life, double-consciousness.

Also in 1964, five years after Hansberry's Younger family courageously, if a bit implausibly, integrated a Chicago suburb, Baldwin's *Blues for Mister Charlie*[45] gave Broadway audiences a view of the struggle for integration they may have been trying to avoid. Samuel Hay reports that Jones was inspired by Baldwin's monumental drama:

> It was one of the great theater experiences of my life. A deeply touching "dangerous" play for Jimmy, it not only questioned nonviolence, it had a gutsy — but doomed — black hero [Richard] and his father go at each other's values, echoing the class struggle that raged between Dr. King and Malcolm X.[46]

Baldwin's instinctive attachment to Locke's Inner Life concerns transforms what should be a conventional protest play into a drama about human futility and, by implication, about the futility of the integration movement. Here, the list of the "doomed" reveals not only the name of Baldwin's "gutsy hero," Richard, but also those of virtually all of his central dramatic figures, white and black. There is depicted in this work the almost violent banality of a segment of the white South that is reminiscent of Tennessee Williams' drama. It is presented with Baldwin's landscape of white-southern Inner Life issues, "mendacity" (Williams' word), duplicity, gender oppression, and sexual repressions; but for economic considerations, one wonders why any reasonable person should want to integrate into such a society? But Baldwin does not play favorites, he not only "questions" Negro "non-violence," he also gives us a view of the startling and, in some ways inexplicable, impotence of segments of Negro culture. This, too, he accomplishes using Inner Life processes: a failed musical career, drug addiction, the loss of a beloved spouse, unrequited and doomed love relationships, and sexuality as an expression of shrunken as well as expanded human consciousness.

In Act II, when Richard tries to purchase soft drinks in Lyle Britten's store with a twenty-dollar bill that Britten cannot change, an argument ensues then ends in Richard knocking Lyle to the floor. All of this occurs in front of Britten's wife, Jo, and Britten will later report to his friend Parnell that the "niggers was laughing at me for days." In the final moments of the play, Britten asks Richard for a simple apology to which Richard's answer is "no." Britten, in his own way, does, as he says, give Richard "every chance to live!" And Richard, in the words of his father, Meridian, "refuses them all." Richard arrived unarmed and unescorted to an appointed meeting with a man he had to know was capable of killing him. Thus, it is difficult not to conclude, especially when accounting for Baldwin's Inner Life tendencies, that to escape the impotence of his own life, Richard acquiesces to a form of assisted suicide.

After Richard's murder and the legal freeing of his killer, Baldwin's blacks continue their struggle for desegregation not so much as an act of faith that their action will change the system, but rather as symbol of their belief in the ultimate righteousness of their cause. Among the blacks in the play there seems to be a collective conviction that in such ethical action, whatever its outcome, lies the essential definition of what it means to be human, the boundary between persons and beasts. Drawing on his formative experiences in that tiny, politically unimportant black church, Baldwin, as a final coda, gives us ethical action for the sake of ethical action. And here, as discussed earlier, the Africanized nature of Negro Christian fundamentalism should be kept in plain view. In particular, his use of ethical action and of sexuality to physicalize both expanded and limited states of human consciousness is evidence of his working with the cultural materials of his own life. He had grown up seeing church women transform sexuality into spiritually (a central motif in *The Amen Corner* and a brief one in August Wilson's *Fences*) and seeing righteousness praised as its own reward. In stepping into his own life for his depiction of ethical behavior and spiritualized sexuality, Baldwin may have unwittingly touched on then unrecognized Africanisms in Negro culture.[47]

Ed Bullins' *Clara's Ole Man* and Harold Cruse's "Lost Generation"

In *Clara's Ole Man* (1965),[48] Ed Bullins executes Locke's Inner Life principles almost with a vengeance. Set in a "slum in Philadelphia," Bullins' characters are firmly locked within their own world. As the play opens, Clara, an attractive girl of eighteen, has invited Jack over to her apartment. Jack is an ex-marine who works for the Post Office and whose "speech is modulated and too elegant for the surroundings," writes Bullins. Jack and Big Girl sit drinking at a kitchen table, and as Jack continues drinking "his words become slurred and mumbled," Bullins adds. Big Girl, who has taken the day off from her hospital job, entertains Jack, and it is clear that he is attracted to Clara. Big Girl continually jokes with him about his interest in Clara; sometimes her jokes have a barely perceptible menacing tone. At crucial moments in the action, Big Girl makes it clear that she has complete control over Clara. The climax of the play comes when Jack, after too many drinks, inadvertently reveals that Clara told him "to come by today when her ole man would be at work," and he discovers that Big Girl is, in fact, "Clara's ole man." The play ends as Bama, Stoogie, Hoss, Big Girl's hoodlum friends, are heard beating Jack in an off stage yard outside of the apartment.

Again, recalling Neal's careful handling of his description of Jones' *The Toilet*, this was a period when homosexuality was not a frequent topic of discussion in Negro life. Bullins subtitled this work *A Play of Lost of Innocence*, and when it was first presented, the revelation of the lesbian relationship in the play gave the work a shock value that it most likely would not have today. However, it is the almost violently insulated world of Bullins' dramaturgy that is of particular theoretical interest. In this work (and others to follow), Bullins comes close to challenging Du Bois' 1927 assumption that "even the lowest black folks" are aware of "the risen black man and the world of white folks."

Bullins' dramatic figures may not be unaware of an outside world of whites and "the risen black man"; it may be that their jealousy and hatred of that world causes them to dismiss its existence. Their hatred of the outside world, especially regarding other Negroes who function in it, Bullins depicts in the way Big Girl and her friends respond to Jack even before his climactic discovery. In one way, however, it is Jack's innocence that falls into question. It is difficult to imagine that an ex-marine, who has traveled the world, as Jack tells Big Girl's hoodlum friends, has no knowledge of lesbianism. It is possible, of course, that Jack is fabricating his story of worldly experience and that his drinking has clouded his perception. But Jack's story of his background seems honest and direct; yet throughout the action there are continuing clues to the nature of the relationship between Big Girl and Clara that Jack, if his ex-marine story is to be believed, should have observed. It appears that to get the shock value he desires, Bullins imposes on Jack a questionable innocence.

Pushing Inner Life strategies to their absolute limit, Bullins reverses Locke's objective for Negro art, which was to foster an art that would establish before the world the total and enviable humanity of African peoples. In this work, Bullins' dramatic figures, if not less than human, seem to have stunted perceptions that are related to the insular nature of their world. It is not enough to say, as Du Bois had suggested, that poverty, lack of education, and middle class morality are the reasons for this kind of shortfall in human perception. For example, Philip Hayes Dean's Stella Mae in *The Owl Killer* is a character that could easily fit in with what Hatch calls "the wretched of the earth" that populate Bullins' dramaturgy.[49] Stella Mae is as guiltless about her "sins" (prostitution, gambling, adultery) as any of Bullins' characters. But she seems keenly aware of the external forces, including her father, that have helped to make her what she has become. It is also clear that she has struggled against those forces, and though she may have lost the battle, it is that struggle that gives her dimension and that links her to the rest of humanity. Big Girl seems almost two-dimensional when compared to Stella Mae.

On the other hand, *Clara's Ole Man* seems an accurate depiction of what Cruse calls the "lost generation":

> But today we do have a Lost Black Generation — very young and very historically conditioned. They are lost within the deep canyons of the Northern urban cities, aliens to white western culture of the American style, whose exile is within themselves. Their alienation is reflected in many ways — in delinquency, crime, sex, drugs, hatred of whites, hatred of the United States, sometimes in hatred of themselves, and sometimes even in poetry and other art forms.[50]

This was a generation of young blacks who were coming of age in the midsixties, and it is the generation that peoples Bullins' play. In a very real sense, Bullins is dramatizing the Bigger Thomases of the late 1950s and 1960s, and in that same sense, he may have been saying, as Wright had said, "look white America, look at what you've created." Bullins' dramaturgy is, despite the rigor of its Inner Life strategies, or perhaps because of it, like Wright's, a form of protest theatre.

The early 1960s saw the disintegration of the interracial alliance that had formed the core of the Civil Rights movement. The postwar economic boom of the fifties had fostered a "white flight" to the suburbs, and federal agencies had pursued policies to help keep the suburbs predominantly white. A decade after the first major Supreme Court desegregation decision, most Negroes did not live in an integrated America and did not expect to do so within the foreseeable future.

A new militancy took hold in Negro America, and a "new generation" was coming of age to expound that militancy. This new generation began anew the discourse on the nature of Negro art. There was a renewed call for a professional theatre in the black community, free from the intermittent exploitations of Broadway. But, as in the preceding decades, no one since Theophilus Lewis quite understood the importance of dramatists in building a black professional theatre. LeRoi Jones called for a black "Revolutionary Theatre" and initiated the separatist Black Arts movement. Jones opened a Black Arts theatre in Harlem, and Douglas Turner Ward premiered two one-act comedies at the St. Marks Playhouse that would later be the beginning of the Negro Ensemble Company (NEC). In the sixties and seventies, NEC would become as important in African American theatre history as the American Negro Theatre had become in the 1940s.

By the end of 1965, Jones' Harlem Company was defunct, and there were questions in his own ranks whether or not the black populace was ready for his Black Revolutionary Theatre. But, arguably, hundreds of community theatre groups had been formed throughout the country in the wake of the new black militancy. And, as in the fifties, there was still the persistence of art-theatre drama. The Art or Propaganda debate was enjoined anew with the vigor of the uninformed. Apparently, in the imprisoning cycle of the oppressed it is a fact of life that each generation must begin again.

VII

Back to the Future: Conclusion

It can be safely concluded that for the first sixty-five years of the twentieth century, the art or propaganda debate and all its implications dominated black dramatic theory. The issue is, of course, an old one, and by no means does it arise exclusively in the twentieth-century discourse on black drama. But a black American history replete with covert and overt struggles for freedom, and social and political equality, arguably, had imparted a magnitude to the art or propaganda debate found in no other area of twentieth-century dramatic theory. Even in the years immediately following 1965, the art or propaganda debate would remain at the center of the discourse on black drama.

Just beyond 1965

In 1966, LeRoi Jones, now Imamu Amiri Baraka, would meet the black philosopher Maulana Ron Karenga and, perhaps realizing that Wittgenstein and Artaud were not appropriate to his purposes, Jones would "transpose," writes Samuel Hay, "each of the seven principles ... of Karenga's *Kawaida* doctrine into drama." *Kawaida* was Karenga's "ideology of culture that proposed to build a [black] nation built on a common value system." A year later Douglas Turner Ward and Robert Hooks would found the Negro Ensemble Theatre Company, a company which proved to be almost totally devoted to Alain Locke's art-theatre principles, and the art or propaganda wars would continue with a new urgency.

Hay's suggestion that Baraka, in imposing *Kawaida* doctrine onto black drama, "deconstructed" both Du Bois' Outer Life and Locke's Inner Life theories seems to sever Baraka from the continuous, sixty-five year flow of the art or propaganda debate.[1] But Baraka's politicized theory of art under Karenga's tutelage seems not so much a "deconstruction" of Du Bois' Protest theatre and Locke's art-theatre — in the sense, for example, that Jacques Derrida deconstructs Antonin Artaud — as it is a rephrasing of Du Bois and a negation of Locke.[2] Baraka's theatre protested for black power and control, while Du Bois' theatre protested for black civil and social equality; the political differences here are obvious, but the aesthetic ones are non-existent. Protesting Outer Life issues was the coin of the realm for both Du Bois' early protest theatre and Baraka's Black Arts drama. Baraka's validation of only black art that was in the pursuit of Karenga's "nation building"[3] is a negation, not a deconstruction, of the viability of Locke's art-theatre's Inner Life concerns.

Hay also suggests that Du Bois' protest drama establishes the superiority of the "other," while Baraka's cultural nationalism does not. But much of Baraka's dramatic work, even after 1965, used propaganda to create plays that would help to overthrow the race that had created and sustained an apparently superior system of aesthetics since, in its modernist form, Baraka himself was using that system. Moreover, his treatment of whites, as in *Experimental Death Unit #1* (1965), often amounts to a castigation of the people whom the white middle class generally finds despicable. Werner Sollors explains: "In Baraka's works, the image of the devil-enemy appears in the shape of bums, policemen, immigrants, homosexuals, Jews, and women, whereas white Anglo-Saxon entrepreneurs are underrepresented."

In other words, as Sollors adds, Baraka's "Black Cultural Nationalism ... retains middle-class traits and prejudices." And these "middle-class traits," according to Baraka's own lights, are Negro inheritances from white bourgeois society. Looked at in this way, Baraka's protest drama, too, had the annoying habit — as Locke would have noted — of subtextually pointing to the superior judgment or power of that oppressive "other." Essentially, Baraka differs from Du Bois in that he added the element of black protest to the aesthetic practices of the Euro-American *avant-garde* of his own era. Political considerations aside, in black dramatic theory, Du Bois remains the twentieth-century father — and Angelina Grimké the mother — of the black dramatic protest theory that fueled the drama of both the Civil Rights and Black Arts movements.

Jones and Karenga would later (1974) discard the *Kawaida* doctrine, finding that it contained an "exaggerated exoticism" caused by their "fierce pursuit" of "Black cultural nationalism," and their "tendency to talk revolution from the partial perception of culture, instead of from lessons learned from global struggle."[4] Baraka would eventually characterize the *Kawaida* doctrine as a confused mixture of "borrowed ideas from Elijah Muhammad ... Garvey, Malcom X," a number of noted modern African political leaders and also "Mao and even Lenin and Stalin and Marx."[5] As Locke undoubtedly would have warned, the politicization of art would ultimately prove unworkable.

Affinities: Integration and Black Arts Theory

This book has indicated, too, that the passage of time has unveiled the similarities in the propaganda of civil rights and that of Black Arts nationalism. Time and Baraka himself have confirmed these affinities. In 1987, long after the bitter divide between the Black Arts and Integration camps, Baraka would write:

> Hansberry had created a family engaged in the same class struggle and ideological struggle as existed in the movement itself and among the people. Hansberry's play was a political agitation. It dealt with the very same issues of democratic rights and equality that were being aired in the streets. But it dealt with them not as political abstractions, but as they are lived ... The Younger family is part of the black majority, and the concerns I once dismissed as "middle class"—of buying a house and moving into "white folks' neighborhoods"—are actually reflective of the essence of black people's striving to defeat segregation, discrimination and national oppression."[6]

It is interesting that Baraka, in 1987, still evaluates black drama solely in terms of its political usages and properties. As with Jim Williams in *Freedomways* (1963), the materialist view of the dominant ideologies of capitalism, communism, and socialism has not left him. A traditional African or African American view of drama had yet to enter his consciousness. Here, too, Baraka dismisses the prevalent view in the black community that integration and civil rights were, as has already been argued here, not the same things. That "the people" made this distinction, even in their initiation of the Civil Rights Movement, is either still beyond Baraka's knowledge or of little import to his still wholly political arts project.

The emotionally gripping, play-ending speeches of Hansberry's Walter Lee and Baraka's Clay both venture outside of their respective dramatic works to promulgate the propaganda of integration on the one hand and of Black Nationalism on the other. Again, the differences here are in politics and not in art; the fact that these strategies of dramatic discourse emanate not from broadly based, traditional African American assumptions, but from a relatively minuscule Negro middle-class intelligentsia reinforces Locke's conclusion that they are strategies that, in fact, function as an address of the few, either to "harangue or to subjugate to" the all-powerful "other." As in the seminal case of Angelina Grimké's *Rachel* (1916), this is the ultimate function of Negro Protest theory.

Social and Art-Theater Drama

However, it can be concluded here, too, that following Inner Life, art-theatre strategies a few black dramatists in the sixties, fifties, and late forties wrote plays that spoke to current social and political issues but also clearly could not be categorized merely as propaganda vehicles. Written from an entirely Negro point of view that investigated the internal stresses of black life, plays like *Our Lan', A Medal for Willie, Take a Giant Step, Trouble in Mind, Purlie Victorious,* and *Happy Ending* were, in fact, the first of the fully developed Negro social dramas that had been called for since the Harlem Renaissance. There were, too, the purely art-theatre works, like James Baldwin's *The Amen Corner* and his *Blues for Mister Charlie,* Philip Hayes Dean's *The Owl Killer,* and Ed Bullins' *Clara's Ole Man,* all plays that have rather stunning social implications.

The relatively few black social dramas and even rarer art-theatre stage works were a result of the paucity of black dramatists throughout the first half of the century, as Theophilius Lewis sadly noted as the decade of the fifties began. Black commentators on theatre had noted this problem early in the Harlem Renaissance, but from 1917, when the white writer Ridgely Torrence's *Three Plays for Negro Theatre* opened on Broadway, to the present, the emphasis in black theatre remains primarily on the actor. Before 1950, the lack of a sufficient black canon of performed dramatic works from which to draw black theory increased the already proscriptive and prescriptive tendencies in the enunciation of that theory. Even after 1950, when a group of new black playwrights were busy expanding the black canon, this tendency would continue and even deepen well beyond 1965, especially on the part of those on the propaganda side of the art or propaganda debate.[7] To Du Bois and especially Locke's credit, in lieu of a canon of black drama, as theorists, they did try to look to black culture for guidance. Unlike Aristotle, they had no century-old canon of performable drama from which to draw their conclusions.

But, according to the former Howard University Professor Margaret Just Butcher, the half-century dearth of black dramatists cannot be looked on as a particular problem of Negro life or culture. Butcher, in her book "based on materials left by Alain Locke," observes that "drama by and about Negroes has developed and matured in relationship to the developing and maturing of American drama as a whole."[8] Butcher cites Carl and Mark Van Doren's *American and British Literature since 1890,* first published in the United States in 1939:

> American literature has always been weakest in the department of drama. Until the present generation there has been little dramatic work worth the serious attention of the historian, and there have been few or no playwrights of deserved eminence. Not until 1890 did any arise of even respectable quality, and not until 1915 did talent of a high order enter the field.

If the Van Dorens' view is accepted, it had taken white America more than a century after the Revolutionary War to produce writers who could create drama of a "respectable quality"; if the full-length black plays of the late forties and fifties are considered to be at least of the same quality as their white, 1890 counterparts, then it had taken Negro America about eighty-five years from the Emancipation Proclamation to accomplish the same task. It would take, according to the Van Dorens, another quarter century for white America to produce dramatists whose work demonstrated "talent of a high order." In Negro America, it would take another decade or so to produce Hansberry's *A Raisin in the Sun* and a decade after that to produce Lonnie Elder's *Ceremonies in Dark Old Men* and Charles Gordone's *No Place to Be Somebody*: all three are award-winning plays, generally thought to be evidence of "talent of a high order" among black dramatists. It seems reasonable to conclude that American culture, heterogeneous, founded and held together basically on materialist assumptions that associate "happiness" almost exclusively with material gain, does not place the emphasis on the arts found in its European predecessors. The paucity of black dramatists haunting Lewis in 1950 was an American problem, not evidence of a special Negro ineptitude in the dramatic arts.

Two Great Truisms of Black Dramatic Theory

However, the lack of a black canon of drama was a small impediment in the development of black dramatic theory as compared to the Great Depression and World War II. The Depression all but nullified Du Bois' 1930 simple but almost elegant management of the art or propaganda issue—"all art is propaganda, but all propaganda is not art." Moreover, the Depression replaced Du Bois' earlier "best face forward" protest strategies with the propaganda of the proletariat, absorbed, primarily, from the white Left. In turn, after World War II a coalition of Negro leaders, white liberals and leftists spear-headed the replacement of proletarian assumptions with the civil rights, integration propaganda of the 1950s. As in the 1930s, this new propaganda was absorbed into black theory. Then, in the 1960s, the Integration movement's political theory of art would help to precipitate the equally political theory of Black Arts, Black Nationalism; this militant black aesthetic would be projected into the seventies and early eighties.

Thus it can be reasonably argued that for almost a half century, historical circumstances, with which blacks as second-class citizens had little to do, defined the propaganda side of the art or propaganda debate. The propaganda component of black dramatic theory was a response to Outer Life, historical circumstances engendered by those in control of mainstream America. The black argument for propaganda in Negro art was an inverted product of the white political power structure that secured and affirmed, in Locke's terms, that structure's primacy. Herein lies the accuracy and prophetic power of Du Bois' 1903 identification of "Negro double consciousness." Black dramatic theory, for most of the twentieth century, is composed of the Outer Life realities and articulations of those realities taken from the dominant forces in the white world and, in Du Bois' terms, the almost diametrically opposed, "warring" Inner Life realities and assumptions of the black world.

Hay argues that both Du Bois' Outer Life protest theatre and Locke's Inner Life art-theatre have informed African American drama, and they have. However, he adds that: "Within the particular contexts of their origins and development, neither school appears more obviously right or wrong, modern or outdated, than the other." But it seems difficult to argue that Du Bois' early, "best face" forward protest theatre was not a product of white opinion about what indeed was the Negro's best face. In fact, this was likely one of the factors behind Du Bois' 1930 revisionism. If Hay and August Wilson's 1990s calls for a rehabilitated black theatre are to be realized, it would seem that such a theatre cannot be established with a black theory of dramatic art that is, like Du Bois' "double consciousness," composed of "two unreconciled strivings; two warring ideals in one dark body" of black dramatic theory.[9] Papering over the historically opposing forces in black dramatic theory will only insure the continued anemic condition of the black theatre.

It is hoped that this entire discussion has at least broached the fact that the two great truisms of black life, and therefore of African American dramatic theory, are Du Bois' century-old notion of Negro double conscious, and Locke's 1929 identification of the debilitating ills that propaganda imposes on the art of a black culture that needs all its energies to survive and replicate itself in a world dominated by a mainstream, primarily materialist, culture. That survival must be accomplished within a larger American system which is itself embroiled in a process of becoming, of sorting out its many heterogeneous influences to arrive at a cohesive cultural identity — and, in the meantime, makes its most significant contribution to the world in the form of the culturally questionable benefits of consumer capitalism.

For these reasons, it is also hoped that the art aspect of black theory's art or propaganda debate will in the future be given closer attention. In the late 1940s and 1950s, Ralph Ellison, James Baldwin, William Couch, Julian Mayfield, Alice Childress and Louis Peterson, to name just a few, gave serious attention to the Inner Life realities of black Americans and thereby seriously questioned the value of both Negro protest literature and the Integration movement. This serious questioning destabilized the philosophy of integration and, in fact, was another factor that helped to lay the groundwork for militant and separatist Black Arts theory. Locke, it will be recalled, had gone public with his art-theatre Inner Life assumptions in 1925, and that began the discourse on African American literature and drama (1925–1929) that constitutes the centerpiece of twentieth century black dramatic theory and therefore the centerpiece of this book. But the art or propaganda issues that dominated the "high" Harlem Renaissance discourse on Negro art had older origins.

Middle-Class Origins of Negro Protest Theory

In 1916, Locke had fought a career endangering battle with the NAACP's Drama Committee over the selection of Angelina Grimké's protest play *Rachel*. He thought the committee should select an Inner Life folk drama that would, potentially, be the beginning of a national Negro art-theatre. But the NAACP was not an arts institution; it had been organized (1909) for the social and political "advancement of colored people." So the Committee chose Grimké's propaganda play, and the art or propaganda war was ignited. Locke immediately launched a nine-year covert campaign to influence Negro writers to create plays that suited his folk-inspired art-theatre goals.

Grimké, on the other hand, in 1920, plainly stated that her play was not for Negroes, but for white women whom she sought as allies in the battle for social and political equality. In the process of defending *Rachel* against mostly Negro charges that it "preached race suicide," Grimké would articulate, in a way that Du Bois never had, the foundations of Negro Protest theory, which essentially held that if Negroes were treated badly they would behave badly; if they were treated well, they would behave well. It was a statement that black life and therefore black art is ultimately determined by whites; virtually the same statement, but this time in Protest theory's militant rephrasing, would be made almost a half century later when Baraka's Bessie Smith, ostensibly, would have given up singing the blues if she could have just gone out and killed a passel of white folks. Of course, the smallest investigation of traditional African American culture and the elements it draws from West African cosmology place Grimké and Baraka's notions somewhere in the regions of the absurd. But it is perhaps the inescapable baggage of an oppressed minority that Grimké's Negro Protest theory should still inform much of contemporary scholarship on black theatre, and much black theatre practice.

Grimké's assumptions about Negro art should not have outlasted her lifetime. But, as has been indicated in the latter chapters of this discussion, Grimké's view of Negro art was a general assumption of a significant group of the Negro middle class. Far more influential than its numbers would justify, the Negro middle class, for the most part, knew little of Negro culture and the art it produced; it was, in fact, a class whose members had to distance themselves from black traditional culture and become immersed in the values and assumptions of the white mainstream. In the United States, even today, this is a price that blacks not uncommonly pay to maintain their middle class status and its material rewards. This circumstance has helped to create the largest black middle class and the biggest black underclass in American history.[10]

Du Bois and Locke, and Cole, Cook, and the Africa Connection

Du Bois and Locke were two notable exceptions to middle-class Negro estimations of the value of Negro art. In both men's cases, the depth of their education and intellect alerted them to the fact that Negro culture could produce art that was beyond the precepts of the white middle class. Further, there is every indication that Du Bois and Locke considered that their intellectual accomplishments had placed them above what were to them the ordinary middle-class considerations of either whites or blacks. Du Bois, determined to prove the viability of Negro culture, worked tirelessly after World War I to shape the Negro renaissance not only into a movement concerned with the defeat of "color line" prejudice but also one in which there would be a flowering of Negro arts and letters.

Early in the Harlem Renaissance Du Bois showed a deep respect for Locke's Negro folk drama when, in 1922, he praised the original works of the young playwrights in Montgomery Gregory and Locke's newly initiated Howard University drama program. In fact, as early as 1913, Du Bois had called for a drama of Negro Inner Life objectives that would teach "colored people the meaning of their history and their rich, emotional life." That he also wanted a drama that would "reveal the Negro to the white world as a human, feeling thing" was evidence of his own double consciousness and, in any case, a feat that could not likely be accomplished in a single play but required a canon of Negro drama on diverse aspects of black life. Du Bois finally accepted this fact in 1930, after four years earlier operating his own Negro Little Theatre company, the Krigwa Players.

It has been shown here, too, that the beginnings of black theory's art or propaganda debate began with the philosophies and theatre practice of Bob Cole and Will Marion Cook, and that, according to James Weldon Johnson, their differences were often the occasion for bitter disputes. Cole, it will be recalled, was concerned with a mastery of his stagecraft such that his performance and his shows equaled or surpassed that of his white competitors. Cook's only interest was the Inner Life objective of bringing the "genuine" Negro to the American stage. For Negro performers to compete with whites in areas that whites could execute just as well or better was, for Cook, an egregious waste of time and the Negro's unique talent. But Cole's concern with mastery of his craft led him to redefine the Negro minstrelsy into Negro musical comedy by the addition of plot and storyline to the minstrel show's dramatic format. And, perhaps more important to a discussion of black theory, his heritage of what has been termed here Post-Slavery Classicism filled Cole's work with notions of humanism and universality, staples of both traditional West African and African American thought. Moreover, Cole, as the producer, playwright, and performer of his stage works symbolized Brander Matthews' "unbreakable bond" of written drama and performance which, as has been argued here, is another feature of traditional African and black American assumptions about the nature of drama.

The fact that Cole and Cook's work and thought, when examined from a theoretical point of view, reveal links to traditional African and African American thought may indicate a need for an entire reevaluation of early twentieth-century Negro musical comedy. The admittedly negative image of black people in blackface has likely and understandably, even in scholarly circles, stirred more outrage than detached scholarly investigation. Nevertheless, had this African American author pursued this investigation with the particular and justifiable angst of the oppressed regarding such issues, the almost startling gems of traditional black American culture embedded in Cole and Cook's dramaturgy and their enduring links to traditional West Africa would have been unavailable to him.

Evidence of the African nature of Cole's aesthetic heritage, the bonding of performance and the text, can be found in Elizabeth Fine's "Aesthetic Patterning of Verbal Art and the Performance-Centered Text."[11] Here, Fine reports on her observations of James Hutchinson, an African American performer who achieves the effectiveness of his verbal performance using a "highly patterned system of stances." Fine reports that as Hutchinson recited the text, the adventures of "Stagolee," a traditional African American folk tale, his verbal performance was dominated by repeated "hip/hand" and "hip/arm" stances. Robert Farris Thompson reports that these stances are, in fact, derivative of the *Kongo* and *Bakongo* gestures (*télama* and *fútika nkome*), and are, respectively, in the *Kongo* and *Bakongo* cultures, associated with "high oratory" and the speaker's need to "escape a negative situation."[12] As with Cole, the writer-actor, in the performance of a traditional African American folktale, the text and the performance are inseparable. Hutchinson's spoken text and "hip/arm, hip/hand" choreography exemplify the "unbreakable bond" of Cole's performance and Cole's written text.

In some ways, Cook's philosophy and early work have taken us more deeply into traditional black American thought and its African origins than has Cole's work. From Cook's early work can be derived West African notions of time; transcultural sources of the function of comedy in both Nigeria (*Eshu*) and Greece (Dionysus); the duality of African cosmological design; the efficacy of dreams in traditional black American culture; the possession rituals in both the black American fundamentalist church and in the traditional religious practices of the *Ashanti, Baganda, Fon,* and *Yoruba* peoples of West Africa. Cook's work also contains a democratic critique of both the white *nouveaux riches* of his period and the Negro middle class.

Back to the Future to a New Black Aesthetic

Cole and Cook's theoretical links to the past reveal a path to the future. That future offers, if one is still desired, a new Black Aesthetic of dramatic art. And this new aesthetic or black theory would not be black because it is cobbled together as a political answer to Euro-American dramatic theory, but because it is actually derived from cultural constructs already existing in a traditional black American culture linked to a West African past. To begin with, notions of universality that have dominated traditional black culture both in America and West Africa would have to be at the core of any such new aesthetic, if it is, in fact, to be black. The assumptions of Carlton and Barbara Molette that define the thought of Europe, Asia, and what is called the "black disapora" as "separately evolved, culturally constructed human realities" would have to be rejected.[13] This concept is not only inconsistent with traditional black thought, either in America or Africa, it fails to account for many of history's significant transcultural events, like Melampus taking the cult of Osiris to Greece, or the Moorish conquest of much of Europe, or the slave trade, or Europe's colonization of Africa. An aesthetic built on traditional black thought would view world cultures as specifically evolved human realities on different paths leading to the same existential discourse with the cosmos, which offers but a single truth: the ultimate duality of the human existence.

On the other hand, such an aesthetic, despite its adoption of the principles of universality, would eschew "melting pot" notions of culture. In the arts, as in the sciences, specificity (the individual paths of cultures) is a necessary strategy in the pursuit of the universal. The universality of atoms and quarks in all matter, water, wood, air, metal, etc., cannot be determined without the specificity of scientific method; that is, elements must be specifically analyzed to reach their universal components. But in the arts, unlike the sciences, it is the journey that is of paramount importance, not the destination. A new black aesthetic will understand that the extraordinary diversity in the manner in which differing human cultures carry out that central discourse with the cosmos is a testimony to human ingenuity and creativity; it will understand that it is, in fact, this ingenuity and creativity that help the members of all cultures to spiritually and philosophically survive in a world in which human existence can only be described as precarious. Like Du Bois and Locke, a new black aesthetic will rejoice in the fact that Beethoven and Bessie Smith are often discussing the same things but have such diverse ways of executing that discourse. And a new black aesthetic will wage war against any "melting pot" notions or postmodern conflations that seek to change Ludwig into Bessie or Bessie into Ludwig. In this sense, this new aesthetic will be an American aesthetic since it is, at least in part, born of a country that is the most culturally diverse nation on Earth; it will celebrate American cultural diversity as a boon to the world.

The necessity of cultural specificity, as would be required in any new black aesthetic consistent with its own cultural history, returns this discussion to the event in current theatre history in the Introduction of this book: The August Wilson-Robert Brustein debate. Cultural specificity argues for the development Wilson's "unique and specific Black art," and against Brustein's call for black theatre's "continued evolution of so-called universal values" within the American theatre. Again, to reach the universal, specificity is required in both the arts and the sciences.

To Be or How to Be?—African American Realism

The non-realist strategies of the black authors Langston Hughes, Paul Carter Harrison, Baraka, and Adrienne Kennedy have been treated here. It has been made clear here, too, that each of these non-realistic strategies were borrowings from the Russian *avant-garde* of the late thirties and forties, from the minstrelsy, in Harrison's case, and from the Euro-American absurdist *avant-garde* of the fifties and sixties in the case of Baraka and Kennedy. As we have seen, both Kennedy and Baraka's major theatre works were developed in Edward Albee's playwrights' workshop, and Albee may be described as a major American absurdist dramatist. It should be recalled, too, that Sandra Richards, in her dissertation on Baraka's dramaturgy, correctly finds analogies in his theatre work and the drama of Jean Genet, the noted European absurdist playwright.

Nevertheless, African American drama has been dominated throughout the twentieth century by realist dramaturgy. This circumstance is due to a strong preference for realist drama on the part of African American audiences and most of the playwrights who serve that audience. In fact, this strong preference raises yet again and makes current the double-audience problem faced by black dramatists that James Weldon Johnson essayed in his 1929 "Dilemma of the Negro Author." On the other hand, and on the other side of the American cultural divide, postmodern, anti-realist views, most especially in academia, have earned the black plays that endeavor to serve the black penchant for realist drama pejorative and debilitating labels, like "old fashioned," "kitchen sink drama," copies of Clifford Odets and Arthur Miller, and so on. Moreover, postmodern anti-realists charge that realist strategies in art are tools used by dominant ideologies to shape public discourse and to advance specific, usually conservative, political and economic agendas.

From a social perspective, these are the evaluations of critics, commentators, and theatre thinkers who do not seem to comprehend that, at least in part, the historical weight of racism and prejudice in the American theatre has created a general black preference for realist drama. For most of the twentieth century, in mainstream American theatre and film, black audiences have not been inundated with realistic black plays and black dramatic figures. Mainstream American media, including theatre and film, have historically, when presenting black subject matter, shown a tendency to anti-realism long before the term was coined. Alice Childress' play *Trouble in Mind* makes the point that the black dramatic figures inhabiting mainstream theatre have historically possessed a healthy dose of the absurd, existing as they do without cultural or even personal histories, except as relates to white objectives and interests, whether conservative or liberal.

For example, for black audiences, the rise of Sidney Poitier's screen persona is perhaps one of the most significant theatrical events in the last half of the twentieth century. And film has had a pervasive influence on black as well as white theatre audiences. But it can be quite successfully argued that, at least initially, the historic mainstream success of Poitier's screen persona was, for the most part, built on the entirely absurd assumption that worthwhile black people exist in the world for the central purpose of assisting white people in trouble.

In mainstream theatre and film black dramatic figures have also been historically symbolist and abstract in the sense that they are most often symbols, or more specifically, signs of foreshortened, abstracted mainstream notions of blackness. Athletes, ghetto dwellers, tragic mulattos (often of loose morals if the mulatto is a woman), people who function as black Tontos to white heroes, absurdly divorced from other black people, comprise the abstractions and sociological generalizations that, even today, dominate much of mainstream American media, including theatre and film. For those who control these media, these anti-realist depictions of the oppressed must remain generalized and abstract. Realism, or realistic strategies when applied to blacks, as Baldwin has suggested, could lead to a self-examination that it is the American habit to almost religiously avoid; that way lies "chaos," given America's deep and historic ambiguities about race, ethnicity, gender, morality, and even democracy itself. We all would rather go to the mall.

Thus, for the overwhelming majority of black audiences, it is an extraordinary, even an *avant-garde,* event in the American theatre when black characters in a realistic scene actually talk honestly to each other about something that really matters to them, something that is other than a rephrasing or subtextual expression of their history of oppression. From a traditional African American point of view, these anti-realists are but a wing of white mainstream ideology, vying for control with mainstream realists, who have themselves, for the most part, imposed anti-realist strategies on the black theatre and drama presented in mainstream venues. And the realists' defection to anti-realism, when it concerns black subject matter, confirms the black suspicion that anti-realism is, in fact, even better equipped than is the realism to avoid, distort, or completely ignore the largely humanist objectives in black drama. To be sure, there are black anti-realists in the theatre, but their work in no way commands the attention of any considerable black audience. These artists are, as we have seen throughout this history of black dramatic theory, for the most part, middle class blacks who have either absorbed the latest fashions from the Euro-American *avant-garde,* or worse, are practicing what they call a "non-traditional art" in the name of a historically traditional African and black American culture.

On a theoretical level the subject of African American realism takes on more complex features. Isadore Okpewho writes that Western critics have almost universally misinterpreted as "abstract" those features in African art that depict what Africans have designed as representations of a "second level of realism."[14] In fact, Kennedy, in *Funnyhouse of a Negro,* fusing the moods of Symbolism, the existential concerns of Absurdism, the Surrealist features of stage lighting and properties design, and Futurist alogical dialogue strategies, may have actually reached this African "second level of realism." Consequently, Kennedy's amalgam of essentially European *avant-garde* aesthetic practices and her possibly African results may make the distinctions between the Euro-American notion of the abstract in art and the African one of second level realism appear slight. But Kennedy's results were almost certainly fortuitously accidental and unconscious. For Okpewho, there is a vast theoretical difference between what is called "abstract" and second level realism.

To begin with, abstract art, in its more accessible incarnations, assumes that the real world is a mundane cloak that hides important and vital understandings about life and existence. It analyzes, dissects and often reconfigures real objects, as they are perceived in real time and space. For example, Picasso uses cubism, in part, to demonstrate that objects in reality have more planes than we are physically able to perceive. A Matisse still life bends the far rim of a teacup to the viewer so that the cup can be seen in a way it could never be perceived in real life. In this sense, much of what is called abstract art tries to mitigate the distance between the limitations of human perception and the complete properties of objects as they actually exist. In fact, this idea is prevalent, too, in ancient Egyptian art. While farmers, laborers, the ordinary members of Egyptian society, were painted in realistic perspective, royalty and other principal figures in Egyptian society are most often depicted with their torsos and one eye painted frontally and head and often legs in profile. The idea is to paint as much of the human being as possible, that is, without destroying all notions of realism. Real people have tops, bottoms, fronts, backs, and profiles. The Egyptians, in painting their lofty personages, unlike Picasso, settled for two of these planes rather than all of them. In abstract art, as the artist seeks to depict the effects of human emotion and thought, the artwork will generally become a progressively greater abstraction of reality.

The assumption at the core of the creation of abstract art is the dichotomy between the real and unreal; they are separate contrasting entities. Abstract art, by its own lights, exists because it abstracts reality and becomes something that emits a truth or a resonance that reality obscures. But in the African notion of art, according to Okpewho, there are only levels of realism; there is no acknowledgment of the existence of the unreal; all things are real and depicted in levels of realism. Cultures that include the dead in the realm of the real have difficulty characterizing what is unreal. All is real; but human perception, unless assisted by religion or art, will remain at the first level of reality. The assumption that there are realities that exist beyond human perception, on a second level of realism, is the same as in abstract art; but because the notion of levels of realities banishes the concept of the unreal, when it is carried to its logical conclusion, it does not produce abstract art. It produces in literature and the dramatic arts what has been called "magical realism": A man of late middle age sits in his living room; his mother enters, though she has been dead for thirty years, and begins chastising him about the way he has been mistreating his oldest daughter. The man takes no notice of his mother as a ghost, but speaks to her just as he would have when she was alive. The man and his mother are both representations of reality; she represents one level of reality, he another, and, if this is a scene in a play, any "abstract" manipulation of sets, lighting, or costume would severely diminish the central assumption at the core of this kind of dramatic art, which is that in the cosmos there are only levels of reality, and that there is nothing that can be reasonably termed the unreal or beyond the definition of one of the levels of reality.

In black American culture this African notion of levels of reality or levels of realism has been spectacularly displayed in the literature of Toni Morrison, which is generally accepted as an interpretation of traditional black American culture. In a very real sense, it is the viability of these equally real levels of reality that effects the synthesizing of the seemingly implacable dichotomies of Judeo–Christian ideologies as practiced in the West: right and wrong, good and evil, purity and sexuality, etc. It bears repeating that this synthesizing process is represented by the Nigerian god *Eshu*, the humor and sadness in the Blues and in other black American music forms, and in "black English"; all contain expressions of the viability of different levels of reality and provide little, if any, space for what is said to be unreal. Speakers of Black English have, for example, used expressions in which, with the correct intonation, "bad" means "good," and "it's the bomb" does not characterize its subject as an explosive disaster but rather as something explosively good or excellent.

This black American penchant for validating different, seemingly opposing levels of reality and fusing them into a single statement is a process that extends deep into the history of African art. A bas-relief of *The Abydos Passion Play* in the tomb of Seti I reveals Horus, the son of Isis and Osiris, depicted as a full-grown man assisting at his own conception. Isis administers to Osiris who is prone, "lying ithyphallic," symbolizing male fertility and that, at this moment, Horus is being conceived. As in Magical Realism, Horus is both an adult and is being conceived.[15] Linear time has been banished. This fusion of the seemingly inverse ideas that one can be an adult and conceived at the same time makes the statement that the ultimate cosmic form is a circle, not a Euclidian line segment, that there is no straight path from birth to adulthood to death. In the act of giving life to his son, Osiris is resurrected; he had been dead, slain by his brother. So Osiris is inscribed with the cycle of life, death, and rebirth. All of which means, of course, as Aristotle would find much later, that all is representational, mimetic, repeated. As in Derrida's deconstruction of Artaud, there is no "first time," no original moment or thought. In traditional

African American art, these assumptions lead to a simple celebration of existence, of being, in an Osirian and later Dionysian duality-ridden world, and these Africanisms, synthesized dichotomies, are observable in contemporary Black English of the 1980s and '90s.

Future Studies and a Final Word About Humanism

While it is hoped that this book has moved the discourse on black dramatic theory closer to the realization of a twenty-first century black aesthetic of drama, the actual establishment of such an aesthetic relies on similar investigations into the remaining thirty-five years of the twentieth century. In this regard, of particular interest is what appears to be Baraka's new internationalist form of socialist multiculturalism and cultural materialism. Indications of this trend in his thinking can be found in his "The International Business of Jazz and the Need for the Cooperative and Collective Self Development of an International Peoples' Culture" (1998).[16] Bhikhu Parekh's *Rethinking Multiculturalism* should also begin to provide some answers to the issue of how black dramatic theory can situate itself within a culturally diverse environment without losing its specificity. Further, when we look at the influence that the plays and other writings of black women (Grimké, Eulalie Spence, Alice Childress, and Hansberry) have had in shaping the first sixty-five years of twentieth-century black drama, at least a familiarity with black feminism seems a necessary step in establishing a viable aesthetic of black drama. Writings by bell hooks, Stanlie James, Delores Williams, and Reverend Katie Cannon will likely provide an adequate introduction to the field. An offshoot of black feminism, "womanism," of which Reverend Cannon is the founder, is likely to have particular importance to any black theory of art. Cannon founded the Womanist Movement based on the writings of the Pulitzer prize-winning author Alice Walker.[17] Womanism appears to make a heavy investment in Locke's beloved black folk culture and in a form of Christianity that revises the faith's male-dominant ideologies.

The 1980s theoretical work of Herbert Blau should also be of interest to future black theatre theorists. Consistent with Derrida's deconstructions of Artaud, Blau's investigations in "The Universals of Performance; or Amortizing Play,"[18] amount to, in part, an affirmation of the "no first time" assumptions in Aristotelian *mimesis* and in the African concept of "levels of realism" in art that fuse opposite or inverse ideas. Blau's work is particularly useful because the biological issues of life and death that have been treated here are central to his conclusions. These issues, the source of the duality embedded in black traditional culture, both in America and in Africa, point to a need for a comprehensive investigation into what has been termed the Africanisms in black American culture. A review of the field might begin with works that have been cited here: Melvin Herskovits' *The Myth of the Negro Past*, Joseph Holloway's *Africanisms in American Culture*, Robert Pelton's *The Trickster in West Africa*, Sandra Barnes' *Africa's Ogun: Old World and New*, and Theophus Smith's *Conjuring Culture: Biblical Formations of Black America*. Herskovits' study has, in many ways, laid the foundation for this field of African American studies.

The consistent biological significances fundamental to traditional black art from ancient Egypt's *Abydos Passion Play* (1868 B.C.) to the Blues have been historically considered, by some, a form of primitivism. For example, S.G.F. Brandon, writing about ancient Egypt, finds that "the primitive mind would naturally have thought of the beginning of things in terms of biological birth."[19] Lucie Lamy provides an explanation of this practice in her description of the bas-relief of *The Abydos Passion Play* that depicts the conception of the god Horus. Lamy writes that Horus is an "eternal principle," which is what permits him to assist at his own conception. By reviving and sexually arousing Osiris and thereby conceiving Horus, Isis gains for her husband not only eternal life but also what Lamy calls "liberation from the incessant cycles of death and rebirth."[20]

When biological elements in traditional black cultures are looked on as metaphors for how the universe works, they are revealed as being far from primitive. In fact, it can be argued that this way of constructing meaning, with its inverse truths and lack of linear theoretical models, is closely related to contemporary scientific method. This biological or physical interpretation of a cosmos of inverse truths is, for example, consistent with a universe in which all lines bend in infinity and resolve into circles, in which, as Lamy points out, light is considered as both waves and as particles, and in which the inverse truths of Chaos Theory, random behavior and infinitely repetitive pattern, are clearly depicted in fractal geometry. On the other hand, Brandon's seemingly "higher minded," non-primitive set of beliefs that relegate the biological to something that has nothing to do with advanced human thinking has constructed a rigid, dichotomous cosmos, almost totally inconsistent with contemporary scientific findings. Accordingly, the British biologist Rupert Sheldrake has proposed an alternative to the anti-biological model that Brandon seems to believe in and that so much of postmodern thought infers. In *A New Science of Life: The Hypothesis of Morphic Resonance*,[21] Sheldrake proposes a kind of cellular consciousness for all living matter. Moreover, he argues that past forms within a species, through what he calls "morphic resonance," influence the behavior of the living forms of that species across space and time. Sheldrake's assumptions are almost startlingly consistent with what has been discussed here about the biological nature of Egyptian and, ultimately West African cosmological design, especially what has been pejoratively termed "ancestor worship" in African and other traditional cultures around the world.

In the United States, slavery and the system of segregation that followed it, tended to reinforce rather than obliterate the African assumptions about the relationship between past and present generations; in such systems, a greater than usual emphasis is placed on future generations, since the present ones have no hope of attaining the simplest of human pleasures and freedoms within their own lifetimes. As with the ancestral assumptions in African *orisa* beliefs and with Osiris, American slaves and their immediate descendants could not have maintained their humanity without a belief system that connected the living and dead, and in which black people saw their own immortality in the birth of their children. Again, this is why many Negroes thought that Grimké's play, *Rachel*, was nothing less than reprehensible. Thus, for those interested in a black theory of drama based on black American cultural history, a further investigation of Sheldrake's work could prove extraordinarily useful.

A final word: In the sixty-five-year history of black dramatic theory, humanism seems to be the unifying element motivating thinkers and practitioners in the field. On both sides of the art or propaganda debate the concerns are for the state of black humanity. While this book has argued that for the purposes of an art form, the propaganda side of the debate has too often and too severely reduced black Inner Life concerns to sociological and political generalizations, the fact remains that propaganda strategies did address the historical inequities imposed on the majority of black Americans. The contemporary world, with its September Eleventh attacks and thousands dying daily from poverty, hatreds, and counter hatreds, the natural historical results of two centuries of colonialism and *de facto* colonialism, is desperately in need of a large dose of humanism. As we have seen, historical black culture is humanist to the point that the gods themselves behave as humans; human sexuality is seen as a metaphor for the secret workings of the universe; time can only be measured by human agency; and jazz, arguably, the most matured form of black music, grounds much of its composing and performance strategies in an African call-and-refrain improvisation style, a musical interpretation of human communication. Given the depth of this millennial devotion to humanism, the establishment of a theatre able to produce the "unique and specific Black art," that August Wilson has called for may not be just a momentous occasion in black theatre history but also a spiritual boon to a country and a world very much in need of it. But finally, no such theatre is possible without an equally unique and specific theory of African American dramatic art.

Chapter Notes

Introduction

1. See James Hatch's "Theatre in Historically Black Colleges," in Annemarie Bean, ed., *A Sourcebook of African-American Performance: Plays, People, Movements* (London and New York: Routledge, 1999), 150–51, and William Edgar Easton, *Dessalines: A Dramatic Tale* (Boston: J.W. Burson-Company, Publishers, 1893), author's dedication cover page.
2. Kenneth R. Manning, *Black Apollo of Science: The Life of Ernest Everrett Just* (New York and Oxford: Oxford University Press, 1983), 20–31, 40, contains a fuller discussion of Just's educational career.
3. See William Edgar Easton, *Dessalines*, vi, vii, for the citations of Easton. See Samuel A. Hay, *African American Theatre: An Historical and Critical Analysis* (Cambridge and New York: Cambridge University Press, 1994), 136–38, for detailed information on Hewlett and Aldridge, and see Herbert Marshall and Mildred Stock, *Ira Aldridge: The Negro Tragedian* (Carbondale: Southern Illinois University Press, 1968) for an excellent biography of Aldridge.
4. See Eric J. Sundquist, ed., *The Oxford W. E. B. Du Bois Reader* (New York and Oxford: Oxford University Press, 1996), 305. See also Roy Strong, *Art and Power: Renaissance Festivals, 1450–1650* (Woodbridge, Suffolk, U.K.: Boydell Press, 1984); Sondra Kathryn Wilson, ed. "Shakespeare," in *The Selected Writings of James Weldon Johnson*, vol. 1 (New York and Oxford: Oxford University Press, 1995), 254–56, and Alain Locke, "The Drama of Negro Life," *Theatre Arts Monthly* 10 (October 1926): 701–6, rpt. in Jeffrey C. Stewart, *The Critical Temper of Alain Locke: A Selection of his Essays on Art and Culture* (New York: Garland Publishing, 1983), 89; the italics in the next citation of Locke are mine.
5. (Urbana and Chicago: University of Illinois, 1993), 2–5, contains the next citations of Hatch used here concerning Dodson's background and gives a fuller discussion about his parents. For Dodson's *Divine Comedy*, see James V. Hatch, ed., *Black Theatre USA: 45 Plays by Black Americans, 1847–1974* (New York: Free Press, 1974), 322–49.
6. Owen Dodson, "Playwrights with Dark Glasses," *Negro Digest*, April 1968, 32, 34.
7. But all of the "classical" elements of the *Abydos Passion Play*, i.e., a so-called linear chronology, and a hero's quest adventure in the form of the "female" hero Isis, must be derived from a careful study of the subject; they cannot be legitimately inferred from what is historically the most well known version of the drama, Plutarch's *De Iside et Osirde*. In Eberhard Otto, *Egyptian Art and the Cults of Osiris and Amon* (London: Thames and Hudson, 1968), 61, Otto warns that Plutarch's account of the play was taken from the "eastern world of the Mediterranean and the Greeks," and that "the myth of Osiris as he [Plutarch] knew it contained a number of non–Egyptian traits."
8. August Wilson, "The Ground on Which I Stand," *American Theatre*, September 1996, 71–72.
9. W.E.B. Du Bois, *The Souls of Black Folk* (first published Atlanta, Ga.: A.C. McClurg, 1903; New York: First Vantage Books/Library of America Edition, 1990), 36–37.
10. See Thomas Cripps, *Slow Fade to Black: The Negro in American Film, 1900–1942* (New York, London, and Oxford: Oxford University Press, 1977), 72–75, for Washington's interest and involvement in film production.
11. Hatch, *Black Theatre USA: Forty-Five Plays by Black Americans*, 61–99.
12. See David Levering Lewis, *When Harlem Was in Vogue* (New York: Vintage Books, 1979), 260–61, for the *Mule Bone* controversy, and Reuben Silver, "A History of the Karamu Theatre of Karamu House, 1915–1960" (Ph.D. diss., University Microfilms, Ann Arbor, Mich., 1961), 501 and 505 for the 1930s stagings of *Sermon in the Valley*.
13. Robert Brustein, "Subsidized Separatism. View of A. Wilson," *The New Republic*, 216 (Au-

gust 1996): 39–42; Wilson, "The Ground on Which I Stand," 14–16, 71–73, and Robert Brustein, "Subsidized Separation with Discussion," *American Theatre* 13 (October 1996): 26–27.

14. "Culture Shock: The Grudge Match as *Kulturkampf*—Extreme Fighting," *New York Village Voice*, 28 January 1997, 46; here, too, are columnist Richard Goldstein's characterizations of Wilson's "celebrity" and Brustein's "contentiousness." The next citation of Wilson is taken from "From Page to Stage: Race and the Theatre," *New York Times*, 22 January 1997, C14.

15. Brander Matthews, *Development of the Drama* (New York, 1903), 16, and cited in Marvin Carlson, *Theories of the Theatre: A Historical and Critical Survey, from the Greeks to the Present*, expanded ed. (Ithaca and London: Cornell University Press, 1993), 310; here, too, is the next citation of Carlson. Also see W.E.B. Du Bois, *The Souls of Black Folk* (Atlanta, Ga., 1903; reprint ed. New York: Library of America, 1986), 8–9.

16. Sandra L. Richards, "Sweet Meat From Leroi" (Ph.D. diss., Stanford University, 1979), 77.

17. All of these studies are in Joseph E. Holloway, ed., *Africanisms in American Culture* (Bloomington: Indiana University Press, 1991). Holloway's work here is based on the pioneering study in this field that introduced the retention argument, Melville J. Herkovits, *The Myth of the Negro Past*.

18. The apparent exception to the rule is Symbolism, the art movement which gained notice in the theatre shortly after the rise of Chehkovian psychological realism in the early twentieth century. But early Symbolism was heavily influenced by Japanese aesthetic thought.

19. See Ardencie Hall, "New Orleans Jazz Funerals: Transition to the Ancestors" (Ph.D. diss., New York University, 1998).

20. In Hatch, *Black Theatre USA*, 34–58; here, too, 225, is the next citation of Hatch.

21. Lewis, *When Harlem Was in Vogue*, 10–11.

22. Joel Elias Spingarn, *Creative Criticism* (New York, 1931), 31, and cited in Carlson, *Theories of the Theatre*, 312; here, too, 311, 312, are the citations of Carlson; Spingarn, *Creative Criticism*, 22; and the citations from Benedetto Croce, *Aesthetics*, trans. Douglas Ainslie (London, 1929), 116.

23. Larry Neal, "The Black Arts Movement," *The Drama Review*, Summer 1968, 30.

Chapter I

1. In Thomas L. Riis, *Just before Jazz: Black Musical Theatre in New York, 1890 to 1915* (Washington, D.C., and London: Smithsonian Institution Press, 1989), 76, Riis reports that *Coontown* had actually been "written by August, 1897 and was given a trial run in South Amboy, New Jersey, on 17 September 1897." Also see Allen Woll, *Black Musical Theatre: From Coontown to Dreamgirls* (Baton Rouge and London: Louisiana State University Press), 10, and David Krasner, *Resistance, Parody, and Double Consciousness in African American Theatre, 1895–1910* (New York: St. Martin's Press, 1997), 55. Here, Krasner indicates *Jes Lak White Fo'ks'* connections to *In Dahomey*.

2. *Along This Way: The Autobiography of James Weldon Johnson* (New York: Viking Penguin, 1933; reprint. ed. Viking Compass Edition, 1968), 173; here, too, is the preceding citation from Johnson.

3. Samuel A. Hay, *African American Theatre: An Historical and Critical Analysis* (Cambridge: Cambridge University Press, 1994), 21, has a discussion of the opposing "Outer" and "Inner" life strategies of Du Bois and Locke, respectively.

4. James Weldon Johnson, *Black Manhattan* (New York, 1930; rpt ed., New York: Arno Press, 1968), 102; *Dramatic Mirror*, 9 April 1898, Theatre Collection of Houghton Library, Harvard University, *A Trip to Coontown* folder.

5. Riis, *Just before Jazz*, 76; here, too, 6, is Riis' next citation of Cole.

6. *Dramatic Mirror*, 9 April 1898, Harvard Theatre Collection, *A Trip to Coontown* folder.

7. *Resistance, Parody, and Double Consciousness in African American Theatre*, 32; this and all my citations of Krasner on the subject of Cole's whiteface performance are taken from his discussion of that issue, 30–33.

8. Mel Watkins, *On the Real Side: Laughing, Lying, and Signifying—The Underground Tradition of African-American Humor That Transformed American Culture, from Slavery to Richard Pryor* (New York: Simon and Schuster, 1994), 150, 167, and 169 contains Watkins' discussion of Cole's Willie Wayside.

9. Krasner, *Resistance, Parody, and Double Consciousness*, 31, and cited from an unidentified clipping, 6 February 1900, Grand Opera House, Harvard Theatre Collection; italics mine.

10. Watkins, *On the Real Side*, 169.

11. The reasons for this affinity have already been taken up in our discussion of Post-Slavery Classicism. Later, an examination of *Kongo* and *Bakongo* oratorical gestures and their relation to the performance of the traditional African American folktale *Stagolee* will expand this specific topic.

12. Otto, *Egyptian Art and the Cults of Osiris and Amon*, 26–30, has a discussion of Osiris as a god who embodies the seeming opposites of spirituality and sexuality, fertility and death. In

Sandra T. Barnes, ed., *Africa's Ogun: Old World and New* (Bloomington: Indiana University Press, 1989), 84, is a brief discussion of the characteristics of *Eshu*. Also, for *Eshu's* good and trickster aspects, see Robert D. Pelton, *The Trickster in West Africa: A Study of Mythic Irony and Sacred Delight* (Berkeley and Los Angeles: University of California Press, 1980), 133–42.

13. Will Marion Cook, *Jes Lak White Fo'ks* libretto, title page, Library of Congress, Washington, D.C.; copy in Hatch-Billops Collection, New York. Here, the title page indicates that the play has "additional lyrics by Paul Lawrence Dunbar." But the size and boldness of Dunbar's name makes one who is aware of the promotional value of "big names" in the theatre wonder just how many "additional lyrics" Dunbar actually wrote. Cook's first musical, the "rousing" success *Clorindy or the Origin of the Cakewalk*, opened three months after *Coontown* at the Casino Roof Garden (July 1898). The book for this work, written by Paul Lawrence Dunbar, was totally excised so as not to strain the attention span of Roof Garden's late night audiences. This reduced the work, reports Woll, to little more than a "musical sketch," and therefore of little use in a discussion of dramatic theory. For more on *Clorindy* see Woll, *Black Musical Theatre*, 7–10, and Riis, *Just before Jazz*, 79–81.

14. See Riis, *Just before Jazz*, "Will Marion Cook," 40–43; here, too, is the next citation from Cook's *Jes Lak White Fo'ks*.

15. In 1938, Cook's critique of the turn-of-the-century American *nouveaux riches* was vividly supported in American literature by D. Appleton-Century's publication of Edith Wharton's (1862–1937) novel *The Buccaneers* (1938); Wharton was critical of the new American industrial aristocracy since she was herself a descendant of the "old money" American upper class who had gained international prominence in business and art in the "gilded age," just after the Civil War; see John Updike, "Reworking Wharton," *The New Yorker*, October 1993, 199.

16. Krasner, *Resistance, Parody, and Double Consciousness*, 58–62.

17. Cook, *Jes Lak White Fo'ks* libretto, 6; italics mine.

18. Allan H. Sommerstein, trans. *Aristophanes: The Acharnians, The Clouds, Lysistrata*, "Introductory Note to *The Acharnians*" (New York: Penguin Books, 1973), 42. Here, Sommerstein reports that the "scathing indictments of Athenian politicians and policies" in Aristophanes' *The Babylonians* (424 B.C.) resulted in Cleon, Athens' leading politician, "prosecuting" the author "on a charge of 'slandering the City in the presence of foreigners'" and Creon "apparently, secured a conviction" of Aristophanes on this charge.

19. Bernard F. Dukore, *Dramatic Theory and Criticism*, "The Birth of Tragedy," by Friedrich Nietzsche (New York: Holt, Rinehart and Winston, 1974), 820–26. Here is the selection of Nietzsche's writings on which this discussion of the "Apollonian" and "Dionysian" is based. This selection has been reprinted from Friedrich Nietzsche (1844–1900), *The Birth of Tragedy and The Genealogy of Morals*, trans. Francis Golffing (New York: Doubleday and Co., 1956).

20. *History of Herodotus*, trans. George Rawlinson, in Robert M. Hutchins, editor-in-chief, *Great Books of The Western World*, vol. 6 (Chicago: University of Chicago and Encyclopædia Britannica, Inc., 1952), 59–60.

21. See Cook, *Jes Lak White Fo'ks*, 4, and 5. Also, Cook based this element of his story on an actual Negro "Vassar Girl" of the period, Anita Florence Hemmings who graduated from Vassar College in 1897; see Vassar Scrapbook, vol. 2, Special Collections, Vassar College Library.

22. Cook, *Jes Lak White Fo'ks*, title page, and see Krasner, *Resistance, Parody, and Double Consciousness*, 57, regarding black audience responses to "Zion and God" on the next page.

23. See Theophus H. Smith, *Conjuring Culture: Formations of Black American Religion in America* (New York: Oxford University Press, 1994), 58, for a discussion of the traditional African American practice of "conjuring God" and making one's self "over in the image of the imagery."

24. I met Baldwin in 1968 when I played the role of Richard in the Brooklyn Apollo production of his *Blues for Mister Charlie*. We had several conversations again when our paths crossed in Atlanta, GA, in the early 1980s and I was directing for the Just Us Theatre Company, then the African American division of Atlanta's Theatre of the Stars.

25. Barnes, *Africa's Ogun*, 206–10, and John S. Mbiti, *African Religions and Philosophies* (Garden City, New York: Anchor Books, 1970), 224–31, contain fuller discussions of West African religious possession practices.

26. Mbiti, *African Religions and Philosophies*, 22–23. Here, too, 21–22, see the earlier citation of Mibiti, and in his chapter entitled "The Concept of Time," 19–36, he launches into an illuminating discussion of the prevailing concepts of time in traditional Africa. Also, 107–19, is the source for the orisa's pantheon relationship to humanity.

27. Krasner, *Resistance, Parody, and Double Consciousness*, 57; see Lovell, "The Social Implications of the Negro Spiritual," in Bernard Katz, ed., *The Social Implications of Early Negro Music in the United States* (New York: Arno Press, 1969), 134–35.

28. Cook, *Jes lak White Fo'ks*, 8, is the next citation of Cook's Pompous; here, too is Pompous' rejection of the prince. Also, in Riis,

Just before Jazz, 80–81, Riis reports on George Walker and Bert Williams' October 1899 opening of the *Policy Players*, a "musical farce" ostensibly based on "number playing" at the Star Theatre at 13th street and Broadway after Cook's summer opening that year of *Jes Lak White Fo'ks*.

29. See *Abyssinia*, Jessie Shipp and Alex Rogers, book and lyrics; Will Marion Cook and Bert A. Williams, music; Library of Congress, 31, for the citation of Rastas' theme song below.

30. The historical circumstance that an enduring feature of slave systems in Africa, Asia, and in Europe is that they often have their origins in tribal wars in which the leading families (i.e., royalty) of losing factions are enslaved, if not killed, gives some validity to this nationalist belief; the lyrics cited here are from Cook, *Jes Lak White Fo'ks*, 6.

31. Riis, *Just before Jazz*, 40–43; here, too, is the source for this biographical information on Cook and the next citation from Riis. Also, see Johnson, *Along This Way*, 173, for the next citation, and Cook, *Jes Lak White Fo'ks*, 3, for the dialogue exchange below.

32. See Alfred L. Berheim, *The Business of Theatre: An Economic History of the American Theatre, 1750–1932* (New York: Benjamin Blom, 1932; 2nd ed. 1964), 50–84, for a complete discussion of "the Syndicate" and its battles with the Shubert organization.

33. See Woll, *Black Musical Theatre*, 12, for the battle between Cole and the producers of Black Patti's Troubadors that resulted in a court battle over the ownership of Cole's music.

34. William Foster, "Pioneers of the Stage: Memoirs of William Foster," in Theophilus Lewis, ed., *The Official Theatrical World of Colored Artists* (New York: Theatrical World Publishing Co., 1928), 48; *Age*, 10 August 1911, 6, has the next citation of Walton.

35. See Esedebe, *Pan-Africanism: The Idea and Movement, 1776–1963* (Washington, D.C.: Howard University Press, 1982), 45–47.

36. Riis, *Just before Jazz*, 91, 113.

37. When and where *The Cannibal King* may have been produced, like so much in African American theatre history, maybe lost to posterity. In Riis, *Just before Jazz*, Riis tells us that it was never produced, while in Errol G. Hill and James V. Hatch, *A History of African Theatre* (Cambridge: Cambridge University Press, 2003), 155, Hill writes that the play was "staged" by Bob Cole and Rosamon Johnson but gives no other details. In Johnson, *Along This Way*, 175, Johnson writes that *The Cannibal King* was never completed and that his collaborator and composer, Will Marion Cook, sold the incomplete manuscript and music to an unnamed producer. And, my investigations of other sources, periodicals and other books, have produced no production record for this work. Here, too, Johnson tells how he and Bob Cole got into *The Cannibal King* project.

38. Krasner, *Resistance, Parody, and Double Consciousness*, 63–66, treats *The Cannibal King*. Krasner agrees that *The Cannibal King* is a long-form version of *Jes Lak White Fo'ks*. But the observations below about the "back-to-Africa" plays come primarily from my examination of copies of the Library of Congress' original texts of these plays in the Hatch-Billops Collection, New York; here, too, 64, is the next citation of Krasner.

39. (Cook), Bob Cole, James Weldon Johnson, *The Cannibal King*, Library of Congress, Washington, D.C., 31–32.

40. Woll, *Black Musical Theatre*, 38.

41. The sentiments of unpretentious American social and political superiority had long before *Abyssinia* been expressed in Tom Taylor's (1817–1880) *Our American Cousin: The Play That Changed History*, 1858 (Washington, D.C.: Beacham Publishers, 1990). While Shipp and Rogers may have been drawing on the popularity of Taylor's ideas, it cannot be assumed that this work also inspired Cook. The specifics of Cook's background and education made him a prime candidate to espouse ideas of American democracy's social and political superiority without reference to Taylor's play or the popularity it achieved.

42. Woll, *Black Musical Theatre*, 42.

43. James Weldon Johnson, *Black Manhattan*, 174.

44. *Crisis*, May 1930, 162, and cited in Darwin T. Turner, "W.E.B. Du Bois and the Theory of A Black Aesthetic," *Studies in a Literary Imagination* 7, no 2 (Fall 1974): 18.

45. Riis, *Just before Jazz*, 117, is the source of this quotation, and here, too, 121–22, and in Woll, *Black Musical Theatre*, 46, Riis and Woll report that *Bandana Land* was the most "successful" of the Cook-Williams-Walker musicals. The *Bandana Land* libretto is not extant.

46. Henry T. Sampson, *Blacks in Blackface: A Source Book on Early Black Musical Shows* (Metuchen, NJ & London: Scarecrow Press, 1980), 241.

47. See Bert Williams, "The Comic Side of Trouble," *American Magazine*, January 1918, 33–35, and George Walker, "The Real 'Coon' on the American Stage," *Theatre Magazine*, August 1906, 224.

48. Krasner, *Resistance, Parody and Double Consciousness*, 142.

49. Woll, *Black Musical Theatre*, 24; here, too, 23, is the earlier citation of Woll. Also, for firsthand reports of the love-making taboo for Negro theatre presented in mainstream venues, see Johnson, *Black Manhattan*, 171, and Robert Kimball and William Bolcom, *Reminiscing with*

Sissle and Blake (New York: Viking Press, 1973), 93.

50. For two notable exceptions to this "no black love story" rule see James Baldwin, *The Amen Corner* (New York: Dial Press, 1968), and Richard Wright, translated from the original play by Louis Sapin, *Daddy Goodness* (New York: Hart Multi-Copy, 1968).

51. *Blacking Up: The Minstrel Show in Nineteenth-Century America* (New York: Oxford University Press, 1974), 120.

52. See Samuel Hay, *African American Theatre*, 241n.14, 18–19.

53. See George A. Thompson, *A Documentary History of the African Theatre* (Evanston, Ill.: Northwestern University Press, 1998), 36; George C.D. Odell, *Annals of the New York Stage* (New York: Columbia University Press, 1928), 70–71, and I.E. Kirby and C.I. Martin, *The Rise and Fall of the Black Caribs* (Kingston, St. Vincent: St. Vincent and Grenadines National Trust, 1997).

54. Hay, *African American Theatre*, 10, 11, 239n.22, contain the discussion from which this information on Brown, The African Grove Theatre, and Brown's *The Drama of King Shotaway* is taken.

55. Jack D. Forbes, *Africans and Native Americans: The Language of Race and the Evolution of the Red-Black peoples* (Urbana: University of Illinois Press, 1993), 189.

56. Walton, "The Awakening," *New York Age*, 6 May 1909, 6.

57. The financial and artistic success of *The Red Moon* is reported in the *New York Dramatic Mirror*, 15 May 1909: 3; James Weldon Johnson, *Black Manhattan*, 109; Ann Charters, *Nobody: The Story of Bert Williams*, (London: Collier-Macmillan, 1970), 95; Woll, *Black Musical Theatre*, 27, and in Riis, *Just before Jazz*, 140.

58. See Charles F. Kellogg, vol. 1, *NAACP: A History of the National Association for the Advancement of Colored People, 1909–1920* (Baltimore: Johns Hopkins University Press, 1967), 145, has comments on *Rachel* as a response to *Birth of Nation* with the supporting evidence of the NAACP Board Minutes of 13 March 1916, 9 April 1917, and 14 May 1917, cited in n. 24. Also, Hatch, *Black Theatre USA, 137*, reports that Rachel was the first full-length African American straight drama produced in the United States. Here, too, 36–58, and, 34, respectively, is Brown's play, *The Escape or Leap to Freedom*, and this citation of Hatch.

59. Hopkins' writings include the musical dramas, *Aristocracy* (1877), *Peculiar Sam, or the Underground Railroad* (1879), and *Winona* (1878). For more on Hopkins see Claudia Tate, "Pauline Hopkins: Our Literary Foremother," in Marjorie Pryse and Hortense J. Spillers, eds., *Conjuring: Black Women, Fiction, and Literary Tradition* (Bloomington: Indiana University Press, 1985); Anne A. Shockley, "Pauline Elizabeth Hopkins: A Biographical Excursion into Obscurity," *Phylon* 33 (1972): 22–26, and see Hopkins' papers at Fisk University Library in Nashville, Tenn.

60. Hatch, *Black Theatre USA*, 137.

61. For the romantic issues in these protest plays see William Wells Brown, *The Escape: or Leap to Freedom*, Act I, Scene iii and Pauline Elizabeth Hopkins, *Peculiar Sam, or The Underground Railroad*, Act I, both in Hamalian and Hatch, *The Roots of African American Drama*, 50–52; and 102–4, respectively; see Angelina Weld Grimké, *Rachel*, Act III, in Hatch, *Black Theatre USA*, 169–72.

62. "The Place of the Negro in the Evolution of the American Theatre," Ph.D. diss., Yale University, 1945, 343 has the first citation of Belcher here, and here, too, 341, 340, 343, 340n.1, respectively, Belcher cites Abbie Mitchell's recollection of Green "as one of the best the race has produced," and also records that some of the "white shows" were Bronson Howard's *Young Mrs. Winthrop* (1882), C. Haddon Chambers' *Captain Swift* (1888), and Paul Potter's *Trilby* (1895).

63. Also, see Sister M. Francesca Thompson, O.S.F., "The Lafayette Players, 1915–1932," in Errol Hill, ed., *The Theatre of Black Americans: A Collection of Critical Essays* (New York: Applause Theatre Book Publishers, 1987), 211–30.

64. Philip S. Foner, ed. *W.E.B. Du Bois Speaks: Speeches and Addresses, 1890–1919* (New York: Pathfinder Press, 1970), 227; the information and citations for *The Star of Ethiopia* are in Hay, *African American Theatre*, 2–3.

65. "The Negro in Literature and Art," *Annals* (September 1913), rpt. in Meyer Weinberg, *W.E.B. Du Bois: A Reader* (New York: Harper and Row, 1970), 231.

66. "The Drama among Black Folk," *Crisis* 12 (August 1916): 169, has the previous citation of Du Bois; here too, 171, is the next citation of Du Bois. Also, in Europe the drama became secular only as a result of bloody religious controversies between Catholics and Protestants. Elizabeth I banned plays on religious subjects in 1559, a year after she was crowned, ending the presentation of England's medieval Cycle plays.

67. *African American Theatre*, 3–4.

68. Locke to Archibald Grimké, undated, Alain Locke Papers, the Moorland-Spingarn Research Center, Howard University, Washington, D.C.

69. "Steps toward a Negro Theatre," *Crisis*, December 1922, 67.

70. "Reactions of a 'Highly-Strung Girl': Psychology and Dramatic Representation in An-

gelina W. Grimké's *Rachel*," *African American Review* 27, no. 3 (1993): 462; here, too, 463, is the next citation of Storm.

71. Schopenhauer, however, finds in tragedy the struggle between individual will and universal will futile, since they are manifestations of the same thing. See Arthur Schopenhauer, trans. R.B. Haldane and J. Kemp, *The World as Will and Idea* (London: Trübner & Co., 1883), reprinted in Dukore, *Dramatic Theory and Criticism*, 516. Also, see Carlson, *Theories of the Theatre*, 191–92.

72. See Otto, *Ancient Egyptian Art*, 28–29, and Oscar G. Brockett, *History of the Theatre*, 5th ed. (Boston: Allyn and Bacon, 1987), 10–11.

73. Storm, "Reactions of a 'Highly-Strung Girl,'" 463; here, too, is next citation of Storm.

74. "*Rachel*: The Play of the Month — The Reason and Synopsis by the Author," *Competitor*. 1 (January 1920): 52.

75. Gloria T. Hull, *Color, Sex, and Poetry: Three Women Writers of the Harlem Renaissance* (Bloomington and Indianapolis: Indiana University Press, 1987), 119–21, is the source for the information about the play and my citations of Hull on this page. Here, too, 225n.35, indicates that Graves' review was printed in the program of *Rachel's* New York performance (April 1917) and published in the *Washington Post*, 19 March 1917. I could find no such review in the *Washington Post*, suggesting that Graves's review may have been written especially for *Rachel's* New York opening as a promotional device; also, on 121, and 122, are the next citations of Hull.

76. Locke to Archibald Grimké, undated, Alain Locke Papers.

77. Locke to Grimké, Alain Locke Papers, has all my citations from Locke on this page. And, again, due to the scarcity of extant Negro dramas of the period, I have been unable to find any of the plays that Locke writes "had already been done."

78. Hull, *Color, Sex, and Poetry*, 120; here, too, are the next quotations from Hull.

79. *Rachel*: The Play of the Month," *Competitor*, January 1920, 51.

80. Archibald Grimké and his siblings were the children of the prominent South Carolinian Henry Grimké and his slave Nancy Weston Grimké. See Hull, *Color, Sex, and Poetry*, 107–10, 115 for more on Angelina Grimké's family background and education.

81. For ithyphallic gods see Otto, *Ancient Egyptian Art*, 69, plates 15–17. And in Pelton, *The Trickster in West Africa*, 283, Pelton writes that *Eshu*'s power of "touching nothing and finding joy reveals" the "moving power of an ordinary human life. In trickster myths this energy appears as a passion for [sexual] intercourse" that is too all encompassing to be described as mere lust. Thus, *Eshu* has a huge and permanent erection and is properly depicted ithyphallically.

82. "*Rachel*: The Play of the Month," *Competitor* 1 (January 1920): 51.

83. Carlton W. and Barbara J. Molette, *Black Theatre: Premise and Presentation*, 2nd ed. (Bristol, IN: Wyndham Hall Press, 1986), 1; and Michael Pinkney, "African-American Dramatic Theory as Subject of Cultural studies," Ph.D. diss., Ohio State University, 1999, ii, 3–4; Krasner's pertinent work has already been cited a number times in this chapter.

84. Du Bois, *The Souls of Black Folk*, 8–9.

Chapter II

1. Du Bois, "Returning Soldiers" *Crisis*, 1919, reprinted in Sundquist, *The Oxford W.E.B. Du Bois Reader*, 380–81. And Lewis, *When Harlem Was in Vogue*, 8–10, has the previous citations.

2. See *They That Sit in Darkness* in Hatch, *Black Theatre USA*, 178–83, and Burrill's *Aftermath* in Hamalian and Hatch, *The Roots of African American Drama*, 134–51. Cotter's *On the Fields of France* is in James V. Hatch and Leo Hamalian, eds., *The Lost Plays of the Harlem Renaissance, 1920–1940* (Detroit: Wayne State University Press, 1996), 21–25. Nelson's *Mine Eyes Have Seen* is in Hatch, *Black Theatre USA*, 173–77.

3. The previous citations from the *Crisis* are in Du Bois, "Negro Writers," *Crisis* 19 (April 1920): 298–99, and Du Bois, "Negro Art," *Crisis*, June 1921, rpt in Weinberg, *W.E.B. Du Bois: A Reader*, 240. "The Emperor Jones," *Negro World*, June 4, 1921, 6, rpt. in Perry, *A Hubert Harrison Reader*, 378–83; here, too, are all the next quotations of Harrison and O'Neill.

4. "Negro Art," *Crisis*, June 1921, 55–56. Italics mine.

5. Dyson, *Howard University, The Capstone of Negro Education — A History: 1867–1940* (Washington, D.C.: Graduate School Howard University, 1941), 147; here, too, 148 and 149, respectively, are the next citations from Dyson, and a record of the presentation of Fitch's *The Truth*, Dunsany's *Tents of the Arabs*, Torrence's *Simon, The Cyrenian*, and O'Neill's *The Emperor Jones*. The previous and next citations of Locke are in "Steps toward a Negro Theatre," *Crisis*, December 1922, 66.

6. Dyson, *Howard University, The Capstone of Negro Education*, 149; here, too, is the next citation of Du Bois; also see *Danse Calinda*, in Alain Locke and Montgomery Gregory, eds., *Plays of Negro Life: A Source-book of Native American Drama* (New York: Harper, 1927), 373–86; see *Genefriede* in Willis Richardson and May Miller, eds., *Negro History in Thirteen Plays* (Washington, D.C.: Associated Publishers, 1935), 220–37.

7. *The Yellow Tree*, Howard University Moorland-Spingarn Library, Character Page, and 2, 7–9, are the sources for this discussion of Beausey's play.

8. Hatch, *Black Theatre USA*, 218; here, too, 219–24, is Toomer's play, the source of the following discussion along with Richardson's *Mortgaged* in Arthur P. Davis and Michael W. Peplow, *The New Negro Renaissance* (New York: Holt, Rinehart and Winston, 1975), 103–17. Toomer's best-known work is the novel *Cane* (1923); he was also a poet, essayist and philosopher. For more on Toomer, see *The Oxford Companion to African American Literature*, s.v. Toomer, Jean; Cynthia E. Kerman and Richard Eldridge, *The Lives of Jean Toomer* (Baton Rouge: Louis State University Press, 1987); and Nellie Y. McKay, *Jean Toomer, Artist: A Study of His Life and Work, 1894–1936* (Chapel Hill: University of North Carolina Press, 1984).

9. "The Hope of a Negro Drama," *Crisis*, November 1919, 338–39. Also see *The Chip Woman's Fortune* in Hamalian and Hatch, *The Roots of African American Drama*, 159–85. The Howard Players also produced (1924) *Death Dance*, Thelma Duncan's "African," a student play; see Locke and Gregory, *Plays of Negro Life*, 321–31.

10. Woll, *Black Musical Theatre*, 75. Also, "Max Reinhardt Reads the Negro's Dramatic Horoscope," *Opportunity*, May 1924, 145–46, has the previous and next citations of Reinhardt.

11. Hay, *African American Theatre*, 4; here, too, 21, is the previous citation of Hay.

12. See *Survey Graphic*, 1 March 1925; rpt. in Jeffrey C. Stewart, *The Critical Temper of Alain Locke: A Selection of His Essays on Art and Culture* (New York: Garland Publishers, 1983), 7, 10, respectively, for the previous citations of Locke; here, too, 13 and 9, respectively, are the next citations of Locke, and see Hay, *African American Theatre*, 5, 21, and Julius Lester, ed., *The Seventh Son: The Thought and Writings of W.E.B. Du Bois* (New York: Random House, 1971), 311.

13. Du Bois, instead, gave his attention to the past, contemporary, and potential contributions of Negro acting to American mainstream drama in "Can the Negro Serve the Drama?" *Theatre*, July 1923, rpt. in Weinberg, *W.E.B. Du Bois: A Reader*, 241–46. See Alain Locke, "*Goat Alley*, by Ernest Howard Culbertson," *Opportunity*, February 1923, 30, for the previous citation of Locke in which the italics are mine. Culbertson was a white playwright.

14. *Messenger*, November 1924, 353; here, too, are the next quotations from Richardson. *Opportunity*, October 1924, 310, has the previous citation of Richardson.

15. See "Criteria of Negro Art," *Crisis*, October 1926, in Weinberg, *W.E.B. Du Bois: A Reader*, 258. See Theophilus Lewis, "The Theatre: The Souls of Black Folks: *The Great Gatsby— The Great Emperor— The Great God Brown, Messenger*" (Review), April 1926, 116, and Theodore Kornweibel, Jr., "Theophilus Lewis and the Theatre of the Harlem Renaissance," in Arna Bontemps, ed., *The Harlem Renaissance Remembered* (New York: Dodd Mead, 1972), 171.

16. Freda Scott, "Five African American Playwrights On Broadway, 1923–1929" (Ph.D. diss., City University of New York, 1990), 159, gives the name of *Bill*'s author as John M. Frances.

17. See *The Oxford Companion to African American Literature*, s.v., "Schuyler, George S."; also see Michael W. Peplow, *George S. Schuyler* (Boston: Twayne Publishers, 1980), and Schuyler, "Ethiopian Nights Entertainment" (Review) *Messenger*, November 1924, 342–43. *Opportunity Magazine* was the organ of the National Urban League and, like the *Crisis* and *Messenger*, it was a major Harlem monthly published during the period of the High Harlem Renaissance. The *Crisis*, too, had a literature and art competition, which Du Bois initiated in 1924. For a discussion of the play contests sponsored by these publications see Addell P. Austin, "Pioneering Black Authored Dramas: 1924–1927" (Ph.D. diss., Michigan State University, 1986), 37–72.

18. *Black Moses: The Story of Marcus Garvey and the Universal Negro Improvement Association* (Madison: University of Wisconsin Press, 1955, rpt., 1969), 15–20, is the source for this information; here, too, 3, are the previous and next citations of Cronon.

19. *Marcus Garvey v. United States*, 4F. 2d 974–76 (2d Cir. 1925); Marcus Garvey, *Philosophy and Opinions of Marcus Garvey* (New York: Arno Press, 1968; reprint of 1923 edition), 2:173–77.

20. *New York News*, 7 February 1925, quoted in *Spokesman*, 1:29. The Black Star Line officers indicted with Garvey were not convicted. Only Garvey went to jail. Garvey was considered a subversive in much of the white community and came to be bitterly opposed by most Negro leadership. His conviction may well have been the result of a "get Garvey conspiracy," as has always been maintained by his followers and their descendants. See Cronon, *Black Moses*, 35–36, 103–118, for background on these issues.

21. Garvey, *Philosophy and Opinions*, 2:128; here, too, 1, 10, 29–30, are the next citations of Garvey. And see *Black Moses*, 41, for Cronon's previous citation of Garvey.

22. Locke, "Enter the New Negro," *Survey Graphic*, rpt. in *The Critical Temper of Alain Locke*, 10; here, too, is the next citation of Locke.

23. See Lewis, "Same Old Blues," *Messenger*, January 1925, 14–15, 62; here, too, 14, is the next citation of Lewis, and 23–24, Owen and A. Philip Randolph's (1889–1979) writings. Owen and Randolph, fellow socialists, were the *Mes-

senger's co-editors. Randolph, as head of the Brotherhood of Sleeping Car Porters, organized in 1925, would become the American labor movement's most influential twentieth-century black voice. See Jervis Anderson, *A. Philip Randolph: A Biographical Portrait* (Berkeley: University of California Press, 1990).

24. John Drinkwater (1882–1937) was the Artistic Director of England's Birmingham Repertory Theatre, where *Abraham Lincoln* premiered. See John Drinkwater, *Abraham Lincoln: A Play* (London: Sedgwick and Jackson, 1918), 26, and Heyward Broun's review of the play's New York opening mentioning Gilpin, *New York Tribune*, 16 December 1919, 13; the play opened, 15 December 1919, at the Cort Theatre on Broadway. Benjamin Brawley was a noted African American scholar, educator and critic. See *Oxford Companion to African American Literature*, s.v., Brawley, Benjamin, and see W.E.B. Du Bois, *The Gift of Black Folk* (Boston: Stratford Co., 1924; rpt. ed. Millwood, N.Y.: Kraus-Thomson Organization, 1975), 311.

25. *Messenger*, January 1925, 14; here, too, are the next two quotations of Lewis, and he also writes that Gilpin was in *The Old Man's Boy* before the Lafayette Players were formed (1915). In Bernard L. Peterson, Jr., *Early Black American Playwrights and Dramatic Writers: A Biographic Directory and Catalog, of Plays, Films, and Broadcasting Scripts* (Westport, Conn.: Greenwood Press, 1990), 9, 223, we find that *The Old Man's Boy* (1914) was a play with songs written by Alex Rodgers (18?–1930) and Henry S. Creamer's (1879–1930).

26. See *Messenger*, January 1925, 23–24, for the citations of Owen, and see *Opportunity*, April 1925, 123, for this and the next quotation of Richardson.

27. "Negro Art," *Crisis*, June 1921, 55. The *Messenger*, January 1925, 15, has the previous citations of Lewis.

28. *Crisis*, May 1925, 8; here, too, is the next quotation of Du Bois.

29. *Opportunity*, June 1925, 183; here, too, are the quotations of Richardson. "The Unpleasant Play" is in *Opportunity*, September 1925, 282, and here, too, are the next quotations of Richardson.

30. *Modern Quarterly*, October–December 1925, and rpt. in Weinberg, *W.E.B. Du Bois: A Reader*, 247–50, has all the quotations from this source on this page.

31. "The Social Origins of American Negro Art," in Weinberg, *W.E.B. Du Bois: A Reader*, 249. And the popular notion of "natural selection" necessarily leading to the evolution of lower biological forms into higher ones that Du Bois seems to be following here is, of course, essentially a misreading of Darwinian theory, especially when applied to human cultures.

32. "W.E.B. Du Bois and The Theory of a Black Aesthetic," *Studies in a Literary Imagination* 7, no 2 (Fall 1974): 8.

33. John Monroe, "A Record of the Black Theatre in New York City, 1920–1929" (Ph.D. diss., University of Texas at Austin, 1980), 33, reports that on 11 May 1925, the Lafayette Players performed a Flournoy Miller comedy, *Pudden Jones*, which seems to be no longer extant; see *Amsterdam News*, 13 May 1925, 6.

34. A notice in *The Messenger*, February 1925, 111, reports that on 20 February 1925, the Renaissance Art Players produced *The Yellow Peril* at the Myrtilla Minor Normal School in Washington, D.C., and the play is in James V. Hatch and Leo Hamalian, eds., *Lost Plays of the Harlem Renaissance, 1920–1940* (Detroit: Wayne State University Press, 1996), 45–60. Anderson's *Appearances* is in James Hatch, ed. *Black Theatre USA*, 100–34; here, too, 102, is the quotation of Anderson on this page, and on, 100, Hatch's report that *Appearances* opened 13 October 1925 at New York City's Frolic Theatre on Broadway.

35. "A Record of the Black Theatre in New York City," 78; also, see *Age*, 7 November 1925, 6.

36. "The New Negro" (Review), *Crisis*, January 1926, 141; here, too is the next citation of Du Bois, and "W.E.B. Du Bois and the Theory of a Black Aesthetic," 9, has the next citation of Turner. The *Crisis*, January 1926, 115, has the next quotations of Du Bois.

37. "Characters," *Opportunity*, June 1925, 183, here, also, are the other citations from Richardson on this page.

38. Willis Richardson, *Forgotten Pioneer of African-American Drama* (Westport, Conn., London: Greenwood Press, 1999), 12.

39. Reprinted in Stewart, *The Critical Temper of Alain Locke*, 79–86, and see n. 13, 15, above for the citation of Du Bois' article.

40. See Locke, "Steps toward a Negro Theatre," *Crisis*, 1922, 66; Locke, "The Negro and the American Stage," in Stewart, *The Critical Temper of Alain Locke*, 79. Here, too, 80, is the next quotation of Locke.

41. See Van Vechten, "The Negro in Art," *Crisis*, March 1926, 219, and the next quotation of H.L. Mencken, and see "The Negro in Art," *Crisis*, February 1926, 165, for the previous citation of Du Bois. Also see Turner, "W.E.B. Du Bois and The Theory of a Black Aesthetic," 14.

42. *Crisis*, September 1926, rpt. in Turner, "W.E.B. Du Bois and the Theory of a Black Aesthetic," 14, and the *Crisis*, May 1926, 36, has the quotation of Sherwood Anderson.

43. The younger Negro literary artists published in *The New Negro* included Willis Richardson, Jessie Fauset, John Matheus, Rudolph Fisher, Claude McKay, Countee Cullen, Langston Hughes, Zora Neale Hurston, and Jean Toomer.

44. *Messenger*, April 1926, 116; italics mine. The *Crisis*, October 1926, rpt. in Weinberg, *W.E.B. Du Bois: A Reader*, 258–60, has the previous citations of Du Bois.
45. Reprinted in Hatch and Hamalian, *Lost Plays of the Harlem Renaissance*, 404–12.
46. Ibid., 404. Schuyler arrived at this view by ignoring the technical relationships of all forms of Black music, i.e., spirituals, blues, jazz, etc., and the hundreds of thousands of Northern and Midwestern Negroes who almost reverentially supported one or more forms of black music. Bert Williams was of Caribbean descent, as are a large segment of blacks that have historically participated in and supported jazz. In 1920s Harlem, Hubert Harrison was among the many "West Indian Negroes" who supported Negro musical comedy; here, too is the next quotation from Schuyler, and on, 405, the rest of his comments from this source. 409, 411, and, 407, respectively, have the next citations of Hughes from this source.
47. "Krigwa Players Little Negro Theatre: The Story of a Little Theatre Movement," *Crisis*, July 1926, 134–36; here, too, 134, is the next quotation of Du Bois.
48. In 1996, a theatre company, based on the premises of a Harlem church, rejected one of my plays solely because of the language of one of its characters; the same play had been awarded first prize in Samuel French's 1995 Off Off Broadway One-Act Play Festival at the Harold Clurman Theatre in downtown New York City.
49. *Messenger* (July 1926), 214–15, contains all of the quotations of Lewis from this source, and *Crisis*, July 1926, 134, has the previous citation of Du Bois.
50. *Theatre Arts Monthly*, in Stewart, *The Critical Temper of Alain Locke*, 87; here, too, 89–91, are the next quotations of Locke from this source. Also, on 91, are some of Locke's essays on African Art. He was one of the first of his peers to become a collector of African art, and the first major Renaissance figure to be published on the subject. Thus, his writings suggesting that American Negro artists investigate their African heritage have a more specific tone than Du Bois' similar encouragements; see Richard A. Long, "Locke, Race, and African Art," in *Grown Deep: Essays on the Harlem Renaissance* (Winter Park, Fla.: Four-G Publishers, Inc., 1998), 113–23.
51. Stewart, *The Critical Temper of Alain Locke*, 21–22, and also reprinted in Charles S. Johnson, ed., *Ebony and Topaz: A Collectanea* (Freeport, N.Y.: Books for Libraries Press, 1971), 117–18; here, too, in *The Critical Temper of Alain Locke*, 21, are the next citations of Locke.
52. "Variation 0137 of Monologue No. 8," *Messenger*, 53; here, too, are the next citations from Lewis.
53. (New York: Robert McBride and Co., 1926).
54. "The Theater—The Souls of Black Folks," *Messenger*, November 1926, 335.
55. *Crisis*, March 1927, 12.
56. Turner, "W.E.B. Du Bois and The Theory of a Black Aesthetic," 15, has this and the next quotation; here, too, rpt. in the *Crisis*, April 1927, is the next citation of Du Bois.
57. *Crisis*, April 1927, 70.
58. "The Theatre—The Souls of Black Folks," *Messenger*, 229; here, too, are the next citations of Lewis.
59. See Hay, "The National Endowment for African American Theatre, Inc.," in *African American Theatre*, Appendix C, 230–35, and see "The Theatre—The Souls of Black Folks," *Messenger*, July 1923, 243, for the next citation of Lewis.
60. *Nation*, April 18, 1928, rpt. in Stewart, *The Critical Temper of Alain Locke*, and here, too, are the next citations from Locke from this source.
61. See, respectively *Opportunity*, February 1923, 30, and "The Drama of Negro Life," in Stewart, *The Critical Temper of Alain Locke*, 90; here, too, 24, are the next quotations from Locke.
62. See Jean Toomer, *Cane* (New York: Liveright, 1923); Eric Waldron (1898–1966), *Tropic Death* (New York: Boni and Liveright, 1926); Rudolph Fisher (1897–1934), *The Walls of Jericho* (New York: A.A. Knopf, 1928), and Claude Mckay (1890–1948), *Home to Harlem* (New York: Harper, 1928). And *Fire*, ed. Wallace Thurman (1902–1934), was published only once, in November 1926.
63. Stewart, *The Critical Temper of Alain Locke*, 24; here, too, is the next quotation of Locke, and "W.E.B. Du Bois and The Theory of A Black Aesthetic," 2, has the next citation of Turner.
64. *Crisis*, June 1928, 202; here, too, is the previous and next citations of Du Bois.
65. *Opportunity*, 180; here, too, are the next quotations from Spence.
66. *Opportunity*, April 1929, 132; here, too, are the rest of the citations from Lewis.
67. "Art or Propaganda?" *Harlem*, November 1928, 12.
68. *American Mercury*, December 1928, 478; here, too, 479 and 481, are the next quotations of Johnson.
69. *Harlem*, November 1928, 12; here, too, is the next quotation.

Chapter III

1. *The Green Pastures* opened on Broadway in the Mansfield Theatre 26 February 1930, and

see "Dramatis Personae — Green Pastures," *Crisis*, May 1930, 162; here, too, are the next quotations of Du Bois.

2. Monroe, "A Record of the Black Theatre in New York City," 129, cited from Walton, *Age*, 20 March 1923, 6; here, too, 135, is the next citation of Monroe; also see *Amsterdam News*, 5 September 1923, and *Age*, 8 September 1923.

3. "Reflections of an Alleged Dramatic Critic," *Messenger*, June 1927; here, too, 193 and 200, respectively, are the next quotations of Lewis.

4. *Messenger*, June 1923, 747; "Drama," *Messenger*, April 1923, 671, has the previous citations of Fort-Whiteman.

5. "W.E.B. Du Bois and the Theory of A Black Aesthetic," 17, 10, has the next citations of Turner; "Dramatis Personae — Green Pastures," *Crisis*, May 1930, 162, has the previous citation of Du Bois.

6. *Crisis*, April 1929, 125. The white authors, DuBose and Dorothy Heyward, adapted DuBose Heyward's 1925 novel, *Porgy*, for the stage; the play was successfully produced by the Theatre Guild in New York City (1927); the play later was the basis for George Gershwin's opera *Porgy and Bess* (1935). See Hollis Alpert, *The Life and Times of Porgy and Bess: The Story of an American Classic* (New York: Alfred A. Knopf, 1990), 53–71.

7. "A Record of the Black Theatre in New York City," 31–33, 131–32. See *New York Amsterdam News*, 11 March 1925; 18 March 1925, and 5 September 1923.

8. William Jourdan Rapp, a white writer, had been a feature writer for the *New York Times* and an editor at *True Story Magazine*. See Obituaries of William Jourdan Rapp, Thurman papers, James Weldon Johnson Collection, Beinecke Library, Yale University

9. Scott, "Five African American Playwrights," 200–203; here, too, 195–98, is a fuller reconstruction of the play based on Wilson's *Brother Mose* (1935), produced by the Federal Theatre Project. The original script of *Meek Mose* appears to be no longer extant.

10. Wallace Thurman and William Jourdan Rapp, scripts and revision notes, Thurman papers, James Weldon Johnson, Beinecke Library, Yale University

11. Scott, "Five African American Playwrights," 160 here, too, 163, are the next citations of Scott; also see W.E.B. Du Bois, "In High Harlem," *Amsterdam News*, 5 October 1927.

12. Willis Richardson, *Compromise*, in Locke, *The New Negro*, 168–95.

13. "Krigwa Players Show Remarkable Progress as 2nd Season Opens," *Age*, 29 January 1927, 6. See "The Theatre," *Messenger*, March 1927, 61–62, for Lewis' praise of *Foreign Mail*.

14. Scott, "Five African-American Playwrights," 175–77, gives a fuller treatment of the demise of the Krigwa Players.

15. Joshua Carter, audiotaped interview with Eulalie Spence, Hatch-Billops Archives, 1973, New York. See "Five African-American Playwrights On Broadway," 164–66, 177, respectively, for the next citations of Scott.

16. See Austin, "Pioneering Black-authored Dramas," 12–34, 50–77; here, too, 84, Austin reports that five contest winning plays, Spence's *Hot Stuff, Foreign Mail, Spears, Four Eleven*, and *The Fall of the Conjurer*, seem to have no extant scripts; Spence's plays, the three Religious Life Plays, and almost certainly *The Fall of the Conjurer* were non-protest plays, which brings the number of non-propaganda prize-winning plays to nineteen, almost two thirds of all the award-winning plays. Bonner's *Purple Flower* is in Hatch, *Black Theatre USA*, 202–7.

17. *Frances* and *Sugar Cane* are in *Opportunity*, May 1925, 148–53, and June 1926, 181–84, and 201–3, respectively.

18. Scott, "Five African-American Playwrights," 41–42. Here, too, 47–48, Scott notes that Montgomery Gregory, Alexander Woolcott, Robert Benchley, Edith Isaacs, Ridgley Torrence, and Paul Green were among those who served as *Opportunity*'s drama judges.

19. "Youth Speaks," 1 March 1925, rpt. in Stewart, *The Critical Temper of Alain Locke*, 14.

20. Mitchell, *Black Drama: The Story of the American Negro in the Theatre* (New York: Hawthorn Books, 1967), 96.

21. *Opportunity*, January 1929, rpt. in Stewart, *The Critical Temper of Alain Locke*, 201–4, and here, too, 201, are the next quotations of Locke.

22. Edmonds, "Some Reflections on the Negro in American Drama," *Opportunity*, 303. Here, too, 305, 304, 303, respectively, are the next citations of Edmonds, and, 305, the next citations of Richardson. For more on Edmonds' award-winning plays, see Austin, "Pioneering Black-authored Dramas," 95, 108, 127.

23. "Some Reflections on the Negro in American Drama," 304. The previous citation of Locke is in "This Year of Grace: Outstanding Books of the Year in Negro Literature," *Opportunity*, February 1931, rpt. in Stewart, *The Critical Temper of Alain Locke*, 207.

24. "We Turn to Prose: A Retrospective Review of the Literature of the Negro for 1931," *Opportunity*, February 1932, rpt. in Stewart, *The Critical Temper of Alain Locke*, 209; also, here, too, are the next quotations from Locke; italics mine.

25. *Opportunity*, January 1933, rpt. in Stewart, *The Critical Temper of Alain Locke*, 215, 217, 219, respectively, have this and the next quotations of Locke.

26. "W.E.B. Du Bois and the Theory of a

Black Aesthetic," 18; here, too, 18, and 19, are the next citations of Du Bois.

27. *Opportunity*, January 1934, rpt. in Stewart, *The Critical Temper of Alain Locke*, 221. Here, too, 222, is the next quotation of Locke.

28. *Crisis*, August 1934, 232, here, too, are the next citations from Edmonds.

29. "Some Reflections on the Negro in American Drama," 305.

30. See Hatch, "Theatre in Historically Black Colleges," in Annemarie Bean, ed., *A Sourcebook of African-American Performance: Plays, People, Movements*, 150–64.

31. *The Critical Temper of Alain Locke*, 238, reprinted from Alain Locke, "Deep River: Deeper Sea: Retrospective Review of the Literature of the Negro for 1935," *Opportunity*, January and February 1936; here, too, 197, is the previous citation of Stewart.

32. (Washington, D.C.: Associates in Negro Folk Education, 1937; reprint ed., New York: Atheneum, 1969), 139, 123, 140, respectively. As recorded in Chapter 2, the precursors of Brown's "plaster saints" argument here were made in a number of the 1925 writings of Du Bois, Theophilus Lewis, and Willis Richardson.

33. "We Win the Right to Fight for Jobs," *Opportunity*, August 1938, 232.

34. See "The New Negro: 'New' or Newer: A Retrospective Review of the Literature of the Negro for 1939," *Opportunity*, January and February 1939, rpt. in Stewart, *The Critical Temper of Alain Locke*, 272. Here, too, 273, 231–32, 249, and 276, respectively, are the next citations of Locke, all reprinted from *Opportunity*: "The Eleventh Hour of Nordicism: Retrospective Review of the Literature of the Negro for 1934," January and February 1935; "God Save Reality! Retrospective Review of the Literature of the Negro: 1936," January and February 1937; and "The Negro: 'New' or Newer: A Retrospective of the Literature of the Negro for 1938," January and February 1939. Also see *The New Negro*, *Opportunity*, 11, 12, respectively for the next citations of Locke; italics mine.

35. "The Negro Builds His Theatre," *TAC*, June 1939, 12.

36. *Negro Playwrights in the American Theatre, 1925–1959* (New York and London: Columbia University Press, 1969), 46; see also Morgan Yale Himelstein, *Drama Was a Weapon: The Left-wing Theatre in New York, 1929–1941* (New Brunswick, N.J.: Rutgers University Press, 1963). And see John Gassner, "Social Realism and Imaginative Theatre: Avant-Garde Stage Production in the American Social Theatre of the Nineteen-Thirties," *Theatre Survey* 3 (1962): 12.

37. *Garden of Time* is in the Hatch-Billops Collection, New York. Peterson, *Early Black American Playwrights*, 58–59, reports that both Dodson's *Divine Comedy* and *Garden of Time* were produced at the Yale Repertory Theatre. Norford's *Joy Exceeding Glory* is in the New York Public Library (NYPL), Rare Manuscript Division, Schomburg Center; James V. Hatch and Ted Shine, eds., revised ed., *Black Theatre USA: Plays by African Americans. The Recent Period 1935–Today* (New York and London: The Free Press, 1996), 226–63, has Hill's *On Strivers Row*.

38. In Hatch and Hamalian, *Lost Plays of the Harlem Renaissance*, 128–99.

39. See Austin, "Pioneering Black-authored Dramas, 134; Dyson, "Howard University Capstone of Negro Education, a History," 150, and Eulalie Spence, *Undertow*, rpt. in Hatch, *Black Theatre USA*, 193–200. In 1932, The Howard Players also presented Richardson's *Compromise*.

40. *Run Little Chillun* is in Hatch and Hamalian, *Lost Plays of the Harlem Renaissance*, 230–79. Here, too, 229, is a production history for this play, and see Kenneth Burke, "The Negro Pattern of Life," *Saturday Review of Literature*, 27 July 1933, 1.

41. Abramson, *Negro Playwrights*, 53.

42. More than one version of *Joy to My Soul* exists. For more on its production history, see Leslie Sanders and Nancy Johnston, eds., vol. 5 of *The Collected Works of Langston Hughes: The Plays to 1942: Mulatto to The Sun Do More* (New York: Columbia University Press, 2001), 407–8. All of Hughes' plays cited here are contained in this volume.

43. John O'Connor and Lorraine Brown, eds., *Free, Adult, Uncensored: The Living History of the Federal Theatre Project* (Washington, D.C.: New Republic Books, 1978), 21–22. *The Trial of Dr. Beck* is in the Hatch-Billops Collection, New York. Other non-propaganda 1930s plays include Arna Bontemps and Countee Cullen's adaptation of Rudolph Fisher's 1932 novel *The Conjur Man Dies* (1936), a mystery comedy; see Hallie Flanagan, *Arena* (New York: Duell, Sloan, and Pearce, 1940), 162; and Cullen and Arna Bontemps' *One Way to Heaven* (1936), in James Weldon Johnson Collection, Beinecke Library, Yale University.

44. See Locke "Deep River: Deeper Sea," rpt. in Stewart, *The Critical Temper of Alain Locke*, 240, and Turner, "Langston Hughes as Playwright," in Hill, *The Theatre of Black Americans*, 138. *Mulatto* is in Hatch and Shine, *Black Theatre USA*, 4–23.

45. Jay Plum, "Accounting for the Audience in Historical Reconstruction: Martin Jones's Production of Langston Hughes's *Mulatto*," *Theatre Survey* 36, no. 1 (May 1995): 5. For examples of *Mulatto*'s negative reviews, see Brooks Atkinson, "The Play," *New York Times*, 25 October 1935, 18; Robert Garland, "*Mulatto* Pre-

sented at the Vanderbilt," *New York World-Telegram,* 25 October 1935, 30; Percy Hammond, "Theatres," *New York Herald-Tribune,* 25 October 1935, 14.

46. Carlson, *Theatre Semiotics: Signs of Life* (Bloomington: Indiana University Press, 1990), 18.

47. "Accounting for the Audience," 12. According to Plum, some of the reviews that "shifted" audience sympathies were Wilella Waldorf, "Mulatto Brings Up the Race Problem Once More," *New York Evening Post,* 25 October 1935, 10; Richard Lockridge, "The New Play," *New York Sun,* 25 October 1935, 34; Atkinson, "The Play," *New York Times,* 25 October 1935, 18.

48. *Negro Playwrights,* 79.

49. "Accounting for the Audience," 7, has the previous citation of Plum. For comments on the effectiveness of McClendon's acting, see Webster Smalley, ed., *Five Plays by Langston Hughes* (Bloomington: Indiana University Press, 1968), xi, and Locke, "Deep River: Deeper Sea," rpt. in Stewart, *The Critical Temper of Alain Locke,* 240–41.

50. *The Political Plays of Langston Hughes* (Carbondale and Edwardsville: Southern Illinois University Press, 2000), 5; cited from Langston Hughes to Noel Sullivan, 29 January 1936, Box 40:1, Bancroft Library, University of California, Berkeley.

51. Duffy, *The Political Plays of Langston Hughes,* 12; here, too, 15, is the next citation of Duffy. And the plays *Bloodstream, They Shall Not Die,* and *Stevedore* can be found, respectively, in Typescript, NYPL, Performing Arts Division (New York: A.A Knopf, 1934, and New York: Covici Friede, 1934).

52. Langston Hughes, *I Wonder as I Wander: An Autobiographical Journey* (New York: Hill and Wang, 1956), 199–200. *Don't You Want To Be Free* is in Hatch, *Black Theatre USA,* 262–77.

53. Hay, *African American Theatre,* 24.

54. Carlson, *Theories of the Theatre,* 323; and Meyerhold, "The Fairground Booth," *in Meyerhold on Theatre,* trans. Edward Braun (New York: Hill and Wang, 1969), 137; here, too, 199, is the next citation of Carlson.

55. "Of Native Sons: Real and Otherwise," *Opportunity,* January and February 1941, rpt. in Stewart, *The Critical Temper of Alain Locke,* 303–4.

56. *Negro Playwrights,* 79.

57. "*Big White Fog,*" *New Masses,* 12 November 1940, 22; here, too, is the next citation of Ellison. *Big White Fog* is in Hatch, *Black Theatre USA,* 278–319.

58. Hatch and Hamalian, *Lost Plays of the Harlem Renaissance,* 331; see also Reuben Silver, "A History of the Karamu Theatre of the Karamu House, 1915 to 1960" (Ph.D. diss., University Microfilms, Ann Arbor, Mich., 1961), 501–9, for 1930s black-authored productions of Karamu House Theatre.

59. "The Negro in the Field of Drama," *Opportunity,* July 1928, 214; here, too, are the rest of the quotations from Jelliffe.

60. *Blueprints for a Black Federal Theatre, 1935–1939* (New York and Cambridge: Cambridge University Press, 1994), 1; here, too, 3, is the next citation of Fraden.

61. Rena Fraden, "The Cloudy History of *Big White Fog*: The Federal Theatre Project 1938," *American Studies* 29, no. 1 (Spring 1988): 10; here, too, 9, is the next citation from Fraden.

62. See Fraden, "The Cloudy History of *Big White Fog,*" 10, and Abramson, *Negro Playwrights,* 45; Frank Wilson's *Walk Together Chillun* (1934 or 35), Allison's *Trial of Dr. Beck* (1937), Ward's *Big White Fog* (1938), and Theodore Browne's *Natural Man* (1937), treated in the next chapter, were all FTP produced. For more on the demise of the FTP, see O'Connor and Brown, *Free, Adult, Uncensored,* 31–35.

63. *African American Review* 29, no. 4 (Winter 1995): here, too, 615, 616, 618–621, respectively, are the next quotations from Nadler, and his discussion of *Liberty Deferred.*

64. Fraden, "The Cloudy History of Big White Fog," 13–17.

65. *Black Drama,* 106.

66. Duffy, *The Political Plays of Langston Hughes,* 6; here, too, 5–6, are the next citations of Duffy.

Chapter IV

1. (New York: Morrow and Company, 1967, rpt. edition, New York: Quill, 1984), 3.

2. Dubois, "The Negro College," *Crisis,* August 1933, 176.

3. Turner, "W.E.B. Du Bois and the Theory of a Black Aesthetic," 20; here, too, are the next quotations of Du Bois.

4. Lee Strasberg (1901–1982), Harold Clurman (1901–1980), and Cheryl Crawford (1902–1986) founded The Group Theatre in New York City in 1931, modeling it after the Moscow Art Theatre; see Brockett, *History of the Theatre,* 498–99.

5. Program of the New York production of *Big White Fog* in Harlem's Lincoln Theatre, New York City. Further citations of Ward on this topic are taken from this source.

6. See John F. Carrington, *Talking Drums of Africa* (London, Carey Kingsate Press, 1949, rpt. ed. Westport, Conn.: Negro Universities Press, 1969).

7. See Brockett, *History of the Theatre,* 14, 24.

8. Theatre Arts, October 1941, rpt. in Stew-

art, *The Critical Temper of Alain Locke*, 93; here, too, 97, are the next citations of Locke.

9. *Catholic World*, April 1942, 51; here, too, 52, 53, 57, respectively are the next quotations from Lewis.

10. "On Stage ... The Younger Generation," *Opportunity*, November 1947, 210–14.

11. Edmonds, "Towards Community Drama," *SADSA Encore*, spring 1948, 28–29.

12. "The Negro Little Theatre Movement," *Negro History Bulletin*, January 1949, 82; here, too, is the next citation of Edmonds.

13. "Towards Community Drama," 29.

14. Abramson, *Negro Playwrights*, 295–96, n.17.

15. Frazier, *Black Bourgeoisie* (Glencoe, Ill.: Free Press, 1957).

16. Abramson, *Negro Playwrights*, 102, and taken from Louis Kronenberger, *PM*, 3 March 1946 in NYPL, Schomburg Collection, American Negro Theatre folder.

17. See Mitchell, *Black Drama*, 135, and Locke, "Of Native Sons," rpt. in Stewart, *The Critical Temper of Alain Locke*, 313.

18. Hatch and Shine, *Black Theatre USA*, 227.

19. Obituary for Richard Wright, *New York Times*, 30 November 1960, NYPL, Schomburg Collection, Richard Wright Folder.

20. Richard Wright, *Native Son* (New York: Harper, 1940), 9.

21. See Brown, "Negro Characters as Seen by White Authors," *Journal of Negro Education* 2, no. 2 (April 1933): 191–92, and Hatch, *Black Theatre USA*, 393.

22. Hatch, *Black Theatre USA*, 408–9 is the source for the next citations from Act I, Scene iv; here, too, 394–431, is the entire play.

23. See Hatch, *Black Theatre USA*, 393; and Abramson, *Negro Playwrights*, 155.

24. Lee is probably best remembered by mainstream audiences for his film roles as Joe in Alfred Hitchcock's *Lifeboat* (1944), and as the Reverend Kumalo in the film *Cry the Beloved Country* (1951), based on Alan Payton's 1948 novel of the same title.

25. See Abramson, *Negro Playwrights*, 162. For the previous citations, see Baldwin, *Notes of a Native Son* (Boston: The Beacon Press, 1955), 43, and Edith J.R. Issacs, *The Negro in the American Theatre* (New York: Theatre Arts, 1947), 115.

26. Hatch, *Black Theatre USA*, 360–81; here, too, 361, is the next quotation of Browne.

27. Program for *Natural Man*, NYPL, Theatre Collection. The final episode in the Hatch anthology is identified as a "scene" so that the ANT production had seven episodes rather than eight; in all others respects the Hatch script appears to be an accurate reprint of the one used in the ANT production.

28. Abramson, *Negro Playwrights*, 106.

29. In Elisabeth Brown-Guillory, *Wines in the Wilderness: Plays by African American Women from the Harlem Renaissance to the Present* (Westport, Conn.: Greenwood Press, 1990).

30. Peterson, *Early Black American Playwrights*, 64–65, is the source for this information on Graham's work; *Dust to Earth* appears to be no longer extant.

31. Mitchell, *Black Drama*, 135–36, and Peterson, *Early Black American Playwrights*, 209, are the sources for the information on Pitcher and Holifield's plays and for some facts about *This Way Forward*. In my interview, 27 June 2002, with Jeannette, she gives the date of the ANT workshop production of her play as 1950; see Gertrude Jeannette, *Artists and Influence* (New York: Hatch-Billops Collection, 1996), 122–36. Also, in 1984, I directed *This Way Forward* for Jeannette's Harlem company.

32. *Our Lan'* with Kenneth Rowe's analysis on alternate pages is in Rowe, *A Theatre in Your Head* (New York: Funk and Wagnalls Co., 1960), 262–424; here, too, 257, is the next citation of Rowe, and, 257–58, and 262, respectively, have examples of the positive response to the play in the mainstream press and historical sources for *Our Lan'*.

33. *Black Drama*, 133; here, too, 133–34, is the next citation of Mitchell.

34. Rowe, *Theatre in Your Head*, 257.

35. Abramson, *Negro Playwrights*, 95–96.

36. *The Theatre Book of the Year, 1947–1948, A Record and an Interpretation* (New York: Alfred A. Knopf, 1948), 48.

37. Abramson, Negro Playwrights, 92.

38. Negro Playwrights Company, 1940, unpaged, NYPL, Schomburg Collection, George Norford Scrapbook.

39. "*Big White Fog*' Closes Dec. 14 with 64 Performances of Play," *Pittsburgh Courier*, 14 December 1940, n.p.

40. James Hatch, interview by author, 21 June 2002; Hatch reports that in a personal conversations with Ward, the writer repeatedly gave this view of the demise of NPC.

41. Negro Playwrights Company, "Perspective" unpaginated.

42. See American Negro Theatre Records, 1940–1982, NYPL, Schomburg Collection, Manuscripts and Rare Books Div, passim., for more information on ANT membership, which included Fred O'Neal, Austin-Briggs Hall, Stanley Greene, Claire Leyba, Alvin Childress, Alice Childress, Osceola Archer, Hilda Simms, Clarice Taylor, Gertrude Jeannette, Helen Martin, Maxwell Glanville, Earl Hyman, Sidney Poitier and Harry Belafonte. For the previous citation of Hill, see Mary Bragotti, "Stagecraft in Harlem," *New York Post*, 29 December 1943 NYPL, Schomburg Collection, Abram Hill Folder.

43. Ethel Pitts, "The American Negro Theatre," in Hill, *The Theatre of Black Americans*, 253; Pitts reports that ANT's nineteen productions included Phoebe and Henry Ephron's *Three's A Family* (1943); Samuel M. Kootz's *Home Is the Hunter* (1945); Kurt Unkelbach's *The Peacemaker* (194?); Walter Carroll's *Tin Top Valley* (1947), and Kenneth White's *Freight* (1949); all of these plays are by white authors.

44. Pitts, "The American Negro Theatre," in Hill, *The Theatre of Black Americans*, 256. Further, Abram Hill adapted *Anna Lucasta* from the Philip Yordan's original play of the same title. Yordan was a white Hollywood screenwriter, and the play was first published, without Hill as co-author, in 1945, after Hill's rewrite and ANT's production of the work made it a Broadway hit. Hill's *Walk Hard* is adapted from Len Zenberg's 1940 novel *Walk Hard—Talk Loud*, and his *A Long Way Home* is based on Maxim Gorky's *Lower Depths* (1902).

45. Abram Hill, Interviewer: Michelle Wallace, 19 January 1974, *Artists and Influence*, 2000, 19.

46. "The Negro Little Theatre," *Negro History Bulletin*, 84.

47. Silver, "A History of the Karamu Theatre," 509.

Chapter V

1. *Fifty Years of Progress in the Theatre* (Pittsburgh: *Pittsburgh Courier*, 1950), 6.

2. "American Theatre and the Civil Rights Movement, 1945–1965" (Ph.D. diss., City University of New York, 1995), 11, 1; here, too, 178–79, 109–10, 163, respectively, are the next quotations from Nadler.

3. "Into the Mainstream and Oblivion," in *The American Negro Writer and His Roots: Selected Papers from the First Conference of Negro Writers* (New York: American Society of African Culture, 1960), 30.

4. David McCullough, *John Adams* (New York and London: Simon and Schuster, 2001), 378.

5. "Into the Mainstream and Oblivion," 32. See, Abramson, *Negro Playwrights*, 166, for the previous citation.

6. Margaret Just Butcher, *The Negro in American Culture* (New York: Alfred A. Knopf, 1964), vii–viii.

7. "Into the Mainstream and Oblivion," 30.

8. There were several nineteenth-century stage adaptations of *Uncle Tom's Cabin*; George Aiken's (1852) was the first and reportedly the most popular adaptation of the book. There was a "craze" for the play during the 1850s and 1870s, when some fifty touring companies performed it throughout the United States; twelve touring companies were still performing only this play in 1927; see Brockett, *History of Theatre*, 408.

9. "Everybody's Protest Novel," *Partisan Review*, July 1949, 578; here, too, 581, 582, respectively, are the next quotations of Baldwin.

10. *Partisan Review*, November–December 1951, 665; here, too, 670, 679, 585, 666, respectively, are the next quotations from Baldwin.

11. *Phylon* 11 (1950): 127; here, too, 127–29, are the next quotations from Couch.

12. Stanley Kramer produced the low-budget film version of *Home of the Brave*; Kramer decided to use a black actor (James Edwards) in the role of what had been in Laurents' play a young "Jewish" soldier; see Donald Bogle, *Toms, Coons, Mulattoes, Mammies and Bucks: An Interpretive History of Blacks in American Film* (New York: Bantam Books, 1974), 202. Here, too, 80–83, and 272, is more on the film productions of *Imitations of Life*. For *Strange Fruit*, see typescript copy, NYPL, Performing Arts Division, and Kathy Perkins and Judith Stephens, *Strange Fruit: Lynching Plays by American Women* (Bloomington: Indiana University Press, 1998).

13. *Phylon* (1950): 130, 131–33, have the previous citations of Couch.

14. *Masses and Mainstream*, February 1951, 61; here, too, 61, 62 and 63, are the next quotations from Childress.

15. Hatch and Shine, *Black Theatre USA*, 226.

16. William Branch, telephone interview by author, 14 July 2002; Phillip Hayes Dean, telephone interview by author, 18, June 2002.

17. *The American Negro Writer and His Roots*, 2; here, too, 35 and 35–36, 37, and 40, respectively, are the next citations of Arthur P. Davis.

18. See *The Oxford Companion to African American Literature*, s.v. Allen, Samuel; the John Henrik Clarke Collection, NYPL Schomburg Collection.

19. *The American Negro Writer and His Roots*, 9–10; here, too, 20, 21–23, 27, respectively, are the next citations of Allen.

20. *Ibid.*, 7–8; here, too, 8, is the next quotation from Redding.

21. Nadler, "American Theatre," 167–70; here, too, 121, Nadler reports that the next play in this discussion, Ted Ward's *John Brown*, was produced by the People's Drama company on Eldrige Street in lower Manhattan in New York City; also see Abramson, *Negro Playwrights*, 256–57; a typescript of *John Brown* is in the Hatch Billops Collection.

22. Nadler, "American Theatre," 149–53, treats *Alice in Wonder*; here, too, 170–78, and 190–92, respectively, is a discussion of *In Splendid Error*, and *Ballot and Me*. *In Splendid Error* is in Hatch, *Black Theatre USA*, 587–617; Abramson, *Negro Playwrights*, 179–88, also has a discussion of the play; see *Ballot and Me* (writ-

ten for a Harlem get-out-the-vote rally), typescript in the Beinecke Rare Book and Manuscript Library, Yale University, New Haven, Conn.

23. *A Medal for Willie*, in Woodie King and Ron Milner, eds., *Black Drama Anthology* (New York: Columbia University Press, 1972), 470–71.

24. In Lindsay Patterson, compiler, *Black Theatre: A 20th Century Collection of the Work of Its Best Playwrights* (New York: A Plume Book from New American Library, 1973), 207–69; here, too, 262–63, 263–64, 240, 236, respectively, are the next citations from Childress' play.

25. "American Theatre," 178–80; 186–90, 202–4, 213–16, respectively, report on Davis' other short civil rights plays performed as dramatic readings at special events sponsored by Local 1199 (New York City's major hospital employees union) for its membership: *What Can You Say to Mississippi?* (1956); *Montgomery Footprints* (1957); and *The Union Democracy Built* (1957). Here, too, 204–5, is the previous citation of Nadler and the information on *The People of Clarendon County*.

26. Mitchell, *Black Drama*, 170–78, is the source for the information on DeLaine and Mitchell's dealings with him.

27. Justice Henry Billings Brown, "Majority opinion in *Plessy v. Ferguson*," in Benjamin Munn Ziegler, ed., *Desegregation and the Supreme Court* (Boston: D.C. Heath and Company, 1958), 50–51.

28. *Black Drama*, 173–74.

29. *A Land Beyond the River*, in William R. Reardon and Thomas D. Pawley, eds., *The Black Teacher and the Dramatic Arts: A Dialogue, Bibliography and Anthology* (Westport, Conn.: Greenwood Press, 1970), 376–77 (Act Two); in Mitchell, *Black Drama*, 174–79, Mitchell reports on the burning of DeLaine's home, but, if DeLaine had a wife, there is no mention of her. Here, too, 384 and 391, are the next citations from *The Land Beyond the River*.

30. Mitchell, *Black Drama*, 179, reports that the play, scheduled for a ten-week run, opened 28 March 1957 and ran for the rest of the year.

31. Hatch and Shine, *Black Theatre USA*, 105.

32. In 1979, I directed one of the many productions of the play to which Nadler refers for the Theatre of the Stars/Just Us Theatre Company; this production opened in the Peachtree Street Playhouse in Atlanta, Georgia. Twenty years after its Broadway premier, the play received city-wide acclaim, and established the Just Us Company, then the black subsidiary of Theatre of the Stars, as a professional theatre; see Scott Cain, "Radiant *Raisin in the Sun* Becomes More Universal," *Atlanta Journal*, 21 September 1979, 11-B; Helen C. Smith, "*Raisin in the Sun* Staging Well Done," *Atlanta Constitution*, 21, September 1979, 1-B; Adele S. Newson, "*Raisin in the Sun* Called Fantastic," *Atlanta Daily World*, 20 September 1979, n.p.; and A. Sanson, "Just Us 'Matures' with *Raisin*," *NewsScope*, 26 September, 1979, n.p.

33. Daniel J. Leab, *From Sambo to Superspade: The Black Experience in Motion Pictures* (Boston: Houghton Mifflin Company, 1976), 226–27. Nadler, "American Theatre," 233, has the quotation from Nadler.

34. "A History of the Chicago Federal Theatre Project Negro Unit: 1935–1939" (Ph.D. diss., School of Education, New York University, 1998), 194. Hansberry's *A Raisin in the Sun* is in Hatch and Shine, *Black Theatre USA*, 104–46.

35. *Negro Playwrights*, 243; here, too, 242 and 243, respectively, are the previous citations.

36. Hatch and Shine, *Black Theatre USA*, 107, here, too, are the sources for my other comments on the opening pages of the play.

37. Italics mine; the poem *Dream Deferred* is in Langston Hughes, *Montage of a Dream Deferred* (New York: Holt, 1951); also see Abramson, *Negro Playwrights*, 239–54, for her reconstruction of the play centering on Walter Lee.

38. "Coping with Conflict" (New York: WNET-TV NewsHour program, 23 January 2002), Online NewsHour transcript, 1. Here Oz applies his Hegelian definition of drama to the current Arab-Israeli conflict as opposed to its also appropriate application to much of ancient Greek drama.

39. Hatch and Shine, *Black Theatre USA*, 104.

40. *The Crisis of the Negro Intellectual*, 278.

41. "Yes I am a Black Playwright, But..." *New York Times*, 25 January 1970, Arts and Leisure Section, 11. For a discussion of Hansberry's life and economic status see Anne Cheney, *Lorraine Hansberry* (Boston: Twayne, 1984); also Cruse, *The Crisis of the Negro Intellectual*, 267–84, has some useful information about the middle-class nature of Hansberry's life, that is, if one keeps to the facts and is careful about Cruse's interpretation of them.

42. *This Life* (New York: Alfred A. Knopf, 1980), 234; here, too, 234 and 235, are the next quotations from Poitier.

43. "American Theatre," 239, taken from Lloyd Richards, interview with Ernest Wiggins, 8 December 1975, Hatch-Billops Collection, New York.

44. *This Life*, 235; here, too, 236 and 237, are the next citations of Poitier.

45. Abramson, *Negro Playwrights*, 239.

46. Peterson, *Early Black American Playwrights*, 153.

47. See Bernard L. Peterson, *Contemporary Black Playwrights and Their Plays: A Biographical Directory and Dramatic Index* (New York:

Greenwood Press, 1988), 31; and Hatch, *Black Theatre USA,* 514. And, see, Nadler, "American Theatre," for information on *Take a Giant Step,* which is in Hatch and Shine, *Black Theatre USA,* 67–103.

48. Phillip Hayes Dean, telephone interview by author, 18, June 2002; see Peterson, *Contemporary Black Playwrights,* 133–36; *The Owl Killer* is in King and Milner, *Black Drama Anthology,* 301–24.

49. Nadler, "American Theatre," 157.

50. Baldwin, *The Amen Corner,* in *Hatch, Black Theatre USA,* 514–46.

51. Langston Hughes, *Simply Heavenly,* in Patterson, *Black Theatre,* 272.

52. Joshua Carter, audiotaped interview with Eulalie Spence, Hatch-Billops Archives, 1973, New York.

Chapter VI

1. *Crisis of the Negro Intellectual,* 362; here, too, 534, 270, and 362, respectively, are the next citations of Cruse.

2. *The Critical Temper of Alain Locke,* xvii.

3. *Freedom,* April 1953, 5.

4. "Me tink me hear sounds in de night," *Theatre Arts,* October 1960, 69; here, too, are the next quotations from Hansberry.

5. "American Theatre," 233.

6. The stage history of the opera *Porgy and Bess* (1935) is plagued with stereotypic performance traditions and black middle class notions of "positive images." But Du Bose Heyward and George and Ira Gershwin made, mainly, an honest interpretation of a unique Gullah community in early twentieth-century black South Carolina; see my "The Drama of *Porgy and Bess*: Director's Notes," George Gershwin's *Porgy and Bess* (Philadelphia: Opera Company of Philadelphia, Education Dept., 2001), 66–68, in the Hatch-Billops Collection, New York. This essay was written in connection with my two directorial outings with the work: Indianapolis Opera, 7 to 15 October 2000, and the Opera Company of Philadelphia, Academy, 25 April to 6 May 2001; see Whitney Smith, "Hoosier Company's Realism Does Justice to *Porgy and Bess,*" *Indianapolis Star,* 10 October 2000, n.p.; Anaré Holmes, "Black Director Breathes New Life into *Porgy and Bess,*" *Indianapolis Recorder,* 26 October 2000, 2; Peter Dobrin, "*Porgy and Bess* with Dignity: Humanity Permeates OCP's Production," *Philadelphia Inquirer,* 27 April 2001, sec. H-1; and Tom Dinardo, "'Bess' Bet: Director Takes Fresh Look at the Gershwin Classic," *Philadelphia Daily News,* 24 April, 2001, 35, all in *Porgy and Bess* folder, Hatch-Billops Collection.

7. "Why Negroes Don't Like *Porgy and Bess,*" *Ebony Magazine,* October 1959, 50.

8. See James M. Hutchisson, *Du Bose Heyward: A Charleston Gentlemen and the World of Porgy and Bess* (Jackson: University Press of Mississippi, 2000), 168.

9. "The Myth of Negro Literature" in *Home: Social Essays* (New York: William Morrow, 1966), 106; here, too, 110, 111, 115, 112 and 109, respectively, are the next citations of Jones. Also see *Oxford Companion to African American Literature,* s.v. Baraka, Amiri; and Peterson, *Contemporary Black American Playwrights,* 34.

10. *Catholic World,* April 1942, 54.

11. *Partisan Review,* November–December 1951, 665; "Many Thousands Gone" is also published in Baldwin, *Notes of a Native Son* (1955).

12. Sadly, concerning black music, the baggage of historical racial and cultural prejudice, even today, fuels the popular, untutored notion that the music of Brahms and Beethoven, for example, is more difficult for musicians to execute than that of, say, Ferdinand "Jelly Roll" Morton (1890–1941) or Edward Kennedy "Duke" Ellington (1899–1974).

13. "Purlie Told Me!" *Freedomways,* 155; here, too, 156, 157, 158–59, are the next quotations from Davis. For a short biography of Davis, see Michael E. Greene, "Ossie Davis," in Trudier Harris and Thadious M. Davis, *Afro-American Writers after 1951* (Detroit, Mich.: Gale Research, 1985).

14. "A Need for a Harlem Theatre," rpt. in John Henrik Clarke, ed., *Harlem U.S.A.,* 157; here, too, 158, 159, 162, 163–64, 165, and 156, respectively, are the next citations of Williams and the next citation of Lofton Mitchell.

15. *Liberator,* 8 August, 1964, 18–19.

16. "The Theatre — The Souls of Black Folks," *Messenger,* July 1927, 229; italics mine.

17. Dempsey, *An Autobiography of Black Chicago* (Chicago: Urban Research Institute, 1981), 124–25.

18. Williams, "The Need for a Harlem Theatre," *Liberator,* 1963, rpt. in Clarke, *Harlem U.S.A.,* 160–61.

19. "The Black Arts," 21; here, too are next quotations from Riley.

20. L.P. Neal, "The Cultural Front," *Liberator,* 6 June 1965, 26; here, too, is the next quotation from Neal.

21. (New York: William Morrow, 1963).

22. "The Revolutionary Theatre," 4; here, too, 4–5, are the next quotations from Jones.

23. See Antonin Artaud, "No More Masterpieces" (1938), in Artaud, *The Theatre and Its Double* (New York: Grove Press, 1958) and rpt. in Dukore, *Dramatic Theory and Criticism,* 760–66.

24. See Ray Monk, *Ludwig Wittgenstein: The Duty of Genius* (London: J. Cape, 1990); Carlson, *Theories of the Theatre,* 462–63.

25. See Schopenhauer, *The World as Will and*

Idea, pertinent selections rpt. in Dukore, *Dramatic Theory and Criticism*, 516–21.
26. "Is Revolutionary Theatre in Tune with the People?" *Liberator*, 12 December 1965, 8; here, too, 9, is the next citation of Ellis.
27. See "Manifesto of Futurism," in R.W. Flint, ed., *Marinetti: Selected Writings* (New York: Farrar, Straus and Giroux, 1971), 41–42.
28. The original one-act version of *Fly Blackbird* was first produced in September 1960 in the Shoebox Theatre in Los Angeles; its two-act version had productions in the Metro Theatre in Los Angeles (1961) and at the Mayfair Theatre in New York City (1962); the full-length version of the play is published in Hatch, *Black Theatre USA*, 671–93.
29. *Raisin' Hell in the Son* was first produced by Maxwell Glanville's American Community Theatre (ACT) in Harlem, opening in May 1961 and running three performances a week, closing in June 1961; it is unpublished, but Nadler, "American Theatre," 283, reconstructs it primarily from reviews. As a former member of ACT and mentored by Glanville (see Dedication, v), I, too, am also aware of this unpublished work.
30. Hughes, *Jerico–Jim-Crow, A Song Play*, typescript, 1963, in NYPL, Performing Arts Collection; also see Folkways Records FL9671 (script published with recording).
31. See, Peterson, *Contemporary Black Playwrights*, 345; Peterson gives no precise date or theatre for the *Star of the Morning*'s first production, but he notes that the play was later produced by the American Folk Theatre in the No Smoking Playhouse in New York City (c. 1971); the play is published in King and Milner, *Black Drama Anthology*, 1972, 575–639.
32. Douglas Turner Ward, *Two Plays by Douglas Turner Ward: Day of Absence and Happy Ending* (New York: Third Press, 1966), and see Nadler, "American Theatre," 392.
33. Ossie Davis, *Purlie Victorius* (New York: Samuel French, Inc., 1961).
34. Nadler, "American Theatre," 196–202, is the source for the information on Farrakhan's *Orgena* and *The Trial*; here, too, 200, is the next citation of Nadler.
35. Ibid., 306–7, and Peterson, *Contemporary Black Playwrights*, 232–34 for information on Harrison's *Pavane for a Dead-Pan Minstrel*; the play is published in *Podium Magazine* (Amsterdam), November 1965. Jones' *The Baptism* opened in March 1964 in the Writers' Stage Theater in New York City; it is a morality play about Jesus posing as a fifteen year old Negro boy in order to find and destroy the hypocritical members of a Negro Baptist church, along with their pastor; see Jones, *The Baptism and The Toilet* (New York: Grove Press, 1967), 8–32; here, too, 62, 57–60, are the citations from *The Toilet*.

36. *CLAJ*, September 1965, 23. And see Hughes, "That Boy LeRoi," *New York Post*, 15 January 1965, 38.
37. *Dutchman* is in Hatch and Shine, *Black Theatre USA*, 381–91; here, too, 381–82, are the next citations from Hatch; see also Peterson, *Contemporary Black Playwrights*, 34. "LeRoi Jones' *The Slave* and *The Toilet*," *Liberator*, 2 February 1965, 23, has the previous citation of Neal.
38. In *Home: Social Essays*, 105–15.
39. Jones, *The Slave*, in Hatch, *Black Theatre USA*, 813; here, too, 812, is the next citation.
40. See Jones, *J-e-l-l-o*, (Chicago: Third World Press, 1970), and Amiri Imamu Baraka, *Four Black Revolutionary Plays* (New York: Marion Boyars, 1998).
41. *Amiri Baraka/LeRoi Jones: The Quest for a "Populist Modernism"* (New York: Columbia Univ. Press, 1978), 210.
42. *Nine Plays by Black Women* (New York: New American Library, 1986), xxii. See Kennedy, *Funnyhouse of a Negro* in *Adrienne Kennedy in One Act* (Minneapolis: University of Minnesota Press, 1988), 1–23.
43. Patrice Lumumba was the first Prime Minister of the Democratic Republic of the Congo, who was assassinated in 1961.
44. Werner Sollors, "People Who Led to My Plays: Adrienne Kennedy's Autobiography," in Paul Bryant-Jackson and Lois More Overbeck, eds., *Intersecting Boundaries: The Theatre of Adrienne Kennedy* (Minneapolis: University of Minnesota Press, 1992), 13.
45. (New York: Vintage Books, 1992).
46. Hay, *African American Theatre*, 95, cited from Amiri Baraka, *The Autobiography of LeRoi Jones/Amiri Baraka* (New York: Freundlich Books, 1984), 187.
47. See Barnes, *Africa's Ogun*, 156, for the West African god *Ogun* as "a crusader against injustice"; and in Lewis Spence, *Myths and Legends of Ancient Egypt* (New York: Dover Publications, 1990), 108–9, see *Maat*, ancient Egyptian system of ethics, truth, and cosmic balance, governed by the goddess *Maat*, "daughter and the eye of Ra"; also see Eberhard Otto, *Egyptian Art and the Cults of Osiris*, 69, photographic plates 16 and 17, bas-reliefs of *Isis*' (as a female hawk) sexual resurrection of *Osiris*.
48. Bullins, *Five Plays by Ed Bullins* (Indianapolis: Bobbs-Merrill, 1969), 249–82. *Crisis*, September 1927, 227, has the next citation of Du Bois.
49. Hatch and Shine, *Black Theatre USA*, 392.
50. *The Crisis of the Negro Intellectual*, 533–34; I, too, am a member of Cruse's Lost Generation." This book is, in many ways, an effort to recoup some of the losses of my generation.

Chapter VII

1. Hay, *African American* Theatre, 97; here, too, 96–97, are the earlier citations of Hay and, in more detail, his explanation of the Kawaida doctrine.

2. For Derrida and Artaud, see Carlson, *Theories of the Theatre*, 502–3, and Jacques Derrida, *Writing and Difference*, trans. Alan Bass (Chicago: University of Chicago, 1978).

3. Baraka, "Black Theatre Forum," *Black Theatre 50* (1971): 27.

4. See "Maulana Ron Karenga Discusses U.S./Panther Conflict and the Tackwood Distortions," *Unity and Struggle*, June 1974, 7, quoted in Werner Sollors, *Amiri Baraka/LeRoi Jones*, 185. Also, see *Amiri Baraka/LeRoi Jones*, 185, for the previous citations of Sollors.

5. Baraka, *The Autobiography of LeRoi Jones/Amiri Baraka*, 187.

6. Baraka, "A Wiser Play Than Some of Us Knew," *Los Angeles Times*, 22 March 1987, n.p.

7. See Addison Gale, Jr., "Blueprint For Black Criticism," *First World*, February 1977, 41–45.

8. *The Negro in American Culture* (New York: Alfred A. Knopf, 1964), 187; here, too, is the next citation from the Van Dorens.

9. *African American Theatre*, 5, has the earlier citation of Hay; here, too, 225–35, Hay gives specific suggestions for the creation of a black theatre criticism workshop, a "New theatre organizational structure," and a "National Endowment for African American Theatre." See the Introduction, "Needs," for Wilson's call for a "unique and specific Black theatre art."

10. See William A. Darity et al., *The Black Underclass: Critical Essays on Race and Unwantedness* (New York: Garland Publishers, 1994); Burt Landry, *The New Black Middle Class* (Berkeley: University of California Press, 1987); Lawrence Otis Graham, *Our Kind of People: Inside America's Black Upper Class* (New York: Harper Collins, 1999).

11. In *Working Papers in Sociolinguistics* 74–80 (Austin, Tex.: Southwest Educational Development Laboratory, November 1980): 31–32.

12. "Kongo Influences on African-American Artistic Culture," in Holloway, *Africanisms in American Culture*, 163.

13. In Carlton and Barbara Molette, *Black Theatre: Premise and Presentation*, 116–22; conspicuously absent from their discussion of "separately constructed" human cultures is the African concept of "Nommo," which finds all things in the universe of the same "essence"; see Molefi Kete Asante, *The Afrocentric Idea* (Philadelphia: Temple University Press, 1987), 96.

14. *The Epic in Africa: Towards a Poetics of the Oral Performance* (New York: Columbia University Press, 1979), 14–16.

15. See Otto, *Egyptian Art and the Cults of Osiris and Amon*, 69, black and white photographic plate 16.

16. Keynote address to the *Jazz Times Magazine* Convention held in World Trade Center in New York City, October 1998, copy in author's personal papers; for writings on cultural materialism, see Raymond Williams, "Social Environment and Theatrical Environment: The Case of English Naturalism," in *Problems in Materialism and Culture* (London: Verso, 1980); and Alan Sinfield and Jonathan Dollimore, "History and Ideology, the Instance of Henry IV," in John Drakakis, ed., *Alternative Shakespeares* (London and New York: Methuen, 1985).

17. See hooks, *Feminist Theory: From Margin to Center* (London: Pluto, 2000); Stanlie James and Abena P. A. Busia, *Theorizing Black Feminisms: The Visionary Pragmatism of Black Women* (New York: Routledge, 1993); Delores S. Williams, "Womanist Theology: Black Women's Voices," *Christianity and Crisis*, 2 March 1987; and Katie Geneva Cannon, *Katie's Canon: Womanism and the Soul of the Black Community* (New York: Continuum, 1995).

18. In *Substance* 37–38 (1983): 143; see also Carlson, *Theories of the Theatre*, 515–16.

19. *Creation Legends of the Near East* (London: Hodder and Stoughton, 1963), 22.

20. Lamy, *New Light on Ancient Spiritual Knowledge*, (New York: Crossroads, 1981), 87, for the previous citation of Lamy; here, too, 18–19, is the source for the next reference to Lamy's work; and see James Gleick, *Chaos—Making a New Science* (New York: Viking, 1987), 29. Also, Isis' second gift, the release from endless "deaths and rebirths" is one of many aspects of pharaonic religion that suggests that it may be an ancient forerunner of a number of East Indian Vedic religious traditions.

21. (London: Blond and Briggs, 1991; rpt. Rochester, Vt.: Park Street Press, 1995).

Bibliography

Anthologies

Baraka, Amiri Imamu. *Four Black Revolutionary Plays.* New York: Marion Boyars, 1998.
Brown-Guillory, Elisabeth. *Wines in the Wilderness: Plays by African American Women from the Harlem Renaissance to the Present.* Westport, Conn.: Greenwood Press, 1990.
Bullins, Ed. *Five Plays by Ed Bullins.* Indianapolis and New York: Bobbs-Merrill Company, 1969.
Green, Paul. *Lonesome Road: Six Plays for a Negro Theatre.* New York: Robert McBride & Co., 1926.
Hamalian, Leo, and James V. Hatch, eds. *The Roots of African American Drama: An Anthology of Early Plays, 1858–1938.* Detroit: Wayne State University Press, 1991.
Hatch, James V., ed. *Black Theatre USA: 45 Plays by Black Americans, 1847–1974.* New York: Free Press, 1974.
———, and Leo Hamalian, eds. *Lost Plays of the Harlem Renaissance, 1920–1940.* Detroit: Wayne State University Press, 1996.
———, and Ted Shine, eds. Revised and expanded edition. *Black Theatre USA: Plays by African Americans, the Recent Period, 1935–Today.* New York: Free Press, 1996.
Kennedy, Adrienne. *Adrienne Kennedy in One Act.* Minneapolis: University of Minnesota Press, 1988.
King, Woodie, and Ron Milner, eds. *Black Drama Anthology.* New York and London: Columbia University Press, 1972.
Locke, Alain, and Montgomery Gregory, eds., *Plays of Negro Life: A Sourcebook of Native American Drama.* New York: Harper, 1927.
Patterson, Lindsay. *Black Theatre: A 20th Century Collection of the Work of Its Best Playwrights.* New York: New American Library, 1973.
Perkins, Kathy, and Judith Stephens. *Strange Fruit: Lynching Plays by American Women.* Bloomington: Indiana University Press, 1998.
Richardson, Willis, and May Miller, eds. *Negro History in Thirteen Plays.* Washington, D.C.: Associated Publishers, 1935.
Sanders, Leslie, and Nancy Johnston, eds. *The Collected Works of Langston Hughes: The Plays to 1942: Mulatto to The Sun Do More.* Vol. 5. New York: Columbia University Press, 2001.
Smalley, Webster, ed. *Five Plays by Langston Hughes.* Bloomington: Indiana University Press, 1968.
Wilkerson, Margaret. *Nine Plays by Black Women.* New York: New American Library, 1986.

Books and Dissertations

Abramson, Doris E. *Negro Playwrights in the American Theatre, 1925–1959.* New York: Columbia University Press, 1969.
Alpert, Hollis. *The Life and Times of Porgy and Bess: The Story of an American Classic.* New York: Alfred A. Knopf, 1990.
American Negro Writer and His Roots: Selected Papers from The First Conference of Negro Writers. New York: American Society of African Culture, 1960.
Anderson, Jervis. *A. Philip Randolph: A Biographical Portrait.* First edition. New York: Harcourt Brace Jovanovich, 1973.
Artaud, Antonin. *The Theatre and Its Double.* New York: Grove Press, 1958.
Asante, Molefi Kete. *The Afrocentric Idea.*

253

Philadelphia: Temple University Press, 1987.

Austin, Addell P. "Pioneering Black-authored Dramas: 1924–1927." Ph.D. diss., Michigan State University, 1986.

Baldwin, James. *Notes of a Native Son.* Boston: The Beacon Press, 1955.

Baraka, Amiri. *The Autobiography of LeRoi Jones/Amiri Baraka.* New York: Freundlich Books, 1984.

Barnes, Sandra T. *Africa's Ogun: Old World and New.* Bloomington and Indianapolis: Indiana University Press, 1989.

Bean, Annemarie, ed. *A Sourcebook of African-American Performance: Plays, People, Movements.* London and New York: Routledge, 1999.

Belcher, Fannin, Jr. "The Place of the Negro in the Evolution of the American Theatre, 1767–1940." Ph.D. diss., Yale University, 1945.

Berheim, Alfred L. *The Business of Theatre: An Economic History of the American Theatre, 1750–1932* New York: Benjamin Blom, 1932. Second edition, 1964.

Bogle, Donald. *Toms, Coons, Mulattoes, Mammies and Bucks: An Interpretive History of Blacks in American Film.* New York: Bantam Books, 1974.

Bontemps, Arna, ed. *The Harlem Renaissance Remembered.* New York: Dodd Mead, 1972.

Brandon, S.G.F. *Creation Legends of the Near East.* London: Hodder and Stoughton, 1963.

Brawley, Benjamin. *The Negro in Literature and Art in the United States.* New York: Duffield and Co., 1921.

Brockett, Oscar G. *History of the Theatre.* Fifth edition. Boston: Allyn and Bacon, 1987.

Brown, Sterling. *Negro Poetry and Drama and the Negro in American Fiction.* Washington, D.C.: Associates in Negro Folk Education, 1937. Reprint edition, New York: Atheneum, 1969.

———. *Southern Road: Poems by Sterling A. Brown.* New York: Harcourt Brace, 1932.

Bryant-Jackson, Paul, and Lois More Overbeck, eds. *Intersecting Boundaries: The Theatre of Adrienne Kennedy.* Minneapolis: University of Minnesota Press, 1992.

Butcher, Margaret Just. *The Negro in American Culture.* New York: Alfred A. Knopf, 1964.

Cannon, Katie Geneva. *Katie's Canon: Womanism and the Soul of the Black Community.* New York: Continuum, 1995.

Carlson, Marvin. *Theatre Semiotics: Signs of Life.* Bloomington: Indiana University Press, 1990.

———. *Theories of the Theatre: A Historical and Critical Survey, from the Greeks to the Present.* Expanded edition. Ithaca and London: Cornell University Press, 1993.

Carrington, John F. *Talking Drums of Africa.* London: Carey Kingsgate Press, 1949. Reprint edition, Westport, Conn.: Negro Universities Press, 1969.

Charters, Ann. *Nobody: The Story of Bert Williams.* London: Collier-Macmillan, 1970.

Cheney, Anne. *Lorraine Hansberry.* Boston: Twayne, 1984.

Clarke, John Henrik, ed. *Harlem U.S.A.* New York: Collier Books, 1971.

Cripps, Thomas. *Slow Fade to Black: The Negro in American Film, 1900–1942.* New York, London, and Oxford: Oxford University Press, 1977.

Croce, Benedetto. *Aesthetics.* Translated by Douglas Ainslie. London: Heinemann, 1929.

Cronon, E. David. *Marcus Garvey and the Universal Negro Improvement Association.* Madison: University of Wisconsin Press, 1955. Reprint edition, 1969.

Cruse, Harold. *The Crisis of the Negro Intellectual: A Historical Analysis of the Failure of Black Leadership.* New York: Morrow and Company, 1967. Reprint, New York: Quill, 1984.

Darity, William A., and Samuel L. Myers, Jr., with Emmett D. Carson and William Sabol. *The Black Underclass: Critical Essays on Race and Unwantedness.* New York: Garland Publishers, 1994.

Davis, Arthur P., and Michael W. Peplow. *The New Negro Renaissance.* New York: Holt, Rinehart and Winston, 1975.

———, and Saunders Redding. *Calvacade: Negro American Writing from 1760 to the Present.* Boston: Houghton Mifflin, 1971.

Demsey, Travis. *An Autobiography of Black Chicago.* Chicago, Ill.: Urban Research Institute, 1981.

Derrida, Jacques. *Writing and Difference.* Translated by Alan Bass. Chicago: University of Chicago, 1978.

Drakakis, John, ed. *Alternative Shakespeares.* London and New York: Methuen, 1985.

Du Bois, W.E.B. *The Gift of Black Folk*. Boston: Stratford Co., 1924. Reprint, Millwood, N.Y.: Kraus-Thomson Organization, 1975.

———. *The Souls of Black Folk*. Atlanta, 1903. Reprint, New York: Library of America, 1986.

Duffy, Susan. *The Political Plays of Langston Hughes*. Carbondale and Edwardsville: Southern Illinois University Press, 2000.

Dukore, Bernard F. *Dramatic Theory and Criticism*. New York: Holt, Rinehart and Winston, 1974.

Dyson, Walter. *Howard University, The Capstone of Negro Education — A History: 1867–1940*. Washington, D.C.: Graduate School Howard University, 1941.

Esedebe. *Pan-Africanism: The Idea and Movement, 1776–1963*. Washington, D.C.: Howard University Press, 1982.

Flanagan, Hallie. *Arena*. New York: Duell, Sloan, and Pearce, 1940.

Flint, R.W., ed. *Marinetti: Selected Writings*. New York: Farrar, Straus and Giroux, 1971.

Foner, Philip S. ed. *W.E.B. Du Bois Speaks: Speeches and Addresses, 1890–1919*. New York: Pathfinder Press, 1970.

Forbes, Jack D. *Africans and Native Americans: The Language of Race and the Evolution of the Red-Black Peoples*. Urbana: University of Illinois Press, 1993.

Fraden, Rena. *Blueprint for a Black Federal Theatre, 1935–1939*. New York and Cambridge: Cambridge University Press, 1994.

Frazier, E. Franklin. *Black Bourgeoisie*. Glencoe, Ill.: Free Press, 1957.

Garvey, Marcus. *Philosophy and Opinions of Marcus Garvey*. 2 vols. 1923. Reprint, New York: Arno Press, 1968.

Gatewood, Willard B. *Aristocrats of Color: The Black Elite, 1880–1920*. Bloomington: Indiana University Press, 1990.

Gleick, James. *Chaos — Making a New Science*. New York: Viking, 1987.

Graham, Lawrence Otis. *Our Kind of People: Inside America's Black Upper Class*. New York: Harper Collins, 1999.

Gray, Christine. *Willis Richardson, Forgotten Pioneer of African-American Drama*. Westport, Conn., and London: Greenwood Press, 1999.

Hall, Ardencie. "New Orleans Jazz Funerals: Transition to the Ancestors." Ph.D. diss., New York University, 1998.

Harris, Trudier, and Thadious M. Davis. *Afro-American Writers after 1951*. Detroit, MI: Gale Research, 1985.

Hatch, James V. *Sorrow Is the Only Faithful One: The Life of Owen Dodson*. Urbana and Chicago: University of Illinois Press, 1993.

Hay, Samuel A. *African American Theatre: An Historical and Critical Analysis*. Cambridge and New York: Cambridge University Press, 1994.

Herkovits, Melville J. *The Myth of the Negro Past*. Boston: Beacon Press, 1958.

Herodotus. *History of Herodotus*. In Robert M. Hutchins, editior-in-chief, *Great Books of the Western World*. Vol. 6. Translated by George Rawlinson. Chicago: University of Chicago and Encyclopædia Britannica, 1952.

Hill, Errol, ed. *The Theatre of Black Americans: A Collection of Critical Essays*. New York: Applause Theatre Books Publishers, 1987.

Himelstein, Morgan Yale. *Drama Was a Weapon: The Left-wing Theatre in New York, 1929–1941*. New Brunswick, N.J.: Rutgers University Press, 1963.

Holloway, Joseph, ed. *Africanisms in American Culture*. Bloomington: Indiana University Press, 1991.

hooks, bell. *Feminist Theory: From Margin to Center*. London: Pluto, 2000.

Hughes, Langston. *I Wonder as I Wander: An Autobiographical Journey*. New York: Hill and Wang, 1956.

Hull, Gloria T. *Color, Sex, and Poetry: Three Women Writers of the Harlem Renaissance*. Bloomington and Indianapolis: Indiana University Press, 1987.

Hutchisson, James M. *Du Bose Heyward: A Charleston Gentlemen and the World of Porgy and Bess*. Jackson: University Press of Mississippi, 2000.

Issacs, Edith J. R. *The Negro in the American Theatre*. New York: Theatre Arts, 1947.

James, Stanlie, and Abena P.A. Busia. *Theorizing Black Feminisms: The Visionary Pragmatism of Black Women*. New York: Routledge, 1993.

Johnson, Charles S., ed. *Ebony and Topaz: A Collectanea*. Freeport, N.Y.: Books for Libraries Press, 1971.

Johnson, James Weldon. *Along This Way: The Autobiography of James Weldon Johnson*. New York: Viking Penguin, 1933. Reprint, New York: Viking Compass Edition, 1968. Reprint with introduction by Sondra K. Wilson, New York: Penguin Books, 1990.

———. *Black Manhattan*. New York: Knopf, 1930. Reprint with new introduction by Sondra K. Wilson, New York: Da Capo Press, 1991.

Jones, LeRoi (Imamu Amiri Baraka). *Blues People: Negro Music in White America*. New York: William Morrow, 1963.

———. *Home: Social Essays*. New York: William Morrow, 1966.

Katz, Bernard, ed. *The Social Implications of Early Negro Music in the United States*. New York: Arno Press, 1969.

Kellogg, Charles F. *NAACP: A History of the National Association for the Advancement of Colored People, 1909–1920*. Vol. 1. Baltimore, Md.: Johns Hopkins University Press, 1967.

Kerman, Cynthia E., and Richard Eldridge. *The Lives of Jean Toomer*. Baton Rouge: Louisiana State University Press, 1987.

Kimball, Robert, and William Bolcom. *Reminiscing with Sissle and Blake*. New York: Viking Press, 1973.

Kirby, I.E., and C.I. Martin. *The Rise and Fall of the Black Caribs*. Kingston, St. Vincent: St. Vincent and Grenadines National Trust, 1997.

Krasner, David. *Resistance, Parody, and Double Consciousness in African American Theatre, 1895–1910*. New York: St. Martin's Press, 1997.

Lamy, Lucie. *New Light on Ancient Spiritual Knowledge*. New York: Crossroads, 1981.

Landry, Burt. *The New Black Middle Class*. Berkeley: University of California Press, 1987.

Leab, Daniel J. *From Sambo to Superspade: The Black Experience in Motion Pictures*. Boston: Houghton Mifflin Company, 1976.

Lester, Julius, ed. *The Seventh Son: The Thought and Writings of W.E.B. Du Bois*. New York: Random House, 1971.

Lewis, David Levering. *When Harlem Was in Vogue*. New York: Vintage Books, 1982.

Lewis, Theophilus. *Fifty Years of Progress in the Theatre*. Pittsburgh: *Pittsburgh Courier*, 1950.

———. *The Official Theatrical World of Colored Artists*. New York: The Theatrical World Publishing Co., 1928.

Locke, Alain, ed. *The New Negro: An Interpretation*. New York: A. and C. Boni, 1925.

Long, Richard A. *Grown Deep: Essays on the Harlem Renaissance*. Winter Park, Fla.: Four-G Publishers, 1998.

Manning, Kenneth R. *Black Apollo of Science: The Life of Ernest Everett Just*. New York and Oxford: Oxford University Press, 1983.

Marshall, Herbert, and Mildred Stock. *Ira Aldridge: The Negro Tragedian*. Carbondale: Southern Illinois University Press, 1968.

Matthews, Brander. *The Development of the Drama*. New York: Scribner's Sons, 1903.

Martin, Tony. *Literary Garveyism: Garvey, Black Arts and the Harlem Renaissance*. Dover, Mass.: Majority Press, 1983.

Mbiti, John S. *African Religions and Philosophies*. Garden City, N.Y.: Anchor Books, 1970.

McCullough, David. *John Adams*. New York and London: Simon and Schuster, 2001.

McKay, Nellie Y. *Jean Toomer, Artist: A Study of His Life and Work, 1894–1936*. Chapel Hill: University of North Carolina Press, 1984.

Mitchell, Lofton. *Black Drama: The Story of the American Negro in the Theatre*. New York: Hawthorn, Books, 1967.

Molette, Carlton W., and Barbara J. Molette. *Black Theatre: Premise and Presentation*. 2nd ed. Bristol, Ind.: Wyndham Hall Press, 1986.

Monk, Ray. *Ludwig Wittgenstein: The Duty of Genius*. London: J. Cape, 1990.

Monroe, John. "A Record of the Black Theatre in New York City, 1920–1929." Ph.D. diss., University of Texas at Austin, 1980.

Nadler, Paul. "American Theatre and the Civil Rights Movement, 1945–1965." Ph.D. diss., City University of New York, 1995.

Nathan, George Jean. *The Theatre Book of the Year, 1947–1948, A Record and an Interpretation*. New York: Alfred A. Knopf, 1948.

Nietzsche, Friedrich. *The Birth of Tragedy and The Genealogy of Morals*. Translated by Francis Golffing. New York: Doubleday and Co., 1956.

O'Connor, John, and Lorraine Brown, eds. *Free, Adult, Uncensored: The Living History of the Federal Theatre Project*. Washington, D.C.: New Republic Books, 1978.

Odell, George C.D. *Annals of the New York Stage*. New York: Columbia University Press, 1928.

Okpewho, Isadore. *The Epic in Africa: Towards a Poetics of the Oral Performance*. New York: Columbia University Press, 1979.

Otto, Eberhard. *Egyptian Art and the Cults of Osiris and Amon*. London: Thames and Hudson, 1968.

Parekh, Bhikhu. *Rethinking Multiculturalism: Cultural Diversity and Political Theory*. Houndsmills and Basingstoke, Hampshire, U.K.: Macmillan, 2000.

Pelton, Robert D. *The Trickster in West Africa: A Study of Mythic Irony and Sacred Delight*. Berkeley and Los Angeles: University of California Press, 1980.

Peplow, Michael W. *George S. Schuyler*. Boston: Twayne Publishers, 1980.

Perry, Jeffrey B. *A Hubert Harrison Reader*. Middletown, Conn.: Wesleyan University Press, 2001.

Peterson, Bernard L., Jr. *A Century of Musicals in Black and White: An Encyclopedia of Musical Stage Works by, about, or involving African Americans*. Westport, Conn.: Greenwood Press, 1993.

———. *Contemporary Black Playwrights and Their Plays: A Biographical Directory and Dramatic Index*. Westport, Conn.: Greenwood Press, 1988.

———. *Early Black American Playwrights and Dramatic Writers: A Biographic Directory and Catalog of Plays, Films, and Broadcasting Scripts*. Westport, Conn.: Greenwood Press, 1990.

Pinkney, Michael L. "African-American Dramatic Theory as Subject of Cultural Studies." Ph.D. diss., Ohio State University, 1999.

Poitier, Sidney. *This Life*. New York: Alfred A. Knopf, 1980.

Pryse, Marjorie, and Hortense J. Spillers, eds. *Conjuring: Black Women, Fiction, and Literary Tradition*. Bloomington: Indiana University Press, 1985.

Reardon, William R., and Thomas D. Pawley, eds. *The Black Teacher and the Dramatic Arts: A Dialogue, Bibliography and Anthology*. Westport, Conn.: Greenwood Press, 1970.

Richards, Sandra L. "Sweet Meat From Leroi." Ph.D. diss., Stanford University, 1979.

Riis, Thomas L. *Just before Jazz: Black Musical Theatre in New York, 1890 to 1915*. Washington, D.C., and London: Smithsonian Institution Press, 1989.

Sampson, Henry T. *Blacks in Blackface: A Source Book on Early Black Musical Shows*. Metuchen, N.J., and London: Scarecrow Press, 1980.

Schopenhauer, Arthur. Translated by R.B. Haldane and J. Kemp. *The World as Will and Idea*. London: Trübner and Co., 1883.

Scott, Freda. "Five African-American Playwrights on Broadway, 1923–1929." Ph.D. diss., City University of New York, 1990.

Sheldrake, Rupert. *A New Science of Life: The Hypothesis of Morphic Resonance*. London: Blond and Briggs, 1991. Reprint, Rochester, Vt.: Park Street Press, 1995.

Silver, Reuben. "A History of the Karamu Theatre of the Karamu House, 1915 to 1960." Ph.D. diss., University Microfilms: Ann Arbor, Mich., 1961.

Smith, Theophus H. *Conjuring Culture: Biblical Formations of Black America*. New York and Oxford: Oxford University Press, 1994.

Sollors, Werner. *Amiri Baraka/LeRoi Jones: The Quest for a "Populist Modernism."* New York: Columbia University Press, 1978.

Spence, Lewis. *Myths and Legends of Ancient Egypt*. New York: Dover Publications, 1990.

Spingarn, Joel Elias. *Creative Criticism*. New York: Harcourt, Brace, 1931.

Stewart, Jeffrey C. *The Critical Temper of Alain Locke: A Selection of His Essays on Art and Culture*. New York: Garland Publishers, 1983.

Strong, Roy. *Art and Power: Renaissance Festivals, 1450–1650*. Woodbridge, Suffolk, U.K.: Boydell Press. 1984.

Sundquist, Eric J., ed. *The Oxford W.E.B. Du Bois Reader*. New York and Oxford: Oxford University Press, 1996.

Thompson, George A. *A Documentary History of the African Theatre*. Evanston, Ill.: Northwestern University Press, 1998.

Toll, Robert C. *Blacking Up: The Minstrel Show in Nineteenth-Century America*. New York: Oxford University Press, 1974.

Vactor, Vanita Marian. "A History of the Chicago Federal Theatre Project Negro Unit: 1935–1939." Ph.D. diss., New York University, 1998.

Van Doren, Carl, and Mark Van Doren. *American and British Literature Since 1890*. 1939. Reprint, New York: Appleton-Century-Crofts, 1967.

Watkins, Mel. *On the Real Side: Laughing, Lying, and Signifying—The Underground Tradition of African-American Humor That Transformed American Culture, from Slavery to Richard Pryor*. New York: Simon and Schuster, 1994.

Weinberg, Meyer. *W.E.B. Du Bois: A Reader*. New York: Harper and Row, 1970.
Wells-Barnett, Ida B. *Crusade for Justice: The Autobiography of Ida B. Wells*. Edited by Alfreda M. Duster. Chicago: Chicago University Press, 1970.
Williams, Raymond. *Problems in Materialism and Culture*. London: Verso, 1980.
Wilson, Sondra Kathryn, ed.. *The Selected Writings of James Weldon Johnson*. Vol. 1. New York and Oxford: Oxford University Press, 1995.
Woll, Allen. *Black Musical Theatre: From Coontown to Dreamgirls*. Baton Rouge and London: Louisiana State Press, 1989.

Periodical Articles

The full publication facts for all articles and chapters printed in books are listed above in the books and dissertations section of this bibliography.

Allen, Samuel W. "Négritude and Its Relevance to the American Negro Writer." In *The American Negro Writer and His Roots*, 1960.
Antonin, Artaud, "No More Masterpieces." 1938. In Artaud, *The Theatre and Its Double*, 1958.
Brooks Atkinson, "The Play" (review of *Mulatto*). *New York Times*, 25 October 1935.
Baldwin, James. "Everybody's Protest Novel." *Partisan Review*, July 1949.
———. "Many Thousands Gone." *Partisan Review*, November–December, 1951.
Baraka, Imamu Amiri. "The International Business of Jazz and the Need for the Cooperative and Collective Self Development of an International Peoples Culture." Keynote address to the *Jazz Times Magazine* Convention at the World Trade Center in New York City, October 1998. In Amiri Baraka and the author's personal papers.
———. "A Wiser Play Than Some of Us Knew." *Los Angeles Times*, 22 March 1987.
Blau, Herbert. "The Universals of Performance; or Amortizing Play." *Substance* 37–38 (1983).
Bragotti, Mary. "Stagecraft in Harlem." *New York Post*, 29 December 1943.
Brown, Henry Billings. "Majority Opinion in *Plessy v. Ferguson*." In Benjamin Munn Ziegler, ed., *Desegregation and the Supreme Court*. Boston: D.C. Heath and Company, 1958.
Brown, Sterling. "Negro Characters as Seen by White Authors." *Journal of Negro Education* 2 (April 1933).
Brustein, Robert. "Subsidized Separatism. View of A. Wilson." *The New Republic*, August 1996.
———. "Subsidized Separation with Discussion." *American Theatre*, October 1996.
"*Big White Fog* Closes Dec. 14 with 64 Performances of Play." *Pittsburgh Courier*, 14 December 1940.
Burke, Kenneth. "The Negro Pattern of Life." *Saturday Review of Literature*, 27 July 1933.
Cain, Scott. "Radiant *Raisin in the Sun* Becomes More Universal," *Atlanta Journal*, 21 September 1979. Review of Just Us Theatre Company's production of the play in Atlanta, Georgia.
Childress, Alice. "For a Negro Theatre." *Masses and Mainstream*, February 1951.
Clark, William. "Krigwa Players Show Remarkable Progress as 2nd Season Opens." *Age*, 29 January 1927.
Clarke, John Henrik. "Reclaiming the Lost African Heritage." In *The American Negro Writer and His Roots*, 1960.
Cole, Bob. *The Red Moon*. Review in *New York Dramatic Mirror*, 15 May 1909, 3.
Couch, William, Jr. "The Problem of Negro Character and Dramatic Incident." *Phylon* 11 (1950).
Davis, John. "We Win the Right to Fight for Jobs." *Opportunity*, August 1938.
Davis, Ossie. "Purlie Told Me!" *Freedomways*, 1962.
Dinardo, Tom. "'Bess' Bet: Director Takes Fresh Look at the Gershwin Classic." *Philadelphia Daily News*, 24 April, 2001. *Porgy and Bess* folder, Hatch Billops Collection, New York.
Dobrin, Peter. "*Porgy and Bess* with Dignity: Humanity Permeates OCP's Production." *Philadelphia Inquirer*, 27 April 2001. *Porgy and Bess* folder, Hatch Billops Collection, New York.
Dodson, Owen. "Playwrights with Dark Glasses." *Negro Digest*, April 1968.
Drinkwater, John. *Abraham Lincoln: A Play*. 1918. Review of the New York opening of the play mentioning Charles Gilpin, by Heyward Broun in the *New York Tribune*, 16 December 1919.

Du Bois, W.E.B. "The Browsing Reader." *Crisis*, June 1928.
———. "Can the Negro Serve the Drama?" *Theatre*, July 1923.
———. "Criteria of Negro Art." *Crisis*, October 1926.
———. "The Drama among Black Folk." *Crisis*, August 1916.
———. "Dramatis Personae — Green Pastures." *Crisis*, May 1930.
———. "In High Harlem." *Amsterdam News*, 5 October 1927.
———. "Krigwa Players Little Negro Theatre: The Story of a Little Theatre Movement." *Crisis*, July 1926.
———. "Negro Art." *Crisis*, June 1921.
———. "The Negro in Art." *Crisis*, February 1926.
———. "The Negro College." *Crisis*, August 1933.
———. "The Negro in Literature and Art." *Annals*, September 1913.
———. "Negro Writers." *Crisis*, April 1920.
———. "*The New Negro*" (review). *Crisis*, January 1926.
———. "Returning Soldiers." *Crisis*, 1919.
———. "The Social Origins of American Negro Art." *Modern Quarterly*, October–December 1925.
Easton, William Edgar. "Foreward to *Dessalines: A Dramatic Tale*." Boston, Mass: J.W. Burson-Company, Publishers, 1893.
Edmonds, Randolph. "The Negro Little Theatre." *Negro History Bulletin*, 1949.
———. "Some Reflections on the Negro in the American Drama." *Opportunity*, October 1930.
———. "Towards Community Drama." *SADSA Encore*, Spring 1948.
———. "What Good Are College Dramatics?" *Crisis*, August 1934.
Ellis, Eddie. "Is Revolutionary Theatre in Tune with the People?" *Liberator*, 12 December, 1965.
Ellison, Ralph. "*Big White Fog*." *New Masses*, 12 November 1940.
Fine, Elizabeth. "Aesthetic Patterning." In *Working Papers in Sociolinguistics* 74–80 (Austin, Tex.: Southwest Educational Development Laboratory, November 1980).
Ford, Clebert. "Toward a Black Community Theatre." *Liberator*, 8 August 1964.
Fort-Whiteman, Lovett. "Drama." *Messenger*, April 1923.

Foster, William. "Pioneers of the Stage: Memoirs of William Foster." In Theophilus Lewis, ed., *The Official Theatrical World of Colored Artists*, 1928.
Fraden, Rena. "The Cloudy History of *Big White Fog*: The Federal Theatre Project 1938." *American Studies* 29 (Spring 1988).
"From Page to Stage: Race and the Theatre." *The New York Times*, 22 January 1997.
Gale, Addison, Jr. "Blueprint for Black Criticism." *First World*, February 1977.
Garland, Robert. "*Mulatto* Presented at the Vanderbilt." *New York World-Telegram*, 25 October 1935.
Garvey, Marcus v. United States, 4F. 2d 974–76 (2d Cir. 1925).
Garvey, Marcus. Article on Marcus Garvey in *New York News*, 7 February 1925.
Gassner, John. "Social Realism and Imaginative Theatre: Avant-Garde Stage Production in the American Social Theatre of the Nineteen Thirties." *Theatre Survey* 3 (1962).
Gershwin, George, DuBose Heyward, and Ira Gershwin. *Porgy and Bess*. 1935. *Porgy and Bess* folder, Hatch Billops Collection, New York.
Goldstein, Richard. "Culture Shock: The Grudge Match as *Kulturkampf* — Extreme Fighting." *New York Village Voice*, 28 January 1997.
Gordone, Charles. "Yes I Am a Black Playwright, But..." *New York Times*, 25 January 1970.
Greene, Michael E. "Ossie Davis." In Harris and Davis, *Afro-American Writers after 1951*, 1985.
Grimké, Angelina. "*Rachel*: The Play of the Month — The Reason and Synopsis by the Author." *Competitor*, January 1920.
Hammond, Percy. "Theatres" (review of *Mulatto*). *New York Herald-Tribune*, 25 October 1935.
Hansberry, Lorraine. "Me tink me hear sounds in de night." *Theatre Arts*, October 1960.
———. Review of Richard Wright's novel *The Outsider*. *Freedom*, April 1953.
———. "Why Negroes Don't Like *Porgy and Bess*." *Ebony Magazine*, October 1959.
Harris, Abram L. "The Ethiopian Art Players and the Nordic Complex." *Messenger*, July 1923.
Harrison, Hubert. "The Emperor Jones." *Negro World*, 4 June 1921.

Hatch, James V. "Theatre in Historically Black Colleges," in Annemarie Bean, ed., *A Sourcebook of African-American Performance*, 1999.

Hill, Abram. *On Strivers Row*. Review by Louis Kronenberger. *PM*, 3 March 1946.

Holmes, and Anaré. "Black Director Breathes New Life into *Porgy and Bess*," *Indianapolis Recorder*, 26 October 2000. *Porgy and Bess* folder, Hatch Billops Collection, New York.

Hughes, Langston. "The Negro Artist and the Racial Mountain." *Nation*, 23 June 1926.

———. "That Boy LeRoi" (review). *New York Post*, 15 January 1965.

Jackson, Esther Merle. "The American Negro and the Image of the Absurd." *Phylon*, Winter 1962.

Jackson, Wallace V. "The Theatre — Drama." *Messenger*, June 1923.

Jeannette, Gertrude. Interviewed by Henry Miller. In *Artists and Influence*. Hatch-Billops Collection, New York, 1996.

Jelliffe, Rowena. "The Negro in the Field of Drama." *Opportunity*, July 1928.

Johnson, James Weldon. "The Dilemma of The Negro Author." *American Mercury*, December 1928.

Jones, LeRoi (Imamu Amiri Baraka). "The Myth of Negro Literature." In Jones, *Home: Social Essays*, 1966.

———. "The Revolutionary Theatre." *Liberator*, July 1965.

Karenga, Maulana Ron. "Maulana Ron Karenga Discusses U.S./Panther Conflict and the Tackwood Distortions." *Unity andruggle*, June 1974.

Kornweibel, Theodore, Jr. "Theophilus Lewis and the Theatre of the Harlem Renaissance." In Bontemps, *The Harlem Renaissance Remembered*, 1972.

Lewis, Theophilus. "The Frustration of Negro Art." *Catholic World*, April 1942.

———. "If This Be Puritanism." *Opportunity*, April 1929.

———. "Main Problems of the Negro Theater" (theatre column). *Messenger*, July 1927.

———. "Reflections of an Alleged Dramatic Critic" (theatre column). *Messenger*, June 1927.

———. "Same Old Blues" (theatre column). *Messenger*, January 1925.

———. "The Theatre" (theatre column). *Messenger*, March 1927.

———. "The Theatre — The Souls of Black Folks" (theatre column). *Messenger*, July 1926.

———. "The Theatre — The Souls of Black Folks" (theatre column). *Messenger*, November 1926.

———. "The Theatre: The Souls of Black Folks: *The Great Gatsby—The Great Emperor—The Great God Brown*" (review), *Messenger*, April 1926.

———. "Variation 0137 of Monologue No. 8" (theatre column). *Messenger*, February 1927.

Locke, Alain. "Art or Propaganda?" *Harlem*, November 1928.

———. "Beauty Instead of Ashes." *Nation*, April 1928.

———. "Black Truth and Black Beauty, a Review of Negro Literature for 1932." *Opportunity*, January 1933.

———. "Broadway and the Negro Drama." *Theatre Arts*, October 1941.

———. "Deep River: Deeper Sea: Retrospective Review of the Literature of the Negro for 1935." *Opportunity*, January and February 1936.

———. "The Drama of Negro Life." *Theatre Arts Monthly*, October 1926.

———. "The Eleventh Hour of Nordicism: Retrospective Review of the Literature of the Negro for 1934." *Opportunity*, January and February 1935.

———. "Enter the New Negro." *Survey Graphic*, 1 March 1925.

———. "*Goat Alley*, by Ernest Howard Culbertson." *Opportunity*, February 1923.

———. "God Save Reality! Retrospective Review of the Literature of the Negro: 1936." *Opportunity*, January and February 1937.

———. "Of Native Sons: Real and Otherwise." *Opportunity*, January and February 1941.

———. "The Negro and the American Stage." *Theatre Arts Monthly*, February 1926.

———. "The Negro Builds His Theatre." *TAC*, June 1939.

———. "The New Negro: 'New' or Newer: A Retrospective Review of the Literature of the Negro for 1938." *Opportunity*, January and February 1939.

———. "1928: A Retrospective Review [of Negro literature]." *Opportunity*, 1929.

———. Resignation letter from NAACP Drama Committee (1916). Locke to Archibald Grimké, undated. In Alain

Locke Papers, the Moorland-Spingarn Research Center, Howard University, Washington, D.C.
———. "The Saving Grace of Realism: Retrospective Review of the Negro Literature of 1933." *Opportunity*, January 1934.
———. "Steps toward a Negro Theatre." *Crisis*, December 1922.
———. "This Year of Grace: Outstanding Books of the Year in Negro Literature." *Opportunity*, February 1931.
———. "Youth Speaks." *Survey Graphic*, 1 March 1925.
———. "We Turn to Prose: A Retrospective Review of the Literature of the Negro for 1931." *Opportunity*, February 1932.
———, and Charles Johnson. "Max Reinhardt Reads the Negro's Dramatic Horoscope." *Opportunity*, May 1924.
Lockridge, Richard. "The New Play" (review of *Mulatto*). *New York Sun*, 25 October 1935.
Long, Richard A. "Locke, Race, and African Art." In Long, *Grown Deep*, 1998.
Lovell, John. "The Social Implications of the Negro Spiritual." In Katz, *The Social Implications of Early Negro Music in the United States*, 1969.
Marinetti, Tomaso. "Manifesto of Futurism." In R.W. Flint, *Marinetti: Selected Writings*, 1971.
Mayfield, Julian. "Into the Mainstream and Oblivion." In *The American Negro Writer and His Roots*, 1960.
Meyerhold, Vsevolod. "The Fairground Booth." In *Meyerhold on Theatre*, trans. Edward Braun. New York: Hill and Wang, 1969.
Mitchell, Lofton. "The Negro Theatre and the Harlem Community." *Freedomways*, 1963.
Miller, Henry. "The Drama of *Porgy and Bess*: Director's Notes." In *Porgy and Bess: Sounds of Learning Education Program*. Philadelphia: Opera Company of Philadelphia, Education Dept. and The School District of Philadelphia, 2001.
———. "*New York Amsterdam News*—Theatre Notes Column: A Sudy of the Activity in Black Theatre from 27 July 1974 to 21 December 1974." Hatch-Billops Collection, New York.
Nadler, Paul. "Liberty Censored: Black Living Newspapers of the Federal Theatre Project." *African American Review* 29 (Winter 1995).

Neal, Larry. "The Black Arts Movement." *The Drama Review*, Summer 1968.
———. "The Cultural Front." *Liberator*, 6 June 1965.
———. "LeRoi Jones' *The Slave* and *The Toilet*" (review). *Liberator*, 2 February 1965.
Negro Playwrights Company. "Perspective." Hatch-Billops Collection, New York.
Newson, Adele S. "*Raisin in the Sun* Called Fantastic," *Atlanta Daily World*, 20 September 1979. Review of Just Us Theatre Company's production of the play in Atlanta, Georgia.
Nietzsche, Friedrich. "The Birth of Tragedy." Translated by Francis Golffing. In Dukore, *Dramatic Theory and Criticism*, 1974.
Norford, George. "On Stage ... The Younger Generation." *Opportunity*, November 1947.
Obituary for Richard Wright. *New York Times*, 30 November 1960.
Owen, Chandler. "New Ideas on Art." *Messenge,*. January 1925.
Oz, Amos. "Coping with Conflict." Online NewsHour Transcript. New York: WNET-TV NewsHour program. 23 January 2002.
Pitts, Ethel. "The American Negro Theatre." In Hill, *The Theatre of Black Americans*.
Plum, Jay. "Accounting for the Audience in Historical Reconstruction: Martin Jones's Production of Langston Hughes's *Mulatto*." *Theatre Survey* 36, no. 1 (May 1995).
Redding, Saunders. "The Negro Writer and His Relationship to His Roots." In *The American Negro Writer and His Roots*, 1960.
Richardson, Willis. "Characters." *Opportunity*, June 1925.
———. "The Hope of a Negro Drama." *Crisis*, November 1919.
———. "The Negro and the Stage." *Opportunity*, October 1924.
———. "Propaganda in the Theatre." *Messenger*, November 1924.
———. "The Unpleasant Play." *Opportunity*, September 1925.
Riley, Clayton. "The Black Arts." *Liberator*, April 1965.
Sanson, A. "Just Us 'Matures' with Raisin." *News-Scope*, 26 September 1979. Review of Just Us Theatre Company's production of the play in Atlanta, Georgia.
Schuyler, George S. "Ethiopian Nights Entertainment" (Review). *Messenger*, November 1924.
———. "The Negro-Art Hokum." *Nation*, 16 June 1926.

Shockley, Anne A. "Pauline Elizabeth Hopkins: A Biographical Excursion into Obscurity." *Phylon* 33 (1972).
Sinfield, Alan, and Jonathan Dollimore. "History and Ideology, the Instance of Henry IV." In Drakakis, *Alternative Shakespeares*, 1985.
Smith, Helen C. "*Raisin in the Sun* Staging Well Done," *Atlanta Constitution*, 21 September 1979. Review of Just Us Theatre Company's production of the play in Atlanta, Georgia.
Smith, Whitney. "Hoosier Company's Realism Does Justice to *Porgy and Bess*," *Indianapolis Star*, 10 October 2000. *Porgy and Bess* folder, Hatch Billops Collection, New York.
Sollors, Werner. "People Who Led to My Plays: Adrienne Kennedy's Autobiography." In Bryant-Jackson and Overbeck, *Intersecting Boundaries: The Theatre of Adrienne Kennedy*, 1992.
Sommerstein, Allan H. "Introductory Note to *The Acharnians*." In *Lysistrata/The Acharnians, The Clouds*. Translated and an introduction by Allan H. Sommerstein. New York: Penguin Books, 1973.
Southern, Eileen. "Clorindy, the Origin of the Cakewalk." In Southern, *Readings in Black American Music*, 1983.
Spence, Eulalie. "A Criticism of Negro Drama." *Opportunity*, June 1928.
Storm, William "Reactions of a 'Highly-Strung Girl': Psychology and Dramatic Representation in Angelina W. Grimké's *Rachel*." *African American Review* 27, no. 3 (1993).
Tate, Claudia. "Pauline Hopkins: Our Literary Foremother." In Marjorie Pryse and Hortense J. Spillers, *Conjuring: Black Women, Fiction, and Literary Tradition*, 1985.
Thompson, Sister M. Francesca O.S.F. "The Lafayette Players, 1915–1932." In Hill, *The Theatre of Black Americans*, 1987.
Thompson, Robert Farris. "Kongo Influences on African-American Artistic Culture." In Holloway, *Africanisms in American Culture*, 1991.
Turner, Darwin T. "W.E.B. Du Bois and The Theory of a Black Aesthetic." *Studies in a Literary Imagination* 7, no 2 (Fall 1974).
Turpin, Waters. "The Contemporary American Negro Playwright." *CLAJ*, September 1965.

Updike, John. "Reworking Wharton." *The New Yorker*, October 1993.
Waldorf, Wilella. "Mulatto Brings Up the Race Problem Once More," *New York Evening Post*, 25 October 1935.
Walker, George W. "The Real Coon on the American Stage." *Theatre Magazine*, August 1906.
Walton, Lester. "The Awakening." *New York Age*, 6 May 1909.
———. "Williams and Walker on Broadway." *Colored American Magazine*, April 1908.
Ward, Theodore. Speech at the Group Theatre's Benefit for the Negro Playwrights Company (NPC) in September 1940. In Program of the New York production of *Big White Fog*. Hatch-Billops Collection, New York.
Williams, Bert. "The Comic Side of Trouble." *American Magazine*. January 1918.
Williams, Delores S. "Womanist Theology: Black Women's Voices." *Christianity and Crisis*, 2 March 1987.
Williams, Jim. "A Need for a Harlem Theatre." *Freedomways*, 1963.
Williams, Raymond. "Social Environment and Theatrical Environment: The Case of English Naturalism." In Williams, *Problems in Materialism and Culture*, 1980.
Wilson, August. "The Ground on Which I Stand." *American Theatre*, September 1996.

Novels

Brooks, Gwendolyn. *Maud Martha*. New York: Harper, 1953.
Dodson, Owen. *Boy at the Window*. New York: Popular Library, 1951.
Fisher, Rudolph. *The Walls of Jericho*. New York: A.A. Knopf, 1928.
Himes, Chester. *If He Hollers Let Him Go*. London: Falcon Press, 1947. Reprint, New York: Thunder's Mouth Press: Distributed by Persea Books, 1987.
———. *Third Generation*. Cleveland: World Publishing Co., 1954.
Hughes, Langston. *Simple Speaks His Mind*. New York: Simon and Schuster, 1950.
———. *Simple Takes a Wife*. New York: Simon and Schuster, 1953.
———. *Sweet Flypaper of Life*. New York: Simon and Schuster, 1955.
McKay, Claude. *Home to Harlem*. New York: Harper, 1928.

Smith, Betty. *A Tree Grows in Brooklyn.* [n.p.]: Everybody's Vacation Publishing Company, 1943.
Smith, Lillian. *Strange Fruit.* New York: Reynal and Hitchcock, 1944.
Toomer, Jean. *Cane.* New York: Liveright, 1923.
Van Vechten, Carl. *Nigger Heaven.* New York: Alfred Knopf, 1926.
Waldron, Eric. *Tropic Death.* New York: Boni and Liveright, 1926.
Wharton, Edith. *The Buccaneers.* New York and London: D. Appleton-Century, 1938.
Wright, Richard. *Native Son.* New York: Harper, 1940.
———. *The Outsider.* New York: Harper, 1953.
Zenberg, Len. *Walk Hard—Talk Loud.* New York: Bobbs-Merrill, 1940.

Plays

Aiken, George L. *Uncle Tom's Cabin.* 1852. Reprint. New York: Garland, 1994.
Anouilh, Jean. *Becket or The Honor of God.* New York: Coward-McCann, 1960.
Bolt, Robert. *A Man for All Seasons.* 1960. London: Heinemann, 1961.
Brieux, Eugène. *The Red Robe.* Translated by Mrs. Bernard Shaw. New York: Brentano's, 1916.
Gorky, Maxim. *Lower Depths,* 1902. Reprint. London: Unwin, 1912.
Hauptmann, Gerhart. *The Weavers: A Drama of the Forties.* Translated by Mary Morison. New York: B.W. Huebsch, 1911.
MacLeish, Archibald. *JB: A Play in Verse.* New York: Samuel French, 1958.
Shaw, George Bernard. *Mrs. Warren's Profession: An Unpleasant Play.* New York: Brentano's, 1913.
Taylor, Tom. *Our American Cousin* (1858): *The Play That Changed History.* Washington, D.C.: Beacham Publishing, 1990.

Significant Early Black Plays

The full publication facts of the anthologies in which plays in this bibliography are published are given above in the anthologies section.

Brown, William Wells. *The Escape: or Leap to Freedom* (1858). In Hamalian and Hatch, *The Roots of African American Drama,* 42–95.
Burrill, Mary. *Aftermath* (1919). In Hamalian and Hatch, *The Roots of African American Drama,* 134–51.
Burrill, Mary. *They That Sit in Darkness* (1919). In Hatch, *Black Theatre USA,* 178–83.
Cole, Bob, and James Weldon Johnson (Will Marion Cook). *The Cannibal King.* 1901. In Library of Congress, Washington, D.C.
Cook, Will Marion. *Jes Lak White Fo'ks.* 1899. In Library of Congress, Washington, D.C., and Hatch-Billops Collection, New York.
Cotter, Joseph Seamon, Sr. *Caleb the Degenerate.*1901. In Hatch, *Black Theatre USA,* 61–99.
Easton, William Edgar. *Dessalines: A Dramatic Tale.* Boston: J.W. Burson-Company, Publishers, 1893.
Grimké, Angelina Weld. *Rachel.* 1916. In Hatch, *Black Theatre USA,* 137–77.
Hopkins, Pauline Elizabeth. *Peculiar Sam, or The Underground Railroad* (1879). In Hamalian and Hatch, *The Roots of African American Drama,* 100–123.
Rodgers, Alex, Will Marion Cook, and Bert Williams. *Abyssinia* (1906). In Library of Congress, Washington, D.C., and Hatch-Billops Collection, New York.
Shipp, Jesse, and Will Marion Cook. *In Dahomey.* 1903. In Library of Congress, Washington, D.C., and Hatch-Billops Collection, New York.

Significant Harlem Renaissance Plays

Anderson, Garland. *Appearances.* 1925. In Hatch, *Black Theatre USA,* 100–134.
Beausey, De Reath Byrd. *The Yellow Tree.* 1922. In the Moorland-Spingarn Collection, Howard University Library, Washington, D.C.
Bonner, Marita. *Purple Flower.1928.* In Hatch, *Black Theatre USA,* 202–7.
Cotter, Joseph Seamon, Jr. *On the Fields of France.* 1920. In Hatch and Hamalian, *Lost Plays of the Harlem Renaissance,* 21–25.
Culbertson, Ernest. *Goat Alley: A Tragedy of Negro Life.* Cincinnati: Steward Kidd Co., 1922.
Duncan, Thelma. *Death Dance* (1922). In Locke and Gregory, *Plays of Negro Life,* 321–31.

Lipscomb, George. *Frances* (1925). In *Opportunity*, May 1925, 148–53.
O'Neill, Eugene. *The Emperor Jones*. New York: Random House, 1920.
Richardson, Willis. *Broken Banjo*. In Locke and Gregory, *Plays of Negro Life*, 302–20.
———. *The Chip Woman's Fortune* (1923). In Hamalian and Hatch, *The Roots of African American Drama*, 159–85.
———. *Mortgaged*. 1924. In Davis and Peplow, *The New Negro Renaissance*, 103–17.
Schuyler, George S. *The Yellow Peril.*1925. In Hatch and Hamalian, *Lost Plays of the Harlem Renaissance*, 45–60.
Spence, Eulalie. *Fool's Errand*. 1927. New York: Samuel French, 1927.
———. *Undertow*. 1927. In Hatch, *Black Theatre USA*, 193–200.
Toomer, Jean. *Balo*. 1923. In Hatch, *Black Theatre USA*, 219–24.
Torrence, Ridgely. *Danse Calinda* (1922). In Locke and Gregory, *Plays of Negro Life*, 373–86.
Webb, Helen I. *Genefriede*. 1922. In Richardson and Miller, *Negro History in Thirteen Plays*, 220–37.
Wilson, Frank. *Sugar Cane*. 1926. In *Opportunity*, June 1926, 181–84, 201–3.

Significant Depression-Era Plays

Allison, Hughes. *The Trial of Dr. Beck* (1937). In the Hatch-Billops Collection, New York.
Burris, Andrew. *You Mus' Be Bo'n Ag'in* (1930). In Hatch and Hamalian, *Lost Plays of the Harlem Renaissance*, 128–99.
Cullen, Countee, and Arna Bontemps. *One Way to Heaven* (1936). In James Weldon Johnson Collection, Beinecke Library, Yale University.
Connelly, Mark. *The Green Pastures*. New York: Farrar and Rinehart, 1929.
Dodson, Owen. *Divine Comedy* (1938). In Hatch, *Black Theatre USA*, 320–49.
Gershwin, George (Music); DuBose Heyward and Ira Gershwin (Libretto). *Porgy and Bess* (1935). United States: Chappell/Intersong Music Group; Winona, Minn.: Distributed by H. Leonard Publishing Corp., 1935.
Hill, Abram. *On Strivers Row* (1939). In Hatch and Shine, *Black Theatre USA*, 226–63.
Hughes, Langston. *Don't You Want to be Free?* (1937). In Hatch, *Black Theatre USA*, 262–77.
———. *Mulatto* (1935). In Hatch and Shine, *Black Theatre USA*, 4–23.
Johnson, Francis Hall. *Run Little Chillun* (1933). In Hatch and Hamalian, *Lost Plays of the Harlem Renaissance*, 230–79.
Norford, George. *Joy Exceeding Glory* (1938). In the New York Public Library (NYPL), Rare Manuscript Division, Schomburg Center.
Peters, Paul, and George Sklar. *Stevedore* (1934). New York: Covici, Friede, 1934.
Schlick, Frederick. *Bloodstream* (1932). Typescript in NYPL, Performing Arts Division.
Ward, Theodore. *Big White Fog* (1938). In Hatch, *Black Theatre USA*, 278–319.
Wexley, John. *They Shall Not Die*. New York: A.A. Knopf, 1934.
Wilson, Frank. *Brother Mose*. In 1934 Publication Number 7, Federal Theatre Project, Works Progress Administration, Sept. 1937.

Significant Plays of the 1940s

Browne, Theodore. *Natural Man.*1941. In Hatch, *Black Theatre USA*, 360–81.
Dodson, Owen. *Garden of Time*. 1945. In the Hatch-Billops Collection, New York.
D'Usseau, Arnaud, and James Gow. *Deep Are the Roots* (1945). New York: Scribner's, 1946.
Graham, Shirley. *It's a Morning*. In Brown-Guillory, *Wines in the Wilderness*.
Green, Paul, and Richard Wright. *Native Son*. In Hatch and Shine, *Black Theatre USA*, 24–66.
Jeannette, Gertrude. *This Way Forward*. 1948. In author's personal papers.
Laurents, Arthur. *Home of the Brave*. 1946. New York: Random House, 1946.
Smith, Lillian. *Strange Fruit*. 1945. New York: Hart Stenographic Bureau, 1945.
Ward, Theodore. *Our Lan'.* 1947. In Kenneth Rowe, *A Theatre in Your Head*, New York: Funk and Wagnalls Co., 1960, 262–424.
Yordan, Philip (Abram Hill). *Anna Lucasta*. New York: Random House, 1945.

Significant Plays of the 1950s

Baldwin, James. *The Amen Corner*. 1954. In Hatch, *Black Theatre USA*, 514–46.
Branch, William. *A Medal for Willie*. 1951. In King and Milner, *Black Drama Anthology*, 439–73.
———. *In Splendid Error*. 1954. In Hatch, *Black Theatre USA*, 587–617.
Childress, Alice. *Florence*. In *Masses and Mainstream*. October 1950, 34–37.
———. *Trouble in Mind*. 1955. In Patterson, *Black Theatre*, 207–69.
Dean, Philip Hayes. *The Owl Killer*. 1958. In King and Milner, *Black Drama Anthology*, 301–24.
Hansberry, Lorraine. *A Raisin in the Sun*. 1959. In Hatch and Shine, *Black Theatre USA*, 104–46.
Hughes, Langston. *Ballot and Me*. 1956. Typescript in the Beinecke Rare Book and Manuscript Library, Yale University, New Haven, Conn.
———. *Simply Heavenly*. 1957. In Patterson, *Black Theatre*, 271–344.
Peterson, Louis. *Take a Giant Step*. 1953. In Hatch and Shine, *Black Theatre USA*, 67–103.
Ward, Theodore. *John Brown*. 1950. Typescript in Hatch-Billops Collection, New York.

Significant Plays, 1960–1965

Baldwin, James. *Blues for Mister Charlie*. New York: Dial Press, 1964. Second publishing, New York: Vintage International, 1995.
Bullins, Ed. *Clara's Ole Man* (1965). In *Five Plays by Ed Bullins*, 249–82.
Davis, Ossie. *Purlie Victorius*. New York: Samuel French, 1961.
Harrison, Paul Carter. *Pavane for a Dead-Pan Minstrel*. 1963. In *Podium Magazine* (Amsterdam), November 1965.
Hughes, Langston. *Jerico–Jim-Crow, A Song Play*. 1963. Typescript in NYPL, Performing Arts Collection.
Jackson, C. Bernard, and James Hatch. *Fly Blackbird*. 1960. In Hatch, *Black Theatre USA*, 671–93.
Jones, LeRoi (Imamu Amiri Baraka). *The Baptism* (1963) *and The Toilet* (1964). New York: Grove Press, 1967.
———. *Dutchman*. 1964. In Hatch and Shine, *Black Theatre USA*, 381–91.
———. *J-e-l-l-o*. Chicago: Third World Press, 1970.
Kennedy, Adrienne. *Funnyhouse of a Negro* (1964). In *Adrienne Kennedy in One Act*, 1988, 1–23.
Mitchell, Lofton. *Star of the Morning*. 1965. In King and Milner, *Black Drama Anthology*, 1972, 575–639.
Ward, Douglas Turner. *Two Plays by Douglas Turner Ward: Day of Absence and Happy Ending*. New York: Third Press, 1966.
Wright, Richard. *Daddy Goodness*. c. 1960. Translated from the original play by Louis Sapin. New York: Hart Multi-Copy, 1968.

Index

Abolitionists 41
Abraham Lincoln (play) 62
Abramson, Doris 103, 108, 112, 126, 130–132, 135, 142, 162, 165
The Abydos Passion Play (1868 BCE) 10, 231, 233
Abyssinia (musical play) 21, 33, 35, 37; *see also* Back to Africa
"actor-dramatist" 63
"actor-showsmith" 63
The Actors Studio 205
Adams, John (president) 140–142
Aeschylus 97
"Aesthetic Patterning of Verbal Art ... Performance-Centered Text" 225
African American folklore 25
African American Theatre (book) 11
African cosmology 40
The African Grove Theatre (c. 1821) 8
African Religions and Philosophies (book) 10, 30
"African Religious Retentions ..." 16
Africanisms 186–187, 213, 232–233
"Africanisms in African-American Music" 16
Africanisms in American Culture (book) 233
Africa's Ogun: Old World and New (book) 30, 233
Afro-American 32
The Afro-American Cultural Association 194
Afro-centric 32
Aftermath (play) 13, 52
The Age (periodical) 9, 34, 40, 87
agitprop 101, 103, 109, 111, 114
Albee, Edward (dramatist) 205, 211, 227
Alda, Alan (actor) 203
Aldridge, Ira (actor) 8
Alice in Wonder (play) 153
Allen, Samuel (writer and lawyer) 150–151
The Amen Corner (play) 143, 173–177, 186, 213, 220
American and British Literature Since 1890 (book) 220
American democracy 32, 33, 40

The American Mercury (periodical) 72, 84
American Missionary Association 7
"The American Negro and the Image of the Absurd" 191
The American Negro Repertory Players 138
The American Negro Theatre 126–127, 131–133, 137, 148, 192–193, 216
The American Society for African Culture 184
American Theatre (journal) 14
The American Theatre for Poets 184
The Amsterdam News (periodical) 87–88
Anderson, Garland (dramatist) 66–67
Anderson, Sherwood (novelist) 70–71
Angelo Herndon Jones (play) 102
Anita Bush All-Colored Dramatic Stock Company 42
Anna Lucasta (play) 137, 192
Anouilh, Jean (dramatist) 192
ANT *see* The American Negro Theatre
The ANTA Theatre 211
anti-realist 228–229
Apollonian dream world (theory) 27
Appearances (play) 66–67
Archer, William (critic) 78
Arena Stage Company 14
Aristophanes 10, 26, 27, 35
Aristotle 1, 8, 9, 10, 12, 220, 231–232
Armstrong, Louis (musician) 198
"art for art's sake" 49, 78
"Art or Propaganda?" 11, 83, 85
Art or Propaganda debate 11–12, 15, 21, 40–41, 43, 50, 57, 82, 84, 90, 104, 113–115, 125, 135, 138, 143, 152, 178, 191, 216–217, 220, 224–225, 234
Art over Propaganda 52, 95
art-theatre 12, 22, 36, 44, 47, 49, 54, 56, 77, 95, 97–98, 101, 103–104, 110, 122, 140, 142, 145, 152, 173, 174, 177–178, 204, 217–220, 222–223, 231
Artaud, Antonin (theorist) 196, 210, 217, 231–232
Ashby, William (dramatist) 116
Atkinson, Brooks (reviewer) 134
Atlanta University 7

267

Attucks, Crispus (American revolutionary) 84
Austin, Adell 94-95

Back to Africa (movement and plays) 21, 35, 37; *see also Abyssinia*; *In Dahomey*
Baldwin, James (writer) 9, 30, 131, 143-145, 146, 149, 152, 156-157, 173-174, 178, 185-187, 211-213, 220, 222, 228
Ballot and Me (play) 153
Balo (play) 55-56
Bandana Land (musical play) 37
The Baptism (play) 205
Baraka, Emamu Amiri (a.k.a. LeRoi Jones) 12, 15, 16, 18, 180-181, 184-189, 194-198, 201, 205, 207-212, 214, 216-219, 223, 227-228, 232
Barnes, Sandra 30, 233
Basie, "Count" William (musician/composer) 198
Beat Generation 181, 184, 196
Beausey, De Reath (dramatist) 55
"Beauty Instead of Ashes" 80
Becket (play) 192
Beebe, Stuart (actor) 108
Belcher, Fannin 42
Benny, Jack (comedian) 210
Bhikhu, Parekh 232
The Bible 7, 9, 29
Big White Fog (play) 102, 110-112, 114-115, 118, 121, 125, 132-133, 136-137, 160-163, 188-189
Bigger Thomas (character) 128-131, 145, 163, 165, 169, 189, 215
The Bijou Theatre 38
Bills (play) 60
Birth of a Nation (film) 41, 128
Black Arts (theory) 18, 179, 205, 219; drama 39, 204; movement 59, 75, 142, 153, 189, 218-219, 223; theatre 194, 197, 216
The Black Arts Repertory Theatre and School 195, 197, 210
black bourgeoisie 126, 128
Black Boy (novel) 181
black Caribs 39
black cultural diversity 39-40
black economics 32, 34-35; determinism 34, 35, 61
black English 231-232
Black Manhattan (book) 22
Black Nationalism 32, 33, 34, 60, 180, 204, 219
Black Patti's Troubadors 37
Black Theatre USA (anthology) 17
"Black Truth and Black Beauty" 98
The Blacks (play) 15
Blake, Eubie 38
Blanche DuBois (character) 45
Blau, Herbert (theorist) 232
Bloodstream (play) 109
Blues (musical form) 16, 19, 24, 25, 110, 231

Blues for Mister Charlie (play) 143, 211-212, 220
Blues People: Negro Music in White America (book) 195
Blyden, Edward W. 151
Bolt, Robert (dramatist) 192
Boni, Albert and Charles (publishers) 67
Bonner, Marita (dramatist) 94
Bontemps, Arna (writer) 106
Booke, Sorrell (actor) 202
Booker T. Washington (play) 116
Boy at the Window (novel) 150
Braithwaite, William (writer) 66
Branch, William (dramatist) 149, 153-155, 165, 178
Brandes, George (critic) 83
Brandon, George 16, 233
Brawley, Benjamin (educator, historian) 62
Brecht, Bertolt 15
Bridges, William 52
Brieux, Eugene (dramatist) 58, 59, 87
Briggs v. Clarendon County 140-141, 159
Brisbane, Arthur 151
"Broadway and the Negro Drama" 122
Broken Banjo (play) 92, 94
Brooks, Gwendolyn (writer) 150
Brooks, Jay 192
Brown, Sterling (writer) 99, 101, 128, 185
Brown, Tom (impersonator) 22
Brown, William Alexander 39
Brown, William Wells 16, 18, 41
Brown v. The Board of Education 140-141, 159
Browne, Theodore (dramatist) 131-133, 136-138
"The Browsing Reader" (column) 81
Brustein, Robert (critic) 14, 17, 84, 227
Bullins, Ed (dramatist) 211, 214-215, 220
Burck, Jacob (journalist) 116
Burke, Kenneth (critic) 105
Burrill, Mary (dramatist) 13, 51
Burris, Andrew (dramatist) 103
Burroughs, Charles (director) 95
Bush, Anita 42
Butcher, Margaret Just 220

Caleb the Degenerate (play) 11
Calvacade: Negro American Writing... (anthology) 150
Cambridge, Godfrey (actor) 192
Campbell, Dick 98, 115
"Can the Negro Serve the Drama?" 70
The Cannibal King (musical play) 28, 35, 38
Cannon, Katie 232
Carlson, Marvin 11, 17, 108
Carnegie Hall 205
Carnovsky, Morris (actor) 118
The Casino Roof Garden Theatre 21
catharsis 8-9
Ceremonies in Dark Old Men (play) 221
Césaire, Aimé (writer) 151
Chambers, Whittaker (writer) 116

Index 269

"Characters" 65
Charles, Ray (musician/singer) 198
Chatoyer, Joseph (Chief) 40
Chekhov, Anton (dramatist) 69
The Cherry Lane Theatre 205
Chesnutt, Charles (novelist) 66
Chicago Conference (1893) 35
Childress, Alice 13, 148–149, 153, 155–159, 173, 178, 187, 222, 228, 232
The Chip Woman's Fortune (play) 9, 56
Church Fight (play) 92
civil rights 4, 12, 28, 140–143, 146–148, 153, 155, 159 173–174, 178, 193–194, 201, 203–204, 215, 218–219, 221
Civil War 4, 7, 8, 9, 39, 134, 141
CLAJ (periodical) 206
The Clansman (novel) 128
Clara's Ole Man (play) 211, 214, 220
Clark, William (journalist) 93
Clarke, John Henrik 150–151, 190, 195
classical 8–9, 28, 190; Greek drama 26–27, 40, 123; stage 37
Clorindy (musical play) 34
CNA *see* The Committee for the Negro in the Arts
Cole, Robert A. 7, 19, 21–25, 28, 33, 34, 35, 37, 38–40, 42, 50, 56–57, 108, 224–226
Coleman, Ornette (musician) 186, 198
"Colored Aristocracy" (song) 35
"Colored Girl from Vassar" (song) 28–29
Columbia University (New York) 17
The Committee for the Negro in the Arts 153
community theatre 124, 138, 190–19
Compromise (play) 92–95
Conjuring Culture: Biblical Formations of Black America (book) 233
Connelly, Marc (dramatist) 86, 89, 97
The Conquest of Mexico (play) 196
"The Contemporary American Negro Playwright" 206
Cook, Will Marion 7, 19, 21–22, 25–35, 40, 42, 48, 50, 56–57, 69, 105, 106, 108, 126–127, 224–226
coon shows 56
Cooped Up (play) 59–60
Cordelia the Crude (short story) 91
The Cort Theatre 188, 203
Cotter, Joseph S., Jr. 52
Cotter, Joseph S., Sr. 11
Couch, William, Jr. 143, 146, 149, 155–156, 222
Cow in the Apartment (play) 133
Creel, Margaret 16
Crisis Magazine 1, 12, 51–52, 54, 56, 64, 67–68, 70, 81, 92–96, 104, 194
The Crisis of the Negro Intellectual (book) 117, 122, 125
"Criteria of Negro Art" 71
"A Criticism of Negro Drama" 82
Croce, Benedetto (theorist) 17, 18, 24
Cronon, E. David 61

Cruse, Harold 117, 121, 125, 132, 168, 170, 179–181, 183–184, 195, 201, 211, 215
Culbertson, Ernest (dramatist) 58, 80, 96
cultural nationalism 218

The Daily Worker (periodical) 116
Danse Calinda (play) 55
Dante (play) 184
Darmouth College 8
Davis, Arthur P. (writer) 150, 152
Davis, John (activist) 101–102
Davis, Ossie (actor/writer) 153, 159, 188–190, 201, 203–204
Day of Absence (play) 202–204
Dean, Phillip Hayes (dramatist) 149, 174, 176, 215, 220
Death of a Salesman (play) 167
Dee, Ruby (actor) 133, 172–173, 203
Deep Are the Roots (play) 146
DeLaine, Joseph A. 159
Demsey, Travis (writer) 193
Dépestre, René (writer) 151
Derrida, Jacques (theorist) 217, 231–232
Dessalines (Haitian emperor) 106
Dessalines (play) 7–8
DeWindt, Hal (actor/writer) 201
"The Dilemma of the Negro Author" 40, 84–85, 104, 122, 228
Dionysus (Greek god) 27–28, 189, 226, 231
Diop, Birago (writer) 151
Diop, David (writer and historian) 151
Divine Comedy (play) 9, 103
Dixon, Thomas (novelist) 128–129
Dodson, Owen (dramatist) 9–10, 103, 136–137, 150
A Doll's House (play) 45
Don't You Want to Be Free? (play) 102, 106, 109–110, 197, 201
Dostoevsky, Fyodor (novelist) 150
double consciousness 15, 16, 18, 21, 22, 42, 50, 83–84, 110, 117, 201, 212, 222, 224
Dougherty, Romeo (journalist) 90
"The Drama Among Black Folk" 83
The Drama of King Shotaway (play) 39
"The Drama of Negro Life" 9, 76, 79
Dramatic Mirror (periodical) 22, 23
"Dramatists in Dark Glasses" 10
Dream books 32
A Dream Deferred (poem) 166
Du Bois, W.E.B. 1, 4, 7, 8, 10–11, 15–19, 21–22, 24, 34, 37, 39–40, 42–44, 49–51, 53–54, 57–59, 62–81, 83–87, 89–91, 93–101, 105, 107–111, 113–115, 117–119, 121–122, 125, 134–135, 138, 141–142, 149, 151–152, 158, 170, 173, 175, 180, 182–183, 185, 187, 194–195, 201, 205, 209, 212, 214–215, 217–218, 220–224, 227
Duffy, Susan 109, 116
Dunbar, Paul Lawrence (poet) 35, 51
d'Usseau, Arnaud (dramatist) 146
Dust to Earth (play) 133

Dutchman (play) 196, 205–209, 211
Dvořák, Antonín (composer) 25
Dyson, Walter 54

Early Renaissance Plays (Harlem) 59, 165
The East End Theatre 211
Easton, William 7, 8, 28
Edmonds, Randolph 96–101, 113, 124–125, 138, 191
Egypt (ancient) 10, 24, 28, 29, 31; art and society 42; goddess Isis 45 48, 79, 231, 233
Eighth Ditch (play) 184, 205
The Eighty-Fifth Street Playhouse 173–174
Elder, Lonnie (dramatist) 221
The Elks Community Theatre 133, 138
Ellington, "Duke" Edward (composer) 198
Ellis, Eddie (writer) 197
Ellison, Ralph (novelist) 112, 121, 222
Emancipation literati 7, 9, 28, 34
Emancipation Proclamation 42
The Emperor Jones (play) 52, 63, 73, 186
"Enter the New Negro" 57–59, 62, 71, 102, 187
Erlanger, Abraham (theatre manager) 34; *see also* The Syndicate
The Escape: Or Leap to Freedom (play) 16, 41
Eshu (*orisa* god) 24, 27, 189, 226, 231
The Ethel Barrymore Theatre 173
Ethiopia 79
The Ethiopian Arts Theatre School 59
"Evah Dahkey Is a King" (song) 35–36
"Evah Niggah Is a King" (song) 26, 33, 36
"Everybody's Protest Novel" 143, 146, 187
Evils of Intemperance and Their Remedies (play) 41
Ewing, Kay (director) 114–115, 142
Experimental Death Unit #1 (play) 210, 218

Farnsworth, William (FTP official) 113
Farrakhan, Louis 204–205
The Federal Housing Administration 193
The Federal Theatre Project 101–103, 106, 110, 113–114, 116–117, 131, 153
Fences (play) 213
Fiedler, John (actor) 164, 201
Fine, Elizabeth 225
Fire (periodical) 80, 91
The Firehouse Repertory Theatre 211
The First Conference of Negro Writers 149, 152–153, 190
Fisher, Rudolph (writer) 80
Fisk University 7
Fitch, Clyde (dramatist) 54–55
Fitzgerald, F. Scott (writer) 72
Flanagan, Hallie (FTP head) 113–114
Floating Bear (periodical) 184
Fly Blackbird (play) 201
folk drama 43, 44, 49, 54, 77
folk plays 1, 44; folk-play movement 75; folk opera 105, 132
Fool's Errand (play) 92–94

"For a Negro Theatre" 148
Forbes, Jack 40
Ford, Clebert (actor) 192
Foreign Mail (play) 92–93
Foreman, Richard (dramatist) 197
Fort-Whiteman, Lovett (journalist) 88–89
Foster, Frances (actor) 192
Foster, William (filmmaker) 34
Fraden, Rena 113–115
Frances (play) 95
Frazier, E. Franklin (historian) 126
Freedom Ways (periodical) 188, 190, 192, 219
The Front Porch (play) 106
"The Frustration of Negro Art" 122, 185
FTP *see* Federal Theatre Project
Fuller, Meta Warrick (sculptor) 47
Funnyhouse of a Negro (play) 211, 229

Gaines-Shelton, Ruth (dramatist) 92
Galsworthy, John (dramatist) 82
Garden of Time (play) 103, 137
Garifuna people 39
Garvey, Marcus ("Garveyism") 60–62, 85, 99, 111, 183, 218
Gassner, John (critic) 103
Gay Harlem (play) 88
Genet, Jean (dramatist) 15, 228
Genifriede (play) 55
G.I. Bill 193
The Gibson Theatre 90
Gilpin, Charles (actor) 54, 62–63; Gilpin Players, 13, 103, 125, 133, 138
Glanville, Maxwell (actor) 133, 192
Goat Alley (play) 58, 80
Goldsmith, Oliver (dramatist) 8
Gordone, Charles (dramatist) 12, 168, 221
Gorky, Maxim (dramatist) 65
Gottlieb, Manuel 134
Gow, James (dramatist) 146
Graham, Shirley (writer) 114–115, 133
Grand Opera House 38
Graves, Ralph 47
Gray, Christine 69
The Great Gasby (play) 72
The Great Northern Theatre 110
Greek drama 1, 9; chorus 10; comedy 26
Green, J. Edward 42
Green, Paul 42, 78–81, 96, 110, 122, 128–131, 139, 162–163, 165
The Green Pastures (play) 86, 88–89, 97–98
The Greenwich Mews Theatre 153, 201
Gregory, Montgomery 7, 19, 44, 47, 54, 92, 100, 224
Grey, Edgar (journalist) 88
Griffith, D.W. (filmmaker) 11, 41 128
Grimké, Angelina 13, 19, 41, 42, 44–50, 55–57, 59, 69, 80, 104, 165, 198, 208–210, 218–219, 223–224, 232, 234
Grimké, Angelina Weld 48
Grimké, Archibald H. 7, 19, 42, 51, 69
Grimké, Sarah Stanley 48

Grimké family 69
The Group Theatre 118
"Gulla Attitudes Toward Life and Death" 16

The H.A.D.L.E.Y. Players 133
Hall, Robert 16
Hamalian, Leo 104
Hampton Institute 100
Handke, Peter (dramatist) 197
Hansberry, Lorraine 12, 13, 111, 153, 161, 163–168, 171–174, 178–184, 187, 198, 201, 212, 219, 221, 232
Happy Ending (play) 202–204, 220
Harding, Warren G. (president) 74
Harlem 4–5
Harlem (periodical) 11
Harlem (play) 82–83, 90
Harlem Experimental Theatre 103
Harlem Players 116
Harlem Renaissance 11, 12, 13, 59, 82–83, 85, 89 101–102, 178, 180–181, 195, 220, 224
The Harlem Workshop 174
Harrison, Hubert 52–53, 82, 183
Harrison, Paul Carter (dramatist) 205, 227
Hartford Stage Company 14
Harvard University 7, 18, 48
Harvest (play) 109
Haryou Act 197
Hatch, James V. 1–2, 5, 7, 8, 9, 17, 41, 55–56, 104, 107, 127–128, 130–132, 148, 167, 201, 207, 210, 215
Hauptman, Gerhart 58, 59, 87
Hay, Samuel A. 11, 36, 44, 56, 57, 79, 109, 212, 217–218, 222
Head of the Family (play) 173
Heath, Gordon (actor) 9
Heglian (Georg Hegel) 167
The Henry Street Playhouse 133–134
Her (play) 92–93
Herodotus 27–28
Herskovits, Melvin 233
Hewlett, James (actor) 8
Heyward, Dorothy (writer) 42, 82, 183
Heyward, DuBose (writer) 42, 82, 183
High Harlem Renaissance 9, 50–52, 57, 85, 87, 89–90, 97, 122, 180–181, 186, 223
Hill, Abram (dramatist) 103, 114, 116, 125–126, 136–138
Hill, Errol 5
Himelstein, Morgan (critic) 103
Himes, Chester (novelist) 150
Hiss, Alger (lawyer) 116
historical discontinuity 179–180, 183–184, 195, 201
A History of African American Theatre (book) 5
Hitler, Adolf 136
Hochschule für Musik (Berlin) 25
Holifield, Harold (dramatist) 133
Holloway, Joseph 233
Holy Ghost 30; *see also* religious possessions

Home of the Brave (play) 147
Home to Harlem (novel) 81–82
hooks, bell 232
Hooks, Robert (actor) 217
Hopkins, Pauline E. 41
Hopkins' Colored Troubadors 41
Horace (Roman philosopher) 8
Horus (Egyptian god) 231, 233
The Howard Players (University) 8, 54, 55, 63, 100, 104, 186
Howard University 1, 9, 25, 44, 54, 100, 173, 185, 220, 224
Hughes, Allison 106, 138
Hughes, Langston 9, 13, 73–75, 84, 99, 101–102, 106–112, 115–117, 121–122, 131–132, 136, 138, 142, 150, 153, 166, 172–174, 176, 182, 184–185, 197, 201, 206, 208, 227
Hull, Gloria T. 46–47
humanism 10, 23, 24, 31, 225, 234
Hurst, Fannie (novelist) 147
Hurston, Zora Neale 13

Ibsen, Henrik (dramatist) 45, 65, 97
If He Hollers Let Him Go (novel) 150
Imitation of Life (book and film) 147
In Abraham's Bosom (play) 78
In Dahomey (musical play) 21, 28, 33, 35, 36, 37; *see also* Back to Africa
In Splendid Error (play) 153
In the Jungles (musical play) 37
Inner Life (theory) 4, 22, 36, 40, 42, 50, 57–58, 95, 104, 106, 110, 132–133, 143, 145, 152, 170, 173–175, 177, 181–182, 204, 211–215, 217–219, 222–225, 234
Integration (movement) 29, 140, 142–143, 148–150, 160, 164, 173–174, 183, 193, 212, 219, 223; cultural 153–154, 178; drama 39; goals 203; propaganda 168, 221
"International Business of Jazz ... Cooperative Self Development of an International Peoples' Culture" (paper) 232
Issacs, Edith 131
Italian Renaissance 89
Ithyphallic gods, 48, 49

Jackson, C. Bernard (writer) 201
Jackson, Esther Merle (writer) 191
Jackson, Mahalia (singer) 198
Jackson, Wallace (journalist) 88–90, 97
James, Allen (writer/lawyer) 134
James, Stanlie 232
Jazz (musical form) 4, 16, 19, 74, 110, 234
JB (play) 192
Jeannette, Gertrude (actor) 133
Jelliffe, Rowena 113, 117, 125
Jelliffe, Russell 112
J-e-l-l-o (play) 210
Jericho-Jim-Crow (play) 202
Jes' Lak White Fo'ks (musical play) 21, 25–29, 31–38, 69, 106, 127
Jim Crow 24–25, 49, 202

Joachim, Joseph (violinist) 25
Jochannen, Ben (historian) 195
John Brown (play) 153
John Henry (Negro folklore) 56, 132–133
John Reed Club 116
Johnson, Andrew (president) 134
Johnson, Billy 22
Johnson, Charles 56, 94
Johnson, Francis Hall 105
Johnson, Georgia Douglas 1
Johnson, J. Rosamond (composer) 38
Johnson, James Weldon 7, 9, 17, 19, 21–22, 33, 35, 37, 40, 51, 72, 82–85, 88, 104, 122, 225, 228
Jones, LeRoi *see* Baraka, Emamu Amiri
Jones, Martin (producer) 107–108
Joy Exceeding Glory (play) 103, 116, 173
Joy to My Soul (play) 106
Joyce, James 150
Just, Ernest 8

Karamu Theatre (Karamu House) 13, 103, 106, 112–113, 117
Karenga, Maulauna Ron 217–218
Kawaida doctrine (theory) 217–218
Keats, John ("Truth and Beauty") 8, 9, 62–63, 67–68, 71, 79, 86, 97–99, 121, 182
Kennedy, Adrienne (dramatist) 211, 227, 229–230
Kilpatrick, Lincoln (actor) 19
Kimball Union Academy 8
Klaw, Marc (theatre manager) 34; *see also* The Syndicate
Kopit, Arthur (dramatist) 166
Kornweibel, Theodore 59
Krasner, David 22–24, 26, 29, 31, 35, 49
The Krigwa Players 74, 76, 91–92, 94–95, 224
Kronenberger, Louis (critic) 126–127

Lafayette Players 42
The Lafayette Theatre 42, 59, 87, 90, 113
Lamie, Lucy 233
"Lamp-blacked Anglo-Saxons" 73, 142
The Land Beyond the River (play) 153, 159, 161
"The Land Question in Georgia During Reconstruction" 134
Larson, Nella (novelist) 81
Laurents, Arthur (dramatist) 146
Lawson, Elisabeth 134
Leaks, Sylvester (writer) 190
Lee, Canada (actor) 130
"legitimate stage" 62–63, 64
Lenin, Vladimir 218
"Let My People Go" (Negro spiritual) 30
Levy, Robert (theatre manager) 42
Lewis, David Levering 17, 51
Lewis, Sinclair (writer) 71
Lewis, Theophilus 59, 62–64, 66, 72–76, 79–80, 82–84, 87–88, 91, 93, 95, 97, 111, 122–125, 135, 140, 142, 148, 177, 180, 185, 193, 204, 216, 220–221

The Liberator (periodical) 194–195, 197
"Liberty Censored: Black Living News-paper" 114
Liberty Deferred: A History of the Negro ... (living newspaper) 114
Lincoln, Abraham (president) 134
Lincoln Theatre 42, 136
Lindsay, Vachel (writer) 80
Lipscomb, George (dramatist) 95
Literary Garveyism (book) 61, 74
living newspapers 114, 153
Liza (musical play) 56
Locke, Alain 1, 4, 7, 9, 11–13, 19, 22, 44, 47, 49, 53–64, 66–73, 76–77, 80–85, 87–88, 91–92, 95–104, 107–110, 112, 118, 122, 124–126, 132–133, 135–136, 141–146, 149, 152, 168, 173–178, 180, 182, 187–189, 195, 204, 210–215, 217–224, 232
Lonesome Road: Six Plays ... (anthology) 78
A Long Way Home (play) 137
The Longacre Theatre 183
"Love Will Find a Way" (song) 38
Lovell, John 31
lovemaking taboo 41
The Lyceum Theatre 173
Lyles, Aubrey (librettist) 137
The Lyric Theatre 105

MacLeish, Archibald (writer) 192
"magical realism" 16, 230–231
"Main Problems of Negro Theatre" 79
The Majestic Theatre 35, 38
Malcolm X 218
A Man for All Seasons (play and film) 192
The Manhattan Art Theatre 192–193
"Many Thousands Gone" 144, 146, 185, 187
Mao 218
Marquez, Gabriel Garcia (novelist) 16
Marshall, Thurgood 141, 159
Martin, Tony 61
Marx, Karl 218
Matthews, Brander 15, 17, 24, 225
Maud Martha (novel) 150
Maultsby, Portia K. 16
The Maxine Eliot Theatre 106
Mayfield, Julian (writer) 141–143, 149, 153, 159–160, 187, 222
Mbiti, John 10, 30, 31
McCarthy, Joseph 153
McClendon, Ernestine (actor) 174
McClendon, Rose (actor) 108, 116; The McClendon Players 115–116, 126
McKay, Claude (writer) 80–82
McNeil, Claudia (actor) 172
A Medal for Willie (play) 153, 155, 165, 220
Medieval Europe 8
Meek Mose (play) 90–91
Melampus 28, 226
Mencken, H.L. 70, 74, 84
The Messenger (periodical) 88
Meyerhold, Vsevolod (director) 109–110

Index

Miller, Arthur (dramatist) 167, 228
Miller, Flournoy (composer) 137
Miller, Irvin (playwright) 87–88
Mine Eyes Have Seen (play) 51
minstrelsy 22, 23, 24, 26
Minturn, Harry (FTP official) 114–115
Mitchell, Lofton 96, 98, 115–116, 126, 133–135, 153, 159–160, 192, 202
Model Studies 11
Molette, Barbara 49
Molette, Carlton 49
Monroe, John 67, 87, 90
Moore–Forrest, Marie 54
Morgan State College 100
Morgue, Efua (writer) 151
Morrell, Peter (dramatist) 102
Morrison, Toni 16, 231
Mortgaged (play) 55–56
The Moscow Art Theatre 69
Mrs. Warren's Profession (play) 58
Muhammad, Elijah 218
Mulatto (play) 106–108, 111, 122, 131
Mulebone (play) 13
multiculturalism 232
"The Myth of Negro Literature" 184, 208
The Myth of the Negro Past (book) 233

NAACP *see* National Association for the Advancement of Colored People
Nadler, Paul 114, 140–141, 146, 159, 171–172, 174, 183, 205
Nathan, George Jean (reviewer) 134–135
The Nation (periodical) 73, 184
The Nation of Islam 204–205
The National Association for the Advancement of Colored People 12, 17, 41–43, 72, 99, 101, 114, 118, 141, 159–160, 223; Conference (1926) 71; Drama Committee 44, 46–49, 51, 54
The National Ethiopian Art Theatre 59
The National Negro Business League 11
National Negro Theatre 54, 79
Native Son (play) 110, 122, 128, 130–131, 139, 145, 147, 161–162, 165, 173, 188–189, 207, 211
Natural Man (play) 131–132, 137
Neal, Larry 18, 194–195, 206, 214
The NEC *see* Negro Ensemble Theatre Company
Négritude 150
"Négritue and Its Relevance to the American Negro Writer" 151
"The Negro and the American Stage" 58, 70
"The Negro-Art Hokum" 73
"The Negro Artist and the Racial Mountain" 73–75, 84
"The Negro Audience" 63–64
Negro audience problems 62–65
Negro comedy 53
The Negro Drama Group 138

The Negro Ensemble Theatre Company 203, 216–217
Negro folk culture 48
The Negro in Literature and Art (book) 62
The Negro Intercollegiate Dramatic Association 101
Negro musical comedy 21, 22, 38, 55, 56
The Negro People's Theatre 116
The Negro Playwrights Company 111, 119, 136, 138, 193
Negro Poetry and Drama (book) 101
Negro renaissance 96, 98, 100, 117–118, 224; *see also* "New Negro"
"The Negro Theatre and the Harlem Community" 192
The Negro World (periodical) 52
"The Negro Writer and His Relationship to His Roots" 149
The Neighborhood Playhouse 46
Nelson, Alice Dunbar 51
Nerny, May Childs 47–48, 49
The New Criticism (theory) 17, 18
The New Heritage Repertory Theatre 4
"New Ideas on Art" 62–64
The New Lafayette Players 9
"New Negro" (Movement) 50–51, 55, 57, 68, 85, 101–102, 118, 141; *see also* Negro renaissance
The New Negro (book) 67, 71, 102, 168, 180
New Republic (periodical) 14
New Science of Life (book) 233
"new theatre" 42, 57
The New Theatre League 119
The New York Age see *The Age*
The New York Amsterdam News see *The Amsterdam News*
The New York Theatre 35
The New York Theatre Guild 134
The New York Times (periodical) 128, 195–196, 198
Nietzsche, Friedrich (theorist) 27
Nigeria 24, 226, 231
Nigger Heaven (book) 70
No' Count Boy (play) 80
No Place to Be Somebody (play) 12, 168, 221
Noah's Dove (play) 174; see also *The Owl Killer*
Nora (character) 45
Norford, George (dramatist) 103, 116, 125, 136, 138, 173
Notes of a Native Son (book) 152
NPC *see* The Negro Playwrights Company

Oberlin College 7, 25
Odets, Clifford (dramatist) 112, 116, 228
The Off-Bowery Theatre 184
Okhlopov, Nikolai (director) 109–110
Okpewho, Isadore 229–230
The Old Man's Boy (play) 63
On Being Forty (play) 59–60
On Strivers Row (play) 103, 116, 125–128, 137–138

On the Fields of France (play) 52
On the Real Side (book) 23
O'Neill, Eugene (dramatist) 42, 52–53, 63–64, 72, 78, 80, 82, 93, 95, 183, 186
Opportunity Magazine (periodical) 56, 60, 64, 94, 96–97, 124
Orgena (play) 204–205
Osiris (Egyptian god) 24, 27, 28, 31, 45 226, 231–234
Ostrovsky, Alekandr (dramatist) 65
Our Lan' (play) 133–136, 139–140, 165, 220
"Our Little Renaissance" 77–78
Outer Life (theory) 21, 22, 24, 36, 39, 40, 50, 57–58, 105, 170, 174–175, 188, 217–218, 222
The Outsider (novel) 181
Owen, Chandler 62–64, 71
The Owl Killer (play) 174, 176–177, 215, 220
Oz, Amos (writer) 167

Pa Williams' Gal (play) 87
Page, Thomas (writer) 128–129
Parker, Charlie (musician) 5, 208–209
Pavane for a Dead-Pan Minstrel (play) 205
The Pekin Stock Company 42
The Pekin Theatre 42
Pelton, Robert 233
The People of Clarendon County (play) 159
People's Theatre (115th Street) 133, 138
Perry, Jeffrey 52
Peterkin, Julia (writer) 71, 78, 81
Peters, Paul (dramatist) 102, 109, 116
Peterson, Bernard 207
Peterson, Louis (dramatist) 173–174, 178, 211, 222
Phylon (journal) 191
Pinkney, Michael 49
Pitcher, Oliver (dramatist) 133
Pitts, Ethel 137
The Pittsburgh Courier (periodical) 136
"pity and terror" 9, 77, 96–97
Plays of Negro Life (book) 92
Plessy v. Ferguson 159
Plum, Jay 107–108, 131
Poitier, Sidney (actor) 171–173, 228
Pompous (character) 25–26, 31–36
Porgy and Bess (opera and film) 183–184
Post-Slavery Classicism 7–11, 19, 23, 28, 100, 225
Powell, Linsay (writer) 138
Preminger, Otto (director) 133
Présence Africaine (journal) 151
The Princess Theatre 90
"The Problem of Negro Character and Dramatic Incident" 146
problem play 44, 47, 49, 52, 56, 58, 77, 122, 133
"Propaganda and the Theatre" 58
propaganda play(s) 59, 72, 77, 82, 87, 97
Protest drama(s) 39, 41, 42, 44, 45, 50, 59, 110
Protest theatre 109–110, 217–218, 222

Protest theory 21–22, 48, 209, 218–219, 223
Provincetown Players 54
psychological realism 104, 177
Purlie Victorious (play) 188–190, 201, 203, 220
Purple Flower (play) 94

Quicksand (novel) 81

race drama 44, 54
Rachel (play) 41–42, 44–51, 53, 57, 59, 67, 69, 104, 165, 198, 219, 223, 234
A Raisin in the Sun (play) 3–4, 12, 111, 153, 161, 164, 166, 168, 170–172, 174, 178, 181, 183, 187–189, 192, 201, 221
Raising Hell in the Son (play) 201
Rapp, William Jourdan (writer) 82, 90–91
realist drama 45, 228
Realists 229
"Reclaiming the Lost African Heritage" 151
Reconstruction 17, 134
The Red Moon (musical play) 38–40
The Red Robe (play) 58
"Red Summer" (1919) 52
Redding, Saunders (writer and critic) 149, 151–152
Reed, John (journalist) 116
Reinhardt, Max (director) 55–56, 66, 212
religious possessions 30; *see also* Holy Ghost
The Renaissance Casino 92
Renaissance Europe 8
Rethinking Multiculturalism (book) 232
"The Revolutionary Theatre" 195–196, 198, 209, 216
Rice, Thomas (minstrelsy performer) 23
Richards, Beah (actor)
Richards, Lloyd (director) 171–172
Richards, Sandra L. 15, 16, 228
Richardson, Willis (dramatist) 1, 9, 55–56, 58–59, 62–66, 68–70, 72–73, 75–77, 80, 91–92, 95–97, 133, 185–186
Riis, Thomas L. 22, 33–34
Riley, Clayton (critic and reviewer) 194–195
Robeson, Paul (actor) 134
Rogers, Alex (librettist) 37
Romanticism 8, 7, 12, 17
Roosevelt, Frankin D. (president) 113
Rose, Philip (producer) 171, 188
Roumain, Jacques (writer) 151
Rowan, Carl T. (journalist) 194
Rowe, Kenneth 134, 136
Royal Entries 8
The Royale Theatre 134, 147
Run Little Chillun (play) 105
Running Wild (musical play) 56

"Sacrificial Practices in Santeria" 16
SADSA *see* The Southern Association of Dramatic and Speech Arts
The St. James Theatre 128
The St. Marks Playhouse 194, 202–203, 205, 216

"Same Old Blues" 62, 64, 149
Santoni, Reni (writer) 201
Sartre, Jean-Paul 151
Sasa time 31
"The Saving Grace of Realism" 100
Schepp, Archie (musician) 198
Schlick, Frederick (dramatist) 109
Schopenhauer, Arthur 45, 197
Schuyler, George S. 59–60, 66–67, 73, 142, 184
Scott, Emmett 10–11
Scott, Freda 92, 94
Semiotics 22, 23, 24
Seneca (Roman dramatist) 12
Senghor, Leopold (writer) 151
Sermon in the Valley (play) 13
Shakespeare, William 7–10, 12, 88, 97
Shaw, George Bernard 58–59, 65, 82, 87
She Stoops to Conquer (play) 8
Sheldrake, Rupert (biologist) 233–234
Shine, Ted 9, 127, 167
Shipp, Jesse (librettist) 35, 127
The Shoo-Fly Regiment (musical play) 38–39, 40
The Shout (religious song) 42, 66
Shuffle Along (musical play) 38, 56
A Sign in Sidney Brustein's Window (play) 183
silent march 51
Silvera, Frank (actor) 9
Silvera, John (writer) 114
Simple Takes a Wife (novel) 176
Simply Heavenly (play) 173, 176
Sissle, Noble (lyricist and playwright) 38
Sklar, George (dramatist) 102, 109
The Slave (play) 205, 209–210
Slaves Escape; or The Underground Railroad (play) 41
Smith, Alfred E. (governor) 113
Smith, Bessie (singer) 208–209
Smith, Betty (novelist) 163
Smith, J.A (dramatist) 102
Smith, Lillian (novelist) 147
Smith, Theophus 233
social documents (drama) 59, 72, 111, 125, 131, 133
"The Social Origins of ... Negro Art" 65–66
"Society" (song) 35
Sollors, Werner 210, 218
"Some Reflection on the Negro in American Drama" 96
Sorrow Is the Only Faithful One (book) 9
South Bronx 3–5
The Southern Association of Dramatic and Speech Arts 124
Southern Road (book) 99
Spence, Eulalie 1, 13, 59–60, 76, 82, 87–88, 91–95, 97, 104, 177, 232
Spingarn, Joel A. 17–18, 24
Spring Beginning (play) 133
The Squires Club 194
Stalin, Joseph 136, 218

Stanislavsky, Constantin 5, 191
Stanton School 7
The Star of Ethiopia (pageant) 8, 42–44, 109, 205
Star of the Morning (play) 202
"Steps Toward a Negro Theatre" 54, 75
Stevedore (play) 102, 109, 116
Stewart, Jeffrey 96, 101, 180
Storm, William 44–46
Stowe, Harriet Beacher 143–145, 147
Strange Fruit (book and play) 147
Strindberg, August (dramatist) 65
Sugar Cane (play) 95
Sugar Hill (musical play) 137
The Suitcase Theatre 109, 116
Sullivan, Noel (writer) 109
Sundquist, Eric 23
Supreme Court 140–141, 159–160, 194, 216
Survey Graphic (periodical) 57, 62
Sweet Flypaper of Life (novel) 150
"Sweet Meat from LeRoi" (Phd. diss.) 15
The Syndicate ("skindicate") 34, 37; *see also* Erlanger and Klaw

Take a Giant Step (play) 173–174, 211, 220
Tanner, Henry (artist) 66
Taylor, Clarice (actor) 133
The Theatre Arts (periodical) 184
Theatre Arts Monthly (periodical) 70
"Theatre Column" 75, 78
The Theatre Guild (New York) 173
"Theatre in ... Black Colleges" 7
Theatre 1964 Playwrights Unit 205, 211
Theatre of Cruelty (theory) 196
Theories of the Theatre (book) 11
They Shall Not Die (play) 109
They That Sit in Darkness (play) 13, 51–52
The Third Avenue Theater 21
The Third Generation (novel) 150
This Way Forward (play) 133
Thompson, Eloise (dramatist) 59–60, 97
Thompson, Robert Farris 225
Three Plays for a Negro Theatre (1917 production) 137
Three Plays for Negro Theatre (book) 220
Throckmorton, Clem 54
Thurman, Wallace (writer) 82, 90–91
The Toilet (play) 194, 205–206, 214
Toll, Robert 39
Toomer, Jean 1, 55, 80
Torrence, Ridgely 42, 54–55, 78, 80, 137, 220
"Toward a Black Community Theatre" 192–193
"Towards Community Drama" 124
traditional black humor 40
A Tree Grows in Brooklyn (novel) 163
The Trial (play) 204–205
The Trial of Dr. Beck (play) 106, 138
The Trickster in West Africa (book) 233
A Trip to Coontown (musical play) 21–22, 24–25, 34

Trojan War 183
Trouble in Mind (play) 153, 155, 173, 187, 220, 228
Troubled Island (play) 106
Turman, Glynn (actor) 3
Turner, Darwin 66, 68, 71, 78, 81, 89, 99, 107, 118
Turner, Nat (slave revolt) 84
Turpentine (play) 102
Turpin, Waters (writer) 206
Tuskegee Institute 10

Uncle Tom's Cabin (novel) 143, 147, 156
Undertow (play) 60, 104, 177
U.N.I.A. *see* Universal Negro Improvement Association
The Universal Negro Improvement Association 61, 74
universality 10, 40, 225, 227
"The Universals of Performance; or Amortizing Play" 232
"The Unpleasant Play" 65
uplift plays 53
The Urban League 114

Vactor, Vanita 162
The Vanderbilt Theatre 107
Vandercook, John W. 151
Van Doren, Carl 220–221
Van Doren, Mark 220–221
Van Vechten, Carl 70, 80
"The Vassar Girl" (song) 28, 35
Vedic traditions (Hindu Scriptures) 24
Vereen, Ben (actor) 4
Vesey, Denmark (slave revolt) 84
The Veterans Administration 193
The Village South Theatre 205
Virginia State College 100–101
Virginia Union College 101

Waiting for Lefty (play) 112, 116
Waldron, Eric (writer) 80
Walk Hard (play) 137
Walker, Alice (writer) 13, 232
Walker, George (performer) 37, 38, 62
Walter Lee Younger (character) 161–172, 189, 219
Walton, Lester 34, 40, 87, 95

Ward, Douglas Turner 202, 204, 216–217
Ward, Theodore (dramatist) 102, 110–112, 115, 118, 120–121, 125, 132–139, 142, 148, 153, 162, 165 173, 182–183, 198–199
Washington, Booker T. 10–11, 19, 34, 61
Watkins, Mel 23
The Weavers (play) 58
Webb, Helen I. (dramatist) 55
Welles, Orson (actor/director) 128, 130
Wesley, Richard (dramatist) 9
Wexley, John (dramatist) 109
"What Good Are College Dramatics?" 100
"What Purlie Told Me!" 190
When the Jack Hollars (play) 106
Wilkerson, Margaret 211
Williams, Bert (performer) 37, 38, 62, 202
Williams, Delores 232
Williams, George 151
Williams, Jim (writer) 190–193–195, 199, 219
Williams, Tennessee (dramatist) 45, 212
Willie Wayside (character) 22–25
Wilson, August (dramatist) 10, 14, 17, 83, 213, 222, 227, 234
Wilson, Frank (dramatist) 87, 90, 95, 97
Witmark, Isadore 34
Wittgenstein, Ludwig (theorist) 196–197, 217
Woll, Allen 21–22, 38, 56
Woodson, Carter G. 151
Works Progress Administration 113
The World as Will and Idea (book) 197
World War I 13, 17, 19, 41, 51, 85, 158, 224
World War II 124, 137, 174, 178–180, 185, 221
WPA *see* Works Progress Administration
Wright, Richard (novelist) 110, 125, 128–131, 136, 139, 162–165, 181, 207, 211, 215

Yale Drama School 9, 133
The Yellow Peril (play) 66
The Yellow Tree (play) 55
Yoruba 24, 27
You Mus' Be Bo'n Ag'in (play) 103–104
Young, Lester (musician) 5
Youth Conference on Afro-American Culture 194
"Youth Speaks" 57–59, 62, 71
Yugen (journal) 184

Zamani time 31

www.ingramcontent.com/pod-product-compliance
Lightning Source LLC
Chambersburg PA
CBHW051212300426
44116CB00006B/542